AN UNCHOSEN PEOPLE

An Unchosen People

Jewish Political Reckoning in Interwar Poland

KENNETH B. MOSS

HARVARD UNIVERSITY PRESS

Cambridge, Massachusetts

London, England

2021

First printing

Library of Congress Cataloging-in-Publication Data

Names: Moss, Kenneth B., 1974– author.
Title: An unchosen people : Jewish political reckoning in interwar Poland /
    Kenneth B. Moss.
Description: Cambridge, Massachusetts : Harvard University Press, 2021. |
    Includes bibliographical references and index.
Identifiers: LCCN 2021014709 | ISBN 9780674245105 (cloth)
Subjects: LCSH: Jews—Poland—Identity—History—20th century. |
    Jews—Poland—Politics and government—History—20th century. |
    Jewish nationalism—Poland—History—20th century. | Antisemitism—
    Poland—History—20th century. | Poland—History—1918–1945.
Classification: LCC DS134.55 .M66 2021 | DDC 943.8 / 004924009042—dc23
LC record available at https://lccn.loc.gov/2021014709

לזיכרון דעם טאַטן, ראָבערט (ראובן) מאָס, עליו השלום, און פאַר אונזערע קינדער צירל רייזל, אהרן וואָלף, און איציק לייב. צוליב זיי האָרן מיר נישט אויף צו גלייבן אז עס וועט קומען אַ בעסערער מאָרגן.

In memory of my father, Robert A. Moss, and for Celia, Aaron, and Isaac. Because of them, we nevertheless believe that a better future will come.

CONTENTS

Note on Transliteration and Translation   *ix*

Map   *xii*

Introduction: Unchosen Times, Unchosen Conditions   1

1 Futurelessness and the Jewish Question   41

2 Toward a Politics of Doubt and Exit   88

3 Minorityhood and the Limits of Culture   114

4 Antisemitism, Nationalism, Eliminationism   154

5 From Ideology to Inquiry   193

6 Palestine as Possibility   221

7 Reason, Exit, and Postcommunal Triage   254

Conclusion: "With a Cruel Logic"   306

Notes   *331*

Acknowledgments   *365*

Index   *369*

NOTE ON TRANSLITERATION
AND TRANSLATION

Most of the sources for this work are in Yiddish, Hebrew, and Polish. I have transliterated Yiddish sources according to the YIVO system and Hebrew sources according to Library of Congress recommendations, albeit without diacriticals. Many of the figures who appear here bore multiple names; I have chosen the form featured most prominently in my sources. I have deviated from transliteration rules for terms with an established English norm (e.g., Warsaw instead of Warszawa, Hehalutz instead of He-haluts). The history examined in this book took place in a region characterized by ethnolinguistic and communal multiplicity. I have chosen to call places by their formal interwar Polish designation, parenthetically noting Jewish usages and Ukrainian, Belarusian, and Lithuanian ones where relevant. The fact that this is a history of Jewish political culture might suggest choosing Jewish toponymic usage as primary. After all, such usage expressed the deep cultural distinctiveness of local Jewish communities—some larger than local ethnic Polish populations, in fact—and bespeaks the centuries-long existence of a distinct East European Jewish ethnic community no less native than any other. I have nevertheless chosen otherwise because this book is in part an argument about power. Jewish at-homeness was not the same as actual power to determine what would become of a place and its people in the age of the nation-state. All translations are mine unless otherwise noted.

AN UNCHOSEN PEOPLE

Poland, 1923–1937

Introduction

Unchosen Times, Unchosen Conditions

"Even Trotsky has begun to believe that Hitler will remain in power some ten to twenty years [. . .]. That which has happened in Germany, with its relatively small Jewish community, is only a hint of the catastrophe that will break out in those lands where Jews make up a population of millions. By the time the storms finally grow still, the Jewish people will be crushed and broken." This dark vision of the future that awaited Poland's three million Jews, and their nearly two million coreligionists in Romania, Lithuania, Latvia, and Hungary, was not voiced in 1939 with German tanks at the border, or in 1936 when those actually in charge of the Polish state began to embrace the ideal of de-Judaizing Poland as far as possible. Rather, the essay that pivoted around this grim prediction appeared in October 1933, at a moment of relative stability in Poland, in a Warsaw Yiddish journal that constituted one of the few relatively independent platforms for serious inquiry in a Polish Jewish public life profoundly divided among bitterly opposed political camps. The author, calling himself Mikhl Astour, had long been a leading youth activist on behalf of Yiddish secular culture in Wilno (Yid.: Vilna; Lith.: Vilnius). This commitment, Yiddishism, was in turn intimately linked to the ideology of Jewish Diasporism, which wagered that a healthy Jewish national-communal future could be sustained in Eastern Europe. That a vision of imminent diasporic collapse would come from a fiercely committed Yiddishist like Astour was especially jarring.[1]

Astour, however, had not come to don sackcloth for a Diasporist faith he now deemed misplaced, but to demand that Polish Jewry take honest stock of things as they were and were likely to *become,* and what Jews could and could *not* realistically hope to *do* about the matter. To those who urged Polish Jews to redouble their famous political activism, to "carry on the old politics" of fighting in Poland's parliament,

1

municipalities, and streets for Jewish well-being or for revolution, Astour responded with scorn that suggested a countervailing certainty: that it was delusion to continue to hope, after a decade of effort, that *any* variety of political effort by a community composing only 10 percent of Poland's population and marked off as a "minority" could substantially determine how the larger society would answer the Jewish Question. So, too, liberal hopes: whether he meant faith in Poland's governing elites, among whom there were liberal spirits, or once-expansive hopes that the Western powers would protect Jewish rights, now Astour had only "a bitter smile" for "the naïve ideas of the Jewish liberals, who believed that the world is becoming nicer and more humanitarian."[2]

Was the answer then revolution? Astour was himself fiercely socialist: "Only under the red flag of socialism," he instructed his elders, "can one gather active and committed youth and inspire them."[3] But he deemed the approach of the two dominant Polish Jewish socialist parties, the Communists and the General Jewish Labor Bund in Poland (the Bund), worse than useless. Both parties insisted that socialist revolution would perforce solve the Jewish Problem and that only it could. Both insisted that the Depression was dialectically strengthening the forces of redemption. Both insisted that class struggle was the only legitimate Jewish politics, cross-class Jewish cooperation was unthinkable, and plans for organized emigration were communal betrayal. In Astour's view, holding to these orthodoxies meant telling Poland's Jews to "wait with our hands in our pockets until the social revolution comes, and then everything will be fine."[4] Socialism, too, had to think about likelihood and duration; the lesson of the ease with which Nazism had won power in Germany, with its enviable constitution and Europe's strongest socialist movement, was that fascism would likely spread far, spread fast, and last long enough to do terrible harm to Jews before revolutionary deliverance.

So what was to be done? The answer, Astour insisted, had to begin neither from hope nor from ideology. It had to begin from a chastened assessment of what Jews really could and could not do with what powers they had in relation to the future they most likely faced. And Astour drew a first consequence of his judgments unflinchingly: "If we take as given that we cannot hope for an improvement in Jewish life in the Diaspora, we must seek another path."[5]

In our histories of the modern Jewish experience, and in our reflections on that history's larger significance, what place is merited by thought like Astour's? Astour was thinking about what it meant to belong to a group seen by many as a grave problem. He was issuing a call to reason from risk rather than from convictions and ideals, and to analyze political dangers based not on utopias or principles but on a clear-eyed reckoning with the resources one's community really possessed.

To begin a book about Jewish history with thought like Astour's is to risk sinking immediately into a morass out of which historians of modern Jewry have long striven to climb, and not only historians of Polish Jewry but historians of all those Jewries undone by political catastrophe in the twentieth century—German Jews, North African, Middle Eastern. It is to risk descent into unilluminating arguments about "the lessons of the Holocaust" or "Zionism versus Revolution" construed ahistorically. Many of my fellow Jewish historians will worry that to open with thought like Astour's is to impose a "teleology" that impedes serious attention to Jewish creativity and to the many species of Jewish politics that imagined Jews and their non-Jewish neighbors building a modern life together in the lands they had all long shared.

Historians of East European Jewry are especially passionate about these issues, and it is no mystery why. From the mid-nineteenth century on, many of the great global Jewish communal debates about how Jewish life should be lived in modernity revolved above all around the capacities and fate of the distinctive Jewish community that spanned the territory we now associate with Lithuania, Belarus, Poland, Ukraine, Moldova, and Romania. Comprising far and away the largest Jewish population in the world—at the turn of the twentieth century it numbered more than six million without even reckoning an ongoing westward migration that removed some two million (more) in the four decades before the First World War—this was a population brimming with creativity and fierce divisions. East European Jewry's sheer size, largely intact ethnolinguistic difference, and still-common pride in its cultural inheritance made it the focus for all varieties of Jewish nationalism seeking "national revival." A confluence of high literacy rates, brutal impoverishment, and region-wide radicalism allowed Jewish socialists to imagine it a great force for revolution. Culturally, intense religious piety flourished alongside bold secular revolt in this community, rendering it the great hope both for traditionalist visions of religious continuity despite modernity's acids and for secularist visions of Jewish cultural reinvention. To pronounce on East European Jewish modernity is to pronounce on Jewish modernity as a whole.

And among historians of East European Jewry, none are more passionate about celebrating the full gamut of pre-war Jewish experience than historians of Polish Jewry particularly. For these historians and for those general historians of Poland who share their passion, the issue is not simply one of historical accuracy, though it is certainly true that one cannot understand Poland's history without serious attention to Poland's Jews, who made up 10 percent of the interwar population and more than a third of Poland's urban population. Rather, many scholars of Polish Jewry are driven by a special pathos about the history of Jewish-Polish relations: a 500-year history of troubled yet intimate entanglement ended only by the Holocaust. One product of this long history was a subculture of Jews in Poland's cities who were as Polish in culture and identity as German Jews were German, Iraqi Jews Arab—and over the past three decades especially, scholars have worked hard to recover this form of life from the neglect to which Jewish historiography often consigns assimilationists. Then, too, many Polish Jewish historians—and even more so many historians of Poland—strongly resist approaches to interwar Poland's history that see the end of multiethnic Poland inscribed in its beginnings, fail to give Poland's progressive traditions due credit, and do not recognize that Poland faced grave problems.

Many scholars of Polish Jewry will insist that views like Astour's were far from universal among contemporaries, and this is true. Much recent work in Polish Jewish history focuses precisely on dimensions Astour rudely dismissed, particularly the blossoming—precisely in the 1930s— of Polish Jewish socialisms of all kinds. Some scholars of religion underscore the resilience of Poland's large pietist-Orthodox Hasidic community. Still others are rediscovering the undimmed political and cultural faith of many Polonized Jews. Marci Shore's history of interwar Poland's aesthetic avant-garde recovers the strange synthesis of revolutionary and integrationist faiths cherished by the many writers of Jewish descent within it. Anna Landau-Czajka offers a respectful reconstruction of the lives and hopes of the liberal-patriotic "Poles of the Mosaic faith" who comprised a sizeable subculture particularly in Poland's great cities. Forgotten forms of Jewish-Polish hybridity are also being rediscovered, as scholars such as Samuel Kassow, Karolina Szymaniak, and Karen Underhill recapture how talents like the journalist-intellectual Rokhl Auerbach, the historian Emmanuel Ringelblum, the poet Debora Vogel, or the critic Naftole Vaynig moved "amphibiously" between Yiddish and Polish culture. New histories of Jewish leisure, architecture, education, art, and religiosity testify to the energy ordinary Jews continued to muster to carve out fulfilling lives.[6]

The second kind of protest we might expect against "the Astour effect," so to speak, proceeds from the complexity of interwar Polish society more broadly. Many historians of interwar Poland will aver that whatever reasons Astour had for his outlook, the objective situation of Poland's Jews was not so clear, the horizons not so dark, not all the factors in play so bad. Poland's fractious society was *not* univocal about the Jewish Question—or anything else. Poland's great sociological complexity—its regionalisms, its multiethnicity, the deep differences between country and city, proletarian and petit bourgeois, peasant and intellectual—was matched by great political-cultural division. Polish nationalism itself was bifurcated: alongside an intolerant and antisemitic ethnonationalism of the Right, there persisted an older inclusive vision of the nation with at least some room for Jews. Although the creation of the new Poland in 1918 was accompanied by much animosity and some violence directed against Jews qua Jews,[7] it was the tolerant tradition that set the constitutional terms: Jews received equal citizenship and the substantial freedoms of all Polish citizens to say most of what they wished (though there was substantial press censorship about politically touchy matters), to organize institutions, and to participate in politics.[8]

In its most assertive version, this historiography paints the interwar period up to 1935 as one of *expanding* possibilities for Jewish integration into Polishness—and especially in the 1926–1935 era, precisely the years on which I focus. In the turbulent first years after independence in 1918, Poland's nationalist Right seemed to be moving toward dominance. Instead, a 1926 coup led by the independence hero Józef Piłsudski put in power a regime committed, more or less, to the civic model of Polishness. There were some signs that this regime, the Sanacja, would seek to improve the state's relationship to Poland's several large non-Polish populations, including Jews.[9] Among Jews, the 1926 coup fed hopes for a breakthrough to real integration and the drawing of antisemitism's poison from the body politic.[10] More generally, Polish Jews understood that their neighbors' attitudes toward them varied widely and that Polish culture was still in flux.[11] And Polish Jews were assimilating rapidly—many wanted to belong.[12]

Yet for all that, it is also indubitably true, to begin with, that Astour was no outlier in his sense of a future foreclosed. Quite the contrary, as we will see, his consuming certainty that worse was coming, his sense that Jewish life in the Diaspora might now for the first time truly be mortally threatened, and his grim conviction of Jews' incapacity to do much about either, were by 1933 mainstream outlooks. This book begins by arguing that even as the transition of the mid-1920s brought greater stability to Poland and sped assimilation among its three million Jews, many began to move toward the conclusion that there was little realistic prospect of a decent future for them in Poland or indeed Europe. We will encounter a range of such people and their evolving thought and see how such "Astourian" perspectives began to transform Polish Jewish politics, fostering a new political sensibility defined by disillusionment with all of the Jewish political movements on offer (Orthodoxy, Jewish Diaspora socialism, liberal Polonism, and in a more complicated sense Zionism too), by a search for a better individual future, and by burgeoning interest in any possibility of exit.

Recovering the forgotten scope of this transformation in Jewish political culture is the first of this book's concerns. But more essentially, what follows is a history of social analysis and political choice—a history of Jewish intellectual confrontation with new intensities of illiberal nationalism; with the unexpected flourishing and mass appeal in Poland as across Europe of ideologies that identified "the Jews" as an enemy of the commonweal or at least a grave burden on it, and in all events a national problem demanding a solution; and with the discovery of just how narrow Jews' own capacities to shape their collective future really were. Much has been written about the many competing political faiths of Polish Jews: Zionist and socialist visions of Jewish agency and transformation, Orthodox steadfastness and creativity in defense of tradition, Polonized Jews' passionate quest for acceptance. This book seeks to rediscover forms of Jewish thinking and choice defined not by ideological certainties but by recognition of weakness, danger, and the need to predict. Its protagonists are not the idealists we often celebrate, but intellectuals and ordinary people who tried to reckon with dangers they could not avert, without illusions, through analysis and hard choices.

To ignore Astour and the many others who began to rethink the Jewish condition in similar terms means to miss four essential dramas of modern Jewish thought, culture, and politics. It means to miss, first, the denouement of an essential tension in twentieth-century Jewish thought about the Jewish Question itself: an intense inner struggle between surprisingly dominant progressive (sometimes Marxist) certainties that History was moving toward Reason and darker intuitions that modernity might be less a cure for old political pathologies than a seedbed of new ones. It means to miss a distinctive chapter in the history of Zionism, wherein new forms of Jewish doubt about Poland intersected with unexpected transformations in Palestine to drive hundreds of thousands of Polish Jews previously distant from any version of Zionist thought to think about how the *fact* of a new kind of Jewish polity emerging in the Middle East might offer a chance at a dramatically different future. To ignore Astour's sensibility means, third, to miss an essential moment in the history of modern Jewish culture in its secularist form. Scholars of secular Jewish culture are often fascinated by its social-critical élan or by its champions' bold confidence that Jews could define their own modernity; the latter was the central concern of my own first book. But in this book I trace sadder reckonings with the idea that Jewish culture might have to reduce itself to psychic first aid in the absence of solutions for Jews' problems.

Finally, to push what Astour represented to the margins means to miss what the Polish Jewish 1930s have to say to two global histories of the twentieth century and our own age: the history of progressivism's ongoing struggle to make sense of the unexpected powers of illiberal politics and the politics of enmity, and the history of minority confrontations with majority pathologies, with the need to manage negative identity and its wounds, with calculations of risk, and with the bleak imperatives of communal triage. The Polish Jews on whom I focus felt compelled by circumstance and danger to shift the focus of their thought from which identity they wished to choose to what the majority national society around them wanted and where it was bound. They were compelled to rethink their politics less in terms of long-held ideals and more in terms of the fact of vulnerability and relative powerlessness. Questions of belonging and homelessness, territoriality and dispersion, home and exit were thrust upon them. They felt compelled to make hard choices and sacrifice some things that mattered for others.

This book thus seeks to reopen classic intertwined questions regarding Jewish experience in the nation-state, the history of Europe's Jewish Question and Jewish efforts to find political answers to it (not least through Zionism), and the history of Jewish worldly political thought and choice in modernity. Many Jewish historians wish to focus on Jewish political thought that remained confident about Jewish agency. Joining a different scholarly line that might be said to stretch from Hannah Arendt to contemporary historians like David Engel, this book focuses instead on Jewish thought that emerged from the forcing bed of endangerment, from the prediction that dangerous phenomena around Jews would likely grow worse before they grew better, and from the growing sense that Jews' assumptions about their capacity to shape their own fate—the defining assumption of modern Jewish politics since the 1890s, if not the 1860s—had been mistaken from the start. And though the East European Jewish situation was of course unique, it may also be understood as one case of an intellectual and political fate experienced by many communities defined as unwanted minorities in the age of the nation-state.[13]

Entering the 1930s in Poland

This is a book about the Polish Jewish late 1920s and 1930s, but I do not claim that the paths of Jewish thought I explore were wholly new to that decade, nor am I interested only in the new per se. Of course, in part I am interested in this particular period because it presented Jewish thought with some genuinely new kinds and intensities of danger. There were new intensities and new syntheses of anti-Jewish vision and feeling diffusing, in Poland as in many European societies, from the radical Right into other parts of the social body, moving from the hothouses of Poland's universities to its high schools, from its cities to towns, from towns to villages. In countries around Poland, fascism and extremist ethnonationalism moved from strength to strength. The Great Depression, which began to wrack Poland in 1929 and would not let go, produced profound frustration and great fear about the future among Poles of all backgrounds; amid such social suffering, and in a framework where popular democratic demands that government serve the people were now fully intertwined with commonsense nationalist presumptions about who the people were and were not, it might not even require strong conviction of Jewish malignity, conspiracy, and power for ordinary folks to conclude that a large "alien" middleman minority with an outsize role (however faltering) in Poland's commercial economy was a blockage on their own narrowing path to a better life—and that of their children. And among political elites, thinkers, and national intellectuals, as the 1920s gave way to the 1930s, decades of thinking about "the Jews" as one of the great geopolitical "questions" or "problems" demanding national and international "solutions" ripened, as Holly Case and Anna Landau-Czajka have shown, into a spreading sense in Poland as across Eastern and Central Europe that the time was *now,* that it was both possible and exigent to find dramatic solutions to this "abiding problem" for the good of the nation.[14]

But if the newness of the interwar era's perceived dangers is indeed one of my concerns, this book equally proceeds from the sense that the era of

Piłsudski's regime, actually the last relatively quiet era in Polish and East European Jewish life, crystallized a countertradition of Jewish thought that had shadowed Jewish modernity since the 1880s—a countertradition predicated not on the conviction of Jews' capacity to make their own fate but on the structural roots of danger, Jewish vulnerability, and Jews' incapacity as a minority to much affect either. Such Jewish thinking had emerged intermittently in Eastern Europe since 1881, but had also been restrained by countervailing hopes. In 1882, amid a sudden storm of anti-Jewish riots in the Russian empire and new forms of essentialist antisemitism in Western Europe, the assimilated Odessa doctor Leon Pinsker wrote his famed *Autoemancipation.* Alongside weird excurses on Jews as a sort of undead community terrifying in its uncanniness, Pinsker offered an innovative critique, presaging that of Hannah Arendt, of key dimensions of the progressive political-cultural faith that had guided Jewish emancipatory politics for decades. The emancipation that Western Jews had won and for which East European Jews wished was never given as "a spontaneous expression of human feeling" but always as a "gift" that could be revoked. Jews were fundamentally "refugees" because they could not return the gift within the comity of citizenship-granting nation-states— and "where is the refugee to whom a refuge may not be refused?"[15] In 1903, a brutal three-day carnival of anti-Jewish murder and rape in Kishinev provoked reactions among East European Jews that were, for all their intensity of feeling, mostly reiterations of longstanding certainties. Liberals saw a plot by the Tsarist regime. The Jewish socialist Bund insisted that "spreading class consciousness, aiding the growth of the socialist movement that will destroy the whole capitalist order" was "the best and only way to bring an end to anti-Semitism and pogroms." But one circle of nationalist intellectuals was driven to rediscover Pinsker's insights in a sociological vein:

> We cannot attribute all blame to the wickedness of some individuals [but to] our situation *in general.* Had we not been deprived of fundamental human rights, had the masses not seen, day in and day out, our humiliation in this country, the hatred and contempt that are poured down upon us *from on high*—the power of a few agitators would not have been so great as to lead the masses to robbery and murder in broad daylight. But as we are degraded [. . .] by the very laws of the land; as we are always being trampled on by anyone who has feet [. . .] it is only natural that this constant education

implants a strong belief in the hearts of the rabble that a Jew is not human, and there is no obligation to treat him justly, like other human beings; that not only his property and his honor, but his life, too, is disowned, and his blood is unaccounted for.[16]

Here was a post-liberal sociological insight for the twentieth century to come: visibility, large numbers, urbanity, and a modicum of wealth combined with rightlessness and powerlessness seemed to be breeding not sympathy but hatred.

Such intimations haunted Jewish thought in Eastern Europe for five decades. But they did not win hegemony in Jewish political culture. On the contrary, if any one conviction can be said to have dominated self-consciously modern Jewish political culture in Eastern Europe from the 1880s until the 1930s, it was that Jews could substantially determine their own communal fate through collective Jewish action. It was this conviction that guided what historians call "the new Jewish politics": a family of nationalist, socialist, and late-liberal bids for individual emancipation or for "autoemancipation" as an autonomous nation in a federalized Eastern Europe. The grimmer vision first propounded by Pinsker haunted this new Jewish politics and found a home in its intermittently dominant Zionist lobe. But especially in the prewar era, even Zionism was driven more by visions of national regeneration than of looming danger.[17]

And talk of national regeneration signals another key feature of this new politics. The energizing conviction that East European Jews had it in their power to determine their communal future extended not only to politics but to other fields of collective endeavor like cultural formation. From the 1880s to the 1920s, two generations of writers, artists, and cultural enthusiasts pursued a vision of secular Jewish cultural reformation, powered by the conviction that they could carve out from the chaos of modernity a sphere of life in which modern Jews would flourish as a creative community.[18]

A full reconstruction of the sources of such hopes for Jewish agency cannot be attempted here. It had something to do with a surprisingly broad and deep progressive faith, sometimes Marxian, sometimes not, that whatever ugliness Jews faced was some form of Reaction that the world was moving past. Some figures like the heterodox Marxist-Zionist thinker Ber Borochov explored the darker possibility that modern developments and processes might themselves be generating dangers to Jewish well-being. But especially from the turn of the century, not only socialists and liberals but many Zionists embraced a progressive historiosophy. Parenthetically, the current book will illuminate how deep this faith was by showing how late and partial was the break with it even in the 1930s.[19]

Yet even as East European Jewry became a watchword for vigorous mass politics and institution building, a second dark worry also emerged: What if in fact all this effort was predicated on a mere *illusion* about Jewish agency and capacity? What if East European Jews—for all their outsize literacy, their deep reservoir of professionals and intellectuals, the collective wealth still held by their merchant class despite communal impoverishment, the vigor of their organizing—really did not have the resources or the weight relative to other collectives and forces in the region to meaningfully determine the shape of their collective fate *whatever* they did (unless it was to *leave* in search of better prospects elsewhere, as some two million were doing)? In 1908 the famed Warsaw Yiddish writer Y. L. Peretz wrote his nightmarish symbolist drama "At Night in the Old Marketplace." Over two decades, Peretz had become the leading tribune of Jewish self-determination through cultural creativity. Hence it was a jarring surprise when he put aside celebrations of Jewish folk culture's vitalizing powers to author a grueling morality play in which stock characters embodying every one of the Jewish political and cultural aspirations that had arisen in Eastern Europe—liberals, Zionists, socialists, and also poets and preachers of cultural rebirth like Peretz himself—proclaim their views in unrelieved cliché and prove equally unable to find "the word" that could redeem Jewish modernity. This, while the unquiet Jewish dead rise, a Catholic priest fulminates, and threatening cathedral statues of Polish nobles come to life.[20]

But such doubts did not triumph in Jewish life even after the failure of the 1905 Revolution. Some of the few thousand young Russo-Polish Jews who left for Ottoman Palestine in that era—among them some who would become Israel's founders—*were* driven in part by a grim sense that nothing could be done to win a decent future for East European Jewry as a whole, and that they were called to be the "saving remnant." But many more Jews remained convinced that progress was coming, however slowly, and that East European Jewry could shape its future. Peretz himself remained a progressive. In that same year, 1908, he affirmed his hopes for a coming multicultural federalism that Jews would help build: "The state, to which small and weak peoples were once sacrificed just as children were once sacrificed to Moloch, the state, which in the interests of the ruling classes and peoples had to level everything else" was "losing its luster [. . .]. And the weak, oppressed peoples awake, and struggle for their language, for their uniqueness against the state. And we, the weakest, have also joined their ranks."[21]

Even amid the worst, bloodiest moments of recorded Jewish history before the Holocaust, this sensibility continued to hold for many, and was even reinforced for some. In 1917–1921, as ideological, civil, and nationalist wars convulsed Eastern Europe, more than a hundred thousand Jews were slaughtered qua Jews by all sorts of actors. "Never before in modern history," as Jonathan Frankel indelibly puts it, "had the inherent vulnerability and weakness of the Jews as a scattered minority been exposed with such insistent brutality and impunity. Yet at the very same time, many Jews—movements, groups, individuals—came to the conclusion that the moment of emancipation or autoemancipation (national liberation, however variously defined) had arrived." Whether buoyed by the collapse of the old regime, the springtime of nations, or the apotheosis of Revolution, numerous Jews preserved the sense that "the Jewish people had it within their grasp at last to solve the Jewish question."[22]

This book does not attempt to reconstruct *why* Jewish thought oscillated between a sense of Jewish vulnerability and a sense of Jewish capacity for so long. Perhaps the only useful general explanation to make is that there were always beacons of hope, events, and processes in the larger world offering horizons of something better than mere exposure and powerlessness. Revolutionary socialism's march toward power between the 1890s and 1917, and the promise of more to come, was one such for many.[23]

So too, the first years of life in independent Poland brought their own mix of good omens with the bad. As noted, the birth of the state saw an upswell of anti-Jewish violence and of ever more chilling anti-Jewish activism, amid larger signs that the once-insurgent right-wing intolerant strand of Polish nationalism was moving toward power. Yet, too, the Polish republic offered Jews of every persuasion a far freer field for political action than they had enjoyed in Tsarist Russia. Jewish parties of all sorts could come out from the underground and compete in national elections in a Poland where Jews were 10 percent of the population, municipal elections in a Poland where Jews ranged from 30 to 60 percent of the urban population, and elections to state-recognized Jewish communal bodies where it could seem like real power was at stake. Jewish hopes flagged between 1922 and 1925 as efforts to forge a political bloc of Poland's minorities yielded nothing, the Right grew both more extreme and more politically dominant, and Jewish society was squeezed by state policies that seemed intended to drive Jews out of the middle class. Yet just as many Jews (and many other liberal-minded Polish citizens) were beginning to despair—indeed, for the first time there was a mass emigration of Polish Jews to Palestine in 1924–1925—Piłsudski carried out his coup from the center. As noted, Polish Jews were universally relieved, many talented Polonized Jews threw themselves into the service of the new regime, and, as Natalia Aleksiun's survey of semiliterate Jewish letters to Piłsudski shows, even many unassimilated Jews felt new hope.[24]

But in fact, in ways we will survey shortly, 1926 did not mark an end to the strife and danger plaguing Poland and its Jews. It is with the rapid waning of the hopes of 1926, as Poland sank into intense ideological conflict and economic crisis beneath a veneer of stability, and Poland's *kwestia żydowska,* its "Jewish Question," grew ever more toxic, that this book begins.

Astour's sense of rapidly rising danger to Jewish well-being across East Central Europe, his grim sense of Jews' incapacity to determine their fate, his scant faith in revolutionary deliverance—these are not the sorts of attitudes that recent Jewish and Polish historiography emphasizes. But a massive corpus of evidence shows that he was no anomaly. In 1933, the Yiddish philologist turned pioneering Jewish social psychologist Max Weinreich began a study of several hundred autobiographies written in 1932 and again in 1934 by youth from every region and milieu of Poland's divided Jewish population. Weinreich was fiercely committed to the Jewish diasporist ideal, and most certainly did not wish to find what he found.

First, Weinreich was forced to conclude, the mass of Jewish adolescents across the community's divides were convinced that they faced a grim future in Poland. Declarations of felt futurelessness were "a leitmotif of a great many of the autobiographies submitted to YIVO." The "young man from Warsaw" who concluded that "fate has sentenced me to suffer" was typical, as was one twenty-two-year-old from "a shtetl between Warsaw and Łódź (Lodz)" who deemed his "a hopeless generation." A second finding was equally decisive: many of these respondents had come to see their futurelessness in terms of not only economic ruination wrought by the Depression but also as a *political* condition deriving from their Jewishness—or rather, deriving from what their Jewishness meant to other people and institutions around them. The sense that Jewishness would ruin individual Jews' life chances was so common that Weinreich deemed it virtually universal to Polish Jewish life: although the advent of what he called "attacks of Jewishness" could be "sped up or arrested according to the concrete situation," they could not "be avoided." Finally, Weinreich discerned only two substantial countervailing tendencies to this general crisis of futurity: Zionism and Communism. He spent much of his book mobilizing psychological theories of compensation to condemn both as irrational, but he could not deny the profound attraction these programs—particularly, he granted, Zionism—were exerting on masses of Polish Jews. "Among us," Weinreich ultimately acknowledged, "each is already leaving, even if only psychologically."[25]

In truth, although Weinreich was appalled by what he found, he was not surprised. His research, though unmatched in the scope of its source base, mostly confirmed things already painfully obvious across Jewish society. One hardly had to immerse oneself in the 1932 and 1934 youth autobiographies to know that vast numbers of Polish Jews were burning to leave. Most notable was the reorientation of hundreds of thousands of Polish Jews toward Palestine's burgeoning Jewish-national community, the Yishuv, as Britain reopened its Palestine Mandate in 1932 to unprecedented (though still sharply limited) Jewish immigration. As 70,000 Polish Jews of all class, cultural, and ideological backgrounds left for Palestine over the next four years (competing for still-scant entry permissions with German and Yemenite Jews fleeing woes of their own),[26] far larger numbers eagerly sought that possibility. Tens of thousands, especially youth, enrolled in Zionist organizations to "get in line" for one of the coveted Certificates through which the British Mandatory allowed an individual without capital to settle in Palestine (the number of these was set semi-annually by British authorities, but their distribution was determined by the Zionist movement). At its height in 1933, the youth pioneer organization Hehalutz had over 50,000 members in Poland; similar numbers joined the opposing right-wing Zionist Betar youth movement. Masses of adults explored the option too. Irith Cherniavsky has made the striking discovery that, by 1939, 200,000 individuals had registered formal inquiries about emigration to Palestine with the Jewish Agency's office in Warsaw. She notes further that this number could not have included those who had taken "steps toward *aliyah* but had not yet registered at the Land of Israel Office: members of Zionist organizations, artisan organizations," and members of Hehalutz. Given that this second pool numbered tens of thousands at minimum, and adding that "it is not clear whether this list also included those registered in the regional Kraków and Łódź offices or whether it included those who had already emigrated to Palestine," it becomes still clearer that hundreds of thousands of Polish Jews actually began to think seriously about Palestine as a possibility over the course of the 1930s.[27] And crucially, though some of this burgeoning turn toward Palestine was fed by preexisting reservoirs of genuine Zionist commitment, this was, as we will see, largely a phenomenon of newcomers to Zionism driven above all by rising doubts about their future in Poland.

Just as crucially, the despairing sensibilities Weinreich reported were *not* new to 1935, or to 1933 when Weinreich began his study, or to 1932 when the first youth autobiographies began to flow into YIVO. Numerous other sources demonstrate that a grim take on the Jewish future in Poland began spreading across Polish Jewish society well before 1932, and that it was not confined to any one generation, region, class, or subculture. In 1930, the sociologist Jakob (Yankev) Lestschinsky (Leshtshinski) embarked on a yearlong investigation of the economic life and political outlook of Poland's Jews. In the 1920s, this ideologically peripatetic man had become sympathetic to the Diasporist ideals of the socialist Bund and its confidence that capitalism itself would dialectically solve the Jewish Question by recasting Jews as a nation of proletarians. But what he found in 1930 was that Polish Jews did not share his confidence. Rather, he reported grimly already in January 1931, Polish Jews across all class and cultural divides had been seized by a "pogrom-mood and panic-mood" and their main question had become "to where should one emigrate?"[28]

And some saw much the same even earlier. In 1928, the Yiddish Hebrew journalist Rachel (Rokhl) Faygenberg began a two-year tour "across [. . .] the Jewish cities and towns" of Poland. Even after several years in Palestine, Faygenberg did not share any of the disdain for diaspora life in general and traditional Jews in particular that was so common among the Yishuv's self-proclaimed New Jews. Proud of her own traditional upbringing, she found nobility in the struggle of small-town Jewish burghers to maintain respectability in the face of economic ruination, and credited traditional Jewish "refinement" and "Hasidic tradition" with sustaining communal strength. But by the end of 1929, Faygenberg was forced to conclude—"though it breaks my heart to say it"—that the chief reality of Polish Jewish life was "deep despair" and that among Jewish youth, the most pervasive "ideology" was readiness "to emigrate to any place that will give them a visa."[29]

Moreover, the contemporaries who saw this included not only scholars and journalists in Warsaw, Wilno, and abroad but also participants at the

Figure I.1 Rokhl Faygenberg. Archives of the YIVO Institute for Jewish Research, Record Group 121, Feigenberg R1.

grass roots. One of these, another figure who will stand at the center of this book, was a young man from the eastern Polish town of Bielsk Podlaski who wrote under the pseudonym Binyomen Rotberg or Binyomen R. Having written one of the 1934 autobiographies surveyed by Weinreich (an autobiography that itself offered an unusually thoughtful analysis of political searching among his peers), Binyomen took the unique second step of directly responding to Weinreich's analysis of his generation in *Veg tsu unzer yugnt*. As we will see at several points, his searching response, preserved in Weinreich's personal archive, compels reassessment of what many historians still imagine Polish Jewish politics to have been. But here, let us note solely what Binyomen R. deemed manifestly correct in Weinreich's findings: indeed, "every Jewish young person feels himself to be without a future"; and indeed, what produced this sense of futurelessness was as much political as economic: "We Jews began to feel a specific national oppression even before the Depression."[30]

In the study of Jewish political thinking and rethinking that follows, not only intellectuals like Weinreich, Lestschinsky, and Faygenberg will guide us, but also young people like Astour and Binyomen. But before we can proceed, we must stop to treat, with at least some due care, the complex Polish and global history which shaped their thought and with which they wrestled. To demonstrate that large numbers of Polish Jews were coming to share Astour's grim outlook on Polish Jewish prospects well before 1939 or 1936 raises the question of why this should have been so. Of course, Polish Jewish doubt about the future was not least a product of the Great Depression that began to afflict Poland already in late 1928 and only deepened its grip in the 1930s, and which savaged the already eroding small-commercial and artisanal sectors where most Polish Jews made a living.[31] But simultaneously, as I have already begun to show, rising numbers of Polish Jews also grew ever more concerned with what seemed to many to be rapidly metastasizing *political* dangers.

Were they simply succumbing to free-floating anxiety, or was there something to worry about? To suggest the latter courts the risk, again, of being declared "teleological." But it is not teleology to recognize that the late 1920s and early 1930s brought much evidence that Poland was not immune to the political pathologies racking so many other countries in Central Europe and around the globe—and that many of the pathologies in question threatened disturbing outcomes for Jewish life. True, Piłsudski's coup from the center installed a tolerant regime keen to consolidate rather than divide Polish society in the face of looming Soviet and German threats, and not afraid to use authoritarian means to hobble political opponents—including its chief competitor, the ethnonationalist and anti-semitic Right. But the Sanacja quickly proved limited in its capacities to remake Polish political culture.[32]

Instead, beneath the seeming stability of increasingly brittle Sanacja control, Polish life seethed with ever more intense political, communal, social, and cultural conflict. First, there was the renewed vitality of the organized mainstream Right (generally referred to across its various formations as the National Democracy movement or Endecja). The Right had been moving toward national political dominance before the 1926 coup; by 1930, it had begun to adapt effectively to regime harassment, as Stephanie Zloch has shown, and was showing renewed vitality and popularity in important constituencies. The Obóz Wielkiej Polski (OWP; Camp for Greater Poland), founded by Endecja leader Roman Dmowski after the 1926 coup, grew dramatically from 1930 and numbered some 250,000 members when the regime dissolved it in 1933.[33] The Sanacja could disband organizations, but it could not undo the fact that Poland's Right was no mere political party but rather a ramified subculture of civic organizations, student groups, and women's auxiliaries counting hundreds of thousands of supporters across the country.[34] Dramatic organizational regrowth was matched by ideological radicalization, led by a youth cohort who believed that power could be won only through open extraparliamentary confrontation with the Sanacja and that a wider Polish national awakening could only happen through new, more violent forms of mass mobilization and action.

And of special concern to Poland's Jews, nowhere was this ideological intensification more marked than in the realm of the mainstream Right's stance on the Jewish Question. Well before 1918, the conviction that "the Jews" were both a grave objective obstacle to Poland's national development and genuinely malign enemies working actively against Polish health and happiness had entered the mainstream of Polish nationalist thought, as historians such as Brian Porter, Grzegorz Krzywiec, and Theodore Weeks have shown.[35] After 1926, as historians such as Alina Cała and Kamil Kijek show, these beliefs became utterly central to Endek ideology, and ever-wilder rhetoric was accompanied by new deeds. Between 1929 and 1932, Poland's universities in Warsaw, Wilno, Lwów, and elsewhere became sites of violent anti-Jewish demonstrations, riots, and attacks. Right-wing students carried this antisemitic energy back to the small towns where some half of Polish Jewry continued to live. Beginning in 1931, as Kijek and Krzywiec have recently shown, Endek organizers launched a concerted campaign to inculcate antisemitic ideas and incite anti-Jewish violence among wide circles of ordinary Poles. Over 1932–1933, the Kielce district, for instance, saw a "massive," well-organized boycott campaign promoted among "city merchants and artisans" and "especially young peasants" through rhetorics of an "existential Jewish threat." In 1933 there began a spate of violent attacks against Jews in "the provincial cities and towns of the Białystok, Kielce, and Łódź districts." The electoral campaign of the spring of 1933 saw mainstream Endek politicians like Sejm member (and priest) Adam Błaszczyk celebrating Nazi policies as a model for how Poland should deal with its Jews.[36]

And it was not just that a revitalized nationalist Right was reemerging as the most formidable competitor to the Sanacja for national power. More deeply, those strands of Polish nationalism that framed all ethnic Others as problems or indeed enemies to the "real" nation not only grew more extreme *within* the organized Right but gained ever greater traction in the wider political culture. "Rightist ideology permeated Polish society ever more deeply," as Joseph Rothschild puts it; Timothy Snyder sees "Polish nationalism [turning] from the confidence of the 1920s to the fear of the 1930s, shifting from the ambitions of state building to worries of powerful neighbors and internal enemies."[37]

What did this entail concretely? Bogumił Grott finds that in its final years (1931–1933), the OWP became a genuine mass party that succeeded in moving beyond the Endecja's traditional constituencies to win support in "all social classes." Neglected sources from the era offer still more granular insights. In 1931, the young sociologist Aleksander Hertz conducted an experimental course in "civic education by correspondence" among some 500 rank-and-file members of Poland's Korpus Ochrony Pogranicza, the Border Protection Corps stationed in Poland's multiethnic eastern borderlands. It was offered with full support from the leadership of the KOP—like Hertz, Sanacja loyalists deeply committed to the goals of the young centrist regime. When Hertz and the Sanacja educational activist Lucja Kipowa sat down to write a book about the course, they also found themselves with extraordinarily "rich material" for investigating "the inner world" (*świat duchowny*) of the KOP men. Not only did they have in hand the 5,000 workbooks in which the 500 participants had sent in short-form answers to textbook questions ranging across every major social question in Polish life, they had also distributed an end-of-class survey enjoining longer and freer responses, encouraging the students to express their personal views by preserving their anonymity. Three hundred and ninety-one of these surveys were returned.[38]

Such access to the "inner world" of these men presented an exciting possibility for a young sociologist because, as Hertz and Kipowa observed, there was good reason to see them "to a large extent" as representative of "Poland's half- and quarter-intelligentsia." These men were of modest, provincial backgrounds, but they were strivers: patriots, family men, keen for education and advancement. They were the backbone of the nation.[39]

But to Hertz and Kipowa's dismay, this representativeness raised terrifying implications. One of the topics that many participants raised often and with "burning" interest was the question of "relations to the national minorities." Here, in a militia under direct Sanacja control, one might have expected the Sanacja's tolerant ideology to have sunk roots. Yet with regard to attitudes toward Poland's minorities, Hertz and Kipowa discovered instead that the "large majority of our students" actually manifested a "profound and sincere" investment in ideas associated with "the most fanatical press organs of the nationalistic camp," Suspicion of ethnic Germans on the western border seemed "theoretical," but the widespread hostility toward Ukrainians, Lithuanians, and Jews was intense. This suggested, alarmingly, that actual *contact* with minority individuals was not serving to lessen hostility but actually adding an element of "passions."[40]

Hertz and Kipowa's findings regarding their students' attitudes toward Jews (as toward Lithuanians and Ukrainians) were sobering:

> Among [the students], we found antisemitic attitudes to a very pronounced degree. This was not true for all of the students, of course, nor was it all to the same degree. Notably, some of the writers have had somewhat closer contact with the Jewish community and have attained a good understanding of its affairs (for example, some showed a thorough knowledge of political trends among [Polish] Jews). In those students, antisemitism was significantly weaker; in some it cannot be found at all [. . .]. However, in most [of our] cases, antisemitism is quite pronounced.[41]

And where the militiamen's hostility toward Lithuanians and Ukrainians was linked to actual ethnonational conflict in the borderlands, the relationship to Jews had a peculiar phenomenology. Beneath a grab bag of charges— "activity damaging to Poles, hatred toward Christians, international influence, support of Bolshevism, exploitation, economic maliciousness, spiritual and physical strangeness, a tendency toward slovenliness"—Hertz and Kipowa discerned three structuring convictions. The first of these was an essentially preempirical certainty about "the harmfulness of the Jews [*szkodliwość Żydów*]," which respondents "try in the most diverse ways to demonstrate." Second, "in general, the students feel the Jews to be something alien, as a jarring and irritating insertion." Third, Hertz and Kipowa found that for their respondents, these sentiments were thoroughly connected to a self-consciously *modern* self-image. The respondents took "the postulate of religious toleration [as] self-evident," and if religion was mentioned at all, it was only to attribute Jews' ostensible hatred of Christians to *Jewish* "religious fanaticism." Strikingly, the respondents worked to justify anti-Jewish sentiments with "rational arguments" in a way that they did not when discussing any of the other groups targeted for suspicion. Some respondents, Hertz and Kipowa stressed, did not manifest "chauvinistic attitudes," taking rather the "state attitude" of tolerance and civic inclusion toward minorities. They even added that these respondents were generally the most "outstanding." But the larger proportion of the respondents who took a robustly intolerant ethnonationalist line seemed, alas, more representative.[42]

What Hertz and Kipowa found suggested several deepening problems in Poland's political life, all feeding each other. The hold of rightist nationalist ideology on civic-minded people like the KOP men was intertwined with a second problem in interwar Poland's polity: deepening ethnonational hostilities along Poland's western and especially eastern reaches. Particularly volatile was the situation in Poland's east, the *kresy,* where Polish national aspirations clashed especially with the burgeoning nationalist movement of the vast population of ethnic Ukrainians in the southeast. This intersected, incidentally, with the Jewish Question in especially volatile ways: in places like the Wołyń/Volhynia/Volin region, both Polish and Ukrainian nationalist actors, colonial and anticolonial as it were, increasingly viewed the region's large Jewish population—poor but dominant in those regions' underdeveloped cities and commercial sectors— as an obstacle to the realization of their respective national hopes.[43]

And the salience of anti-Jewish convictions was the third problem about which Hertz and Kipowa's findings left little doubt. That Polish culture was not immune from the global malady of Judeophobia could not have surprised Hertz or Kipowa or their readers; it was neither rare nor hidden.[44] Ireneusz Jeziorski's study of the image of the Jewish in Polish culture tarries with a local paper of the mid-1920s, the *Gazeta Żywiecka.* Published under the slogan "With God and the Nation," it aimed to give "the citizens of Żywiec" local news. But the paper was also pervaded by charges of Jewish malignity and threat of every imaginable variety marked by a promiscuous combination of forms of antisemitism that we sometimes imagine as separate strains: religious and secular-national, objectivist and intentionalist. A short passage from an early issue combined the trope of Jews as a "non-creative" people destroying for the sake of destruction, a "parasitic form of life," and an enemy operating with special "hostility against the Polish people and its national tradition." These ideas were communicated through a "surreal" multiplication of repulsive metaphors: plant-parasites, leeches, excrement.[45] Hertz and Kipowa found less lurid anti-Jewish discourse among the KOP men, but it had the same disturbingly protean and experience-resistant character. The danger Jews posed was hydra-headed, but it was definitely a danger.

Neither these convictions nor these rhetorics were marginal. They flowed across the Polish cultural sphere in copious amounts. In the late 1920s, serious readers could "learn" from Wilno professor Feliks Koneczny about the "objective tensions" between the Polish and Jewish "ethos"— but also "discover" in his work that the *Protocols of the Elders of Zion* reflected an actual malevolent global Jewish conspiracy.[46] The 1932 *Zmierzch Izraela* (The twilight of Israel), a "history" of the eternal Jewish drive to "corrupt the non-Jewish world" that "revealed" Jewish conspiracy behind the Russian Revolution, the Protestant Reformation, even the fall of the Roman Empire, sold out twice within the year.[47] Not only secular people articulated this vision. As numerous scholars have shown, similar convictions pervaded a good portion of the vast discourse articulated under the sponsorship of the Polish Church, Poland's most important popular institution. While some church-sponsored discourse hewed to papal injunctions against ethnonational hatred, much of it resounded with claims like those of the rector of Lublin's Catholic University from 1925 to 1933, who taught both priests and laymen that "Jews bound by the Talmud were united together to plot against and destroy other nations."[48] Ronald Modras finds that conceptions of the Jews as a force inimical to Polish Catholic well-being resonated among many of the parish priests in regular contact with a large part of Poland's population. He also finds that "the charge of a Masonic-Jewish conspiracy was a staple" in the church-affiliated press, which reached hundreds of thousands of readers at many levels of sophistication. Cała also finds the "motif of conspiracy" widespread and particularly linked to Zionism, as when, in 1929, the important clerical journal *Przegląd Katolicki* offered a conspiracy-theory account of the Sixteenth Zionist Congress. And one did not have to be devout to encounter these teachings: the image of Jews as enemies of Catholic Poles made its way into some of the clergy-written textbooks used in Polish public schools. Taken as a whole, religious discourse about the Jews in Poland was less total and less directly aimed at incitement than the anti-Jewish rhetoric of the nationalist Right. It could be hedged by reaffirmation that Jews as individuals could of course redeem themselves through conversion, and even sometimes by a certain admiration for religious Jews' deep faith. But overall, the weight of religious discourse also fell on framing the Jews of Poland as a genuinely serious problem, both spiritual and social.[49]

It is important to register that Poland's civil society and culture offered far more tolerant visions as well. As the experimental pedagogue Henryk Goldszmit gained growing fame in Poland (albeit under his markedly un-Jewish penname Janusz Korczak), the rightist press responded furiously: in 1926, *Kurier Poznański* "outed" him as a "Jew-Zionist," and in 1929 *Myśl Narodowa* attacked his children's writings for undermining national identity.[50] But these sensibilities did not win the day outright: in 1933, Korczak received government honors, was included in a postcard series of "famous Polish doctors," and was even given a program on Polish radio.[51] Korczak's case reminds us that parts of Poland's cultural milieu arguably remained more closed to antisemitism than many. Polish literature never suffered the indignity of having its greatest interwar writers turn out to be Judeocide cheerleaders like Pound, Celine, or much of the Romanian avant-garde. Polish urban popular culture like cabaret was saturated with attention to Jews, but humorous defanging of antisemitism seems to have been the predominant tone (due not least to the many Jews involved). There were some Catholic thinkers and activists who argued for civic inclusion even on religious grounds, like another Wilno professor, Marian Zdziechowski. Numerous ordinary Poles evidently felt perfectly comfortable letting their children read Korczak's writing (or for that matter that of Julian Tuwim, who did not even conceal his manifestly Jewish name).[52]

And civic ideals could still seem formidable not only in the cultural sphere but in the political sphere too. Not only the Right but also the Sanacja had many devoted supporters, especially early on; historian Eva Plach cites letters to Piłsudski from regular Poles showing real enthusiasm for the Sanacja's vague program of national renewal and deep opposition to the Endecja.[53] Then there was the mainstream Left. As the atmosphere thickened, the Polish Socialist Party (PPS) overcame some of its earlier hesitancy to be seen as too close to the Jews. PPS university students aided Jewish fellow students against attackers. In 1932, the prominent PPS Sejm member Kazimierz Czapiński (later killed in Auschwitz) offered working-class Polish readers *Faszyzm Współczesny,* a simple account of fascism that for all its narrow class-struggle rhetoric did acknowledge and indict the Nazi obsession with Jews.[54] By 1934, the PPS was open to cooperation with the Jewish Bund, though Bundist leaders noted some tensions among the rank and file.[55]

But the question—at least for the Jews who figure in this book—was not whether there was tolerance as well as enmity in Poland's civic culture. The question was: Which way was all this going and likely to go? Historian Szymon Rudnicki observes that the "autumn of 1931" brought "a new stage in anti-Jewish propaganda and activity" in Polish life, as the pace of "anti-Jewish occurrences" accelerated, moved beyond the universities, and included new "unexpected" forms: flagrant beatings, library burnings, and a school principal in Baranów nad Wieprzem shaving a cross on a Jewish student's head.[56] More broadly, antisemitism was clearly moving toward popular political-cultural dominance. As Cała puts it, the late 1920s and early 1930s saw "wider popularization of antisemitic ideology among the middling and petty bourgeoisie, [in] peasant-clerical and worker-clerical circles, right-wing parts of the intelligentsia, and among the officer corps of the army and the police."[57] Kijek's aforementioned research on the Endek antisemitic campaign of 1931–1932 reveals government reports that the violent preachment was gaining many new followers among "young peasants and young clergy."[58] We cannot measure precisely the impact of the streams of antisemitic discourse flowing through public life, but Modras's note regarding church discourse seems apposite: "How much influence the church's pulpit exerted on Catholics at the time is [. . .] indeterminate," but it was "hardly negligible."[59] It seems clear that, as Landau-Czajka concludes, although many Poles continued in the early 1930s to "simply [see] Jews as co-citizens," this pool of tolerant people was "declining."[60]

And many contemporaries recognized this trajectory. Rudnicki notes the rising worry about a metastasis in Polish civil society between 1931 and 1934 in principled conservative journals like *Dzień Polski* and *Czas;* by 1934, *Czas* had concluded that antisemitism was "incredibly strong, incredibly deep" and that the Endeks were building on sentiments already widespread in the larger society.[61] Looking back at his own experience coming of age in the early 1930s, Czesław Miłosz went so far as to claim that, "in general, Poles were unusually aware of Jews and anti-Semitic."[62] Miłosz's own memoirs actually nuance this claim. But he was far from the only one to register a crisis. The aforementioned sociologist Hertz, a Polish patriot born of Polish patriots, certainly was not eager to pronounce a grim verdict on the Jewish-Polish relationship. In 1932, he and Kipowa had contained their grim findings with a declaration of undimmed "faith" that "the modern Polish state" could yet engineer "peaceful, just, and self-less cooperation of the groups and individuals" who composed Polish society. But by 1934, Hertz was sounding terrifying alarms in *Wiedza i życie* (a redoubt of the most liberal elements in the Sanacja, which, Hertz later noted, was "under constant criticism for being 'Jewified'").[63] There was now "no doubt" that an "antisemitic atmosphere" was spreading rapidly. "Anti-Jewish slogans are becoming more and more popular," and even political groupings for whom the Jewish Question had previously been marginal were taking them up as well. More fundamentally, the Jewish Question in Poland had come to be treated as a *"unicum,"* different in *essence* from "other national, religious, confessional, socio-economic or cultural" questions. And "thousands, millions of people" were proving open to the most bizarre conspiratorial convictions about

24

Jewish destructiveness: "Even people who manifest a certain mental level and critical thinking believe in the legends of the 'Elders of Zion.'"[64]

Clearly, as some historians will be quick to emphasize, the terrible conjunctural accident of the Great Depression played a significant role in all of the aforementioned cresting political enmities. Some contemporaries inclined to treat the Depression as the essential cause of the political pathologies in question. In autumn 1933, Warsaw's left-leaning Institute for Social Economics (Instytut Gospodarstwa Społecznego) gathered for analysis several hundred diaries by Polish peasants. The institute director Ludwik Krzywicki was disturbed to find the diaries suffused by growing "dislike, even hatred," toward outsiders (he also noted that although this could extend to all sorts of "outsiders"—the village schoolteacher, the constable—it seemed to apply "above all" to the "Żyd-pośrednik," the Jew middleman and creditor). But Krzywicki, a man of the Left, deemed this burgeoning hostility the product of the Depression, the "Crisis" that had "engulfed" peasant life ruinously and completely.[65]

Polish Jews were of course well aware that millions of their fellow Poles were suffering terribly from the Depression, and that the political pathologies taking shape around them were undoubtedly fed by mass social suffering. Jewish newspapers across the political spectrum keenly followed new research on the psychological and political effects of the Depression in Polish society broadly, like the aforementioned Instytut's groundbreaking 1933 sociology of Poland's unemployed, *Pamiętniki bezrobotnych*.[66] And if one imagined that growing mass openness to political enmity was largely due to crisis rather than more long-standing pathologies, it was possible to hope that when the Depression subsided, political pathologies would too.

But there were good reasons to worry that in fact the ramified politics of enmity taking shape in Poland had deeper roots. The Depression worsened but did not create profound structural problems of underdevelopment coupled with rapid population growth; by one estimate, in the 1930s, in a population of 30 million, "there were 4.5 million people for whom work needed to be found."[67] And the processes of ideological and cultural formation that unsettled Jews had been moving toward hegemony in Polish political culture not for years but for decades, and rather steadily. Historians like Krzywiec, Cała, Porter, Weeks, and others have established that the ethnonationalist "Poland for the Poles" idea, and the anti-Jewish ideologies grafted to it at the root, had been winning hearts and minds not since 1930 but since the 1890s; in Timothy Snyder's words, "Dmowski's definition of Polishness was all but hegemonic by 1914, and his National Democratic movement the most important in Polish lands."[68] And this had carried over into the first years of the young Polish state. As the organized Right moved toward predominance, the anti-Jewish sensibilities it championed continued their seemingly inexorable move to the center of Polish political culture, even as the state extended equal rights to Jews in a constitutional democracy. Rightist verbal and physical political violence—most famously the execration and assassination of President Gabriel Narutowicz as a "president for the Jews"—had rapidly set the terms of debate about the Jewish Problem. Anti-Jewish attitudes seemed pervasive enough among Poles of all classes that in the 1922 elections even the socialist PPS advertised that its candidates were "real Poles."[69]

And it wasn't simply antisemitism as a brew of toxic attitudes and suspicions that demands attention. Landau-Czajka suggests that more relevant in our assessments should be whether discourses and visions of Poland's Jews as a grave *problem* for Poland's development, health, and happiness—a *kwestia* that needed some solution—were mainstream. And clearly, they were. Landau-Czajka's study of discourse about "the Jewish Question" across Poland's political spectrum leads her to conclude that if there was a single moment that brought "a fundamental change in thinking about the matter," it was the Nazi demonstration to the world in 1933 that the terms of a country's Jewish Question could be changed far more quickly and profoundly than most thought possible. Yet she also reminds us that "throughout the entire interwar period in Poland, the Jewish Question was a subject of analysis and debate—whether with lesser or greater intensity," demand for "solutions to the Jewish Question did not appear suddenly," and "the majority of conceptions [of the Jewish Problem and solutions to it] in one form or another were present in Polish publicistics already in an earlier period." Extending his gaze beyond the secular realm, John Connelly suggests that within Polish Catholic religious thought too, the regnant view by the 1930s was that the sheer "size of Jewish communities—in some urban settings one-third of the population—[ruled] out compromise. The 'Jewish problem' was thought to require a radical solution, and the consensus on this matter was so overwhelming that one can count alternative views on the fingers of one hand."[70]

The problems looming ever larger after 1929 had long predated the Depression. And then, too, even in the 1930s the question of how much all of this was "just because of the Depression" was misleading in a second sense, as some began to recognize. Even granting that some of the rising tide of enmity flowing along channels dug by the Right flowed simply from Depression-era social suffering, did this mean that it would evaporate quickly when the Depression ended? Some Jews thought so, and all certainly hoped so—but others began to ask questions that presage our own hard-won recognition that economic crises can not only intensify but also solidify political pathologies long in the making. And some asked: Even if there is a reversal eventually, or even a breakthrough to something better, what will happen to us in the meantime? This was, the reader will recall, a key premise of Astour's text.

Then, too, the early 1930s not only intensified old problems but brought new terrors. Events abroad undid any lingering Jewish hopes for substantial protections from the international community even before the Sanacja withdrew from the Minorities Treaty in 1934.[71] Just over the border, the unexpected success of extreme-right politics in Germany and Austria between 1932 and 1934, and the unexpected weakness of socialist and liberal resistance in those places, suggested that the sociopolitical calculi with which reasonable Europeans had assessed the stability of their political order throughout the 1920s were terrifyingly inaccurate. And not only Poland's *Jews* saw how easily extremist or reactionary visions could win power even in liberal constitutional orders, with well-organized socialist parties to boot, and transform the terms of the Jewish Problem overnight.[72] Other Poles did too. As noted, Landau-Czajka concludes that if there was a moment of "breakthrough" in the idea that Poland could "solve" its Jewish Question, it was not Piłsudski's death in 1935 but "the year 1933."[73]

And then there was the terrifying generational issue. In Poland as in many Central European states, antisemitism was particularly pervasive, virulent, and ambitious in the generation coming of age after 1926. Signs of openness to virulent anti-Jewish views among Ukrainian and peasant youth were worrisome enough. But even more worrisome was that the most extreme antisemitism was flourishing—had long been flourishing—among *elite* Polish youth, students in Poland's universities and increasingly its gymnasia, those destined for leadership of state and polity. By 1934, the aforementioned sociologist Lestschinsky reflected grimly that while it was infuriating that the regime-men now targeting the Jews for extrusion were often "a part of that same generation with which we stood on the barricades, with which we sat in prison," there was good reason to be far more worried about the *rising* generation, the sons of the new elites: "a new younger generation 'which did not know Joseph,' which did not see the Jews on the barricades and did not itself stand on the barricades [. . .] a generation for whom personal and national egoism, chauvinism and cruelty constitute its fundamental makeup." Jews had to ask what would happen in coming years as this rising youth began to inherit state power?[74]

And what of the Sanacja, which still, after all, held the levers of power? Some in the regime were genuinely committed to an inclusive vision of Polishness with room for Jews. But there were worrisome signs. As Emmanuel Melzer and William Hagen have shown, the sense that Jews posed a serious obstacle to Polish development was never fully evacuated from the Sanacja, a regime knit together from many parts. By the early 1930s, some affiliated with the regime were ready to enunciate such ideas, from the editor of the semiofficial regime paper *Gazeta Polska* Bogusław Miedziński to Poland's ambassador to Germany Alfred Wysocki, who already in May 1933 was defending Nazi views internally.[75] But more to the point, already by the end of the 1920s, there was growing reason to doubt that the regime would even try to impose a tolerant answer to the Jewish Question. A weak regime "increasingly isolated from society," as Antony Polonsky puts it, it surely did not have the power to uproot antisemitism systematically; and as Daniel Heller reminds us, it never tried.[76] Was the regime supposed to go out on a limb for a minority seen as dominating the commercial economy while regular Poles faced joblessness, poverty, and desperation, after years of effective efforts by the revitalized Right to convince ordinary Poles that the regime was actually the "servant" of "the Jews" and their supposed power?[77] By early 1934, the circumspect chief officer of the Joint Distribution Committee in Warsaw, Yitshok Giterman, a deeply committed Diasporist eager to believe in a Jewish future in Poland, privately reported that antisemitism had become so robust in Polish society that the Sanacja *had* to follow: "Any minister who treated the Jews fairly would cease to be minister."[78]

And again, as Polish Jews themselves understood, the problem was not simply antisemitism as some discrete free-floating ideology. Multiple pathologies were feeding one another. In 1937, a rising star of Polish sociology, Józef Chałasiński, launched a major research project on the outlook and inner lives of Poland's peasant youth. He found among many other things that extremist antisemitism had made dramatic inroads among quite a few. Chałasiński added to this two careful sociological points that more recent scholars sometimes make less carefully. First, this antisemitism was not random but closely linked to membership in rightist organizations; it was not "drunk with one's mother's milk" but incited and weaponized by connection to a specific politics. Second, Chałasiński insisted that to understand why some young peasants were embracing radical antisemitism, one had to understand a larger set of experiences and blockages. For two ethnic Polish peasant men in Wołyń, a twenty-seven-year-old from Horochów and a twenty-five-year-old from Łuck, violent antisemitism was part and parcel of a larger bundle of urges to "fight sectarianism, fight the Orthodox [Christians], fight Ukrainians, fight Jews, fight Communists." While not denying that their antisemitism was heartfelt, Chałasiński attributed their "emotional antagonism[s]" to wider social-psychological problems attendant on Poland's sputtering modernization. Their sense of "the Jew [as] the main culprit" behind their troubles stemmed from a sense of "powerlessness" that "occurs not only in relation to Jews, but to strangers generally; it always occurs easily among individuals [. . .] with a sense of superiority who find themselves in a strange environment [in which they] have no place or significance. For individuals in this situation, finding the guilty enemy who must be fought [. . .] is often the only way to salvage a threatened sense of importance."[79]

Leaving aside how fully Chałasiński's 1937 findings can be applied to the 1929–1935 period, his larger insight is undoubtedly correct: *of course* anti-Jewish antagonism in Poland—as in every other case—was not some self-contained phenomenon but rather interwoven with all sorts of other worries, enmities, fears, and societal blockages. But if *we* can appreciate Chałasiński alongside Hertz as another exemplar of prewar Polish sociology's precocious capacity to think toward theories of prejudice that American and refugee German sociology developed only after World War II, the Polish Jews we are studying had to ask a different question: Did the fact that the spread of far-reaching, potentially violent eliminationist and redemptive antisemitism was multifactorial mean that it was less dangerous to them?

So too, they had to ask: As the Depression worsened and fear among ordinary Poles grew greater, would antisemitism decline in significance or grow? As a generation of millions raised to be members of the Polish nation looked to their state to meet their needs in an era of desperation and fear, how could any regime respond except to put "real Poles" first? The future was in question for everyone, not just Jews. But this hardly guaranteed mutual sympathy. If anything, the opposite appeared far more likely for the foreseeable future, regardless of whether the Sanacja held power or the Right won it back.

Danger, Minority Social Thought, and Political Reason

Did all of this mean that a bad future for Polish Jews was carved in stone as of 1929? No one can make that pronouncement. Some of the unsettling phenomena limned above could lead in multiple directions. The Depression was driving some peasants toward antisemitic bromides, but then too there were signs that it was driving others toward critique of capitalism and the state.[80]

But to say that multiple possible futures remained in play should not give us license to ignore thought like Astour's or Binyomen R.'s, the kind of thought that Faygenberg, Lestschinsky, and Weinreich were finding across Polish Jewish society. As we will see, there were growing numbers of Polish Jews of quite varied political backgrounds who *did* begin to take cognizance of the phenomena limned above, who tried to comprehend them with new tools, and who began to reckon with their significance and with that fact of Jewish incapacity to avert them. Given our own ever-deepening understanding of just how grave the tensions racking Polish society were, we should not sequester such thinking as somehow beyond analysis.

Yet such sequestration is precisely where the field of Jewish history seems to be headed. In the decades following the Holocaust, the question of which Jewish movements had understood the situation in Europe and which had not seemed to many to have been answered with terrible clarity. Even in scholarly circles, few were prepared to take seriously pre-war diasporist, integrationist, and traditionalist convictions that it had been reasonable to hope for a safe and healthy Jewish future in post-imperial Central and Eastern Europe. Today, in the Jewish scholarly world at least, the ground is shifting rapidly in the other direction: a glance at the contents of Jewish studies, journals, and conferences leaves little doubt that scholarship on twentieth-century diaspora Jewry in Europe and (perhaps even more so) North Africa and the Levant is now dominated (at least in the United States) by passionate revisionist engagement with pro-diasporic ideologies and hopes previously dismissed. How far this shift extends beyond the walls of the academy is unclear, but much anecdotal evidence testifies that it does. Teachers like myself can see it in the many undergraduate and graduate students who come to Jewish studies classes already surprisingly aware of the once-invisible Diasporist tradition and eager to learn more. Suggestive too is the fact that in 2013, *The New York Times* marked the seventieth anniversary of the Warsaw Ghetto uprising not by invoking it as a tragic symbol of a foreordained Jewish doom, but by running an essay by a leading scholar that compared the views of Poland's socialist-diasporist Bund to those of Zionism and averred that "in the 1920s and 1930s, the Bund's program seemed much more grounded, sensible and realistic."[81]

It seems obvious that present-day concerns are the driving force behind this quickening shift in common wisdom, and that changing attitudes not only toward nationalism in general but toward the terrible situation in Israel and Palestine in particular are decisive factors. Just as clearly, the mere fact of this presentism does not invalidate any of the historical claims made within the frame of the new paradigm, any more than we can simply dismiss earlier historical analysis written within the frame of recent catastrophe. My claim is more modest, if untimely: This new common wisdom should not lead us to overlook an entire universe of twentieth-century Jewish historical experience and thought.

There are many ways to approach the thorny problem of assessing the realism of historical actors. One approach, central to the new common sense, is to compare the programs offered by the competing movements in interwar Jewish life and to maintain that those that promised to help the largest numbers of Jews with as little alteration of their condition as possible must be adjudged the most realistic (once we suspend "teleological" sensibilities).[82] The approach taken in this book stems from a different conviction: that we miss much that is essential in the modern Jewish experience—and perhaps that of any number of modern political subjects in dangerous times— if we ignore historical actors who sought to determine what is "realistic" not within the space of ideological faiths but from the standpoint of dangers they saw emerging around them and sober assessment of the limits of their own agency.[83]

One of the chief empirical contentions of this book is that in the seemingly stable Sanacja era, growing numbers of Polish Jews came to think of political realism *not* in terms of *any* of the ideological blueprints on offer in Jewish life since the 1890s, but as a problem of trying to extrapolate what trajectories in Poland's and Europe's messy present were likely to win out—and what, if anything, Jews could do about it collectively or individually. Again, it is *not* my argument that all Polish Jews felt this way.

Many continued to believe that traditions of tolerance in Polish political culture would win out eventually. Others retained a faith in the providence of God or History for Jews who organized and behaved correctly. Even great stumbling blocks placed before the socialist faithful, like the easy victories of rightist forces in 1933 and 1934 over the vaunted socialist movements of Germany and Austria, did not always erode Marxist certainties. When the Bundist leader Henryk Erlikh set out to reiterate the "the essence of Bundism" in late 1934, he found no reason to rethink his belief that class struggle would bring revolution in Poland and solve its Jewish problem.[84]

Nor is it my goal to insist that these forms of faith had no grounding in reality. Socialists in particular could point to concrete reasons to hope for a decisive turn for the better in the not impossibly distant future. Communists were of course correct that the Soviet regime on Poland's eastern border could transform societies profoundly, if it wished. Bundists could point to the fact that they were the one party in Jewish life with a real partner in the mainstream Polish political field, the repressed but unbowed Polish Socialist Party (PPS).[85]

But many others traversing the 1928–1935 era could not abide in such hopes. Max Weinreich, a committed Bundist in his youth and still a supporter in the 1930s, reacted rather less confidently than Erlikh to events in Austria, which he happened to witness while studying with the Viennese youth psychologist Charlotte Buehler. In March 1934, in a letter written in ungainly English to an American colleague, he acknowledged: "The Vienna tragic events of February haven't affected us directly, but the imponderabilia of life have changed immensely."[86]

In his chastened sense of the need to rethink cherished assumptions not only about socialism's powers but about the progress of human culture and the reach of Jewish agency, Weinreich embodies one of the impulses that this book seeks to recover. Chapter 1 of this study takes up the phenomenon revealed and concealed by Weinreich's invocation of the Malinowskian term "imponderabilia." Gathering a variety of sources that testify to deepening doubts about a viable future across Polish Jewish society well before 1939 or 1936, Chapter 1 also lays groundwork for an argument that runs throughout this study: that for a substantial number of Polish Jews, these doubts emerged not only from economic woe but from reflection on *political* developments taking shape around Polish Jews, whether over the border in Germany and Austria or at home. Concomitantly, Chapter 1 begins to recapture a profound shift in Polish Jewish political thought that will also preoccupy us throughout this work: a growing sense that Jewish political thinking had to begin not from ideological certainties but from an appreciation of rising dangers to Jewish well-being.

Chapter 2 turns to the history of organized Jewish politics, but does so to recover a neglected phenomenon that unfolded *outside* the familiar Jewish political movements and troubled all of them. I argue that in the late 1920s and early 1930s, the same sense of growing danger spurred a genuine transformation of Polish Jewish political culture at the grassroots. I recover mass disillusionment with the existing political programs on offer as incapable of charting any realistic path to a better Polish Jewish future, coupled with ever-widening interest in the possibility of individual exit from Poland (and Europe) in search of something better. These factors provoked substantial "desertion" from Orthodox and Diasporist movements and a sudden explosion of interest in "pioneering" Zionism that grew not from serious engagement with Zionist ideology but from the first two factors coupled with newly concrete possibilities for Jewish life in Palestine.

Readers interested in the history of Polish Jewish politics may find frustrating the kind of political history assayed in Chapter 2 and taken up again in Chapters 5–7. Poland's great Jewish socialist leaders barely appear, Orthodox leaders show up only in the conclusion, and even major Zionist figures are wedged into minor roles alongside unfamiliar journalists and sociologists, provincial activists, heterodox socialists without party home, and young people wholly without influence. This omission is, however, not an oversight. With the partial exception of the Zionists, in the early 1930s the great Jewish movements generally did not rethink strategies, assumptions, and ideals born in the 1920s or even the 1890s. The Orthodox Agudes Yisroel (Agudat Israel) party remained committed to quietistic loyalism and quiet lobbying toward whichever regime ruled. The Bund and the Communists remained committed to the view that revolution was the only meaningful goal and that in the meantime, politics meant unrelenting "class warfare" with Jewish "bourgeois" elements.[87]

This book is not about true believers. Its protagonists are self-selected by their demonstrated sense of the need to rethink old assumptions. Where Chapters 1 and 2 acquaint us with some of these voices and their inchoate efforts to find different options in organized politics, Chapters 3 and 4 turn our attention to Jewish intellectuals who began to engage these questions in more analytically ramified terms. Taken together, Chapters 3 and 4 offer an intellectual history of a painful and partial recasting of Jewish social thought about the nation-state, minorityhood, antisemitism, and political rationality. The figures on whom these chapters focus—some in Poland, some in an East European Jewish "near-abroad" of peripatetic scholar-intellectuals—were both Zionists and Diasporists. Looking beyond siloed histories divided between Zionist and Diasporist camps, I investigate the thought produced when heterodox thinkers in both camps were impelled to abandon old certainties and grope toward new understandings of the Jewish condition and of where the society around them was going.

But was the key issue the former or the latter—what Polish Jewry was becoming, or rather what Poland and Europe were becoming and what that would most likely mean for Jews? The analysis bifurcates in accordance with the national intelligentsia's divided answer. Pained awareness of the sense of crisis gripping many Polish Jews drove some—especially Diasporists—to think more urgently about how subjectivity itself could be wounded, what that might mean for individuals and the community, and what might be done about it. Thus, the aforementioned Weinreich became an informed, if reluctant, participant in a comparative sociology of global minorityhood: pulled away from the comfortable tradition of imagining Jewish nationhood as like that of other "historical nations," he began to think about Polish Jewish subjectivity in relation to African American experiences of violent exclusion and imposed identity. Tracing new lines of thinking about psychology and politics, Diaspora and minorityhood, Chapter 3 also reaches beyond intellectual history to investigate how Diasporist activists and artists hoped to shore up embattled Jewish subjectivity. Focusing on figures *not* armored in Marxist certainties, this chapter aligns with work on Diasporist praxis at its most complex by scholars such as Szymaniak, Kassow, Efrat Gal-Ed, and Cecile Kuznitz. But where they explore ways in which Diasporism's *Kultur* ideal retained vitality amid the era's challenges, I explore how visions of Jewish self-reinvention through culture began to give way to a sad sense that Jewish culture could only help Jews bear up to psychic woe.[88]

As some Polish Jewish intellectuals confronted embattled subjectivity, others found themselves driven to search for new tools to understand unexpected trajectories of the political world around them. Chapter 4 examines a motley assortment of heterodox intellectuals, mostly Zionists, who looked past reassuring truisms about the economic determination of politics and the essential rationality of human interests to wrestle with the unexpected powers of anti-Jewish myth in Europe, the changing relationship between mass politics and the choices of political elites in the nation-state, and illiberal nationalism's unexpected capacity to redefine the terms of public life. Tracing the movement of this thought, I suggest a deeper shift at its heart: an inchoate move from the slow work of trying to explain political phenomena toward an urgent sense of the need to think *extrapolatively, predictively,* about the likely trajectories of Poland, Europe, majoritarian nationalism, the population politics of nation-states, and the situation of middleman minorities.

The Polish Jewish thinkers featured in Chapters 3 and 4 were provincial participants in the central drama of twentieth-century social-political thought. Most were steeped in Marxian assumptions about the tight linkage of ideology to material interest or progressive convictions that society was groping (however fitfully) toward rationality. Their belated confrontation with the powers of hatred and resentment makes their 1930s part of a larger history of progressive and Left thought groping to understand political pathologies that defied long-standing assumptions in their rapid spread, intensity, and social reach. The rethinking these Jewish thinkers achieved was partial. But perhaps it offers something to our own present-day rediscovery that old models of who will do what to whom and why seem inadequate to the tempo and mobility of modern political hatred.[89] Perhaps, too, they can speak to concrete contemporary thinking about the nation-state. Wrestling with why hostility to Jews should become such a political power, some of these Jewish inquirers vectored on models that took cultural and psychological factors more seriously than progressive thought had done previously. Others moved toward sharper structural intuitions about what could go wrong for minorities in nation-states and why. Living in a republic where some elites genuinely sought to balance service to the Polish nation with equality for all, Jews became precocious observers of how this might be undone both by some citizens' enmities against "dangerous" minorities and by a powerful tendency within majoritarian nationalism toward demanding that the state serve only the "real nation."[90]

It was one thing to think about what was going wrong in the larger society around one, and another to ask what, if anything, one might do to find a path forward with the resources one had within the space of the possibilities available. By 1929, the aforementioned sociologist Yankev Lestschinsky had become a supporter of the Marxist-Diasporist Bund and a welcome presence in its party press. But he was also worried. In

October 1929, he sought to place an essay in a Bundist organ calling on the Bund and the Zionist movement to "together consider ways and means and seek a way forward." In one sense, Lestschinsky's request was profoundly unrealistic. As he well knew, the Polish Jewish political sphere was so divided by class politics that such a sit-down would have been unthinkable for Bundists; and indeed, his piece was rejected by the Bundist leader Erlikh despite its admirable "tone of calm and concrete practicality" because the Bund had to fight "the Jewish middle class, the Zionists" just as it expected class to trump nation among "'gentile' socialists." Yet in a different sense, Lestschinsky's piece bespoke precisely a search for realism: a call for Jewish politics to begin anew by figuring out what resources Jews really had to affect their own situation.[91]

Lestschinsky's argument crystallized a growing awareness that Jewish political resources were worrisomely limited. He was not the only one to wonder whether Polish Jews could substantially affect the choices the surrounding society would make about them. Like scholars today, some contemporaries were aware of Jewish predominance in Poland's film industry, which (as rightists lamented) kept Polish cinema free of antisemitism.[92] But how useful was this bulwark if the local prelate was preaching antisemitism to the fathers and local youth groups to the sons? Some knew of towns where Jewish Revisionist-Zionist youth marched as Polish scouts, complete with state-issued weaponry (provided with an eye toward the Soviet threat). But some also dwelt in towns where "all of the local [Gentile] students" were "pro-Endek."[93] And extending one's gaze beyond Poland offered no reassurance: Could Polish Jews affect choices made in Germany, France, Britain, the League of Nations, the United States? As the essay by Astour with which we opened demonstrates, some were beginning to think not.

Urgent extrapolative thinking about unexpectedly intense dangers, rising doubts about explanatory assumptions that had dominated Jewish social thought since the 1890s, a hard second look at the assumption that Jews could have a substantial impact on their collective future if they but organized—these were, I suggest, three key ingredients of a largely homeless Jewish political realism very different from what the main Polish Jewish movements offered. Chapters 5–7 look beyond formal intellectual discourse to ask how such hard reckonings fed new forms of Jewish political thinking and choice. Chapter 5 returns to the grass roots to argue that we have largely missed a quiet revolution in the character of popular Polish Jewish political thinking. Most histories of Polish Jewish politics in the 1930s remain focused on the old, long-established Jewish ideologies and camps. But several recent revisionist histories—most spectacularly Kijek's *Dzieci modernizmu*—have shown that there was actually a profound upending of Jewish political sensibility and faith in the early 1930s, especially among youth. Chapter 5 joins this discussion, combing through grassroots political thinking to argue that a significant number of Polish Jews moved not only toward skepticism about the old ideologies but also toward a new praxis of chastened inquiry—a keen drive to understand the processes taking shape around them, a practical-minded hunger to know what was actually possible, and a readiness to search along multiple channels for reliable information.

Chapter 6 takes up a more concrete political watershed of the era: how Polish Jews across the political spectrum negotiated a new kind of relationship to Zionism and to the perhaps-unique Jewish national community it was shaping in Palestine, the Yishuv. In part, of course, interest in the Yishuv was driven by fulsome Zionist propaganda. And no doubt growing Polish Jewish attention to Palestine also reflects the impress of Polish or Ukrainian nationalism on Jewish thinking.[94] But in our period, I argue, Polish Jewish engagement with Palestine was ever more defined by what was taking shape in Poland and Europe. One emissary from Palestine who arrived in Poland immediately after Arab-Jewish violence in August 1929 was struck by how tightly Polish Jews' view of the Palestine situation was intertwined with worries about their place in Poland: "One Jew, a provincial intellectual, said to me with real pain: 'The most terrible thing for us during the "disturbances" was not the fallen in themselves—we got used to that—but above all the feeling of shame vis-à-vis the Poles, because, behold, even in [Palestine] they can't stand us . . .' I encountered this insulting and painful feeling among many Jews here."[95] Between 1932 and 1936, when an unexpected British reopening of Palestine rendered it the world's most open destination for Jewish immigrants, Polish Jewry became one of the first Jewries to engage en masse less with Zionism as *idea* than the Yishuv as a new kind of *fact*—and potential. Debates about Zionism that had long pivoted on cultural issues of identity became instead for many an inquiry about where Jews, or at least *some,* were most likely to find a chance at a decent life.

Finally, Chapter 7 investigates the painful emergence of new forms of Jewish political rationality defined by emergency, renunciation, and triage. Under the pressure of the belief that Jews faced imminent danger they could do little to avert, some Polish Jews groped toward the unhappy sense

W Palestynie.

— Ojoj, panie Anglik, ja bardzo dziękuję za takie załatwienie kwestje żydowskie.

Figure I.2   "In Palestine: 'Oy oy, Mr. Englishman, sir, thank you very kindly for this solution to the [Jewish] Problem.'" Cartoon on the ethnic violence in Palestine in *Mucha,* a long-running Warsaw satirical journal. *Mucha* 61:38, 20 September 1929. Reproduction courtesy of Polona.

that political reason meant putting aside ideals and hopes—including cherished ones—to ask coldly what could be done (if anything) to improve *some* Jews' lives and life chances. Within the space of this kind of thinking, it became possible, I argue, to grapple consequentially with a series of tightly linked propositions: *exit* from Poland might be the only consequential way of really improving Jewish lives. The fact that exit was hard to find did not render this less true. There was no realistic chance of finding a happy solution for Polish Jewry as a whole (much less one that Jews could effect through their own agency). Therefore, however much one believed in the value of community or one's obligations to it, to better one's

Figure I.3   A Polish journal's commentary on the Zionist project. *Mucha* (Warszawa) 61:39, 27 September 1929. Reproduction courtesy of Polona.

own life chances might require seizing individual opportunities and leaving the community to its fate.

These new forms of political thought and choice, I argue, took shape in the interstices of organized Jewish politics, though they found some expression in youth-dominated movements like Hehalutz, the Territorialist movement, and the Frayhayt socialist-Zionist organization. They were expressed in partial forms, perhaps because they involved the painful recognition that things of value, even culture, community, and one's own identity, might have to be sacrificed for the sake of individual life chances. For the actors in Chapter 7, the problem of political choice was redefined by the painful recognition that Jews faced not one unitary danger but two different kinds. We might call these, following Eric Oberle, dangers of communal imperilment and individual vulnerability. The early 1930s laid bare the imperilment of the *communal* life to which the aspirations of many Polish Jews were bound. Yet that same period in Poland, as in Europe as a whole, forced back to the surface something brutally manifested during the 1914–1921 cataclysm but papered over in the hopeful 1920s: the growing multisided *vulnerability* of Jews as *individuals* to the whims of those who deemed them a threat or problem to be solved.[96]

We often indict nationalists—including the Jewish nationalists among whom most protagonists of this book must be reckoned—for thinking only of communal imperatives and always being ready to sacrifice individuals to them. But in the Polish Jewish case, worrying about the fate of the Jewish nation was arguably the only idiom that enjoined serious thought about either the community as a whole or all of the individuals who composed it. In all events, it was there that the tension between communal and individual need manifested itself.[97]

Chapter 7 thus takes up Jewish debates about communal solidarity against individual evacuation, traces new kinds of judgments about the claims of Zionism and its competitors against new standards like how much time remained, and traces the process of choice on the part of a few individuals and families who have left the sources to begin to do so. It enters, finally, a murky middle ground between the individual and the collective: Is a politics focused on one's children an especially narrow and selfish communality? Or an especially selfless approach to addressing vulnerability?

1

Futurelessness and the Jewish Question

In late 1931, after ten years in Palestine, the folklorist and veteran Zionist activist Alter Druyanov traveled back to Eastern Europe on behalf of Zionism's Jewish National Fund. In part, his task was to strengthen ties with committed Polish Zionist circles. But he was also charged with investigating the larger situation among "all segments" of Polish Jewry.[1] Druyanov took his charge seriously. In the six months that followed, he traversed "sixteen centers, including great and mid-sized cities and small towns," and evidently spoke to a wide array of interlocutors: not only Zionists of all sorts but also Orthodox Jews (*"haredim"*) and above all the "householders," the small merchants he viewed with a respect that was increasingly uncommon among fellow Zionists.[2]

The publication this trip yielded, the 1932 *Tsionut be-Polanyah* (Zionism in Poland), is half-remembered for its hearty defense of Polish Jews' grace under pressure and its rebuke to other emissaries from Palestine's Jewish community wont to make brutal indictments of Polish Jewish brokenness. But in fact, Druyanov could not disguise that he too found everyday Polish Jews gripped by fear and doubt about their prospects. Both those already impoverished and those who still only "heard the call of their hunters around them" were sunk in "the woe of today and the woe of the tomorrow drawing near." He summed up what he found thus: "The Polish Jew [. . .] whose day has darkened [. . .] lives in constant fear—not without reason—lest his tomorrow be still darker."[3]

Druyanov never got to the old eastern market town of Prużana (Yid.: Pruzhene; now Pruzhany in Belarus), but if he had, he would have had nothing to say to Gershn Urinsky. If there was one subculture in Polish Jewish life that Druyanov could not abide, it was the socialist-Diasporist milieu, which he found repellent for its revolutionary sentiments, anti-traditionalism, and anti-Zionism alike.[4] Urinsky was the sort of person

Druyanov could not stand. He was the dynamo behind the founding of Prużana's well-respected secular Yiddishist school and its tireless principal for two decades, in a setting where some parents were so poor they had to pay teachers in kind and Urinsky opened a paint store to support the school. Urinsky was founder and editor of the region's chief left-wing Yiddish newspaper. In 1931, he played the leading role in producing a unique Yiddish communal history of Prużana, the *Pinkes fun der shtot Pruzhene,* which impressed contemporaries as a great Diasporist achievement for its demonstration that the Jews of Prużana had sustained a vibrant communal and cultural life on their own terms over many generations. And Urinsky combined these Yiddishist cultural endeavors with a leading role in Prużana's Jewish Left, dominated by the Marxist Bund. A colleague at the school remembered Urinsky as no less a socialist than a Yiddishist. Though Urinsky himself was not a card-carrying Bundist, he was connected to it not only personally (his sister Yente Uryevitsh played a major role in the local Bund, as did Urinsky's closest school collaborator, Yente's husband Zalman) but also by strong sympathy. Indeed, in Prużana's 1929 Jewish communal board election, he was the top candidate for the "Radical Group" list, essentially a front for the Bund (which at the time still faced dubious legality in Poland's eastern provinces).[5]

Druyanov and Urinsky, thus, were loyal activists in two ever more bitterly opposed camps. But had they somehow chanced to talk, Druyanov would have discovered that the malady of felt futurelessness he found among so many Polish Jews in Zionist and Orthodox circles was spreading across working-class, leftist, and Diasporist circles too. From his vantage at the heart of Prużana's Diasporist milieu, Urinsky saw something unfolding that moved him by 1934 to a cri de coeur. Prużana's youth and parents alike, he averred, were consumed by a plague of "despair," had given up on Yiddish culture, and while a few had "fallen so far" that they were turning to religious Orthodoxy, most were vectoring on a different "extreme" solution: they were beginning to see exit from Poland as the only chance to win a decent future. The "fever" of exit that consumed the youth was not determined by any of the familiar ideological commitments that so cleanly divided older figures like Druyanov and Urinsky. Many of Prużana's youth regarded a Certificate allowing immigration to British Mandate Palestine as "the 'big win,'" but they were ready to leave for *anywhere:* "A few go to Argentina, but there's a crisis there too and it's difficult to establish oneself. Every so often someone gets to Cuba, once in a blue moon to the US," and even those waiting in "large numbers" for a Certificate to Palestine were open to leaving for what would seem to have been Palestine's polar opposite in the Jewish political imagination, the far eastern Soviet territory of Birobidzhan. There, the Soviet government claimed to be building a Jewish autonomous zone not least to compete with the Zionist endeavor for Jewish hearts and minds. "[Then] in the newspapers there appeared a notice about Birobidzhan, the young people gave a start: can you [actually] go to Birobidzhan? We're ready, give us the visa and we'll go."[6]

Strikingly, a report from 1936 or 1937 on the economic situation of Prużana's Jews preserved in the archives of the YIVO Institute attests to the accuracy of Urinsky's claims. Of the 183 Jews who had graduated from "the local schools over the past five years" (1932–1936), some 31—17 percent of the total recent graduates—had actually emigrated despite the incredibly high legal-administrative and economic barriers to doing so. Even Urinsky's list of destinations was not literary license: thirteen of these young people had gone to Palestine, eight to the United States, eight to Argentina, and two to Cuba.[7]

Thus, between 1931 and 1934, proceeding from profoundly opposed points of view, Druyanov and Urinsky discovered the same thing: a growing sense of futurelessness among Jews old and young, Zionist and socialist, culturally conservative and culturally radical. And as we saw in the introduction, they were far from alone: much the same was becoming visible to the ideologically peripatetic journalist Rokhl Faygenberg as early as 1929, the once-hopeful socialist-nationalist-Yiddishist sociologist Yankev Lestschinsky from his continental vantage between Berlin and Warsaw by 1931, the Yiddishist-Diasporist stalwart Max Weinreich in Wilno by 1933, and the twenty-year-old Binyomen R. in provincial Bielsk no later than 1934. And in turn, these were only a few of the many who registered some version of this same sea change in Polish Jewish political consciousness between 1929 and 1935. Over those years, numerous participant-observers from every camp and background—Zionists and anti-Zionists; visitors from abroad and deeply rooted Polish Jews; intellectuals, activists, and ordinary people; people at home in Warsaw, Wilno, and Łódź, in small towns in the Lithuanian and Ukrainian kresy, and in western Galicia and central Poland—recognized that large swaths of Polish Jewry, Jews of every social and ideological stripe, were growing convinced that there was little realistic prospect of a decent future for them or their children in Poland. Many of those who thought in these terms moved, moreover, toward a more ramified sense of their condition à la Astour: toward a concomitant sense that there were quite realistic prospects of a distinctly bad future awaiting them and that this was in some critical and perhaps determinative respect linked to the ascriptive fact of their Jewishness and what it might come to mean in the eyes of others and in the unfolding of larger processes around them.

This chapter undertakes four linked tasks. It aims, first, to help demonstrate the sheer scope and social reach of Polish Jewish doubts about the future. But, second, it also begins to show something more specific: Polish Jewry's emerging doubts about the future were not simply some unreflective reaction to the raw economic suffering visited on Poland by the Great Depression, but were for growing numbers also widely, deeply, and ever more coherently shaped by *political* fears and understandings. Contemporaries of course recognized that Jewish worries about the future in the 1930s were powered in part by brute economic disaster. But as we will see, Jewish concerns about the future in the 1928–1935 period articulated themselves around not only economic concerns but also political ones.

The dangers unfolding in and around Poland from the late 1920s on were many, and Jewish fears and inchoate analyses were fed by many sources. To reiterate, Poland's relatively stable regime sat atop a magma of hostilities and tensions: political, ethnopolitical, class-political. As Eva Plach has observed, the 1926 coup did nothing to abate the long-running conflict within the Polish national movement and self-consciously Polish society as a whole. On the contrary, it sharpened the struggle within the divided national mainstream as the sense that Poland's future and Polishness itself were utterly at stake compelled both supporters of the new regime and supporters of the nationalist Right toward a more uncompromising struggle.[8] Ethnopolitical tensions in Poland's east, particularly in the Polish Ukraine, threatened once again to spill over into violence after a decade of calm. The Depression generated not only ever-deepening class conflict along multiple lines—workers and bourgeoisie, country and city—but also ambient despair, fear, and anger across society. Though the antirightist Sanacja regime consolidated its hold on political institutions, the larger political culture was ever more permeated, as elaborated in the introduction, by ethnonationalist enmity, conspiracy thinking, and visions of radical societal transformation through mass politics and violence. Thus, it is unsurprising that some of the political fear that gripped Polish Jews was, as we will see, framed not in terms of antisemitism or the Jewish

Question but in direct relationship to a larger sense of things spinning terribly out of control.

At the same time, many of the voices we will encounter tied their deepening worries to awareness of a special kind of problem—the Jewish Problem—in the eyes of many and perhaps of the age. Historian Szymon Rudnicki sees the "autumn of 1931" as the beginning of "a new stage in anti-Jewish propaganda and activity" in Polish political life, marked by a burst of "anti-Jewish occurrences" across the arc of the new Poland—traversing the regions of Nowogródek, Białystok, Lublin, Warsaw, Łódź, Kielce, and Silesia—that were concentrated, notably, not in the kresy but in central Poland. He perceives popular anti-Jewish discourse in the press spreading from dedicated Endek organs to local papers from Poznań to Kraków. But Rudnicki also underscores the important point that not only historical retrospect allows us to see this shift: *contemporaries* perceived it too. Rudnicki cites disgust giving way to growing worry in principled Polish conservative journals like *Dzień Polski* and *Czas;* by 1934 the latter had concluded that antisemitism was "incredibly strong, incredibly deep" and that the Endeks were building on sentiments widespread in the larger society.[9]

And, as Rudnicki adds, Polish Jews were seeing this too. In the introduction, I tried to pull together a reasonable historical account of the complex but undoubtedly tension-ridden Polish political and cultural reality in which our actors swam, including the rapidly changing texture of the *kwestia żydowska*. Here, we will proceed from a different point of departure, examining what particular things various Jewish actors were starting to see as special or surprising dangers. If growing Jewish concerns about the future becoming present were not merely misdirected economic woe, as a few contemporaries on the left occasionally suggested,[10] still less should they be dismissed as free-floating anxiety unconnected to processes unfolding around Jews in Poland, Central Europe, and across the continent and globe. A third task of this chapter, which cuts against a certain skeptical vogue in some recent work on Jewish political culture, is to investigate seriously how real political processes were becoming visible, if always partially, in the evolving thought of Polish Jews. In numerous ways, Polish Jewish fears reflected real experience, whether direct or mediated, of a range of troubling gestures, events, promises, and threats that compelled recognition that Jews were objects of forces that seemed likely to render their lives considerably worse rather than better, and that were beyond their control.

In concentrating on what we might call the anatomy of Polish Jewish fears, I ultimately seek to get it out of the way, so to speak, so as to focus on the Polish Jewish *thinking* that grew out of sociopolitical experience—and thus investigate the Polish Jewish part in the larger modern story of how being targeted as a problem and a danger leads to particular kinds of social thought and political reason. The chapter's fourth and final goal is to embark on that undertaking. Moving among texts from 1926 to 1935 by Polish Jews of the most various sorts and varied locations, we will begin to see in inchoate form some emerging models of the Jewish political predicament—of what Jews ought to expect and prepare for.

The Scope of Felt Futurelessness

Few general claims about what people felt and thought can be stretched across a population as socially and culturally diverse and fissured as the three million Jews of interwar Poland. But as we have already begun to see, if there is one thing that a mass of observers of all social locations and ideological stripes agreed on, it was what the Zionist Druyanov and the anti-Zionist Urinsky, the populist Faygenberg, the waffling Diasporist Lestschinsky, and the Diasporist stalwart Weinreich all came to recognize between 1929 and 1935, several much against their will: a mass of evidence testifying to a cascading collapse of Polish Jewish hopes that they could attain a decent future in Poland, across all social and ideological lines in the community's life. The evidence of this shift is a case of unity in diversity, of many "blind men" tapping an undeniably real "elephant." Observers described different phenomena, laid different emphases, groped for understanding. But within this variety, all shared a sense of much Polish Jewish political outlook, argument, and thought reorganizing itself around a growing sense of no good future for most Polish Jews.

Some observers dilated on widening disillusionment regarding the hopes once placed in organized Polish Jewish politics as a means of defending Jewish rights and status in Poland's public sphere. In June 1932, Moyshe (Mojżesz) Polakiewicz wrote a private letter from Warsaw to his "rebbe" Yitshok Grinboym (Yitzhak Gruenbaum). Throughout the 1920s, Grinboym had been the leading figure in that wing of Polish Zionism that sought most assertively to mobilize Polish Jews not only in service of the Zionist project in Palestine but also to demand Jewish national minority rights in Poland. But by the end of the 1920s, such hopes had essentially collapsed; despairing of the broken promises of minority rights and the political process, Grinboym left Poland in 1932.[11] Polakiewicz wrote him shortly after his departure to report on the political situation: "Silence, lifelessness, and apathy reign in our little Jewish political world [. . .]. The indifference and the apathy make the impression either that everything is so happy and good for [Jews] that it isn't worthwhile to engage in serious activism and [conduct] a long-term struggle, or that things are so bitter that our hands won't lift themselves to work."[12] A similar account of the hollowing out of Jewish political hopes can be found in a 1932 police report from Poland's great industrial center Łódź: "More and more, one can see that the political life of the Jewish citizenry is slowly dying."[13]

Others, like Urinsky, focused on the intense and widespread desire to emigrate, which all observers understood as driven overwhelmingly not by any positive agenda about the destination country but by a growing conviction that Jews could not reasonably hope for a decent future in Poland. All sorts of data drawn from multiple realms attest to a strong ambient readiness across wide swaths of Polish Jewry to think seriously about leaving. The 400,000 Jews who did leave Poland between 1921 and 1938 made up some 50 percent of permanent emigration from Poland in this period as against the 10 percent of the population that Jews composed.[14] And inarguably, the raw number of actual emigrants represents only a small portion of those who grew interested in leaving. Between 1928 and 1931, more than 100,000 people—adults, obviously, and many heads of households—contacted the Jewish Central Emigration Society in Poland (YEAS); between 1924 and 1934, it received nearly 300,000 letters. This was an organization with no pull and very few resources; those who contacted it were seeking information, a bit of administrative assistance, perhaps small loans to ease emigration. Memoirs, contemporary observations, and even government reports all record that whenever a Jew from a small town managed to emigrate *anywhere,* however unfamiliar, others were seized by intense interest in the possibility of leaving for the same place.[15]

And the fact that most Polish Jews did not actually emigrate is hardly counterevidence of continued certainty about their future in Poland. There were massive obstacles to actual Jewish emigration. Most obviously, substantial parts of the world had no interest in East European Jewish immigration and worked actively to forestall it. The United States had closed itself off to all but a trickle of Jewish immigration in 1921, and by the 1930s, American consuls on the ground apparently shared a well-developed word-of-mouth culture enjoining special stringency when it came to Jews, in the context of a visa system whereby consular representatives could enforce strict country quotas at the point of origin.[16] Pioneered by Britain well before World War I and turned into US policy immediately after, the drive to constrict large-scale Jewish immigration began to spread to other intake countries as well, like South Africa.[17]

And there was also a tremendous barrier to Jewish emigration *from* Poland even where a destination might be found: sheer poverty. By dint of his position as the chief official in Poland for the American Jewish philanthropic giant the Joint Distribution Committee, the aforementioned Yitshok Giterman had an intimate and probably unequaled knowledge of the Polish Jewish economic situation in every sort of locale. Then, too, his position required that he maintain close contact with representatives of every Polish Jewish camp (and they with him), and few could have been as informed about the sentiments and situation of Polish Jews of every sort. By 1934, he was reporting not only that large numbers of Polish Jews were desperate to leave but also that many were simply too poor to act on that desire.[18]

Everyone who recognized the upsurge in Jewish eagerness to leave Poland recognized too the unique scope of interest in leaving for Palestine particularly. As Giterman observed in a private letter in 1935, even many Polish Jews who had previously been "distant or even antagonistic to Zionism" had grown interested in "practical Palestinist" activity owing to "events of very recent years."[19] As noted in the introduction, Britain's 1932 reopening of its Palestine Mandate to Jewish immigration at hitherto unprecedented (though still quite limited) levels after three years of near closure moved at least several hundred thousand Polish Jews to engage with the possibility of leaving for Palestine with some degree of seriousness over the next few years. Yet most everyone, Zionist and non-Zionist alike, also agreed (defensively or triumphantly, worriedly or accusingly) that much of this sharply rising interest in Palestine was driven less by any preexisting commitment to some version of Zionism than by grim assessment of individual and collective Jewish life chances in Poland. As the Hebrew poet Chaim Nahman Bialik toured Poland in late 1931, he was moved to write to his wife, Manya: "Poland, that is Jewish Poland, is completely destroyed. I've now visited ten cities"—these were Warsaw, Łódź, Kalisz, Sosnowiec, Częstochowa, Będzin, Kraków, Bielsko, Tarnów, and Lwów—and "one sees the ruination everywhere." What this meant for Zionism was double-edged: "The Jewish youth have no prospects in Poland—and [so] throw themselves to Zionism [. . .]. If no door can be opened in the Land of Israel, we will lose every one of them" to "the Left, from despair."[20] In 1934, the sociologist Lestschinsky put it thus: "Even Zionists admit that it is less that people are running *to* the Land of Israel and more that they are running *from* Poland, Romania, Lithuania, Latvia, Germany, Austria—and from where aren't they running?"[21] In 1933, when David Ben-Gurion arrived in Poland to mobilize support for Labor Zionism in the elections to the next Zionist Congress, he recognized the same: "The masses are not flocking to our ideology [. . .]; they are coming because they think that we are the channel to immigration."[22]

Of course, it was not the case that everyone who joined a Zionist organization in this period was simply seeking exit from Poland and felt no investment in Zionist ideals. Equally important, the turning of so many Polish Jews' attention to Zionism for whatever reasons often provoked thereafter serious thought about the Zionist project and about what the emerging Jewish Yishuv in Palestine did and did not offer in comparison with Poland—a point I return to in Chapter 6. But contemporaries could see and hear what Zionist organizational statistics also confirmed: that many and soon most of the growing number of Polish Jews who began to flow into Zionist organizations in the post-1928 period were not part of Poland's distinct Zionist subculture(s), were not products of the closely affiliated Tarbut Hebrew school system, and indeed did not have a previous connection to a Zionist organization of any sort. The first Zionist organization on the ground in Poland to register an upswing in Zionism's fortunes was Hehalutz, "The Pioneer," a Zionist-socialist youth-training movement affiliated with Palestine's newly burgeoning kibbutz movement that sought to direct Jewish youth toward "national regeneration" through settlement in a socialist Jewish collective. Already well before 1932, Hehalutz found itself facing an unexpected grassroots resurgence in its Polish ranks. This resurgence was unexpected because as of 1928 the Zionist project still seemed to be in a crisis of recent vintage: 1924 and 1925 had seen the first mass Polish Jewish emigration to Palestine, the so-called Fourth Aliyah, but what had begun as a triumph for Zionism had ended in economic collapse in Palestine's Jewish sector, driven the number of Polish Jews who formally took membership in the Zionist movement from 110,000 in 1925 to 10,670 a year later, and sent many recent arrivals back to the Diaspora bearing furious stories of expectations betrayed.[23]

In 1928, to the delight but also surprise of many kibbutz-movement activists, Hehalutz's fortunes in Poland began to turn around. By 1931 it had nearly 10,000 members; by 1933, this had more than doubled to

21,000 and was continuing to climb even as some actually managed to leave for Palestine. But one thing that was clear to all was that, as one activist put it in April 1929, many of those coming were "new people" possessing "neither written Torah nor oral Torah"—that is, coming to Hehalutz with no substantial previous Zionist engagement.[24] Tellingly, this grew truer after Palestine's reopening in mid-1932. In January 1933, as a massive new influx made itself felt, G. Ayzenberg reported from Galicia that many of the young people "lately streaming into Hehalutz" came "from outside any framework whatsoever." In some Hehalutz branches, "for instance in Kosów Huculski [Yid.: Kosev; Ukr.: Kosiv]," the majority consisted of "*stam-halutsim*" (just halutzim), meaning halutzim unaffiliated with any of the ideologically ramified party- or movement-affiliated youth groups that cooperated under the Hehalutz umbrella.[25] Two censuses of Polish Hehalutz membership conducted in July 1931 and again in April 1933 bespeak the general accuracy of these observations. Already in 1931, 41.37 percent of 9,862 members had not previously been involved in any Zionist youth organization. As of 1933, across a membership that had more than doubled and continued to grow rapidly, this was true of 59.3 percent.[26]

And as everyone understood, it was no accident that Hehalutz particularly was the address to which so many young people previously indifferent to Zionism (or indeed, antagonistic to it) now turned. On its face, Hehalutz was actually a strange choice for anyone unenthusiastic about Zionism as a program of rigorous self-transformation. The kibbutz movement in Palestine to which Hehalutz was connected saw itself as the avant-garde of a secular, socialist, Hebraic nation and imposed intense ideological demands on those who joined: a cultic embrace of manual labor as not only economic necessity but also supreme moral value, radical commitment to a Hebraist and secularist Jewish cultural revolution in one's own personal life, and an ethos of self-sacrifice.[27] But as everyone understood, many young people were joining Hehalutz *despite* these demands for transformation because—for reasons having to do with the balance of forces in Jewish Palestine—the kibbutz movement and Hehalutz had disproportionate access to the coveted Certificates: the permissions doled out by the British Mandatory to the Zionist organization every six months that allowed immigration to Palestine even by someone without means, as long as he or she had some guarantee of employment upon arrival. In Poland during the period under discussion, joining Hehalutz was

widely seen as the most practical choice for young people without resources seeking a chance to emigrate.[28]

Nor was the massive upswing of interest in Palestine as a possibility
confined to youth. When the aforementioned Polakiewicz wrote to Grinboym in late 1932 to lament the terrifying resignation he saw around him,
he noted one great exception: vast public interest in possible emigration
to Palestine. "Here it's heaven and earth and . . . Certificates. Everywhere,
in Warsaw and in the provinces, in the larger as well as the smaller towns.
The issue of Certificates has become the talk of the day."[29] Significantly,
Polakiewicz did not write triumphantly; worried about how much access
Palestine could really provide, he wished to reinvigorate the old-style
Polish Zionism concerned no less with Polish Jewry's needs than the
Yishuv's.

Not every Polish Jewish observer agreed that Polish Jewry was consumed by a crisis of futurity, and dissent from this picture was particularly strong among some socialists and Diasporists. Bundists seem to have
been particularly reluctant to acknowledge any sort of crisis of political
belief in their own ranks, though as we will see, there were plenty of signs
of it among those the Bund called "the Jewish working class," and indeed
substantial evidence of grassroots defections from the party to Zionism.
But even Bundists did not consistently deny that there was a crisis of
confidence in some parts of Polish Jewry. Sometimes, instead, they contained the unsettling implications of the phenomenon by insisting that
only the Polish Jewish "bourgeoisie" was seized by "panic," whereas
working-class Jews were ostensibly immune to doubts. This claim received
its most fulsome elaboration in the late 1930s, in the Bundist youth-
movement leader Moyshe Kligsberg's book *Youth Psychology and Socialist Education,* which insisted that those flowing into Hehalutz were
"bourgeois" youth moved by frustrated "careerism."[30] But the argument
was already emerging in the early 1930s. At a February 1935 teachers'
conference, the leading Bundist pedagogical activist Shloyme Mendelson
declared, "We must have a solid ideational foundation in order to swim
through the current of danger that is flooding over us. The Jewish bourgeoisie is gripped by panic and is lost spiritually. Our only bulwark is the
working class."[31]

Yet there were open admissions by figures on the left that in their circles too there was plenty of rising doubt. As we have begun to see in the
case of Weinreich, a Bundist since his university days in Petersburg, even

those who stood close to the Bund could not always convince themselves that any class of Polish Jewry was immunized against doubt. In 1929, teacher Shloyme Bastomski asked his students in Wilno's leading Yiddishist school to write an essay about how things would be a hundred years in the future. The thirteen-year-old Shmuel Murshteyn responded with a utopia in which there was "neither poor nor rich," essentials were free, work was ensured, and ethnic difference was neither bad fate nor something that had to be transcended. Murshteyn's essay sported sweet-natured technophilia: airships took students freely from Wilno over France to North America, and each of the "many Jewish farming villages, where only Jews live," used "electrical machinery" by day and attended local cinemas in each "Jewish village" at night. But there was a dark shadow over Murshteyn's Diasporist-socialist utopianism. In the essay's present moment, 2029, the Jewish farm families sadly watch a documentary film about "life a hundred, two hundred years ago" (that is, Murshteyn's 1929): "Every worker comes home exhausted, sucked dry [. . .]. Here is an artisan—a shoemaker. He gets up before daybreak, slaves a whole day, and lays down late, exhausted. Even in sleep he cannot rest, for he is thinking about paying bills, paying back loans, obligations and taxes [. . .]. Then one sees how the state grabs taxes from everyone. It's hard to watch."[32]

Der veg tsu unzer yugnt, Weinreich's uniquely sourced empirical investigation of Polish Jewish youth attitudes—based on a substantial cross section of more than 300 Jewish youth autobiographies from across Poland in 1932 and in 1934—demonstrated the accuracy of all the grim diagnoses by participant-observers like Polakiewicz, Giterman, Lestschinsky, and Faygenberg. Indeed, Weinreich was compelled to acknowledge, declarations of felt futurelessness were to be found in "a great many of the autobiographies submitted to YIVO." An "18-year old young man from Congress Poland" declared that "everyone is convinced that we have no prospects," dilated on the absence of professional possibilities of any sort for young shtetl Jews, and also registered what was already a growing sense of desperation regarding the possibility of emigration: "Overseas? But where to, and who would take us?" A twenty-two-year-old "from a town between Warsaw and Łódź" declared that "Jewish youth is roasting in a hermetically sealed pot and cannot release its energy. Every path is closed before it, it is not allowed in anywhere." And though such terms allowed in principle for a critique of this felt futurelessness as self-defeating—and this was the move that

Weinreich qua Diasporist would ultimately make at the end of *Veg*—here he allowed readers to see that this second respondent not only shared this despair but deemed it simply a *realistic* assessment of the situation: "Were one to ask that I describe my outlook on the era in which we are living [. . .] I would answer thus: a hopeless generation." A third autobiographer reflected, "It would be a great achievement for YIVO should it be able to clarify the dangers that arise when there emerges a youth without a tomorrow."[33] Weinreich himself was desperately eager to find more optimistic voices. He celebrated those he found who had not yet given up a stubborn commitment to the Diaspora.[34] But he came away convinced that these latter were a minority.

Weinreich was clearly distraught by these findings, but that he was not surprised he himself admitted in a moment of pained directness: "But it is not only from these autobiographies that we know Jewish life, and every one of us sees often enough the extinguished eyes and hanging heads." Nor did he come to recognize this phenomenon only in 1935, as he completed the book in which his findings were laid out; notes for the study dating to 1933 bespeak his awareness already that something was—from a Diasporist standpoint—profoundly awry.[35]

Between the Depression and Political Danger

In March 1930, after several months in Poland, the kibbutz-movement activist Lova Levita lamented that the "situation of the Jews of Poland" was defined by "a degenerative poverty that imposes its sentence on everyone without distinction." He was shocked by the "terrified anxiety over [every] cent, the concentration of every thought and worry on [. . .] unpaid promissory notes, tax rates."[36] This horrified assessment by someone who was no stranger to hard living—he had come of age in revolutionary Russia—will not surprise students of Polish Jewish life in the early 1930s. Was it not the case, as some contemporaries argued, that the felt crisis of futurity among Polish Jews was in the first instance a result not of political but economic woes: the Great Depression or a deeper process of declassing linked to the final collapse of long-moribund Jewish economic niches?

Yet Levita also offered a striking coda to his reflections: "And all of the superhuman efforts—which abase all self-worth—to hold on in life, to pull [oneself along], to survive, are done without even a minimum of faith in tomorrow." "Faith in tomorrow": Levita points us to the vital recognition that the transformation in Polish Jewish outlook was driven not only by brute material woe but also by a sense of a future foreclosed.

It is easy enough to assume that the factor shaping Jewish worries about the future was raw economic woe, for such woe was indeed severe for vast numbers of Polish Jews (as of course for vast numbers of non-Jewish Poles). A full-fledged collapse in the circumstances of many Jews, particularly in small towns, was already visible by the end of 1929, and the ensuing years would see the economic ruination of a good part of the Jewish population.[37] In October 1930, the Warsaw office of the Jewish industrial training organization ORT received the following grim report from Kowel in Poland's southeast (now Kovel' in Ukraine): "One of the largest industrialists in [the Volin region] Mr. Mikhoel Faynshteyn [. . .] has gone into a bankruptcy of more than half a million zlotys, and for our small provincial city this is truly a death-blow. Moyshe Kagan, the only member of our organization who paid 5 *gildn* a month membership dues and contributed $10 to our campaign, shot himself this week due to material difficulties."[38] In Buczacz (Yid.: Bitshutsh; Ukr.: Buchach) in Galicia, a local (Gentile) official reported that "commerce and trade, which are largely in the hands of the Jews," had collapsed in the midst of a more general economic crisis hitting the peasantry particularly hard, and there was now "an enormous number of needy Jews in the district."[39] These reports were symptomatic of currents from the smallest towns to the main business thoroughfare of Jewish Warsaw, Nalewki Street, where by 1935, as one observer put it, for every prosperous merchant, "ten, twenty" Jewish *luftmentshn* were eking out a shoestring existence as suppliers and agents.[40] In 1933, Leon Vulman, a leader in the Jewish public health organization TOZ, commented that the Polish Jewish masses' failure to adopt hygiene prescriptions was due less to opposition of "those strata [. . .] that still stand distant from a modern world-view" than to the fact of "the great poverty and material lack of the Jewish population, which is ruled by worry over a simple piece of bread to still one's hunger, and where there can be no talk at all about buying soap, detergent, toothpaste, brushes."[41]

Ezra Mendelsohn sums all this up with data from the 1931 census: "Between 1921 and 1931 one important change took place. That by the latter date more Jews derived their income from 'industry' (42.2 percent) than from 'commerce' (36.6 percent) was a most unusual situation so far as Jews were concerned and unparalleled in any other country in East Central Europe. Some observers called this a process of 'proletarianization,' while others, more realistically, termed it a process of pauperization."[42] Undoubtedly such material woe had a powerful effect on outlook, both among those plunged into ruinous poverty and among those living through a less brutal but still dizzying declassing.

But it is equally clear that for large and growing numbers of these same Polish Jews, distinctly political concerns about the political trajectory of the world around them also grew ever more central to their thought. One of the 1934 autobiographies collected by the YIVO Institute issued from the pen of a twenty-year-old woman calling herself "Forget-Me-Not." Like so many of the YIVO autobiographies, this one is organized around two poles: life trajectory from childhood to education to the world of work, and rising engagement with political ideology in the context of deepening material woes and political worries. In Forget-Me-Not's case, the former was marked by grinding poverty and family tragedy, an education sharply curtailed by both, and entry into full-time work as an adolescent. The latter was defined by what the author represents as a deep conversion to socialism as a faith. This occurred, evidently, sometime in her mid-adolescence, in the late 1920s or early 1930s. Barely out of elementary school, she was tasked with running the household for her father and six siblings while also working as a pea sheller. During evenings spent at a local Jewish library, she was approached by a young Communist—drawn perhaps by the fact that she was reading a novel by Upton Sinclair—and exposed for the first time to the argument that her woes stemmed from "the capitalist system." Within days she had joined "an illegal political organization"—a Communist Party cell. What followed was a conversion in the sense of coming to see a new truth and understanding the world anew through it: "For the first time, I became interested in life [. . .]. I learned that there were hundreds more like me." In short order, Forget-Me-Not moved into a position of authority within the small world of a political cell: "Assigned various political activities," she "devoted all [her] youthful energy to the movement." She also adopted the mandatory intra-Jewish antagonisms of Polish Jewish Communism toward both Zionism (an antagonism activated when the older male leader of her first cell actually "joined a Zionist organization to get a Certificate to emigrate to Palestine") and the Bund (an antagonism activated when one of her younger sisters declared that she wanted to join the Bundist SKIF youth group).[43]

But by the time Forget-Me-Not submitted her autobiography in 1934, she was mired in deep political doubt and had broken with Communism.

And the key factor in her telling was the victory of the Nazis in Germany. "The events in Germany affected me profoundly. When my friends shouted 'We were not defeated,' I realized how great the defeat was, because the masses were leaving us. At the moment when everything has reached a climax, fascism has triumphed and not the proletariat." Driven by a desperate desire to understand what had gone wrong, she had "spent entire evenings poring over various books and pamphlets, looking for an answer." She was also cast into "deep depress[ion]" by "these internal doubts" and, "for the reasons I've mentioned," left "the political group to which I'd belonged for a long time."

In Forget-Me-Not's case, the disillusionment was not complete. Her associational life remained connected to socialist activism: by the time she wrote in 1934, she had joined the Bundist sports organization Morgenshtern despite anti-Bundist feelings from her Communist days, and was devoting her evenings to union work. And her thought, even in its more critical mode, remained framed by socialist analytical categories. Thus, her analysis of the rising power of fascism—offered to the reader in several long present-tense asides—vectored on the Trotskyist account: the chief causes of the masses' seduction by fascism were "ignorance," a lack of adequate "education," and "lack [of] a common language" among "the workers." There is no articulation here of any thinking about ways Nazism and Austro-Fascism might have tapped into powerful nationalist, racist, and antisemitic enmities, hopes, and fears thickly woven into political imaginaries. Yet even within the limits of the frame set by historical-materialist ways of talking about the politics and ideology, Forget-Me-Not's text registers a disorienting turn from ready-made answers to new and pressing kinds of questions and a terrified sense of how near the danger was: "Starting with Germany, a fascist wave is now spreading over the entire world. Because of the ignorance of the masses, fascism is able to appropriate the proletariat's left-wing slogans and use them to attract the masses."

We should note that Forget-Me-Not's analysis did not frame the problems that consumed her in terms of antisemitism. Indeed, she had nothing but good to report of one of the few actual Catholic Poles she seems to have known—the supportive principal of her elementary school, a man committed to the liberal-integrative tradition of the Polish national idea. Rather, she framed her worries in terms of extremist nationalism's terrifying popular draw. We will now see that many of her contemporaries expressed worries that entangled such concerns with more specific intimations of the Jewish Question's metastasis. But Forget-Me-Not offers a valuable point of departure for two reasons. First, she reminds us in advance that Polish Jewish political fears had to contend not with one danger but with many interwoven ones, shifting, fast-moving, feeding on one another. Other observers bound to the fate of Polish or East European Jewry also foreground at times a sense of general rather than a specific crisis. Like Forget-Me-Not, the socialist-Diasporist activist Avrom Rozin was moved by what he called "the unbelievable catastrophe" of Nazi victory in 1933 and the shockingly easy victory of the clerical-nationalist Right over Austria's vaunted socialist movement in February 1934 to a vertiginous conclusion that right-wing nationalism had gone far further toward winning the hearts and minds of "the masses" in Central Europe than he could have imagined, for reasons and in ways that socialist theory was simply not well equipped to explain: "Why has the modern labor movement, without distinction of right and left, and not only in Germany and Austria but also in other lands, failed to command the soul of the worker-masses, to call forth from them that deep and abiding enthusiasm, that readiness for sacrifice, as various religious movements in earlier times were able [to do], for instance, and as still today is achieved by the apostles of patriotism, whom masses follow to the slaughter, driven not only by force but often by inner conviction?"[44] But Forget-Me-Not also offers an essential bridge to the next part of our discussion because she embodies the inchoate Jewish political thinking to which we now turn: though living in real poverty, she was engaged enough to understand that the problems of her age were far more than economic ones.

Forget-Me-Not and Ben-Adir wrote in the wake of Nazi victory on Poland's border. Others gave voice to deepening worries about what was going on inside Poland, and did so notably earlier. In January 1930, Jakob Appenszlak, Warsaw editor of the leading Polish-language Jewish newspaper *Nasz Przegląd,* proclaimed that much of Polish Jewry in all its variety—"worker, merchant, artisan, student, scholar, doctor, lawyer, engineer, industrialist, writer, and artist"—was coming to experience its life as a form of "ghettoization" within "invisible yet impassable boundaries." The forms of this new "ghetto" were various, but all involved the experience of large swaths of life possibilities being fenced off, of exclusion and closure—from factories whose Polish workers kept a closed shop against Jews, from state-owned industries and state-controlled internal markets, from state-backed loans and support, from inclusion in a longed-for Polish society itself. In turn, this present closure fed a sense that the future would only bring even more foreclosure. Appenszlak conceived the situation as variegated by the specificities of class but also *unified* by a shared experience of a future foreclosed by Jewishness. "Pauperization of the mass of Jews" was of course part of the problem, to varying degrees based on one's resources. But across all differences, Appenszlak suggested, the Jewish "worker, merchant, artisan, student, scholar, doctor, lawyer, engineer, industrialist, writer, and artist" increasingly shared an understanding that the forms of closure they were experiencing derived also from the decisions and desires of other actors—by a *politics* that related to their Jewishness and over which they had vanishingly little control.[45]

Not everyone who recognized that disturbing changes were afoot shared Appenszlak's sense of general siege. The 1 January 1930 issue of *Nasz Przegląd* that carried Appenszlak's diagnosis also carried a somewhat less grim assessment of the "Kwestia żydowska w Polsce w r. 1929" by his colleague Samuel Hirszhorn.[46] Like Appenszlak an intellectually serious and supple national progressive committed to Jewish collectivity but equally committed to the ideal that Polish Jews could be full participants in the young Polish commonwealth, Hirszhorn opened by sounding what could be read as more direct notes of warning than those by Appenszlak. He began by reviewing (for readers who could hardly have needed a review) the previous year's ominous uptick in more radical antisemitic agitation on the part of a newly reconstituted Endek movement and energetic university student circles eager to be its shock troops. But Hirszhorn's conclusions were guardedly optimistic: though the organized Right had spent the year trying to fan the flames of anti-Jewish sentiment *beyond* its ranks, Hirszhorn maintained, it had not had much apparent success. Efforts by right-wing students to foster a "pogrom atmosphere" in Lwów, Poznań, and other cities had backfired, in Hirszhorn's view, moving not only the representatives of the Sanacja state but also elements in the Polish public to push back against "excesses." Hirszhorn framed other rightist initiatives as a hope-inducing sign of retrenchment: rightists were now focusing on more modest campaigns against "overrepresentation" of Jewish students in universities, against Jewish medical students' access to cadavers, and against kosher slaughter because they had "suffered a defeat on the pogrom battlefield."[47]

Written at the very beginning of the period at stake in our discussion, Hirszhorn's guarded optimism captured a key assumption central to much Polish Jewish thinking about the Jewish Question going into the

1930s: that the really dangerous attitudes toward the Jewish Question were largely confined to the organized Endek Right and that the key question for the Jewish public was *virological*—that is, were rightist efforts to "spread the virus" of antisemitism to the broader society succeeding or not? Even for those who maintained this strangely reassuring view of a virus not yet diffused in the body politic, the coming years would undermine the sort of optimism Hirszhorn articulated, for multiple reasons.

First, with every passing year, perhaps every passing month, it became harder to remain confident that the Right was failing to disseminate its message and reshape the public culture. As early as 1931 there were signs of a growing optimism, even a sense of breakthrough achieved, in rightist circles. The year 1931 saw the publication of a new work by the preeminent ideologue of the mainstream nationalist Right, Roman Dmowski, *Świat powojenny i Polska*, which reiterated his long-standing vision of Poland and the world subjected to a Jewish-Masonic conspiracy driven by the Jews' lust for power. But as Jewish commentators noted at the time (see Chapter 4), Dmowski now wrote with new optimism that, finally, global forces were aligned to allow this evil to be overcome and undone. Closer to the ground, Rudnicki cites the happy comments of an Endek student in an August 1931 issue of *Myśl Narodowa* that he and his fellows were changing the youth culture beyond right-wing circles: they had not only excluded Jewish students from youth organizations but also "created a mood" wherein "today the friendship of a young Pole with a Jew is almost impossible to contemplate. Even those hostile to the national idea have had to adopt this attitude."[48]

Some Jewish observers began to perceive not only growing rightist commitment and strength but also disturbing signs that elements in the larger society, and perhaps even elements in the service of the state, were not dependably opposed to the Right's political incitement. In November 1931, reacting to a wave of anti-Jewish "excesses," the Galician Zionist Sejm deputy Fiszel Rottenstreich used the occasion of a budget debate to enter "an overview of the ongoing anti-Semitic campaign" into the parliamentary record; he warned his fellow lawmakers that "Hitlerism" was finding followers in Poland too. In response, the minister of the interior reiterated the regime's determination to "ruthlessly" suppress any further "excesses"—a reassuring sign that the regime resistance to antisemitic agitation was intact à la Hirszhorn. But Rottenstreich's fellow

Jewish deputy Yitshok Grinboym was left concerned that all was not well with "the state": he accused the police of inactivity. In response, another minister dismissed Grinboym's account as based on faulty press reports.[49]

At the same time, in more intimate and internally directed Jewish discourse, other observers were giving voice to the different and perhaps deeper fear that Appenszlak had been sounding in January 1930: that pathologies of anti-Jewish sensibility, suspicion, and hostility had taken wider hold in Polish society well beyond the Endek's propagandists, provocateurs, and student thugs. Whether this was a product of recent "spread"—of the Right's active campaign to inculcate its ideology of Jews as a many-faced existential threat to Poles and Poland (which government reports recognized to be bearing fruit among social groups far from its old urban commercial, white-collar, and clerical base and among young people of all classes especially), of a longer-term diffusion, or of multiple upwellings from multiple sources—was unclear. But nor was it clear that that analytical question was the most important one.

In 1931, the thirty-four-year-old Polish gymnasium teacher Mikhoel Burshtin published a particularly distressing novel, his first, titled *Iber di khurves fun Ployne* (Upon the ruins of Ployne). *Ployne* was a sociologically acute portrait of a small-town Polish Jewish community's economic ruination over the course of a year and the concomitant undoing of communal bonds, cultural norms, and individual morale and integrity. The ethnographic and sociological eye of the novel was not novelistic background but foreground: *Ployne* was not meant to be a novel of individual experience but a portrait of what Burshtin deemed a community in crisis. As Burshtin noted, he modeled Ployne on an actual town, Błonie (Yid.: Bloyne). A small town in Warsaw's orbit, Błonie was Burshtin's birthplace. Beginning circa 1925, Burshtin had begun—after many years living in a Polonized milieu in Warsaw and elsewhere—to rediscover the town in its present form through repeated visits that soon became compulsive. What he found, as he recalled in 1936, was grim: "inferiority, surrender, and brokenness." In a 1932 letter to a fellow writer, Burshtin revealed that his very turn to fiction had grown from this shattering late-1920s encounter with "the terrible decline [of Jewish life] in Poland's provinces." This open admission of the novel's presentism helps us understand too that although technically *Ployne* could be called a historical novel—its action was set over the course of 1924–1925, a *previous* moment of upheaval in Polish Jewish life—it was not a history but a chronotopy, a reflection on

Figure 1.1   Cover of M. Burshtin, *Iber di khurves fun Ployne* (Vilna: Kletskin Farlag, 1931), artist unknown. Author's collection.

the present of 1926–1931. It was not just that Burshtin's actual representation of Błonie's life was based on what he had found in the town *beginning* in 1925 or 1926. More than that, Burshtin plainly wrote the book out of acute worry about Polish Jewry's *current* situation as the 1920s gave way to the 1930s. As he put it in the aforementioned 1932 letter: "It is not only Ployne that lies in ruins now. We are being rolled back from the positions we once held and are tumbling down. It is thus in all areas of life."[50]

And, importantly, Burshtin regarded this current situation not only as one of Jewish economic and communal collapse but also of rising *political* danger around Jews. Literary historian Chone Shmeruk (who himself grew up in 1930s Poland) reads *Ployne* as essentially *about* antisemitism in interwar Poland.[51] This seems an oversimplification, but unquestionably, what Ployne's—and Poland's—non-Jewish Poles were thinking about their Jewish neighbors was a central concern of the novel.

The Jewish Question pulses through *Ployne* in both short metonymic set pieces and more elaborate portraits of Polish characters' inner lives as well as their actions.[52] A late chapter in *Ployne* follows a pathetic mass of Jewish men and women hiking to the local train station to go peddling in Warsaw. When they arrive, the Polish passengers in the second-class cars stroke their mustaches and laugh as the Jews push each other to get on the train. Someone shouts down "Asiatics!" and then, sharing in the mockery, the conductor sets off a few minutes early to amuse the "mustaches" at the Jewish panic. Here the anti-Jewish sensibility most familiar to Burshtin's readers is invoked in a few strokes: the "mustaches" in "the second-class cars" are Poles somewhere in the middle stratum, the affect is contempt, the epithet is racial-civilizational-national in its force. Elsewhere Burshtin represented more alarming forms of discourse. The chapter that follows takes the reader to the well-known Warsaw Church of All Saints: "Inside the cathedral, in its hollows, there lies a great arched hall. The worshippers descend to it after the pacem requiem eternam, to hear the fiery sermons of Monsignor Galewski. The priest hurls fire and brimstone against the enemies of the Church and ignites in the hearts of the faithful the torch of faith. That fire burns, burns, and then it dies out, guttering faintly . . . until there comes a time, until there comes a time, oh, the time will come. The faithful feel it, they know it."[53]

As befits a novel claiming to represent the distinctive world of a Polish small town, still rooted in rural life, Burshtin offered more fine-grained attention to the Polish as well as the Jewish denizens of Ployne. In Burshtin's depiction, Ployne's Polish milieu is not monolithically antisemitic. The Polish townsmen, whom he calls the "obivateles" (*obywateli*), "the citizens," have complex feelings toward their Jewish neighbors. Some Polish characters are depicted as bearing a relationship to the town's Jews marked not by an intense enmity but rather by a mix of distaste and intimacy. Thus, at a key juncture of the book's second arc focusing on the "revolutionary action" of a small group of local radical Jewish youth—

an action that consists, laughably, of secretly meeting to eat cheese-cake during Passover in order to insult their fellow Jews in the name of Revolution—the reader encounters the town's police sergeant, evidently a man of peasant background. Burshtin does not represent him as provoked to any sort of profound enmity or reflections on Jews' ostensible innate radicalism and anti-Polishness as per the burgeoning "*żydokomuna*" (Communism as a Jewish plot) discourse of the era. Rather, Burshtin presents him as someone who finds excessive contact with the town's Jews off-putting but who knows them intimately enough to understand the nature of the violation, and who ultimately proceeds by delivering the contraband to the town's rabbi with a firm but polite rebuke to the latter for not properly watching over "your Jews." [54]

Yet Burshtin's *obywateli* are also already open to newer and more complicated sentiments. In the book's final chapter, the Zionist counterprotagonist, Levi, the father of the Diasporist protagonist, Mateusz, leaves town to begin his journey to Palestine. He is accompanied by Jewish well-wishers jealous of his Certificate, who are then met by a small angry crowd of Jewish radicals come to denounce him in the name of class struggle. Looking on all the while are the town's Polish denizens:

> In the foyers and on the doorsteps of the shops, the *obivateles* stood and looked on with curiosity at how the Jews were working themselves up over the departure of one of their own to Palestine. Some were affronted, felt that it injured their honor that a Jew should up and leave Ployne of his own will. Others, seeing how the young people were loading luggage onto the cart, grew suspicious that something wasn't right here. Who knows what's packed in there—maybe the Jews are transporting gold out of Ployne? And when Levi climbed up on Shmil Betke's cart, they tipped their hats. Suddenly it seemed a shame to the *obivateles* about this Jew, who was leaving Ployne forever, it seemed—a quiet Jew, so many years we've lived together. [55]

The novel's most elaborate and worrisome representation of what is transpiring in Polish hearts and minds revolves around the character Stach Biliszewicz, a peasant farmer made good through hard work who is now "the richest citizen of Ployne." The reader has first met Biliszewicz earlier in his capacity as a municipal councillor, where we were made privy to his confident sense that the noble-born chief councillor to whom he still has to defer will soon be forced to step aside for the new rising Poland embodied in Biliszewicz's son, a peasant boy now studying law in Warsaw. We are reintroduced to Biliszewicz as he readies himself to manure the fields. Told that he is now "the richest citizen of Ployne," we gain access to his thoughts and memories as, with "watery, smiling eyes," he inspects the milkmaids milking his cows, mounts his cart "with a single jump," and thinks with pleasure about the social distance he has traveled since the war, before which he had lived "in a peasant's hut in Kopitow." Turning his thoughts from past to future, he meditates with equal pleasure on his son Wacek, who approaches wearing his "fraternity cap." Wacek, thinks his father, will soon be a lawyer and then "who knows how far he can go. Best would be that he become mayor of Ployne." But here the ruminations on social mobility take a political turn: reminded of the current mayor, Biliszewicz reflects angrily that he is "too good to Jews." Biliszewicz by contrast has driven all the Jews off his holdings ("except for the doctor, of course, who's almost like a Catholic anyway"). Here the language that Burshtin ventriloquizes through Biliszewicz is striking: his holdings, he thinks, are now "*Judenrein.*"

Possessed of these thoughts, and the certainty that his son Wacek will treat the Jews otherwise when *he* becomes mayor, Biliszewicz asks Wacek whether "we can take the Jews' houses? You're a lawyer, you know the laws." Wacek's response is a measured one: "Why should we take them, father? They'll give them away themselves. A hundred thousand Jews are leaving Warsaw for Palestine, and the Ployne Jews are getting ready to do the same." This provokes an exchange in which father and son discuss whether the Jewish project in Palestine is a real change or a "swindle," Biliszewicz remaining convinced that it must indeed be a new "swindle" of some kind since it is unthinkable that Jews will "manure fields, plow and sow with their soft white hands."

Interestingly, rather than leaving the scene of peasant father and educated son at this juncture of their comments about Jews, Burshtin remains with them a while longer, allowing us to hear how Biliszewicz tells his son to stay home lest he dirty his clothes and how Wacek gently insists on helping his father. To his evident filial piety, however, Wacek adds an ideological motivation: "No, dad, this is our land, our Polish earth, and one must not be ashamed of it." Biliszewicz is both moved and amused by his son's remark: "Ah, when you start to talk like the newspaper, there's nothing I can do. You're the educated one."

At this point, the scene shifts from Polish-national idyll to Jewish political debate and searching: several Jewish young people are having a measured political debate at the edge of Biliszewicz's fields, among them Bur-shtin's mouthpiece Mattias. In the midst of Mattias' Diasporist argument to his Zionist interlocutors, "Biliszewicz drew near to the edge of the field. Seeing that some bunch of Jews were sitting on his property, he stepped in front of them with fury, with his pitchfork in hand. His watery smiling eyes suddenly took on a murderous light, his face reddened, then grew pale, and the pitchfork in his hand raised up to strike. He awaited only the arrival of his son." Biliszewicz does not strike, but contents himself with driving the Jews away:

> "Look Wacek, how the Jew-gentlemen [*zhidovske panes*] sit here in the middle of the week, dressed for holidays, and read newspapers. That's what you call leaving for Palestine? They would rather, the lazy bums, stretch out in the middle of the day on our fields, and want us to work for them. Bolsheviks, get off of my field!" Little Hershl stood up in fright. Mattias and Binem tried to say something to the old Biliszewicz, but his fury grew still stronger and the two friends instead silently stepped off the edge of the field and remained standing in the middle of the road.[56]

Why did Burshtin devote such attention to incising this terrifying portrait of peasant turned prosperous farmer Biliszewicz particularly? One great question mark for Jewish observers in interwar Poland was where Poland's still-vast peasantry with its opaque worldview was headed. The populist leaders who managed to mobilize masses of peasant voters periodically were fairly labile—though one of the chief figures in that scene, Wincenty Witos of the Piast Party, manifested a marked convergence with Endek sentiments in 1928 when he characterized the Sanacja as a party of "saboteurs, Jews, and aristocrats."[57] But what of the millions of peasants themselves? Scholarship on Jewish-peasant relations in the interwar era shows that certainly there remained space for livable relations between Jews and peasants not appreciably different from the intimate relationship of suspicion-but-symbiosis that had obtained for centuries.[58] On the other hand, William Hagen's recent revelations about peasant and peasant-soldier millenarian anti-Jewish violence during World War I powerfully demonstrate that peasant *allo*semitism went deep and allowed for openness to far-reaching extrusive antisemitism under the right circumstances.[59] By the time Burshtin wrote his novel between 1926 and 1931, the question had become: Which way were things tending as Poland's vast peasantry was being transformed along with the new Poland itself? As noted en passant in the introduction, the 1930s brought several grand sociological projects aimed squarely at gaining insight into what was going on in the life and thought of Poland's peasantry. The first of these, the aforementioned peasant diary project initiated in 1933, contained much to worry about for Jews who were paying attention. Project director Krzywicki's acknowledgment that the pervasive anger he found in the diaries manifestly did not exclude Jews was put more triumphantly by the right-wing politician-academic Władysław Grabski, who noted that nearly a third of the fifty-one essays ultimately selected for publication in a 1935 anthology voiced negative views of Jews, that this was a remarkably high proportion given "how few" among the diarists felt moved to express negative views of "other groups in the population," and that nothing positive about the Jews could be found in any of the diaries.[60]

As both Grabski and Krzywicki agreed, the anti-Jewish animus in these diaries revolved mostly around money grievances—charges of cheating, usury, ruthlessness. A more optimistic analyst might hope that such traditional charges, still distinct from the eliminationist antisemitism of the nationalist Right, would yet remain politically inert. Yet among the diaries one could also find a more "developed" form of anti-Jewish ideology turning on presumptions about a special Jewish malignity toward Poles. One diarist moved seamlessly in the space of a paragraph from complaining about the hard work and slow pace of acquiring land that ought to have been given to veterans at a discount, to laments about how the "Independent Poland" for which he longed as a child is treating its citizens, to complaints that the local government favors "the Jews" to such a degree that "if a Jew beats a Pole, even if he's not in the right, it's the Pole who will be punished," to allegations that Jews were organizing militarily for what can only be nefarious reasons: "Poles are not allowed to organize themselves, the peasants in the countryside are not allowed to organize themselves, and the Jews already have their militias." There follows a remarkable screed about a summer visit to the big city, Łódź. Recalling the Yiddish signage for "doctors and midwives" on the side of an ambulance, the diarist declares his certainty that the "city [municipality] pays" for said Yiddish inscription on the ambulance "because in Polish it would insult Jewish honor." But he is equally revolted by the spectacle of Łódź Jews cheering the parade of a militia unit marching under the banner of Berek Joselewicz, the Napoleonic-era Jewish fighter for Polish independence who was the very symbol of Jewry's Polish patriotic bona fides: "Only Jews are stomping down to Piotrkowska Avenue, the central street in Łódź, and the Jews are all applauding. I ask what kind of unit this is, and they tell me this is our Jewish unit, [dedicated to] some Jew, Colonel Berek Joselewicz." The municipal health-care fund reveals itself to have "special departments" for Jews. Finally, a visit to a municipal credit union reveals the outlines of a secret world in which "a Jewish gentleman shows up every second and each of these gentlemen borrows two thousand, three thousand, five thousand zlotys each," the bank clerks speak to clients in Yiddish so as to conceal what they are saying from real Poles like the diarist, and deals are concluded elsewhere over dinner. And the dirty dealing is not merely dishonest, not even merely objective parasitism, but the vehicle of a veritable Judeo-Zionist subjection of the new Poland. It was not simply that "the Jew [who] enriches himself at our expense" was "building Palestine [. . .] not Poland," but that "today in Poland" *itself*—the Poland for which the diarist had given his blood "for the Polish future," the Poland of veterans, "orphans, widows, and cripples"—"there is being built a Palestine with great freedoms for the Jews, and Egyptian slavery for the Poles."[61]

Several features of this screed deserve note. First, it conflates unrelated and even opposing versions of Polish Jewish identity into one multifaceted Jewish malignant otherness: Jews keen to celebrate their Polishness and commitment to Poland, Jews keen to build the Yishuv. Jewish doctors who post Yiddish signage—all are the same Jews underneath. Second, the author is consumed by a sense not only of Jewish dishonesty, greed, and swindle but also of Jewish domination over banks, government, and public space. Third, classic anti-Jewish tropes are wedded to a deeply felt personal grievance that in turn is channeled into nationalist idealism and anger. If this was not Biliszewicz poised with a pitchfork in hand, it was also not the old allosemitic "peasant mentality" in which suspicion and periodic fury were interwoven with respect, dependence, and a generally passive worldview about the order of things. For diarist 12, Jewish malignity was inarguable and the Jews enemies of Poland.

To come back to *Ployne*, one thing is certain: Burshtin by background and ideology cannot be suspected of having reason to invent fears he did not actually feel, for novelistic or ideological purposes. Burshtin was no Zionist like Rottenstreich and Grinboym or even a friend to the movement like Appenszlak (not that we should presume that those ideologies intrinsically obscured the truth of the diasporic situation). On the contrary, he could be said to have been doubly invested in an ideal of Polish Jewish at-homeness. Burshtin's engagement in Jewish matters including

Yiddish literature had begun only recently after some fifteen years of immersion in Polishness. Beginning when he moved to Warsaw in 1912 at age fifteen, Burshtin immersed himself, apparently, quite totally in the Polish cultural milieu. That he landed a position as a teacher in a Polish-language gymnasium in the early 1920s testifies to full Polonization; a more direct testament comes from the description of the Warsaw Yiddish writer and critic Meylekh Ravitsh, to whom Burshtin in the early 1930s seemed a "returnee" coming from a great social distance and bearing an impressive *rekvisit* of metropolitan culture with him.[62] Sometime around 1929, Burshtin had begun to move away from this assimilatory project and turned to active engagement in Jewish cultural life—tellingly, initially still in Polish rather than Yiddish. But if his turn to Jewish engagement involved a break with assimilation, it did not involve a renunciation of hopes for a Jewish future in Poland. On the contrary, Burshtin's turn to Yiddish fiction in the mid-1920s coincided with a fulsome embrace of Diasporism. Burshtin was a committed proponent of *doikayt*, "here-ness," who would spend the entire 1926–1939 period working in multiple ways, not only as a writer but also as an activist in Diasporist cultural work of multiple sorts, preaching to Polish Jews the necessity and rightness of working for a Jewish future in Poland.

And if the last thing Burshtin would have wished to do was invent worries about dangerous anti-Jewish sentiment where none existed, his trajectory in the years that followed shows a person who could not stop worrying about the issue. The 1932 letter cited above clearly renders his sense that the grim vision in *Ployne* was, alas, not fictional. And upon completing *Ployne*, Burshtin immediately embarked on a second novel still more tightly focused on troubled relations between Poles and Jews. The resultant book, the 1934 *Goyrl* (Fate), was a genuinely historical novel set in pre–World War I Poland; but its attention to toxic attitudes and their imperviousness to what Jews did or said bespeaks the track of Burshtin's concern. As Ravitsh wrote after *Goyrl*'s appearance, this was a man who had been pushed back into Jewish life "by a wind that blew cold and angry from foreign peoples."[63]

The point is not to insist that Burshtin's specific representations of allo- and antisemitism were *accurate*, as though *Ployne* was an ethnography. Rather, the point is that his worry was no fiction. And the specific interest in looking *beyond* the familiar world of Endek discourse, to try to imagine what might be transpiring behind the eyes of neighbors one thought one knew, captures a central worry in Polish Jewish thinking about the Jewish Question.

It is important to note the range of sensibilities—and uncertainties—these various texts bespeak. Where Hirszhorn remained firmly focused on the Right and its noisy, performative moves in a "war of position," Burshtin worried about hostilities welling up largely out of sight, in houses of worship and the hearts of one's neighbors. Where both Burshtin and Hirszhorn focused on attitudes, Appenszlak attached his chief worries neither to the affects and passions of Jews' neighbors nor to the terrifying enthusiasms of the radical Right, but to a sense that there were "colder" forces consolidating in Polish society, and perhaps even the state, that would work to push Jews out of the economy, culture, and society. The case of Forget-Me-Not demonstrates, in turn, that even those focused with profound worry on the triumphs of Nazism in Germany did not necessarily center their worries around the Jewish Question. But all of these efforts to take the measure of disquieting changes marked paths toward recognition that Polish Jews were facing real dangers that had something to do with the intentions, programs, and choices others were making—toward thinking politically.

In turn, Appenszlak's essay, Burshtin's novel, or Grinboym's Sejm interpolation are not only interesting as instances of a certain way of thinking about the nature of the danger Polish Jews might be in. They also function as chronological markers, showing currents of deep worry about changing attitudes toward Jews and the Jewish Question in Polish society quite a bit earlier than 1933–1934, to say nothing of the post-Piłsudski era.

Nor was 1931 the first moment such worries could be heard. In 1926, reflecting on the 1924–1925 outflux of Polish Jews and what had driven it, Wilno social relief activist Moyshe Shalit, who played a leading role in interwar efforts to create a Polish Jewish cooperative movement and to bring order to the chaotic world of Jewish emigration and resettlement, concluded that recent years had in fact seen a profound transformation in Polish Jews' outlook on their future in Poland. He saw the emergence of a keen interest in emigrating among masses of Jews drawn from *all* parts and geographic segments of the varied Jewish population, including elements (notably Jews in Congress Poland) that had shown little such interest in the prewar era: "Circles and groups for whom the word 'emigration' was until recently a distant and foreign concept are now being pulled into the emigration-stream: householders established on solid foundations for generations, small industrialists, entrepreneurs and the like, for whom the emigration is becoming an attempt at salvation." Pivotally, although economic travail remained the chief motivation here, sociopolitical changes were moving to the center of Jewish outlook in Shalit's experience: among the factors that differentiated the emigration hunger of now-Polish Jews from that of prewar East European Jews were the "awakening" of the Polish "petit bourgeoisie" and the "outspoken national-aggressive character" of the Polish cooperative movement. Worries like Shalit's may have been blocked out for a few years by renewed hopes after the 1926 coup, but the processes they registered did not cease.[64]

Here, surprisingly early, was the beginning of a sense that one did not have to be narrowly focused on the question of antisemitism's *intensity* as attitude and its *depth* as conviction to begin to think ever more seriously about how the Jewish Question in the minds of others might profoundly affect Jewish lives. Shalit seems to have been thinking more in terms of the weight of common sense and indeed interest than in terms of hatred and imagination. But maybe a commonsense view that "the Jews" were an obstacle to Polish development and the happiness of Poles by dint of their economic role and urban concentration, let alone their alien morality and sensibility, was just as dangerous? The very commonsensicality of conceiving the Jewish presence in Poland as one of the questions to be redressed through rational and organized action by society and state presented the danger of a self-fulfilling prophecy.

Whatever the status of such political fears in 1926, or even in 1931, clearly they spread and deepened rapidly across Polish Jewish society in the early 1930s. Weinreich's uniquely sourced research based, again, on substantial selection of some 300 Yiddish, Polish, and Hebrew youth autobiographies collected in 1932 and 1934 leaves no room for doubt that political concerns about the trajectories of the Jewish Question in Poland (and beyond) played a key role in the changing outlook of Polish Jewish youth. The twenty-two-year-old from a "town between Warsaw and Łódź" who declared that his generation was being driven "toward mirage and despair" not only by "social upheaval" but also by "insult" on "national-human" grounds was far from alone. Weinreich found clearly (and unhappily) that many of his young subjects had come to perceive Jewishness as "bad fate"—a stigma that made life uncomfortable as well as a major factor shadowing their future. Whether the youth were right or wrong in their assessment—a question to which Weinreich was not the only one to return to obsessively—it was a social-psychological fact that Polish Jewish youth (and, evidently, many parents too) pervasively understood itself to be a "youth without a tomorrow" for both "social" (that is, socioeconomic) and "national" (that is, political) reasons. Weinreich found this view so ubiquitous in the autobiographies that he deemed it the defining structure of Polish Jewish youth experience by the early 1930s:

> There are two moments when [the fact of] national belonging impacts the development of the entire personality with special force. The first time: as the child becomes conscious of his fundamental belonging to a marked community. The second time: when one begins [adult] life. These moments can come a year earlier for one person, a year later for another; the development can be sped up or arrested according to the concrete situation. [. . .] But these experiences cannot be avoided. I call them "attacks of Jewishness" [. . .]: "The older the young person gets, the more he sees that there follows from the oppression of his community a powerful shrinkage of his personal chances as well.[65]

Weinreich's analysis in the uniquely sourced *Veg* allows us to see not only the spread of Polish Jewish political worries between 1932 and 1934 at a minimum. Weinreich's findings also testify, reluctantly, to two further facts about these worries that taken together confirm that a genuine transformation of Polish Jewish political culture and perception was under way. First, although Weinreich struggled to deny at times what he himself articulated so clearly above, his findings actually showed that a growing sense of political threat and Jewishness as was spreading among young Jews of *all* backgrounds and ideologies. It was not some cultural effect of a certain ideology. Second, Weinreich's findings begin to show us that what he and so many others were seeing was not some modish discourse of despair but, often enough, real and deep wrestling with perceived and experienced danger—something we will reconfirm many times in the course of this book.

Regarding the first of these, faced with findings that challenged all his Diasporist hopes, Weinreich was tempted at times to characterize the youths' views as a psychologically unhealthy *over*reaction to the objective situation (which was, he granted, grim). This meant different things at different junctures in his work. Weinreich's confrontation with this phenomenon brought him at one juncture in *Veg* to the cusp of an interesting social-theoretical argument that a kind of minority consciousness comparable to that of minorities immiserated, stigmatized, and in many ways defined by racism (particularly African Americans) might be taking root among the Jews of Poland. What seemed comparable to him was not least, as we will see, the woeful sense that one was fated to suffer "without compensation." Less analytically interesting but more strongly pronounced in *Veg* was a second tendency, noted by Kijek: Weinreich toyed with the suggestion that such a sense of Jewishness as bad fate afflicted *assimilated* Jews more than those imbued with proper national consciousness, self-respect, and love of Jewish culture, by which Weinreich meant Yiddish. Other nationally minded Jewish analysts entertained the same possibility. The once well-known psychoanalyst Fishl Shneurson, more catholic than Weinreich in his appreciation for Jewish self-respect of any sort, suggested in his *Jews and the Psychology of Nations* that *any* sort of thickly Jewish upbringing—Yiddishist, Zionist-Hebraist, or Orthodox— seemed to shield one against hopelessness to which, presumably, assimilated folk were prone.[66]

But even if this "inferiority-complex" model captured some part of the emerging Polish Jewish condition, it can be deemed only part of the story, and indeed a small part. When push came to shove, Weinreich's own findings led him to conclude that a felt sense of Jewishness as an "attack" or bad fate had become near universal in Jewish youth life, an "unavoidable" stage of experience and consciousness. He could not ignore the fact that the sense of futurelessness attaching to Jewishness could be found in Yiddish-language autobiographies by proud Jewish small-town youth (and among Orthodox youth too) no less than in autobiographies by Polonized youth in Lwów or Warsaw. One of the autobiographies Weinreich analyzed was that of Binyomen R., the young man from Bielsk mentioned in the introduction. Binyomen did not suffer from any sort of inferiority regarding his Jewishness: his ego-documents reveal an avid consumer of Yiddish culture who also found it a gateway to more general knowledge and insight about the world, and more generally a person with little interest in what the Gentiles around him thought *of* Jews; indeed, he was not free of attitudes of superiority of his own.[67] What bothered Binyomen, as we will see, was not a mixed relationship to his own Jewish *identity* but that the world around him seemed to be moving toward a structure of relations to people like him defined by antagonism and a desire to "solve" them as a problem.

Second, Weinreich helps us see more clearly—perhaps, again, against his own ideological preferences—that the Jewish Question was something that weighed heavily on plenty of ordinary people, shaping their outlook and decisions, rather than a mere discourse of despair. It is no doubt true, as some scholarship on popular culture, consumption, and everyday life suggests, that the fact of one's Jewishness could at times be sequestered, or recede into irrelevance even in the fraught interwar era. Any glance at the Polish Jewish press in all three languages, with its ads for the latest fashions and products, reveals that Polish Jews were eager participants in the global transethnic "dream world of mass consumption."[68] Many Polish Jews, both assimilated and nonassimilated, were avid filmgoers, and it was not only in Hollywood film that they could escape Jewish concerns; interwar Polish film, as Sheila Skaff observes, largely elided ethnic conflict (not least owing to the heavy representation of Jews at every level of the industry).[69] Even where Jewishness was "activated" in such settings, this was doubtless intermittent: spectacle sports like wrestling were pervasively ethnonationalized in the interwar era, but we cannot assume that most Jews who consumed these things related to them in exclusively national terms or let ethnic matters spoil their fun.[70] On a more quotidian level, clearly there were interactions between some Jews and some of their non-Jewish neighbors that did not problematize Jewishness or indeed involve any marked ethnic component. There were Jewish-Polish relationships of respect, friendship, and love.

But for substantial numbers of Jews of the most varied sort, a sense of contracting horizons in Poland (and Europe) was anything *but* a ritual utterance with no purchase in everyday life, thinking, and choice making. Here Weinreich's uniquely researched *Veg* shows its value beyond its power to confirm the general picture of doubt and exitism manifest in so many other sources. Weinreich was well aware of the readiness of his youthful subjects to find pleasure in movies, sports, and literature; in his introduction to *Veg,* which opened by disclaiming any special crisis in Polish Jewish life and maintained that calm tone until about page 10, Weinreich even gestured toward ranking consumption of cinema, where youth "absorb[ed] the ideals, interests, and gestures of Hollywood," as no less a factor in shaping the massive desire of young Polish Jews to break with the world of their "fathers" than anything else. But within a few pages, he acknowledged the "intensity" with which "idea-oriented" (*ideishe*) Jewish youth were "dreaming" en masse of "escaping from the old forms of life."[71]

Though this could mean dreams of cultural rupture as much as flight from the Jewish condition, Weinreich further acknowledged finding that for young Polish Jews, questions of political consciousness and choice loomed above all else: "In the circumstances of the Eastern Jewish community, the sociopolitical reactions of the individual primarily pour out in the form of taking part in [political] parties [. . .]. A fact is a fact: the political party stands at the top of our youth's organizational life." Though it was "a bit of an exaggeration to say that there is *no* [Jewish] public life outside politics," one of the realities disclosed by the youth autobiographies "whether one likes it or not" was that "not sports nor projects of economic productivization nor self-education nor any other sort of sociocultural activity has the magnetic power over our youth that the political party does."[72]

Finally, although Weinreich played at length with the notion that all this engagement with "politics"—and above all *Zionist* politics—registered a sort of psychic immaturity, he recognized that this turn to politics had much to do with how his respondents were thinking about the darkening situation around them. One attraction of joining a Jewish youth movement of *any* hue, Weinreich observed, was that such organizations "bring the members onto the streets, and that has a special significance in our circumstances. The Jewish youth, in whom since earliest childhood there has taken root the feeling that the street belongs to 'the Gentile hooligan', suddenly feels—if perhaps only for a short time—that he too belongs." He noted further that "under the conditions that obtain in Jewish life [. . .] one feels so easily and so often painfully helpless regarding the outside world." In short, though there is much evidence to suggest that economic suffering and prospectlessness composed the chief worry that many of these respondents faced on a quotidian level, many were also becoming convinced that "Jewishness" guaranteed that their current woes would only deepen in years to come—and this in turn concatenated layers of deepening worry about the political trajectory of the world around them and the trajectories of attitudes and policies toward them as Jews.[73]

One 1934 YIVO autobiography, by a Polonized young man writing under the pseudonym "Rex," clearly articulated some terms of the deep political worries in play. This autobiography focuses almost exclusively on the economic problems afflicting him and his generation. But as the text draws to a close, the author turns to deeply disturbing political reflections. Two sorts of threats loomed large. First, the Polish nationalist Right was growing ever more extreme: "The Endeks and ONR people are not satisfied with nasty articles against the Jews but now attack Jewish passersby." Even more frightening was that, as he saw it, the Polish *state* was moving in the same direction. At the grassroots level, Jews could not trust the police to defend them; rightist attacks "almost always end in blood and . . . arrests of *Jews*." And in the Sanacja regime proper, Rex saw an unmasking taking place. The regime might "promise equality to all by law," denounce antisemitism now and again, and repress the most extreme rightist youth. But as he saw it, the regime itself was turning toward a policy of nativizing the economy on the model of the Nazi regime next door: "The government aspires openly toward pushing the Jews out. The situation here is not like that in Germany, because we don't have so many Jewish professors or managerial types, and the press is not entirely in Jewish hands as it was in Germany. Thus, the work of the [Polish] government is easier: it's just the commercial sector." Thus, even if Polish Jewry's troubles were largely *caused* by the Depression, those troubles, Rex predicted, would be rendered permanent by state policies going forward even if Poland managed to avoid "'nationalist revolution' of the sort that just took place in Germany."[74]

For this young man, then, it seemed clear that substantial forces in both society and the state were already targeting Jews for extrusion—the specifics and extent of which were yet to be determined but which would certainly not be determined by him and his fellow Jews. Rex was already convinced that antisemitism was a powerful force across Polish society, and well beyond the Right—as evidenced in his intemperate but anguished comment: "Because almost every Christian is an antisemite." Just as notable, though, is his strong extrapolative orientation: what drove his analysis was the effort to understand where state policy was likely to go in light of the sociocultural trajectories he saw unfolding around him.

Experience, Observation, and Judgment

Some sources of the time allow us to see clearly how evolving political worries could grow out of personal experience and careful attention to what was transpiring around one. Here we turn in earnest to a figure already mentioned several times, a guiding figure throughout this book, Binyomen R. of Bielsk. Binyomen offers us a unique degree of access to the transmutation of experience into judgment because he left a unique pairing of sources. In 1934, he joined hundreds of other Polish Jewish youth in writing an autobiography (in part actually a *diary*) for YIVO's youth autobiography project; he focuses on political life in the 1931–1934 period with particularly acute detail. Uniquely, though, a year later, he responded to the portrait of his generation laid out in Weinreich's *Veg tsu unzer yugnt* with a second, unique text: a long chapter-by-chapter commentary on *Veg* that offered his own searching reflections on his sociopolitical experience and that of his peers. He sent the latter text to Weinreich, who saved it in his personal archive. For us, the earlier 1934 autobiography serves as a kind of control text that shows which claims made in the 1935 commentary were rooted in Binyomen's real social experience long before he felt moved to respond to Weinreich's *Veg*. In a hermeneutic virtuous circle, the autobiography thus read allows us in turn at least some understanding of the real-life coordinates and settings of the socio-logical empirical elaborations made in the later commentary.

And thus to the point: the central presence of the Jewish Question in Binyomen's own political thinking is registered in several places in the 1935 text, and nowhere more assertively—even angrily—than in a re-sponse to what he read as a suggestion in Weinreich's *Veg* that Polish Jewish doubts about the future were really just economic in character, responses to the Great Depression little different from those of European young people belonging to majority nations, including ethnic Poles. Actually, Weinreich entertained this argument from the Left only briefly and soon rejected it as simplistic; Weinreich knew full well that Jews faced real po-litical troubles in East Central Europe, having lost use of his left eye in a November 1931 anti-Jewish riot in Wilno.[75] That Binyomen was mis-reading Weinreich's intent is of little relevance here, though. The point is the vehement clarity of the young man's counterassertion:

> It is indeed true that things are bad for everyone ["alemen iz shlekht," Weinreich's chapter title] [. . .]. But it's nonsense to com-pare the situation of Jewish youth to the situation of Polish [youth]. I imagine that it's even worse in this respect in the big cities than in a small shtetl. If [Poles] suffer, they suffer only from the bad eco-nomic conditions but don't know any national oppression. All eco-nomic positions are open to them and they feel themselves to be rulers in their land. The drive to emigrate among them is small, and they certainly don't make of it an ideal. [But] we Jews began to feel a specific national oppression even before the [economic] crisis. At every step we are abused, at every step we are given to feel that we are second-class citizens [*tsvey-rangike birger*]. Is it then so strange that our youth does not feel at home in its "home," which is in fact no home at all?[76]

Elsewhere, the 1935 text offered ground-level descriptions of ethnic relations in Bielsk itself that bespeak how this outlook was rooted in direct experience of a changing Polish civic society. Whereas Binyomen's Jewish peers in Bielsk devoted themselves to socialist or Zionist activism, read newspapers, and included some substantial number of intellectually serious people, the mass of the "White Russian and Polish youth" of the town organized themselves in "patriotic organizations" and read nothing at all, boulevard press papers, or (most alarmingly) papers with a "clerical-Endek" line. The Polish youth of Bielsk who attended gymnasium "display some amount of intellectual seriousness," but this was hardly to the good since "all (!) of the local [Gentile] students are pro-Endek and hooligans of NARA," the right-wing nationalist youth organization. And this extended to Polish adult society as well—a claim he motivated by describing the efforts of local "powers that be" like the veterinarian Tadeusz Fuks ("who is always saying 'ja żydków nie lubię'" [I don't like the sheenies]) to drive the Jewish musicians out of the fire-department orchestra.[77]

In turn, Binyomen's earlier 1934 autobiography clearly demonstrates that his pointed insistence that Polish Jewish youths' perspective on the future was linked not only to economic collapse but to a growing sense of *political* danger was not something provoked into being by his reading of Weinreich. Furthermore, the observations about the matter dispersed richly across his autobiography not only support the claim that deepening concerns about antisemitism in Polish society played a significant role in his political thinking about the Jewish future in Poland, but also capture his sense that antisemitism—and rightist politics more generally—was *metastasizing* in the double sense of spreading and changing its form. Reconstructing his educational trajectory, Binyomen's autobiography notes that circa 1930 his father had sent him to study Polish with a Polish Catholic language tutor Stepan Jackiewicz. In passing, Binyomen, speaking in the present of 1934, notes that Jackiewicz had since become an Endek. In the meantime, Binyomen had had the chance to experience a more robust iteration of the Polish Right's rising youth movement and its developing efforts to incarnate extrusionary antisemitism in newly confrontational forms. In the winter of 1931–1932, several Polish young men who were back in Bielsk for the New Year's holiday from their university studies in Wilno carried out a "boycott action" in front of the town's Jewish-owned cinema, seeking to persuade Christians not to support Jewish businesses. When one of the young men pushed his way into the cinema, Jews responded with blows. In response, the Endek supporters broke windows of Jewish homes, including Binyomen's own. Local police arrested some of the Endeks but soon freed them, and briefly arrested eight local Jews instead.[78]

By the spring of 1934, Binyomen was himself serving as a Polish tutor to several Jewish children in the nearby village of Dunki, and his interlude in a village where the rest of the population was composed of Christian peasant farmers left disturbing impressions of how Poland's large and still-distinct peasant population was shifting its attitudes about the Jewish Question.[79] Binyomen's Jewish employer in Dunki, he remarked, hoped that his neighbors would remain ignorant of "events in Bialystok and of the anti-Semitic wave that is flooding Poland," lest they be influenced by example to turn on him and his family. Binyomen allowed that this hope was not altogether ridiculous because nobody in the village subscribed to a newspaper, but he reflected that his employer's hopes would likely be dashed because during the peasants' periodic visits to town "they hear the stories." And he suspected these particular peasants were ready to act on them: "These *goyim* are no friends of the Jews and it is already an 'established truth' to them that all Jews are capitalists and bloodsuckers. The frustration of the peasants is tremendous and with a 'wink' from the regime, this agitation could turn itself not against the regime but against the Jews, the old scapegoat."[80]

Significantly, Binyomen's analysis of peasant attitudes was not one-dimensional. He did *not* take anti-Jewish enmity to be a given of peasant culture: noting reports that peasants in the villages of Ploski and Adrinki had recently attacked Jewish property and persons, he ascribed those cases not to antisemitism but to class grievances against "executors," and indeed opined that peasants of Byelorussian ethnicity were less given to antisemitism than their counterparts ("the White Russian peasants don't let themselves be fooled"). As for the peasants of Dunki, Binyomen recognized their very real material want and the better living conditions of the local Jewish family: "My employer *does* live better than the peasants. He hides the hallah baked for the Sabbath so that the *goyim* won't 'God forbid' notice that [his family] eats" white bread. But although Binyomen acknowledged the material woes and social injustices out of which deepening peasant frustration grew, he resisted falling into the rather undialectical materialist sociology he saw among his Communist friends and interlocutors. Perhaps the anti-Jewish convictions of Polish (and Ukrainian) peasants were not sufficient to cause violence; perhaps in some causal sense the necessary condition of peasant violence was material injustice.

But regardless, as that injustice deepened, it rendered the peasants open to ideologically refurbished accounts of Jewish perfidy and enmity— accounts that offered a powerful social logic that gave sanction, meaning, and *targets* for restitutive violence.

Binyomen's grim sense of antisemitism and political extremism spreading across provincial Polish public life and youth culture and transforming itself in the process manifested itself acutely in a comment made about his own moment. Informed by a friend about the arrest and beating of a number of Bielsk Jewish youths following the June 1934 assassination of Interior Minister Bronisław Pieracki (by, it later turned out, Ukrainian insurgents), he commented: "Poland is really going 'forward', they're thinking of us, they're building camps. One talks about the NARA folks but one means the workers. Just like with Dollfuss." Recent research by Kijek resonates closely with Binyomen's perceptions and helps us appreciate the larger realities Binyomen was seeing from the local perspective.

Rediscovering untapped archives, Kijek demonstrates that as early as autumn 1931, Endek youth activists in the Kielce province, aided by adult movement leaders both local and central, launched a concerted and effective campaign to inject far-reaching "redemptive" antisemitism, hatred of the Sanacja, and fascist ideas of national regeneration through violence into already existing rightist youth organization branches in the province's provincial towns (Kielce, Częstochowa, Opatów, Opoczno) *and* to spread this violent vision among wider constituencies, particularly the vast rural population. The core ideas to be inculcated were that "the Jew was an absolute and deadly threat who stood behind the gravest calamities and sins of the world," Poland's Jews were a "state within a state," the Sanacja was the Jews' "puppet," and "[Jews'] elimination from Polish political and social space was the only way to save Poland." Mining confidential government reports, internal Endek records, and a bulletin put out illegally—and thus without government censorship—by local extremist youth, Kijek reconstructs how Endek activists worked to implant this vision both in the provincial towns and in "the very different social context [of the] Polish countryside." While openly organizing a major multisite anti-Jewish boycott campaign, Endek activists undertook a twofold conspiratorial program. In 1932, university students home for break worked with local activists to imbue their more ramified ideology among youth groups in the towns and train them to use violence. In the spring of 1933, town activists inundated the countryside with a flood of leaflets and an illegal bulletin that used "very simple [. . .] language designed to promote a millenarian version of anti-Semitism among the least educated inhabitants of the countryside": Poles were "being 'murdered' by the Jews, or [were] to be 'murdered' in a systematic way if Jewish communism were to take over. Jews were 'scum,' 'criminals,' 'thieves,' and the Sanacja regime was their 'puppet.'" In the summer of 1933, five organizers from Poznan who were brought in with coordination from Warsaw Endeks toured the region, guided radicalization work in existing cells in towns, and, with local activists, visited "many villages, recruiting peasant youth." Local elements took up the project with enthusiasm: the branch in Częstochowa, which was well organized and armed, underwent fighting training led by "local worker Florian Markowski." Throughout the region the activists worked to make acts of violence against Jews and other enemies a central part of every young nationalist's praxis, both to strengthen the movement ideationally and psychologically and to force the regime to respond, which in turn would "show Polish society that our current government protects Jews more than the other citizens."[81]

And all this brought impressive results. First, "from the end of 1931— as attested to by hundreds of local authorities' reports, the *Endecja* press, and especially posters and leaflets, as well as the proceedings of criminal courts dealing with attacks conducted upon Jews—urban, redemptive anti-Semitism, along with other elements of fascist political culture, [began] to be promoted constantly through acts of daily anti-Jewish violence." This sudden and sustained program of violence—nonlethal until Markowski, apparently under direction from Endek higher-ups, murdered a Sanacja-affiliated Jewish journalist in Częstochowa in August 1933— was mostly the work of "old or freshly recruited members of the nationalist movement." Meanwhile, the massive propaganda campaign had substantial effects on "normal people" too. Already visible as early as late 1932, this effect was acknowledged in a report by Kielce's provincial administration admitting that in "the second half of 1933 and beginning of 1934," the Right had achieved "greater success in the countryside."

Between 1932 and 1934, this new kind of "anti-Jewish campaign" changed the texture of politics across the Kielce region. Kijek's important findings relate solely to the Kielce region; Binyomen was somewhere else. Whether Binyomen knew anything about violence in Częstochowa or Kielce is unclear—Kijek offers the critically important reminder that regime press censorship was quite heavy as regards the Right and interethnic violence, and one could learn only so much from the press. Binyomen may not have known of similar antisemitic political violence in "the provincial

Figure 1.2   Isaac (Yitshok) Giterman (glasses and mustache) and four others at table, Warsaw 1937. American Jewish Joint Distribution Committee Archives, NY-15844.

cities and towns" of the Łódź district to his west. But he did know of anti-Jewish violence closer to home; his writings reference the burst of anti-Jewish violence that convulsed multiple towns in his own Białystok region in 1933 and 1934. So too, he had no way to gain the kind of precise sociological insight into the changing form, character, and reach of the rightist politics that scholars like Kijek can now recapture, and he did not necessarily know, as Joseph Rothschild puts it, that the Endecja in its various forms was "interwar Poland's geographically most universal party," able to draw support across Poland wherever ethnic Poles were to be found, though particularly "in ex-Prussian western Poland, in [Congress Poland], and among the Polish urban islands in the Ukrainian peasant [and Jewish] sea of eastern Galicia." But he clearly had a sense that what he was witnessing in Bielsk and Dunki was a manifestation of something far larger and deeper.[82]

And figures with a far better national vantage than this twenty-year-old provincial young man were coming to share his deep concerns. It was in the hope-filled year of 1926 that the aforementioned Isaac Giterman became the Joint Distribution Committee's chief agent in Poland. A supremely competent relief worker, Giterman met the Depression creatively, becoming a moving force throughout the 1930s behind a program of microloans upon which hundreds of thousands of Polish Jews came to depend.[83] Then, too, it is important to register that Giterman was a fiercely committed Diasporist. Scion of an old Hasidic line of which he remained proud despite his own secularization, he was an enthusiastic Yiddishist in cultural life, and in civic life an outspoken defender of the essential Diasporist principle that world Jewry as a whole should commit itself to building and maintaining healthy Jewish communities wherever Jews lived. This was not a man who wished to believe that Polish Jewry had no future. But to a visitor in mid-1934, as William Hagen has discovered, Giterman confided a profoundly grim sense of the situation in both economic and political terms. It was not just that the economic ruination continued to deepen to the point of possible irreversibility (Giterman noted that "in one place the Jewish public health agency TOZ 'gave cod-liver oil to the children and found that whole families were putting it on bread as a luxury'"). It was also that Giterman, a figure with robust connections across the Polish Jewish world, had come to believe that antisemitism had become "inherent" in multiple sites of Polish life and was now thoroughly woven into how many Poles thought about their own well-being, that Poland's intelligentsia was "wholly anti-Semitic," and that substantial numbers of Poles sought a situation of "no contact with Jews however they may be dressed."[84]

The State in Question

In this troubled political, economic, and discursive context, another question that loomed ever larger for many Jews was whether the Sanacja regime would hold the line against antisemitism. There were reasons for concern. Already by the late 1920s, growing numbers of Jewish observers were charging that for all its anti-antisemitic posture, the new regime was in fact continuing many of the same efforts to Polonize the economy as the Right-dominated governments of the early 1920s had: sectors brought under state monopoly hired only Poles, tax laws and debt repayment rules seemed to target Jews, the credit policies of state banks seemed aimed at helping Polish businessmen and disadvantaging Jewish ones—all these and other policies were read by some contemporaries as "betraying an intent to harm Jewish interests."[85] By 1933, cracks in the regime's anti-antisemitic stance were visible. But some Jewish observers understood that the issue might be more complicated still—that it might rather be an issue of what the regime was *able* to do in light of where the larger society seemed to be headed. As mentioned, by 1934 Giterman had come to believe that despite the fact that the Sanacja leadership mostly continued to reject antisemitism, the breadth of popular antagonism toward Jews meant that "any minister who treated the Jews fairly would cease to be minister."[86] Giterman's dire comment reflected views that other observers were developing in greater analytical depth: the possibility that some sort of anti-Jewish policy might be hardwired into the project of the nation-state in Eastern Europe. Moreover, the kinds of worries Giterman voiced did not have to wait until 1934 to ripen. As the aforementioned Druyanov traversed Poland in late 1931 and early 1932, he encountered not only the grinding Depression but also anxious Jewish discussions behind closed doors as to how *political* conditions would limit any Jewish recovery. His conclusion was an insight into state capture:

> Not a single million but tens of millions of unemployed people are now wandering hungry and thirsty in [every] land on the globe. [But] they are only unemployed, only hungry and thirsty, and not *unwanted,* and for that reason their cry is heard [. . .]. Whereas *our* 'million' of hungry and thirsty people in Poland, [because] they are unwanted [. . .] their cry is not heard [. . .] among the masters of the state, who have it in their power to offer much or at least a little salvation [. . .]. The government will not appoint a Jewish official, no Jewish person will be hired as a teacher in a general public school.[87]

Druyanov reported a substantial difference of opinion among his Zionist interlocutors in Galicia (Lwów, Kraków) as opposed to those in Warsaw: the latter had suspicions about the subjective motivations of state policy makers and bureaucrats themselves, whereas the former defended Sanacja motives against imputations of subjective antisemitism. But notably, both agreed that either way, Jews should expect that the state would not act to aid them, because it could not, given the shifting weight of attitudes in the larger society. This anticipation of how societal forces of intolerance would serve to shape state policy even in a situation where those running the state were actually relatively tolerant was an insight into the shifting character and rising power of nationalism that other Jewish observers were taking up in more analytically far-reaching ways, as we shall see in Chapter 4.

The End of Old Assumptions

In the early 1930s, Burshtin, Forget-Me-Not, Shalit, Appenszlak, Bin-yomen R., Rex, Giterman, and Druyanov's interlocutors were just a few of the Polish Jews who were registering, however inchoately, some very real dangers emerging around them. They were groping toward knowledge—knowledge of the Jewish condition and knowledge of the larger social condition, and perhaps particularly knowledge about minority life in an age of nationalism gone off the rails, or nationalism coming into its own, depending on how one looked at it.

Of course, the grim things they saw were not the only things one could see. In the early 1930s, the Jewish Society for Knowing the Land in Poland (Żydowskie Towarzystwo Krajoznawcze, ZTK) began to enjoy dramatic growth under the new leadership of a talented cluster of activists who sought to use the organization to inculcate Polish Jewish pride in Yiddish, in Jewish rootedness, and in Polish Jews' centuries-old culture. In 1933, the leadership exulted that their "movement" had "grown greatly in the last few years"; the Warsaw branch alone had grown from a "handful of people" to "nearly 2000 members"; there were branches in Kraków, Łódź, Lwów, and Wilno, "dozens of branches in the provinces," and "thousands of members" all told alongside "hundreds of sympathizers and friends"; the "popularity of the society" was "growing from day to day"; and "hundreds" were joining "at a constant rate." Unhappily, though, the young leaders of the ZTK acknowledged that this influx had more to do with the grim political situation rather than with attraction to Yiddishist and Diasporist ideals. The newcomers, it turned out, were largely Polonized Jews lacking even the most basic "Jewish knowledge"; many related to Jewish cultural matters with indifference or "distaste." Why were such Polonized Jews joining the ZTK? It was because, the editors admitted, "the Polish tourism societies do not accept Jews happily, or at all."[88]

Of course, if that fact speaks to the political troubles that began to reshape the outlook of growing numbers in the late 1920s and early 1930s, it might just as easily be invoked to argue something else. After all, if the ZTK's occluded social history tells us that Jewish encounters with growing ugliness in the surrounding society were common enough, the choice to join the ZTK can be read as a way to *maintain* faith in a Jewish future in Poland—or at least to not let the bastards spoil one's life, a chance at travel, leisure, romance, or happiness.

This same double valence can be read in the bilingual journal of the ZTK, *Landkentenish / Krajoznawstwo*. Overall, the journal was free of political reference; unless one read carefully, one finds almost no direct reference to anti-Jewish sentiment or to the great internal questions of Polish Jewish political life, like Zionism. When politics did intrude, it communicated not unanimity but division.

The April 1935 issue included a fierce critique by Y. Toyb of a 1927 Polish-language guidebook to Łowicz, a storied town west of Warsaw with beautiful Baroque churches that was also, with a population of 4,400 Jews, 25 percent Jewish. The guidebook, by Łowicz teacher and school inspector Aleksander Bluhm-Kwiatkowski, was remarkable, Toyb wrote bitterly, for "the exactitude with which the 'scientifically objective' author has surveyed all that is Polish, from historic monuments all the way to a modern bakery" but stubbornly "omitted everything that carries the faintest trace of Jews and Jewishness." For Toyb, the intentions that lay behind this omission were clearly revealed by another omission that defied economic sense but made political sense: the listing of local businesses sought out as sponsors of the booklet was "not polluted by even one Jewish firm" in a town where, as was typical, much of the commercial class was Jewish. The guide, Toyb concluded, was "another ring in the chain that calls itself 'the elimination process.'" The fact that the 1927 guide had been initiated by the Łowicz branch of the "*Polish* land-tourism society," of which Bluhm-Kwiatkowski was chairman, suggested that this promotion of a "*Judenrein*" Łowicz to tourists was a collective act by some of Łowicz's most dedicated publicly minded citizens.[89]

Toyb's little review is far and away the most explicit reference to anti-Jewish politics to be found anywhere in *Landkentenish / Krajoznawstwo*. What to make of this? The mystery grows deeper when we realize that a larger issue lurked beneath this 1935 review of a 1927 book: Łowicz had been the site of an intense anti-Jewish riot in early 1933 in which a crowd of local high school students led by several of their teachers alongside student-teachers from the local teachers' seminar marched down the "main Jewish street Zduńska," threw rocks through the windows of the synagogue and Jewish stores, and "in some cases attacked Jewish passersby and beat them mercilessly." Writing from Melbourne in the late 1940s, one former resident of Łowicz recalled that the riot had been organized in support of Endek university students in the big cities—that is, it was connected to the national political scene—and that it had grown from fertile soil: Łowicz's high schools had been "steeped in anti-Jewish incitement" led by a fair number of teachers, as everyone from the school director to the local Jews seems to have known. The memoirist—who was writing in a memorial book in Yiddish for fellow former Lovitshers rather than polemicizing with anyone—recalled further that not only had "no police" been involved on the day of the event but also that, although witnesses identified the attackers easily enough and the town magistrate pushed initially for some sort of punishment under brief pressure from the interior ministry in Warsaw, "as was usual in such matters, the whole thing ended with a few light punishments." Once "the local administrative organs concluded that the central regime did not take the matter as seriously as they had first thought [. . .] the whole thing was slow-walked."[90]

The mystery grows deeper still when we note that the memoirist's name, Y. Toybenfeld, makes it very likely that this author and the author of the 1935 review are one and the same. Here is reason to suspect that censorship as much as mixed feelings may have trammeled more open discussion of anti-Jewish politics in the ZTK's journal. But it wasn't just censorship. If the growing worries of the early 1930s thus made their way, sotto voce, into the ZTK journal, the very same April 1935 issue offered reinforcement to more optimistic outlooks by foregrounding a countervailing image of the Polish-Jewish relationship. The Polish-language side of the issue was fronted by an essay on the "democratization of tourism" and its environmental consequences. This was fairly bland stuff, but what mattered was the author: the prominent Polish socialist leader, progressive, and opponent of antisemitism Kazimierz Czapiński (whom we met in the introduction as the author of a 1932 PPS pamphlet about the dangers of fascism). To publish Czapiński in *Krajoznawstwo* was to offer its readers an embodiment of Poland's most genuinely tolerant, welcoming, and progressive ideals. And Czapiński's only comments on the Jewish Question in this context reinforced that message precisely in their cheerful normality: as he listed Poland's proliferation of touristic societies, he defined some as "Jewish" ("żydowska 'Kulturliga,' etc.") in a manner that was not stigmatizing, but quite the contrary, an act of inclusion in which Jewishness was marked as a normal part of Polish touristic endeavor.[91]

If events like those in Łowicz raised fear, figures like Czapiński offered hope. It was possible to see healthy developments alongside the dangerous ones and to invest great significance in them, especially if one had a progressive or socialist worldview to begin with. But as the 1920s gave way to the 1930s, it became ever more difficult to think that Poland's Czapińskis were headed for victory. For growing numbers, what was happening in Łowicz, in Kielce, Częstochowa, and Opatów, in the Grajewo and Łomża districts, in the Łódź region, and abroad in Germany and Austria challenged enduring assumptions about what politics was *about* and what Jews could reasonably hope for. As readers began to see in the introduction and have seen further here with the guidance of scholars like Kijek, there was growing evidence of a more consequential anti-Jewish politics taking root in hearts and minds, including those of people with real social power and in position to win political power, if not electorally than by generational transition. This was a politics of national salvation: it pulsed with the growing sense that a future without Jews was achievable, and certainly worth striving for. Simultaneously, evidence was growing that Jews could not hope to really affect the terms of the surrounding society's relationship to them. And now, for those Polish Jews without messianic or revolutionary faith, it simply no longer made sense to *assume* that things would move in the right direction. Rather, some concluded, it was necessary to think analytically and extrapolatively about the situation unfolding around Jews, about minorityhood and majorityhood in an age of nationalism—to reckon soberly with danger.

2

Toward a Politics of Doubt and Exit

Lova Levita had left his native Eastern Europe for Palestine in 1924. He returned in 1929, a young father and a leader in Palestine's fledgling kibbutz movement. The task for which the United Kibbutz leadership at Ein Harod had dispatched Levita was to help make sense of reports that thousands of Polish Jewish young people were spontaneously flooding into the Zionist Hehalutz youth-pioneer movement. Levita's four-month trip across Poland's northeast (Białystok, Lida, Grodno) and its center and south (Częstochowa, Kalisz, Sieradz, Będzin) confirmed what other emissaries had reported: despite the fact that organized Zionism's fortunes in both Poland and Palestine were at low ebb—by the time he arrived, the economic crisis of the Yishuv in Palestine was overshadowed by the outbreak of unprecedentedly bloody Palestinian-Jewish ethnic violence in August 1929—there was growing influx into Hehalutz. And Levita also reconfirmed what previous emissaries or *shlihim* had quickly discerned: relatively few of these young people were driven by anything like recognizable Zionist ideals and ideologies.

Levita did find a few driven by ideals of Zionist revolution: he perceived this especially in the young women joining Hehalutz, whom he saw as seeking to "escape from the chains" of traditional Judaism and seeking "with all [their] heart a new life." Levita noted too those few cases where he encountered young people deeply informed about Zionism's inner tensions: at a discussion in Będzin (Yid.: Bendin) he faced sharp questions about Jewish-Arab relations from all ideological directions. But mostly the youth drawn to Hehalutz whom he met in town after town lacked any robust relationship to Zionist ideology of any sort. This in turn led him to recognize what virtually every observer of Zionism's resurgence in Poland recognized, as we have already begun to see: that the real driver of

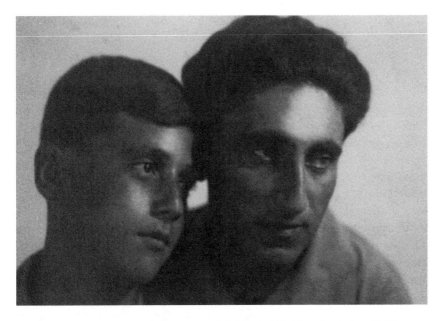

Figure 2.1 Lova Levita with son (Nimrod, b. 1925, killed by a landmine, 1949), early 1930s. Yad Tabenkin Archive, photo 145125.

youth "Zionism" was an emerging conviction of Jewish futurelessness in *Poland*.

Levita found this sense of futurelessness across Jewish Poland; in the fourth month of his trip, writing from central Poland, he reported a "general sense" among Jews that "the Judgment has been made . . . truly, the face of Jews here is like the face of the condemned." This sense of futurelessness could be merely destructive: Levita lamented that it was the root of "the great apathy and skepticism here toward any assertive Jewish politics." But this same sense of futurelessness was spurring young people toward Zionism: "A sense of all of the vaporousness and insecurity that inheres in all of their dealings" was producing "the desire to leave this as quickly as possible, to escape. And truly they are escaping."[1]

If Levita's close encounter with the youth led him to an understanding of Polish Jewish felt futurelessness, it also led him to appreciate some transformations under way in Polish Jewish political culture and political choice that were not always visible to more distant observers. First, Levita discovered that despite all of Polish Jewry's profound geographic and cultural divides, a single, shared evolution of political outlook was under way across the country. It is perhaps unsurprising that a burning interest in the possibility of leaving Poland for Palestine was spreading among the Jewish youth of Poland's eastern reaches, where Polonization had made the fewest inroads; after all, their distance from Polish language and culture was an objective disadvantage in the struggle for a future.[2] But Levita found much the same sensibility in some of Poland's *most* Polonized Jewish communities too. Traveling through the storied old towns of Częstochowa, Kalisz, and Sieradz, and the village turned industrial town of Zawiercie with its 7,000 Jews, he found Jewish youth who studied overwhelmingly in Polish state schools, no knowledge of Hebrew to speak of, and linguistic Polonization proceeding so fast that some young people who attended his discussions could not understand Yiddish. But Levita also discovered that of this youth too, "a large part wants to escape from here. They are also drawn to the Land of Israel and our organizations."[3]

Second, Levita was particularly struck by the discovery that not only were many of those flowing into Hehalutz coming from *non*-Zionist backgrounds, but that a nonnegligible number were coming from *anti*-Zionist backgrounds: "former 'Reds'" (Communists) and "readers of the *Folkstsaytung*" (Bundists). That is, Hehalutz was drawing both previously apolitical newcomers and young people from the Polish Jewish Left's most ideologically ramified—and anti-Zionist—parties.[4]

Finally, Levita discovered a sea change in how young Jews related to something central to his own political life: to the promises and powers of *ideology* as a blueprint for political action that would (ostensibly) change the world if properly directed:

> The forces that are driving our youth and its masses to our movement are somewhat different from those we once knew. Not the storminess of the era, not wars and social movements, not civic life and not ideological thought—these are neither active nor determinative here. The causes are different, maybe less conscious, but no less fundamental. [. . .] The youth sees with complete clarity— cannot *fail* to see—what their parents also understand but struggle to deny because they have no other choice, namely: the total lack of a foundation for their continued existence [here], all of the

vaporousness and insecurity that inheres in all of their dealings. From this derives the desire to leave this as quickly as possible, to escape. And truly, they are escaping.[5]

If this held true even in the kresy, where a thickly ethnic Jewishness still predominated, it was even truer in the more Polonized swaths of Congress Poland that he visited. Relative to the kresy, there were even fewer frameworks of preexisting Jewish national identity to account for the reorientation to Palestine, and the ideology of escape was even less crosscut by the positive Zionist agenda of *livnot u-lehibanot* (to build the new Hebrew society and be remade in it) that Levita and his comrades hoped to find. But Levita did not therefore conclude that all of these young persons' choice of Hehalutz was something *unthought,* some form of panic. In his letters about his journey across Poland, Levita was certainly quick enough to unleash sharp indictments of shallowness and anti-intellectualism where he found it; thus, he dismissed the particular *halutzim* he found in Kielce (Yid.: Kelts) and Siedlce (Yid.: Shedlits) as anti-intellectual ("they don't try to think at all") and inclined to a merely performative version of Zionist youth politics that appalled him ("everything is superficial, shrill, 'stormy powers' [spilled] over nothing, 'war' against each other"). But by contrast, some young people he encountered in the northwest and later in central Poland inspired his respect: "With all that said, we have here a fresh, good youth from every stratum." What impressed him, evidently, was a kind of political seriousness different from ideological faith; their distance from what he called "ideological thought" coexisted with a capacity to "*see,*" which is to say, sober judgment.[6]

Levita's claims point us toward changes in Polish Jewish political consciousness and choice that have not received the attention they deserve. He correctly perceived that the upsurge in Zionism was in fact for many an "exitism," a judgment about Poland that preceded any formed judgment about Palestine—though importantly it did not preclude such judgment; on the contrary, it invited and provoked it as we shall see in Chapter 6. This chapter assays a social history of Jewish political behavior and choice to argue that Levita was also seeing the birth pangs of a more general and ambient new political sensibility among many young Jews— and not only the young. Across Polish Jewish society, the same factors that produced deep doubts about the future and provoked new lines of thought also drove a spontaneous grassroots search for a new practical

Jewish politics framed by two grim judgments. First, this search was driven above all by a keen interest in exit from Poland (and Europe) in search of something better. Second, and closely related to this, growing numbers of Polish Jews were gripped by the sense that no Polish Jewish politics—except *perhaps* and in a very specific way Zionism—could do much to secure a decent future for them as a community or as individuals. The concrete expression of this feeling was not only the sudden incandescence of interest in particular versions of organized Zionism that was, as everybody recognized, distant from any positive Zionist ideology, but also substantial defection from the great non- or anti-Zionist camps of Orthodoxy, the Diasporist Left, and assimilationism.

This double stance was, I hasten to add, only the starting point of the new politics, and much of what we examine here will be unpacked phenomenologically and intellectually in Chapters 5–7. Here I undertake a more straightforward social history of politics, drawing together a wide range of sources that capture what seems to have been quite widespread, cross-site, cross-region, and cross-class political reorientation at the grass roots away from existing political faiths and toward a desperate search for some form of organization that might help one secure a future. I then draw together a set of sources that show how the specifically *political* worries, fears, and judgments we began to investigate in Chapter 1—to put it crudely, fears and judgments not only about the Depression but also about where the Jewish Question in Poland and Europe was headed—played a major role in reshaping this political reorientation. We will see that some of the individuals actively seeking and making this new politics also embarked on the same stony paths of thought about the Jewish Question and the Polish Question, antisemitism, nationalism, and Poland's political trajectories that preoccupied the figures in Chapter 1.

Socialists, Hasidim, Integrationists, Zionist Believers, and the Eruption of Doubt

To claim in essence that Levita's 1929 impressions capture the beginnings of a major grassroots change in the ecology of Polish Jewish political consciousness and choice provokes a twofold historiographical question that we must limn before we turn to the sources: How can Levita's (and my) sense of a rapidly spreading new politics of doubt, exit, and Jewishness as bad fate be reconciled with the two more familiar and dominant images of interwar Polish Jewry that certainly seem well grounded in the sources (too)? The first of those images is that of Polish Jewry as Europe's ideologically activist Jewry par excellence, a community of activists thronging to movements that, beneath competing ideals, shared a single magma of ideological fervor and idealism. The second (and rather different) image is that of Polish Jewry in the Piłsudski years as a population straining toward *integration* within the framework of real, if scattered, regime outreach to minorities and galloping Polonization among Jews themselves. In this section, I argue that although there is truth in both of these long-established images, Polish Jewry historiography has gravely underestimated the presence of the third reality limned above, and the ways it constituted an emerging alternative politics of doubt and searching that cut across all the old Jewish political faiths.

It is of course undeniable that many Polish Jews remained or became committed supporters of one of the many ideological camps on offer. In Warsaw, by the late 1920s Bundist demonstrations could call thousands into the streets, and the city's branch of the Bund's Tsukunft youth movement counted between 800 and 1,500 members. Concomitantly, just a few streets away, there existed an impressive network of Hasidic houses of study that, by one account, "year after year [. . .] would turn out hundreds of Torah youth, pious and God-fearing, armed with the weapon of the Torah, Hasidic enthusiasm, and a deep Hasidic worldview, ready for the temptations of life in all their forms."[7] Meanwhile, in 1931, nineteen thousand Varsovians declared in the Polish national census that Hebrew was their mother tongue; since this was sociolinguistically impossible and came as a response to a nationwide request by Poland's Zionist movement, we can safely assume that virtually every one of these 19,000 Varsovians was a committed Zionist of some sort, active in one of at least six distinct Zionist subcultures with its own universe of ideals, credos, and certainties.[8]

Conversely, we can also find substantial evidence of how the "third politics" detected by Levita—a politics of the *non*committed—not only coexisted with all these movements but substantially affected each as the 1920s flowed into the 1930s. As we have already begun to see, this is most obvious with regard to Zionism. Of course, some of those who joined Zionist organizations in this era, as earlier, did so primarily because they found some version of Zionism's ideals and myths compelling. A rich source base of memoir, autobiography, and historiography attests to the growing attraction exerted over Polish Jews by the strident urgency of right-wing Revisionist Zionism and its performatively militant Betar youth movement—and to the equal attraction, for others, of the leftist Ha-Shomer ha-Tsair youth movement, famed for the passionate intensity with which its members sought to invent a new form of life that would reconcile A. D. Gordon's Tolstoyan-agrarian Zionism, Baden-Powell's paramilitary scouting ideals, Freudian psychoanalysis, and Marxism.[9] Even with regard to Hehalutz, the organization to which many were clearly turning primarily in hopes of getting the coveted aliyah Certificate, it is clear that positive ideological attractions did play a powerful role for some. The "sisters Strausberg" (later Sarah Gafni and Miriam Vainshtein) were daughters of a Belzer Hasid so "religious-extremist" that he rejected even the Orthodox political party the Agudah as "too 'progressive.'" Inspired by the ideas of halutzim who found work in their father's bakery during the pre-Passover rush, and "enchanted" by illicit visits to the Dror training kibbutz in Kraków while their parents slept on the Sabbath, the Strausberg sisters chose to leave for hakhsharah and try for aliyah despite the pain this "shame" visited on a father "whom we respected so deeply."[10] Theirs may be a case of a larger phenomenon emphasized by Hehalutz historian Rona Yona, who suggests that Polish Jewish youth from declining middle-class families were especially moved by Hehalutz's "cult" of manual labor as regenerative—a cult embodied in encounters with young people like themselves who had indeed transformed themselves into laborers.[11]

But scholars of Zionism in post-1928 Poland have long been aware that "push" factors were far more determinative than "pull" in the movement's grassroots resurgence, even as they continue to focus for the most part on positive ideology. Work on Zionism that begins from the grass roots, be it work on Hehalutz by Yona and Yisrael Oppenheim or Irith Cherniavsky's more general study of Polish Jewish relations to Zionism in this era, reveals that recognizable ideological engagement held for only some of those involved, and probably not most. Historians can reasonably argue about proportion: how much of the sudden turn of Polish Jewish attention to Zionism was fed by a widening judgment about narrowing horizons in Poland as opposed to an enthusiasm for some Zionist vision of Jewish self-transformation. But that the former determination was profound, especially in driving people to join Hehalutz and other organizations seen as giving enhanced Certificate access (like the artisans' organization Ha-Oved), is inarguable. As Yona puts it, the elements that flooded into Hehalutz after Palestine's reopening were made up more and more of a "public that was barely acquainted with the values of the movement and the kibbutz, did not really assimilate them, and it is doubtful that [this public] was in its entirety even interested in [these values]."[12]

Thus, one thing that struck activist after activist was just how many newly minted "Zionists" knew little about the Zionist project and had little connection with central Zionist myths. In mid-1933 the emissary Miriam Shlimovits (late Shalev) visited the fifty-strong Hehalutz group in Galicia's Nowy Sącz (Yid.: Nays-Sants) and was appalled to find that "most of the comrades only know about one place in the Land of Israel, [namely] Tel-Aviv [. . . .] About the Emek [the Jezreel Valley], of course, they knew nothing—this was the first time they'd heard the name." Recent Jewish settlement of the fertile Jezreel Valley (also a center of Palestinian life) was such a central theme of Zionist achievement, enthusiasm, and myth all through the 1920s that we may safely assume that only people utterly distant from *any* sort of Zionist framework before joining Hehalutz would never had heard of it.[13] Even before the reopening of Palestine, in 1930 the emissary Haim Ben-Asher noted that of the 130 young people in Prużana's branch of the Hehalutz-affiliated youth movement Hehalutz ha-Tsair, 70 percent needed remediation "even in elementary matters" regarding Hehalutz "concepts and connections with the movement."[14] Prescriptive sources acknowledged the same. In September 1933, a mimeographed newsletter from Hehalutz activists in Białystok "to all regional branches and kibbutzim" confirmed that "the branches have not ceased to expand. A new element is coming to us which is distant from the question[s] of the movement and it is necessary to fit the work of the branch[es] to [this element] in order to bring it closer to questions of the Land of Israel and to educate it toward pioneering tasks."[15]

Indeed, some would-be halutzim did not even bother to project interest in Hehalutz ideals. In autumn 1932, a new Hehalutz group in Koluszki, outside Poland's suffering industrial center Łódź, reported that "several comrades came to us and declared: 'we want to join Hehalutz, when will you send us to training and how long will it take until we can go to the Land of Israel?' Naturally we explained to them: we are ready to sign you up for the ranks of Hehalutz, but a halutz must not ask 'when' and 'how long,' and we tried to make clear to them the goals and paths of halutzim. Our answer did not satisfy them; the thought of halutzim is too difficult for them and doesn't pay and they left us."[16] The gap between genuine Zionist ideals and "mere" emigrationist sentiment among those joining Zionist organizations was so visible that it generated its own terminology. In late 1933 or early 1934 the Hehalutz ha-Tsair group in Włodzimierzec

(Yid.: Vlodimirets; Ukr.: Volodymyrets) boasted that there were no "conjuncture-pioneers" in *its* ranks.[17] A young man writing his YIVO autobiography in the same period complained that while he wished to *"make aliyah to the Land of Israel,"* his comrades merely wanted to *"emigrate to Palestine."*[18]

The portrait elaborated so far of a mass turn to the "politics of doubt" will no doubt receive sharper skepticism from historians of the other two great camps of Jewish collective politics, identity, and culture in Poland, namely religious Orthodoxy in its various forms, especially Hasidism, on the one hand and, on the other, Poland's robust Jewish socialist camp—especially the Social Democratic Bund but also competing socialist subcultures of anarchists, the sectarian Marxist-Zionist Poalei Tsion Left, and the Communists. Recently, scholars of both the Bund and Hasidism have argued that both movements not only maintained mass influence in the 1930s but expanded it. Scholars such as Gertrud Pickhan and Jack Jacobs argue that the Bund's sway over Polish Jewry "grew [. . .] quite markedly over the course of the interwar period."[19] Concomitantly, historian of Hasidism Glenn Dynner argues that historians wedded to a secularization-thesis historiography have substantially underestimated Hasidic demographic and institutional staying power in the 1930s.[20]

How convincing the revisionist arguments about the robustness and expansion of both the Bund and Hasidic Orthodoxy I leave to others to determine. Jacobs is careful to note that even in the late 1930s at the unquestionable peak of its influence, "the Bund did not attain hegemony," much less the adherence of a majority of Polish Jews. This is certainly truer still for our 1928–1935 period. As for Hasidism and Orthodox Jewry more generally, it seems hard to ignore the evidence of real crisis and cascading decline in observance demonstrated by many scholars and acknowledged by some Hasidic leaders themselves—as when, circa 1931, Kalonymous Kalmish Shapiro, the Piaseczner Rebbe, remonstrated that if his fellow religious leaders were to "stick their heads outside the four cubits of their yeshivas" they would see a "great mass of freethinkers," recognize that the "younger generation" was in the grips of "heresy," and discover that "even the artisans and the merchants who once, though they were never Torah scholars, were at any rate faithful Jews [. . .] have now embraced heresy and become wayward and fallen into a pit of falsehood."[21]

Of course, substantial numbers of Polish Jews did remain or became committed adherents of socialism or of Hasidism, with their very different but equally expansive arguments for why Jews should continue to invest in a future in situ. The Bund's Tsukunft youth movement took root not only in major cities but also in some smaller towns.[22] Conversely, Hasidism continued to win adherents not only in small towns but also in cities.[23] There were whole towns where either socialism or Hasidism commanded local hegemony. In February 1934, the Hehalutz emissary Haim Biber reported a town "entirely under the strong influence of the Reds" and anatomized its distinctive features: Zalman Reyzen's pro-Soviet Yiddish daily the Wilno *Tog* circulated widely; enough local Jewish youth were active in Communist activity that even some Hehalutz members had older siblings in jail; the town supported a Yiddishist school but no Hebraist one.[24]

And to the Jewish socialist and Orthodox camps, we must add one more substantial and internally variegated Polish Jewish subculture that, to a considerable degree, proved able to sustain hopes for a better future in Poland even as matters worsened: the assimilationist camp. Throughout our period, substantial numbers of Polish Jews clearly continued to aspire to be fully Polish. Cities such as Warsaw, Lwów, and Kraków boasted distinct communities of Polonized Jews for whom Polishness was a nonnegotiable value; multigenerational families of deeply patriotic "Poles of the Mosaic faith" functioned as a supportive framework in which offspring and even newcomers to Polish culture could affirm Polishness regardless of rising antisemitism.[25] Some such families could be found even in small towns.[26] Larger cities could sustain a Polish Jewish version of that most peculiar modern Jewish formation: Jewish organizations constituted to further Jewish assimilation. As many as a third of Jewish university students in the 1930s continued to identify as Poles of the Jewish faith, and such students built their own organizations to sustain and further their Polishness in multiple ways. The Związek Akademickiej Młodzieży Zjednoczeniowej (ZAMZ) organized lectures about Polish culture, summer retreats, and even financial aid for needy Jewish students who adhered to assimilationist goals. PPS, anarchist, and Communist organizations of varying degrees of legality provided a parallel assimilationism-positive framework, conjoining support for Jewish Polonization with a *Zukunftbild* of revolutionary social change coming that undoubtedly fortified the faith of many that they would ultimately find their place as Poles in Poland. On a day-to-day level, organizations like these served as sites for vigorous critiques of Jewish nationalist separatism, contact with sympathetic ethnic Poles, and affirmations that assimilationists were an "avant-garde of Jewish-Polish solidarity."[27]

There is some reason to think that such assimilationist hopes eroded more rapidly and widely than fully countercultural religious or socialist views in the 1930s.[28] But clearly assimilationism did not simply evaporate. Some of its number, looking back, underscore signs of health and perhaps even growth; Joseph Lichten claims that "at one of the Warsaw chapter meetings" of the ZAMZ "there were upwards of 400 members."[29]

In turn, this sketch of assimilationism as a still-vibrant subculture brings us to the second overarching image of Polish Jewish political consciousness in the late 1920s and 1930s that some historians will counterpose to my portrait of a politics of doubt—namely, the argument that the 1926–1935 period under the tolerant Piłsudski was one of *expansion* of Jewish hopes for real integration into Polish political society rather than contraction. Undoubtedly, some Jews did experience this period (or at least its early years) in this way. Thanks to the work of Kijek, Heller, Aleksiun, Szymaniak, Underhill, Kassow, and many others, it is also clear that such expanded aspirations to integration were not limited to already highly Polonized circles. As Kijek emphasizes, the YIVO autobiographies across the 1930s are replete with cases of thickly Jewish young people—Yiddish speaking, traditionally educated, even Hasidic—moved by encounters with the symbols of Polish nationhood and in some cases drawn to identify with Polishness by the encouragement of genuinely tolerant teachers.[30] One of the most striking of the 1934 YIVO autobiographies is that of "Esther," who, while living the daily life of a Hasidic woman with little contact with the larger world, nonetheless came to identify with Polish national myth deeply, helped along by illicit reading of Sienkiewicz's novels.[31] Heller convincingly argues that one of the driving forces behind the massive growth of the militaristic and parade-obsessed Revisionist Zionist Betar youth movement in the early 1930s was a yearning to participate in the martial cult central to *Polish* national ritual. Betar's febrile ideology of Jewish pride through power certainly attracted some who felt persecuted, but, paradoxically, others (or perhaps indeed the *same* people) were attracted by the fact that Betar paramilitary units sometimes won permission to parade alongside Polish youth and *as* Polish youth. In Poland's disputed southeast, Betar youth could even participate in a Polishness defined by paramilitary action against Ukrainian separatism.[32]

Concomitantly, recent cultural-historical scholarship has shown us just how many and how various were the Jewish intellectuals who continued to aspire to both individual and collective Jewish at-homeness in Poland

and to see themselves as participants in a Jewish-Polish dialogue about a shared future. Since the 1980s, scholars of interwar Polish-language culture following in the footsteps of Eugenia Prokop-Janiec and Michael Steinlauf among others have been rediscovering an ever-expanding subculture of Polish-language yet expressly Jewish-directed journalism, opinion, and even literature and children's literature written by and for people who identified as Jews despite their cultural-linguistic Polishness. The famed pedagogical theorist Korczak chose both to participate in organizations that embraced Jewish identity and to identify fully as a Pole seeking to build a better Poland. He sometimes published his writings for children in Jewishly identified journals even as he worked to speak to all parents and children. Clearly, he hoped that in doing so he was not simply ignoring contradictions but unifying worlds.[33]

And just as clearly, he was far from alone. More recently, scholars of culture on the seam between Polish and Yiddish culture like Szymaniak, Underhill, Kassow, and Aleksiun have shown us a world in which intellectuals like the poet Debora Vogel, the critic Vaynig, the young historian Ringelblum, and a not-insignificant number of others not only moved back and forth between Yiddish and Polish letters but worked consciously to render Polish culture more open to what we might call multiculturalism. In Yiddish, they elaborated a capacious vision of Polishness, while in Polish they defended Jewish humanity to a Polish literary milieu that was liberal in principle but often intolerant in practice. In some places—Lwów, for instance, with its Austro-Galician heritage of multiethnic tolerance—figures like Vogel helped shape cultural milieus genuinely open to Yiddish and Ukrainian culture as part of Polishness.[34] The rediscovery of these "amphibious" figures in turn illuminates how extensively some Polish cultural actors of Jewish background whom we might once have regarded as wholly distant from Jewish questions also participated actively in negotiating a place for Jewishness within Polishness. Underhill's archaeological reconstructions of Bruno Schulz's Galician Jewish youth and of his intense formative conversations with Vogel allows her to show how Schulz's famously hermetic short stories encode his growing concerns about the Polish Jewish situation and the problem of preserving complex selfhood in a nationalist age.[35]

I have dwelt on these alternative accounts of Polish Jewish political consciousness at some length in order to dispel any misunderstanding of my argument so far: I am *not* claiming that the two familiar images of an ideologically mobilized and "positive" Polish Jewry or of a growing population of Polish Jews aspiring to civic and cultural integration are simply illusory. Indeed, in my own work elsewhere I have attempted to contribute, via a focus on urban niches, to our understanding of why and how both such perspectives could flourish throughout the interwar period.[36]

My claim here, rather, is that from the late 1920s on, a *third* mode of Jewish political consciousness predicated on increasingly ramified doubts about the possibility of a Jewish future in Poland began to emerge, spread rapidly, and gain traction on a massive scale in Polish Jewish life. This shift is not only evident in historical retrospect; contemporaries saw it too. We have already encountered Binyomen R. of Bielsk as a young person moved to respond to Max Weinreich's searing analysis of Polish Jewish youth political culture with searching reflections of his own. As noted, Binyomen reaffirmed Weinreich's most basic insights that Jewish youth were indeed seized en masse by despair about the future, and that this despair derived not only from economic woe but from political experience. And if those aspects of Binyomen's response essentially confirm the scope and character of Polish Jewry's crisis of futurity, his grassroots perspective also equipped him to see something Weinreich could not about a broad transformation in Jewish political culture.

First, Weinreich did not understand how profoundly grassroots Jewish political consciousness was changing relative to the 1920s. Throughout *Veg,* Weinreich operated on the assumption (still regnant, as we can already clearly see, in much historiography today) that Polish Jews were divided into four camps: a "traditional" camp, "a Yiddish-secular [camp . . .] permeated by mostly socialist or Communist influences," "a Zionist-Hebraist stratum," and "the assimilated environment."[37]

In response, Binyomen R. offered a thoroughgoing corrective. First, those divisions into siloed camps defined by homologously structured competing ideologies were a thing of the past: "The boundaries of the social-cultural environments are highly liquid. The same individuals can traverse all of the environments." And the political choices of his peers had little to do with *any* of the famous competing ideals. Many "Zionists" both "right" and "left" had little interest in *any* elemental East European Zionist vision of Jewish cultural revolution and self-reinvention, and "90%" of the Communists "were people who have left other organizations"—including the Orthodox Agudah and the Bund as well as all lobes of Zionism—"in despair."[38]

Rather—Binyomen's second point—much of the new politics turned on a shared search for some better future. What drove most youth into right-wing Zionism was little different from what drove them into left-wing Zionism, and had little to do with the myths of either: the martial violent New Jew of the former or the productive laboring New Jew of the latter. Rather, most in both camps were driven by a sense that Palestine likely offered a better future than Poland for Jews who could get there: "Is the struggle between the League for a Laboring Land of Israel and the Revisionist movement a class-struggle? It's a 'secret' that absolutely everyone knows that it is first and foremost a struggle for Certificates."[39]

Binyomen's 1935 contention that the political consciousness of Jewish youth across ideological lines was reorienting itself en masse away from old ideologies and toward an urgent will simply to leave Poland came as a response to Weinreich's *Veg*. Thus, we might suspect that his intentions were polemical. But the fact that this is how he actually *experienced* the Jewish world around him *before* he read *Veg* is copiously demonstrated by the 1934 autobiography, where, in unstudied fashion, the sections that focus on the recent past and present of 1932–1934 (roughly, the first quarter and last third of the text) bespeak a situation in which quite substantial portions of Bielsk's youth were turning both to Hehalutz and to the Revisionists in frank hopes of securing a Certificate. Thus, the autobiography records without adornment the sudden growth of Bielsk's Hehalutz branch from thirty to seventy members in 1933 and its more recent decline to fifty. By the same token, and with equal grounding in personal experience, the autobiography notes the virtual collapse of the local Bundist Tsukunft youth group amid mass outflux to either Hehalutz or the Communists. Binyomen's experience as well as his testimony thus captures as largely self-evident by 1934–1935 what Levita saw in 1929 and what I have traced across multiple sources above: an ever-widening realm of Jewish experience and thought that found *all* of the existing ideologies and parties inadequate and perhaps even irrelevant—irrelevant in the precise sense that they could not provide a better future for the individual. Instead, the organized parties operated in denial of what more and more Polish Jews were coming to understand—namely, that Jews were objects of forces beyond their control, forces that were moreover likely inimical to Jewish well-being.

The Search for a Future and Political Defection

As suggested by Binyomen R.'s comment on the 1933 collapse of the Bundist Tsukunft group in Bielsk-Podlaski, there is much evidence that

this emerging "third politics" not only coexisted with older Jewish ideologies and more recent integrationist hopes but actually undercut both
of those in no small way in the 1929–1935 period. Diverse sources suggest that substantial numbers of the newly minted Zionists were coming
from the two great redoubts of coherent *anti*-Zionism in Poland: from
the subculture of the Jewish socialist-Diasporist Left and from Orthodox
society, including Hasidic communities. Other sources suggest the same
kinds of "defection" from both Polonized and aspirationally integrationist
circles. I note that this chapter makes no hard claims about the scope
thereof, but I also note that even the most desultory search through ego-
documents and sources like *yizkor-bikher* (collectively authored community memory books created by survivors of the interwar generation after
the Holocaust) suggests that in the 1929–1935 period, this threefold flow
from socialist, Orthodox, and Polonized circles into Zionism as exitism
happened on a large scale and across the entirety of Jewish Poland. My
goal here is to show some of the contours of this "defection" as further
evidence and explication of the emerging politics of doubt.

First, as per Binyomen's experience, there was evidently substantial
defection to Zionism from socialist and Diasporist circles and organizations. This involved Bundists, Communists, and elements close to both,
reached small towns and large, and applied both in the kresy and in
Congress Poland. In April 1933, a letter from Poland's Hehalutz to the
leadership in Palestine aiming to give an overview of the situation described
"a great inflow of people into Hehalutz branches" consisting of "widely
varied human material (ranging from party-members to those belonging
to no party, Zionists and non-Zionists, and including Bund [members]
and Reds [Communists]."[40]

For a concrete example, let us return to Urinsky's Prużana, a town of
about 8,000 circa 1930, 55 percent of whom were Jews alongside roughly
equal minorities of ethnic Polish and nominally Byelorussian inhabitants.
Though Zionist institutions dominated Prużana's internal Jewish politics,
it also developed an unusually ramified Diaspora-socialist milieu for a
town that size, at the core of which stood the Yiddishist Peretz school (cofounded and run by the aforementioned Urinsky) and a well-organized
Bundist scene significant enough to draw regular lectures by Bundist
leaders from Warsaw, build a chapter of the Tsukunft youth organization,
and win a significant minority of the Jewish vote in local elections (in
Prużana's 1927 municipal elections, the Radical Group, stalking horse for
the still semilegal Bund, won about 40% of the Jewish vote with 759

votes; the Zionists won the other 60%, with 1,003).[41] And Prużana's Bund was fiercely ideological. Its electoral campaigns featured unbridled class-warfare attacks against the rest of the Jewish community, as when its propagandists averred that the local Poalei Tsion youth were "a Black-Hundreds gang of upper-class oppressors"—thus charging a wide swath of Prużana's Jewish young people not only with wealth that most individuals certainly did not command (only 35% of the children in Prużana's Zionist-Hebraist schools belonged to anything that could be called the merchant class, and most paid 50% or less of the tuition) but even with kinship to the pogrom agitators of Tsarist Russia.[42]

But for all its fervor, Prużana's socialist-Diasporist scene clearly faced troubles across our period. When the Yiddishist and socialist leader Urinsky wrote woefully in 1934 about the turn toward exitism among Prużana's Jewish youth, he was most perturbed by the evidence of this among the young people he knew best, which is to say, people raised in cultural and political institutions devoted to Diasporism and *doikayt,* products of the Peretz School, and members of the Bund. Sources produced on the other side of the battle lines support his account. Already in 1930, the aforementioned Zionist emissary Ben-Asher noted that Prużana's Hehalutz ha-Tsair had "proven able to draw 30 comrades" from "Left Poalei-Tsion" as well as "from Tsukunft" (that is, the Bund).[43] A memoirist who came of age in Prużana in the late 1920s recalls that especially after 1932, the town's Zionist youth movements began to draw "many boys and girls [. . .] from the anti-Zionist organizations." Another recalls that the Hehalutz organization he helped re-create actively "strove to connect with the youth in the anti-Zionist circles organized around the Peretz school," and "saved many souls raised in the ideological bosom of Bundism or Communism for activist Zionism." A third recalls that the Gordonia "pioneer-popular youth movement," founded by students at the Hebrew gymnasium, also attracted "boys and girls who studied in the Y. L. Peretz school" (and "in the Polish schools," a point I return to below).[44]

And large-scale defection from socialist-Diasporist to Zionist affiliations did not obtain only in smaller towns. In October 1934, the long-time Yiddishist activist Zelig Kalmanovitsh reported to his brother-in-law that Wilno's storied Diasporist movement could no longer hold on to "a youth for ourselves."[45] The same despairing note had been sounded in June by the unyielding Diasporist ideologue Avrom Golomb, writing in the internal-circulation newsletter of Bin (The Bee), a Wilno-region

Yiddishist-Diasporist and Bund-oriented youth movement founded in 1927. Though formally nonparty, Bin's pro-socialist stance plus its Yiddishism naturally aligned it with Bundist sensibilities, and these seem to have been widespread in its ranks. Thus, the 1928 movement notebook of a fifteen-year-old Bin circle leader, Sima Meyerovitsh, demonstrates a clear Bundist line: discussion themes included anti-Zionist and anti-Hebraist but also anti-Communist excurses ("why the Reds want to destroy Bin") and the prison memoirs of the just-deceased Bundist hero Beynish Mikhalevitsh.[46] Wilno itself was the heart of Bin, and Golomb one of the organization's most devoted adult advisers. But, apparently basing his assessment on internal organizational data, Golomb grimly concluded that by mid-1934 "in Vilna itself, there are no more committed Bin members—all have left."[47] Golomb's comments came particularly in relation to one of Bin's signal initiatives. Beginning in 1931, the organization had begun to create work camps for older members. The model was the Zionist training kibbutz, but the ideology was its exact inverse, to prepare Jewish youth for a life of agrarian labor in Eastern Europe: "'There where my house is built, that is my land'—so we sing in one of our songs, and it is not necessary, we say, for Jewish youth to go so far as to uproot itself in order to be able to accept the ideology of labor."[48] By 1934, the endeavor was in crisis. Not only was "the disappointment among Bin's members tremendous," wrote the young Mikhl Astour, a leading figure in those circles, but the "participants in the work-camps have for the most part left either for the Soviet Union or for Palestine."[49] The YIVO archives preserve the autobiography of one of the young people who took this latter path.[50]

Nor was such defection to Zionism from the anti-Zionist Jewish Left limited to any one region, such as Poland's eastern kresy. That it was taking place in central Poland as well is evident from sources found essentially at random from Czyżew-Osada (Yid.: Tshizsheve).[51] Halfway between Warsaw and Białystok, Czyżew-Osada was solidly planted in core Polish territory and in Warsaw's economic orbit. One of those drawn to Warsaw from Czyżew-Osada was Yitzhak Gura. In the early 1920s, he and "dozens of other young Hasidic men" in Czyżew-Osada had embraced Zionism. Time in Warsaw then led Gura to Communist ideals, and these he brought back to Czyżew-Osada, where they proved attractive to some young people. But in the early 1930s, Gura and many of his fellow Hasidim turned Communists reversed course and joined the Zionist Hehalutz. In his telling, this choice was driven both by disillusion-

Figure 2.2 "A group of Frayhayt-movement members in 1931" in Czyżew-Osada (Yid.: Tshizsheve) from *Yizkor-bukh nokh der khorev-gevorener yidisher kehile Tshizsheve*, ed. Shimon Kanc (Tel Aviv, 1961), 375–376. Reproduction courtesy of New York Public Library.

ment with events in the Soviet Union and by a growing consciousness of the Jewish plight in Poland: "The other communists who went with me also understood it this way and little by little sobered up until we finally became active members of the [Zionist] pioneer movement in all its shades [. . .]. We saw everything more clearly, what was happening in the world, looked more closely at Jewish wounds and felt a new responsibility for our people."[52]

Nor, finally, was such defection from the socialist-Diasporist camp to be found only among youth. In February 1934, the Hehalutz emissary Aryeh Tsvik arrived in Warsaw. A visit to a meeting called by Poalei Tsion situated him among adult workers: "men as old as 50, 60, with years of work behind them." He was struck by the special respect accorded a "Jew from the Land of Israel" and by the fact that these were workers who had hitherto been "under the influence of the Communists and the Bund" and now listened with deep interest to the socialist-Zionist message.[53]

And what of integrationist, Polonizing circles, however defined? Here again we find ample evidence of hopes giving way to doubt among many

Jews embarked in some way or another on a trajectory toward assimilation. Once again, sources on Prużana speak powerfully to this phenomenon. Throughout the interwar period, numerous Jewish students attended the key institution of *Polish* national culture in the town (and the only institution to crosscut the town's three-way ethnonational divide, apparently): the Adam Mickiewicz Gymnasium, founded in 1922 not least as part of the young Polish state's project of Polonizing its borderlands. In the 1927–1928 school year, the school's 113 students "of the Jewish religion" made up nearly 40 percent of the total, though in later years the percentage seems to have fallen.[54] Sociologically speaking, these students were taking the most important step available toward a chance at incorporation into Polishness.[55] But just as youth from Prużana's socialist-Diasporist scene evidently defected in substantial numbers to exit-Zionism, so too did youth from the gymnasium. Already in 1930, Ben-Asher noted that a sizable contingent of the newcomers to Prużana's He-halutz ha-Tsair—the ones who needed the most basic remedial ideological education—came from the Polish gymnasium. Prużana native Yosef Fridlander recalls that the Gordonia "pioneer-popular youth movement," founded by students at the town's competing Hebrew gymnasium, attracted not only "boys and girls who studied in the Y. L. Peretz [Yiddishist] school" but also youth from "the Polish schools."[56]

A July 1935 letter from the Joint Distribution Committee's man in Warsaw, Yitshok Giterman, provides us a more far-reaching and definitive testimony to a shift in Polish Jewry's most assimilated and assimilationist circles. The letter was elicited by a query from Werner Senator of the Zionist Executive in Palestine. Senator wrote politely to ask Giterman whether it made sense to revive "the Jewish Agency idea" in Poland—meaning, to revive efforts initiated in the late 1920s but quickly paralyzed by the onset of the Depression to win support for Zionist efforts in Palestine among non-Zionist but sympathetic Polish Jews of means. No doubt Senator turned to Giterman for information because the latter's position at the apex of relief work in Jewish Poland gave him an especially informed take on the Polish Jewish scene. We have noted too that Giterman, a committed Diasporist, had no reason to overemphasize Zionism's popularity among Poland's Jews.

In this double context, Giterman's response is striking. Reframing the question as whether it would now be possible "to create an array of practical Palestinist [*palestinezishe*] movements parallel to" but separate from the "ideational" Zionist movement, Giterman offered a full-throated answer that went well beyond Senator's apparently modest inquiry both in scope and in social-analytical specification. "In the context of the current situation there is virtually no line at which agitation [raising public support] for the work of the Agency would have to stop." In Giterman's view, two distinct social groups were now open to participation in "Land-of-Israel work" in a way that they had never been previously: "the Jewish intelligentsia" and "the money-aristocracy." Nor, he stressed, did he have in mind only "closely [aligned]" elements who had always been sympathetic to Zionism, but indeed major swaths of those elements in both groups who were "yesterday distant or even antagonistic" toward it. Speaking on the one hand primarily about the "money-aristocracy"—the industrialists and businessmen in whose support Senator was presumably primarily interested—Giterman pointed to what he saw as a more general transformation in how active Jewish support of the Zionist project was viewed by *non*-Jewish political elites or governments (this last dimension he left unspecified, but the implication of the non-Jewish gaze was clear): of late, it had become "the case that work for Palestine no longer seems an anti-patriotic act, but quite the opposite: it is now seen as an act of patriotism vis-à-vis the various lands where Jews live." The obvious point left unspoken in this anodyne formulation was that the patriotism attaching to such an act inhered in helping Poland find ways to reduce its Jewish population. Speaking on the other hand about the Jewish intelligentsia, Giterman saw at work a less narrowly calculative and more far-reaching reorientation: work on behalf of Jewish society building in Palestine stood a good chance of "bring[ing] in those elements who have been alienated from the Jewish environment and interests and who are psychologically ready to return [. . .]. To this category belongs the majority [*rov minyen un rov binyen*] of the Jewish intelligentsia in Poland." He detected such a reorientation even in highly assimilationist circles— "even [. . .] the sort of assimilationist intelligentsia circles to which Prof. Szymon Ashkenazy or other such belong."[57]

Finally, similar sorts of reorientation toward an interest in Zionism/Palestine and exit are found easily enough in sources on Orthodox Jewry, despite a powerful censorious impulse on that score. This seems most obviously true of *non*-Hasidic Orthodoxy, often called Lithuanian or yeshiva Orthodoxy. Hehalutz emissaries operating in the northeastern stretches of Poland encountered so little Orthodoxy among the young people of the region that when they did find it, they deemed it extraordinary. When Yisrolik Kopit visited the great Jewish religious center of

Novardok (Pol.: Nowogródek; Bel.: Navahrudak) in 1934, he found it remarkable that "the environment here is very stringent. The entire mature generation [young adults] belongs either to Mizrahi [the religious Zionist movement] or to the Agudah. To eat they demand of you a hat—and other similar sorts of nonsense." This report came after Kopit had visited many other sites; this was evidently the first time that he had seen anything like the very thing that would have once been a strictly enforced norm. Meanwhile, when the aforementioned Tsvik visited Radun (now in Belarus) the site of an especially stringent yeshiva and a town famous in the 1920s for its militant Orthodoxy, he found that the yeshivah "is no longer bubbling" and that Radin's children, "in their conversations and games, when they need to swear to something, [. . .] no longer use an oath to God—in its place they use the Hehalutz or Betar oath."[58]

And what of Hasidic Jews? Scholars of Hasidism sometimes claim that Hasidism's intensely communalist, high-affect, pietistic, and charismatically organized version of Orthodoxy proved hardier in the face of secularizing forces than the non-Hasidic variety, and there is reason to think this is true to some degree. But in the early 1930s, even Hasidism could not stanch the leakage of the young (and even some not so young) to Zionism. To some degree, such leakage no doubt owed something to Zionism's *ideological* pull: Zionism's activation of Judaism's traditional mythologies sometimes resonated powerfully for Hasidic Jews (like other tradition-immersed Jews) despite the Hasidic leadership's general and often fierce ideological-theological opposition to Zionist ideas.[59] But clearly some of the Hasidic individuals drawn to Zionism in the 1920s–1930s were driven less by ideological attraction and more by darkening assessments about Jewish prospects in Poland. Once again, Czyżew-Osada offers an arresting case. Czyżew-Osada entered the interwar period a stronghold of Hasidic commitment. Spiritual and social life revolved to a considerable degree around highly organized local communities affiliated with Poland's two largest Hasidic dynasties, Ger (Góra-Kalwaria) and Aleksander. The memoirist Berl Szajes warmly recalled his feeling as a child that the local prayer house of the Aleksander Hasidim, where he "spent the best years of my youth," had "existed since the creation of the Jewish community in Tshizsheve."[60] Politically, religious elements in Czyżew-Osada embraced the rising efforts of East European Orthodox leaders to mobilize Orthodox Jews as a political force under the banner of the new traditionalist political party Agudes Yisroel (Agudat Yisrael): "We can assert with absolute certainty that our town was one of the first to enthusiastically take up the call to found an organization of Orthodox Jews."[61] A third memoirist, Malka Szajman, testifies to a mobilized Hasidism willing to assert itself beyond the prayer house:

> The [League] for a Laboring Land of Israel quickly grew into one of the largest party organizations in Tshizsheve and in the surrounding region. Despite the persecution that we endured from the religious and Hasidic elements in Tshizsheve, the organization grew stronger in quantity and quality every day. Of the many incidents and conflicts that occurred between us and the religious, I will only relate one. It was shortly after the events in the Land of Israel in 1929. When our party's leading activists [. . .] held a meeting to consider the question of how to honor the fallen heroes who had defended the Jewish communities in the Land of Israel as well as the question of the Congress of [the League for] a Laboring Land of Israel that was supposed to take place then in Berlin, several Gerer Hasidim and others suddenly arrived and began to demolish our premises. They had come to rescue their children. Fights broke out. The police came, then trials.[62]

Szajman's memoir attests to a mobilized local Hasidism. But she and other memoirists also record that one of the factors inciting this was, precisely, substantial defection to Zionism from within Hasidic ranks. The memoirs are agreed that this was first visible in the younger generation: "Hehalutz [. . .] included in its ranks a large portion of the student youth, the younger workers, young men from the yeshivas and Hasidic prayer-houses"; these last were the children that the town's Gerer Hasidim sought to "rescue."[63]

More interesting is the convergence of memoirists' recollections that the 1930s brought a substantial reorientation toward Zionism, or at least tolerance for Zionism, not only among the ever-expanding youth cohort but also among pious members of the older generation. It was not simply that the town's Aleksander Hasidism "tolerated worshippers who thought differently, like Zionists for instance," or that "among the prayer-house attendees, one could find many whom the idea of the Return to Zion enchanted and succored and shored up." Even among those who had opposed Zionism, the period in question brought a marked change. Of those Hasidic elements that disrupted Poalei Tsion proceedings in 1929, Szajman recalls, "But as it turned out, they ultimately grew convinced that our struggle for 'Zionism' was correct. Their children, who later joined our ranks, later became the activist core of the Zionist organizations in Tshizsheve." Another memoirist, Leah Dimentman, recalls the "thirst to make aliyah with the help of Certificates" growing "terribly strong even among those who were waiting for the Redemption and the coming of the Messiah," and pinpoints 1932–1935 as the inflection point. Here, although residual traditionalist romanticism about the Land of Israel may have played a role for some, deepening worries about the Jewish future in Poland were clearly central.[64]

The openness of Hasidic Jews to Zionism—and exitism—was clearly not unique to Czyżew-Osada. As the Fifth Aliyah period unfolded, Agudes Yisroel (Agudat Yisrael)—the traditionalist political party dominated by the Ger Hasidic community—confronted what one Agudah youth leader called a growing "psychosis for *aliyah*" among young members.[65] Some observers saw this even before the 1932 annus mirabilis of renewed aliyah possibilities; in late 1931, the aforementioned Zionist activist Druyanov, who respected Orthodox Jewry and worked to meet with "*haredim*" during his six-month tour of Poland, recorded in a notebook that "even the *haredi* youth" were "distancing themselves" from Agudes Yisroel. Interestingly, he deemed this "not [because of the Agudah's relationship] to Zionism" but "because of its relationship to the Land of Israel" (that is, to Jewish emigration and settlement in Palestine).[66] By 1935, a writer in the newly founded Agudes Yisroel publication *Darkeinu* felt empowered to "demand [!] from the leaders of Agudes Yisroel at their meeting in Basel" that they throw the weight of the organization behind persuading "*haredi* Jewry in the diaspora" to "bring their contribution and [do] their part in the building" of "the Land of Israel."[67]

The Jewish Question in the Politics of Exit

And why were these and other religious Jews turning to Zionism, or better put, seeking a practical politics of exit? No doubt many factors were in play, but clearly one of them was a dark judgment about where Poland was headed politically. Looking back, memoirist David Frankel describes his choice to join Hehalutz in the 1932–1935 period in raw political terms: "My father [. . .] was a fervent *Hasid* and until the age of eighteen I absorbed the spirit of Hasidism in all its variety. As I matured it became clear to me that there was no future in our town for Jewish youth, for many of the Christian citizens were antisemitic."[68] A 1934 YIVO youth autobiography by a second Hasidic youth sounds the same note in its striking conclusion. Noting that "formally I am connected to the framework of the Agudah," the author nonetheless declared, "I would leave for the Land of Israel without the slightest hesitation." As Ido Bassok notes in his insightful analysis, this is an autobiography with almost no political content otherwise; it focuses largely on the author's pained relations with his strict rabbi father, on his peregrinations from the local Aleksander Hasidic study hall to a *Musar* yeshiva, and on inner struggles over belief and sexuality. At no point does he register *any* substantial engagement with Zionist ideas and arguments. Why then the readiness to go to Palestine by the time he concluded his writing? What had "awakened me to this" desire for aliyah, the author relates, was the antisemitism of local Endek youth and their "constant insults."[69] Nor was the connection between reorientation toward Zionism-as-exit and a sense of rising antisemitism among Hasidic people exclusive to youth. The aforementioned Leah Dimentman from Czyżew-Osada recalls that "the thirst" for emigration to Palestine "with the help of Certificates" became "terribly strong" among local religious people "particularly after the antisemitism in Poland became wilder and more brutal."[70]

I close this chapter by drawing from some of the sources we have examined here and in Chapter 1 an important fact: that while many factors shaped Polish Jewish political thinking and choice in the 1929–1935 watershed, there was clearly a robust connection between the widespread grassroots turn to a politics of doubt and exit and a rising sense of *political* danger. This was true not only of religious Jews, of course, but of all sorts of Jews. In Chapter 1, we met a Polonized young man who called himself Rex in his 1934 autobiography. We noted how his autobiography closed with a grim and sharply pessimistic account of his perception that both Polish society and even the Polish state were being drawn toward a robust anti-Jewish politics. Here let us note a further dimension: Rex framed his own choice to become a Zionist not in terms of visions of self-making in Palestine or merely in vague terms of tough times in Poland, but in political-extrapolative terms about where the situation for Jews in Poland was headed: "We shouldn't have any illusions. In order to see the situation of the Jews of Poland as it is we have to say openly: bad times are before us."[71]

In turn, Binyomen R.'s case testifies that similar forces were at work in nonassimilated small-town youth with broadly socialist affiliations. Binyomen's own trajectory exemplifies how everyday experience in Poland coupled with analytical attention to what was going on across the country and the continent could provoke and shape the politics of doubt and exit no less so, and perhaps more so, than raw economic woe. Binyomen too chose Zionism after much hesitation, joining Hehalutz in 1934. Because of the unique richness of the testimonies he left, Binyomen's political thinking and the reasoning behind his choice of Zionism reward close phenomenological attention, which I will revisit later. Here I simply want to underscore one step along that path of rethinking. Binyomen was a socialist by conviction and serious engagement. Marxian categories infused his thought, class and class conflict were part of the optic through which he viewed the world, he read Yiddish and Polish Marxist and socialist journals and newspapers seriously as part of a wider voracious political reading practice, and as we will see, most of his closest interlocutors were Communists serious about their Communism or otherwise socialist. But Binyomen's grim sense of an antisemitism spreading across multiple social spheres of Polish life and transforming itself in the process compelled him to question the socialist analytical assumptions that were close to his heart and common sense for his most respected interlocutors. It was easy enough to accommodate the antisemitism of the veterinarian Fuks or the Endek choices of his former Polish tutor Stepak Jackiewicz within socialist categories, as the antisemitism of the middle class, mobilized for nakedly selfish ends within the dog-eat-dog world of capitalism. But Binyomen saw the same ideas finding new resonance and spread among peasants and, more than that, among the regular folk whom Marxist theory endowed with the world-historical task of bringing human liberation, "the workers." This was the force of his packed comment: "One talks about the NARA [Endek youth] folks but one means the workers. Just like with Dollfuss." His peculiar formulation of this point is also intriguing: the idea that one privately believed that antisemitism was spreading among Poland's working class but publicly confined one's worries to the nominally "middle-class" and student youth who joined the Endek youth movement suggests a growing critical unease about the analytical limits of political discourse in Binyomen's *own* left-leaning circles. He may have meant Jewish public discourse in general, but he likely meant Bundist and Communist discourse in particular, where the idea that the Polish working class would resist antisemitism and other forms of "reaction" was both dogma and a necessary condition for belief in the brighter future those movements promised Polish Jews. That Binyomen had this deeply fraught question for the Left in mind is clear from the curt closing phrase invoking the leader of the Austro-Fascist and antisemitic regime that had seized power in nearby Austria just a few months earlier. For those around the globe who identified with Marxian ideals and sensibilities, the most distressing feature of the easy victory of Austria's nationalist-Catholic-corporatist Right over Europe's most impressively organized and armed socialist movement was the degree to which Austria's nominally radical working class outside Vienna had ignored the calls of Austria's Social Democratic Party for a general strike and mass mobilization.[72]

Let us finally return to Yitshok Giterman's private acknowledgment that elements of the most Polonized sectors of Polish Jewry had suddenly grown interested in the Zionist project. At the root of this shift, Giterman suggested, was a double development. First, "the expanded absorptive capacities of Palestine" had themselves become a factor capable of inspiring real, practical interest in what was transpiring there. But then, too, there was what we might call a push factor—what Giterman called, as pointedly as this reticent man was capable of doing, "the rise of open and hidden Nazism." For assimilated Polonized Jewish adults no less than provincial Yiddishist youth like Binyomen or Hasidic youth like David Frankel, rising doubts about the salvageability of the Jewish situation in Poland, interest in the Zionist project in Palestine, economic woes, and political fears had all become bound together in a new constellation of political thinking that cut across all the old political, cultural, and class divides of Polish Jewry.[73]

In January 1933, a Zionist activist from Równe (Yid.: Rovne; Ukr.: Rivne) named Leah Vidrovits wrote to Druyanov in Palestine regarding Zionist lectures she was delivering in Romania: "This year has been a year of economic and spiritual crisis in the diaspora—a hard year for our work despite the sparkling situation in the Land of Israel. But nevertheless, masses of people come to listen. It's been my lot to give talks in many places this year—in synagogues in the men's section (only once did I have to speak in the women's gallery). And I can't communicate [to you] how exalted is the mood of those who gather from every part of the people [when they] hear the good word from the Land of Israel."[74] But by mid-1935 she saw no exaltation, only a politics of despair. As she wrote from Równe, "Several times I have wanted to send you a few words and I was not able to do so. The main reason, spiritual exhaustion from one sees and hears all around [. . . .] The poverty, the despair, the persecutions, and the mass thirst for emigration to the Land of Israel, all of this is mixed together."[75]

3

Minorityhood and the Limits of Culture

Among Polish Jews committed to Diasporism, none was more unwave-ring than Avrom Golomb. Golomb's take on the Diaspora's political situation was not Pollyannaish: by mid-1933 he was convinced that Germany's turn to "Hitlerism" was "a process with deep roots which will repeat itself elsewhere" and that Jews in Eastern Europe would now face "a stable, permanent, and chronic uprooting-politics." But neither then nor later did Golomb renounce his credo that "no winds" could "uproot" Diaspora Jewish communities, "transfer them, or destroy them," that Jews not only lived but "*wish*[ed] to live all across the world," and that they were called to be an exemplary "superterritorial people."[1]

But would Diaspora Jews acknowledge this calling, given the worsening situation? Through mid-1933, Golomb hoped that hardship would force Jews toward ideological "maturity." Under "permanent and chronic" siege, Polish Jews would unite around a politics of communal self-help. They would demand that the international community recognize in *law* that "the many Jewish communities of the entire world constitute one bound corporation and one part may always protect the rights of another part."[2]

But by October 1933, Golomb had concluded that rather than rising to face the age, Polish Jews were responding pathologically: "All circles of Jewish thought are ruled by apathy, collapse, and a lack of will."[3] The Polish Jewish crisis was also a crisis of Jewish subjectivity.

Golomb was far from alone in his view that alongside ever graver economic and political crises, Polish Jewry also faced a crisis of subjectivity demanding redress. The youth autobiographies collected by YIVO are replete with claims of psychic crisis among one's peers and in oneself. Many activists in both the Zionist and the Diasporist lobes of the divided Jewish *gezelshaftlekhkeyt*—the transnational but Poland-centered intelligentsia which conceived East European Jewry as a *folk* (a nation) and felt called to guide it—were pulled toward the same view. In 1931, Łódź educator Abram Perelman concluded that "to some degree almost every [Polish] Jewish youth" was "suffering from [an] illness" of pathological escapism "expressed in [. . .] dreams of a marvelous solution of life-questions" via deus ex machina—though Perelman, a Zionist, conveniently maintained that Zionism was a different sort of fantasy that incited "heightened energy" and "creative work."[4]

Of course, Polish Jews did not speak in one voice. In both the Diasporist and the Zionist camps, some rejected the charge that Polish Jews were descending into self-defeating despair. In 1933, Yitshok Bernshteyn—a thirty-three-year-old educator in Płock (Yid.: Plotsk) who combined religious, Zionist, and Yiddishist sympathies—insisted in Poland's leading Yiddishist cultural journal that what might seem like signs of psychic breakdown (and he granted that such signs were manifest) were rather the birth pangs of "new values arising" in "the depths of the folk-masses."[5] A year earlier, the Zionist activist Druyanov had taken it upon himself after his six-month tour of Poland to dispute the view of many other Palestinian Zionists that Polish Jews were psychically broken. Druyanov insisted that Polish Jews were demonstrating great psychic resilience in the face of prospectlessness; he cited the steadfastness of shopkeepers who, though pushed to collapse by state-imposed Christian-holiday and Sunday closures, nevertheless refused to open their stores on the Jewish Sabbath.[6]

On balance, it is hard to dismiss the view that there was some crisis of subjectivity playing out in the lives of many Polish Jews. Even defenders of Polish Jewry's good name like Bernshteyn and Druyanov worried in the very same texts that Polish Jewish subjectivity was buckling. Bernshteyn warned that intimations of mass despair should not "be presented openly as a problem to the masses" lest they become self-fulfilling prophecies. Druyanov warned his fellow Zionists not to criticize Polish Jewry overmuch because "'one must not utter to the ear anything but what the ear is able to hear.' The Polish Jew [. . .] whose day has darkened, and who lives in constant fear—not without reason—lest his tomorrow be still darker, his ear cannot hear words of fury and chastisement."[7]

It is, however, *not* my goal here to assess the accuracy of the view that the 1928–1935 period saw the emergence of a Polish Jewish psychic "condition" of debilitating fear and despair. Rather, I am interested in the social thought this worry provoked. This chapter investigates new kinds of thinking about psychology and politics, about diaspora and minority-hood, and about the powers and limits of culture that began to emerge in relation to the pervasive *sense*—correct or not—that Polish Jewry was gripped by a crisis of subjectivity.

And amid the varieties of such thought, I am interested particularly in how the perceived crisis of subjectivity challenged Diasporist thought. Diasporists who perceived such a crisis unfolding could not accept or even welcome it like some Zionists could, for the obvious reason that a collapse of Polish Jewish faith in any future posed a mortal threat to Diasporist efforts. More particularly, I am interested in the thought of a particular type of Diasporist intellectuals: those *not* fully convinced of revolutionary Marxism's blueprints for deliverance.

By the 1930s, many Diasporists intellectuals were socialists, and most were sympathetic to socialism. For some, revolutionary Marxism as instantiated in Bundism or Communism was armor against doubt and provided a clear blueprint for meaningful action in the present. In 1930, the young poet Moyshe Knaphays began drafting a grim *poema* about Warsaw's poorest Jewish neighborhood, known as the *Mokem*. By the time he completed it in 1935, he was on his way toward Communism, and he prefaced the work with an apologia. The poem, he acknowledged, might still bear the marks of the "unrest and confusion in my youthful spirit" from which it had grown. But in the meantime, he had learned "to understand sociopolitical problems differently" and "rearm[ed] myself ideationally and artistically."[8] We see this same "rearming" effect in several youth autobiographies written by Marxists of various sorts. The 1934 autobiographer "Greyno" encountered plenty of antisemitism—from the landlord, local gentile youth, and police. But unlike the autobiographers Rex or Binyomen R., encountered earlier, Greyno's embrace of Communism armed him with a faith that allowed him to understand even his suffering in redemptive terms. Even being jailed for Communist activity only reinforced his optimism, allowing him to meet "older Christians, tall and healthy, some of them intellectuals, teachers, academicians" who concretized the Party's promise of the coming supernational brotherhood. Another 1934 autobiography, by a Bundist, recorded the psychic exaltation of participating in an ethnically mixed socialist demonstration in the Polish national-religious center (and right-wing bastion) Częstochowa: "The holiest Polish city, and here is a torch-lit procession of Jewish socialist youth and nobody attacks them because they are strong [. . .]. Polish and Jewish [socialists] with one goal! The size gives strength, the commonality undergirds. A holy shudder passes through my body. . . . One such demonstration instills greater strength than a hundred lectures."[9]

Then, too, revolutionary ideology provided a rich array of ready-made subject positions that could offer meaning in daily life, however grim. In 1931, the Warsaw poet Hirsh Gutgeshtalt declared to his fellow Polish Jews that "I take upon myself your burden,/bound up in your fate/and want to sing the song of your spilled-out blood/your burning infected woe." This involved as much indictment as sympathy: Jews were "black clouds of bats" who had "poisoned" themselves with "submissiveness and imagined chosenness." But to his "leprous" readers, Gutgeshtalt, a long-time Bundist activist and founder of Warsaw's Bundist Tsukunft youth movement, offered Revolution as the cure:

> And if we were not then that—/We will yet be—/If not today, tomorrow./We—without bread or rights,/Or home./Abandoned and to contempt exposed,/Despoiled, covered in lice,/We will,/ We want/To be the arsonists of your world,/To bring the world-conflagration./We—foundationless/ pathetic-poor,/We—the Jewish millions.[10]

Here was a Sorelian myth of Polish Jewish revolutionary agency that offered an exalted subjectivity: one was not some unemployable artisan at the margins of Poland's floundering industrial economy, but a central player in humanity's redemption.

But those Diasporists who could not feel real belief in revolution and utopia—and there were many such even among those sympathetic to socialism—had to seek *new* paths of understanding and intervention as they faced a Polish Jewish subjectivity in crisis. They are of special interest both because their thought was of necessity more original than that of their revolutionary contemporaries and because they represent *symptomatically* how a spreading sense of Polish Jewish crisis put tremendous pressure on existing Jewish thought, assumptions, and hopes.

Shoring up the Jewish Subject, Reeducating Jewish Subjectivity

One of the few committed Jewish Diaspora nationalists outside of the Soviet Union ever to wield some real institutional power was the aforementioned Yitshok Giterman. As head of the Joint Distribution Committee's Warsaw office, Giterman played a significant role in shaping key Jewish

relief efforts in 1930s Poland, including "the Joint's" single most important intervention in Poland in the early Depression years: its sponsorship
of a vast network of Jewish microloan funds or free-loan *kasses*.[11]

Giterman was keen to use the kasses to stave off the quite physical
woes of poverty. But he also came to see in them a powerful tool of psychic reconstruction. In articles addressed to the broad Polish Jewish public
in 1932, Giterman suggested that the kasses had a twofold regenerative
potential. First, they were already having a profound impact on the inner
as well as the outer lives of their beneficiaries, the petty merchant class.
Operating in some 600 locales, kasses had helped "more than 100,000
families" and could look forward to helping an additional 15,000 families a year. But this was not only help for the stomach; these tiny loans
not only helped keep small merchants afloat but could also "save their
human countenance." What Giterman meant by this was clear from
what he counterposed to it. While some on the Jewish Left reasoned that
declassing was necessary, the antechamber to the desired proletarianization of Polish Jewry, Giterman maintained that such declassed
ex-merchants would cease to be "socially active [. . .], entirely lost to
the community as an active element," and instead "sink to beggary." A
microloan that helped them keep their sense of self helped them retain
aspects of bourgeois investment culture that served the Jewish commonweal: they would, for instance, continue to invest in educating their
children.[12]

Second, Giterman focused with special excitement on how the kasses
might recast the consciousness of the thousands who volunteered for them
locally. Invoking reports sent to him and his own direct encounters with
kasse volunteers from around Poland, Giterman claimed that kasse
volunteerism was becoming a distinct popular "movement" with a special
"social content" and "essence." It was hard, he claimed, to find another
effort in Polish Jewish life that "has so many devoted and fanatic supporters." Kasse volunteer work seemed thankless: constant fund-raising,
picking among the desperate applicants, having to collect from failed bor-
rowers. Yet the volunteers were filled with "joy" that was infectious. A
report from the Buczacz *kasse* averred that the "joy of those who tax
themselves voluntarily for the *kasse* is greater than the joy of those who
benefit from it"; in Zawiercie, "glaziers, carters, and other artisans undertook the building of an office for the local *kasse* with joy and wouldn't
accept any payment." Here was a spontaneous upwelling of "folk-mass
powers that pit themselves against the ruination and attempt to lessen its

Figure 3.1 Regional conference of Free Loan Kassas Society with Joint Distribution Committee representatives including Isaac (Yitshok) Giterman, Sosnowiec (Yid.: Sosnovets), May 1930. American Jewish Joint Distribution Committee Archives, NY-01686.

depredations." This upwelling was also helping to reeducate Polish Jews about where they needed to direct their national energies: "The two years have shown us too that the very fact of the existence of the kasses plays a huge role in unifying and cementing Jewish society around the terribly neglected [. . .] economic problems." Giterman was convinced that this transformed outlook on the project of communal economic self-help would abide even after the current "crisis" subsided. When it became possible to use the kasses to create "new economic positions" for Jews, they would call forth the same "incredible devotion and enthusiasm."

It is hard to know how seriously to take Giterman's claims. He wrote not as a disinterested analyst but as an organization man fighting a two-front struggle within the divided national Jewish intelligentsia: trying to convince socialists that buoying the despised petit bourgeoisie in the near term was actually necessary, and trying to convince those inclining toward hopelessness about the Polish Jewish situation to support the kasse effort. More relevant here than the accuracy of his account is the fact of his distinct concern for regenerating Jewish economic subjectivity as a policy goal. This concern permeated Giterman's work through the 1930s. In 1935, he noted his long-standing desire to see a kind of Diasporist version of Hehalutz: an organization that would offer Polish Jewish youth of any ideological persuasion the transformative effects that Hehalutz seemed to be having on Zionist youth "here at home."[13]

Other Diasporists, too, even those close to the Bund, remarked on what seemed the extraordinary power that Hehalutz unleashed in its young cadres. Already in 1930, the die-hard Diasporist Moyshe Zilberfarb, head of ORT's Polish branch, floated the argument that ORT should reorganize itself as a kind of Diasporist "Hehalutz" for Poland's mass of the unemployed. Whereas ORT functioned merely as a "midwife" easing "the birth-pangs attendant on the rise of new economically productive groups in Jewish economic life," what impressed Zilberfarb about the Zionist Hehalutz was how it "united only elements ready to carry out a revolution in their *own* lives."[14]

Zilberfarb and Giterman were participants in a particular productivizationist "scene" of formally neutral but actually Diasporist organizations focused on lifting Eastern European Jewry out of "unproductive" petit bourgeois professions and growing poverty. But the idea that Jewish economic subjectivity had to be recast if Jews were to weather the storm resonated more broadly. One effort to implant a new economic subjectivity among Diasporist youth was the aforementioned Wilno-centered Bin (The Bee) scouting organization, founded in 1927 by the already much-discussed Max Weinreich.

Weinreich had initially intended Bin—which apparently numbered several thousand at the organization's height[15]—to combine the scouting ideals of Baden-Powell and *Wandervogel* ("sound mind, healthy body," the humanizing impact of contact with nature) with intense Yiddishism and Diasporism irreducible to specific party affiliations. But although Yiddishism and Diasporism were certainly still priorities when Weinreich wrote the first formal statement of "who we are and what we want" in November 1931, that text also resonated with new concerns. First, it was permeated by the sense of a deep problem in Polish Jewish youth subjectivity: an incapacity to commit to sustained *action,* which Jewish youth covered over with a hypertrophy of talk and pointless argument. "Our Jewish youth is too deeply sunk in words. It has little energy for deeds. Bin wants to create a form of youth-life where there will be far less engagement in merely speculative inquiry."[16]

Figure 3.2   "Members of the Bin (Bee) Jewish youth movement with founder and leader Max Weinreich (in white shirt and white tie), physician Tsemah Szabad [. . .] Vilna, before 1935." YIVO Encyclopedia of Jews in Eastern Europe Online, ed. Gershon Hundert. Archives of the YIVO Institute for Jewish Research, Photo 2389i1.

No doubt this hostility to a surplus of words was fueled in part by Weinreich's worry about premature politicization, whether socialist or, worse, Zionist. But he also believed that there was a genuine problem of *will* demanding intervention. The reality descending upon Polish Jews was grim, and Polish Jews would need a youth equipped for self-transformation. Bin was called to inculcate capacities of critical thinking yet also a capacity to *adapt* to circumstances one could not change—"to be able to adapt properly to the environment in every situation."

More specifically, Weinreich shared the spreading view that declassing was an irreversible fact and that self-productivization had to be placed at the center of the Polish Jewish communal agenda. This required a two-fold transformation of Jewish subjectivity. It was not simply that Polish Jewry had to be reeducated to embrace the ideal of labor. Weinreich was also coming to believe that there was a dangerous flaw in East European Jewish political culture: an incapacity to mobilize one's will for day-to-day struggle with hard realities except insofar as one embraced some grandiose myth, be it Revolution or Zion.

By 1931, Weinreich and other Wilno Diasporists had begun to develop new emphases in Bin's practices to meet this multilayered need for inner transformation. A monthlong summer retreat for members in which daily life was largely run by the adolescent "Bees" was intended to break "*through that wall of felt inability to take care of oneself.*" More ambitiously, 1931 saw Bin's leadership create two work farms where a small cadre worked all summer and a much larger group came to assist with the harvest for several weeks. Weinreich saw this as the first step in a larger process of transforming Bin into an organization for productivization and self-reinvention within a Diasporist rather than Zionist frame:

> For our Jewish youth today, unfortunately, it is still to a great degree the case that work is either something experienced as imposed, a grim necessity—and it can be done with appetite only if it is connected to a plan to emigrate. Bin wants to bring the Jewish youth to believe that [manual] work in general and farm work in particular are holy not only in faraway places, but also here, where we live and will live. In one of our songs we sing "where our house is built, that is our land," and we say that is not necessary that the Jewish youth should have to uproot itself before taking up the ideology of work.[17]

Weinreich ended his late 1931 statement on a double note of optimism. First, in 1932, Bin would resume this agrarianist experiment on a much larger scale. Second, though in its first four years Bin had been slow, selective, and above all local in its project of "humanization through Yiddish culture," scouting, and productivization, the time had come to project its practices across Poland and beyond. The former would come to pass and exert a powerful attraction (albeit briefly) in Wilno youth circles; one youth participant, the previously mentioned Astour, testified in October 1933 that Bin's agrarianist experiment had awoken tremendous hopes the year before—a hint of the kind of psychic effect that Weinreich hoped to have.[18] In the event, this was short-lived and gave way to a general despair about Diasporism in the same circles. But this only deepened Weinreich's sense that the salvation of Polish Jewish Diasporism could only come through an interior revolution of Jewish subjectivity—that the most urgent task for Diasporists was to find a psycho-cultural "path to our youth."

If problems of *economic* subjectivity loomed large for Diasporists in the late 1920s, they were increasingly joined by a growing concern with how political pressures were impacting Jewish subjectivity. In Chapter 1, we met the writer Mikhoel Burshtin as a figure especially concerned with antisemitism's reach in Polish society. Despite his deep worries, however, Burshtin remained a committed Diasporist. And in the face of rising socio-political hostility and economic disaster, he held, Jews had to find new psychic resilience while pursuing long-term programs of self-help and economic reconstruction.[19]

But Burshtin also feared that Polish Jews were reacting to their rising troubles in ways that were genuinely counterproductive. If his 1931 *Iber di khurves fun Ployne* was in part worried reflection on antisemitism, it was also an insistent indictment of both Zionism and Jewish socialism as counterproductive fantasies. Much of the narrative traces how Ployne's Jews embrace fantasies of Zionist escape or imminent socialist revolution rather than seeking practical ways to bear up under indefinite political and economic pressure. The Zionism that spreads from the margin of Ployne's Jewish community to "all classes," "young and old," leads many to waste meager savings on a plot of land in Palestine. Meanwhile, the radicals of the Tailors' Union, unable to convince Polish socialists to insist that Jews be hired as well at two nearby factories, instead undertake a farcical "action" against Jewish "clericalism" by hosting a desecration of the Passover holiday. The farce turns serious when appalled religious Jews report them to the local gendarme, and becomes tragedy when one of the ringleaders gets sent to prison for Communism. Although the novel allows a more moderate Diasporist protagonist to articulate Burshtin's preferred alternative, part of the novel's grimness inheres in the fact that this character is a "failed prophet" whose arguments are wholly without effect. The novel ends with two crowds of Jews scuffling at the train station over the same Zionist and revolutionary escapisms that have only worsened their plight.[20]

Burshtin's fears that the worsening situation was doing new kinds of damage to Polish Jewish subjectivity deepened as the 1930s wore on. After writing a second novel, *Goyrl*, which narrates the history of prewar Jewish efforts to integrate into Polish society as self-abasing delusion,[21] he began a third novel set in the present. Provisionally titled *A Guest from the Land of Israel*, this novel (apparently abandoned) revisited *Ployne*'s concern with the outer and inner crisis of futurity in small-town life—but this time without the shock-absorbing chronotopic retrojection to 1924–1925 and with an even more unsettling juxtaposition of Zionist possibility against Diaspora collapse.

Set in the same sort of central Polish small town featured in *Iber di khurves,* but in the present, the novel's opening chapter reads as a virtual endorsement of Zionist claims about the Diaspora. A young man of poor family who had left for Palestine ten years earlier returns to seek a wife. He is shocked to find the community reduced to a pathetic assemblage of ruined people. In the meantime, the young man, who has taken the properly Zionist name Ben-Eliezer, has grown so radiantly healthy that he is initially taken for either an American Jewish visitor (of the sort whose remittances the town's Jewish community now depends on) or the representative of the Polish state's onslaught, the tax assessor. The ruination is also psychological. The people of the shtetl treat Ben-Eliezer with child-like respect: "The less he spoke, the more their respect for him grew." Once-wealthy relatives, now declassed, "gulp his every word." Locals parade their "gussied-up" daughters before him in hopes that he will pick one for marriage and life in Palestine. All of this has little to do with views of Palestine, about which the townspeople have absurdly divergent and vague assumptions. Rather, it has to do with raw despair about the absence of a Jewish future in Poland, a despair that even the daughter of the town's wealthiest man shares.[22]

Arguably, such fiction itself was meant to have an prophylactic impact on readers. But Burshtin was also driven to try to identify other forms of cultural practice that might offer psychic shoring-up. We can detect such lines of rethinking in his relationship to a Diasporist cultural praxis in which he had long been involved: Jewish educational tourism, the practice of *krajoznawstwo* or *landkentenish* (knowing the land).

Burshtin had been involved in the aforementioned Żydowskie Towarzystwo Krajoznawcze (ZTK) since its founding in 1926. In 1930, the organization's leadership passed to a circle of young Diaspora nationalists—the historians Emmanuel Ringelblum and Filip Friedman, the literary critic Naftole Vaynig, and the public health activist Leon Vulman—who believed that an organized program of Jewish tourism in Poland could instill in Jews a sense that Poland was theirs too while also connecting them to the specific cultural treasures of the Jewish *folk,* its Yiddish language, folklore, architecture.[23]

Burshtin shared these commitments. But essays from 1933 and 1934 in the ZTK's journal suggest a shift away from faith in collective identity formation through culture and toward a search for new ways to heal wounded Jewish subjectivity. Burshtin opened a 1933 essay with a hoary set of tropes. "Historical and economic factors" had "torn Jews from Nature," confinement to a purely urban life had caused "physical degeneration and spiritual crippledness," and some Jews had even come to believe the charges of "our enemies" that they were irredeemable and must disappear in accordance with "Nature's immutable law, so to speak."[24] But here Burshtin's account of the tasks of Jewish *turistik* turned from this familiar half-Spencerian discourse to grapple with the present. In the process he sketched new lines of thought about both how to defend Polish Jewish futurity and how to recast Diasporism itself as an ideology.

Jews' "one-sided city life" had rendered them vulnerable to the ongoing "collapse of our economic life." Against this, Burshtin imagined a first new task for *landkentenish*: in reacquainting Jews with nature, it would midwife what now could not be avoided, a systematic program of "productivization" that was the only sensible response to the massive declassing of East European Jewry. The declassing had already begun in earnest yet Jews were "productivizing ourselves at a terribly slow rate." The problem was at least in part a problem of subjectivity: it demanded "inner, psychological preparation." This is what *turistik* could provide: "Among us Jews, this can become an important psychological moment in our striving toward productivization, to earth."

If this first lobe of Burshtin's argument cast the Jewish Problem in material-economic terms, *political* factors were also not far from his thoughts. While Jews had remained yoked to old economic roles, "circumstances had changed" and "new social strivings" had emerged in the society around them—and now "we are left hanging in mid-air, dependent in the best case on the mercy of those who have the say in this new conjuncture." "New social strivings," an obscure "they" who exercised determining power over Jewish fate—the references to the unhappy non-alignment of the Jewish socioeconomic profile with the economic-political imaginary of Poland's society and state could hardly be missed. Here, *turistik* had a special political role. Polish Jews "love to point to historical documents when our civil rights are attacked," but how much use were such "testaments to our lineage" really? Jews had lived "on

Polish earth [. . .] 800, 900 years, but" more effective than any documentary evidence would be "actual connection with the land." "Jewish mass tourism" would also serve to render visible, tangible, and less easily deniable a Jewish claim to belonging in Poland: "Contact with the earth is an unconditional necessity to maintain our existence. It strengthens and 'citizenizes' us in the land [*farbirgert unz in land*], and roots more deeply in our neighbors the concept of our equality and the justice of our claim."

This essay, resonating with a grim vision of the Polish cultural world Burshtin had once aspired to join, suggested that Jews should cease hoping for any sort of acceptance by their Polish neighbors in the foreseeable future. A 1934 essay titled "Regionalism" also resonated with a sense of the need to distance *doikayt* ideals from any continued assumption of Jewish-Polish intimacy and dialogue. A prolonged discussion of regionalism as a kind of counterhegemonic ideology to the nation-state climaxed with a declaration that the true "liberal spirits" of Polish culture were writers like Kazimierz Tetmajer or Stefan Żeromski, who embraced the cultural diversity of Poland to the point of embracing regionalism in *place* of a unitary Polish culture. Quoting Żeromski's testament that "I myself see a guarantee of a better tomorrow in regionalism, that is, is the striving to decentralize the economic and cultural life of Poland," Burshtin endorsed an image of Poland as made up of "quite separate ethnic groups (the national minorities) with specific characteristics and needs."[25]

Burshtin was thus also turning against a particular *Polish*-Jewish Diasporist vision of special Jewish-Polish national intimacy. The idea of a special Jewish-Polish synthesis was cherished by many Diasporists from Yoysef Opatoshu (the author of *In Polish Woods*) to Yehezkl Viltshinski, whose 1928 *Yidishe tipn in der poylisher literatur* posited a deep history of intimate Jewish-Polish reciprocal influence.[26] Burshtin, though specially equipped to take this stance by his own deep history of Polonization, closed his 1933 essay by turning away from the specifically rooted cultural dimensions of *doikayt* and toward an ideal of converting the very "extraterritoriality" of Jews around the globe into a source of communal strength rather than weakness. "The tasks of Jewish tourism [. . .] are not confined to Poland alone. We are an extraterritorial people. The growth of Jewish communities in various lands and their decline appears to be a permanent phenomenon, an unending process." This was not an intrinsically positive fact: "At the current moment, we are being ground down into ever-smaller groups, cast to the shores of every ocean. What unifies [these groups] now?" What could connect Jews and maintain "a unitary Jewish ethnicity" (*etnishkayt*)? Only face-to-face contact would bind Jews together. "He who aims for the concentration of our national powers must now turn his gaze in the direction of mutual exchange among Jews in various lands."[27]

From Diasporic Nationhood to the "Minority Complex"

While Burshtin was pursuing this evolving agenda for the reconstruction of Jewish subjectivity in the face of hostility, another figure with the same general commitments, politics, and hopes—Weinreich—was immersing himself in the youth research project that would eventuate in the 1935 *Veg tsu unzer yugnt*. As we have seen, Weinreich emerged from that project (begun in 1932–1933) convinced, reluctantly indeed, that a baleful transformation of Polish Jewish subjectivity into something wounded was well under way, especially among the youth. While Weinreich shared hopes that this subjective dimension of the disaster could be combatted— indeed, the close of *Veg* declared that the overriding task of Jewish social science was to help Polish Jews adapt to their new difficult circumstances and find new inner resources of resilience—he also allowed himself to explore a darker possibility: that the transformation of Polish Jewish subjectivity might be vectoring on a new *kind* of immiseration and debilitation that would be hard to reverse. Weinreich explored this possibility in the middle of the study's most empirically substantial section, at the intersection between two sets of obtrusively peculiar terms, "miutishkayt" and "miutimshaft," on the one hand, and "kompensatyses" and "fargitikung," on the other. The first two, complete neologisms, can be translated as "minorityhood" and "minoritieshood"; they connoted a general form of social experience on the part of minority communities in which the shared dimensions of minorityhood were more salient than the particularities of any individual community's history and identity. The latter two were almost, but not quite, synonyms: the internationalism "compensations," here meaning both a psychological effect and the cultural form that produced it, and the native Yiddish term "recompense," being paid back in some way to make up for one's loss or suffering. At the intersection of these terms, Weinreich began an intriguing, original, yet also deeply ambivalent inquiry into how Polish Jewish consciousness was being permanently recast in relation, perhaps, to a structure of immiserating and debilitating ascriptive minorityhood.

At the point in *Veg* that began to elaborate the grim conclusion that Polish Jewish young people now could not avoid the experience of coming to see their Jewishness as a future-crippling misfortune ("these experiences cannot be avoided"), Weinreich suddenly expanded the sociological purview of his comments: "I call [these experiences] 'attacks of Jewishness'; if we wish to speak about minorities in general, we can call this attacks of minorityhood." With that jarring shift, Weinreich made a further move that—as a contemporary press account confirms—could only set Polish Jewish readers back on their heels.[28] With an equally tight-lipped note that he would now offer "a few more considerations regarding the question of how the first attack of minorityhood strikes the members of a minority community," he launched into an unexpected excursus on the consequences of psychic suffering among African American youth and professionals in the contemporary United States.[29]

Veg's engagements with the African American experience—what Weinreich called the "Negro" experience—were substantial.[30] Weinreich translated for Yiddish readers a wrenching account by a young woman raised in the North who first discovered that she was a racial Other to some when a white classmate responded to her success in school with a vile epithet; neither the girl's teacher nor her mother could bring themselves to explain it. Weinreich also related the story (heard, he noted, at Alabama's Tuskegee Institute, which he had made a point of visiting) of a southern Black doctor who had sent his son to Paris to spare him a Jim Crow upbringing. Weinreich reported too a conversation with a history student at Fisk University who hoped to document that Africans had discovered the Americas before Columbus—a project Weinreich initially deemed foolish but that upon reflection, he told readers, reminded him of the Russian Jewish liberal scholar Alexander Harkavy's admission years earlier that his pioneering research on Jewish presence in early modern Russia had sprung from a sense that such evidence of long nativity was essential to winning rights for Russian Jews. All of these excurses were fruits, Weinreich noted, of some serious study of African American life during a fellowship year at Yale in 1932–1933. Over intersession, he had traveled south specifically to spend time in African-American academic institutions; at Fisk and Tuskegee, he had conducted "long-ish discussion [. . .] with the students and teachers" and read "a collection of autobiographies by the students." He took substantial research notes.[31]

But what was at stake in Weinreich's choice to interrupt his analysis of Polish Jewish wounded subjectivity with this unexpected turn to the life and thought of African American students, and then to interweave African American and Polish Jewish cases still more directly (interpolating, significantly, the histories of other ethnically demarcated communities—Poles, Greeks, German Jews—at key junctures)? The quiddity is deepened further when we note that at an earlier juncture in the book, Weinreich had taken pains to deny that East European Jews should be assumed to share in the "inferiority complex" that (he claimed) afflicted African Americans, Native Americans, and Poland's small Kashubian community simply by dint of being a "minority." Yet at the book's critical empirical juncture, Weinreich forcefully dramatized the opposite sense: there was *some* sort of comparability between Polish Jewish and African American subjectivity in the present. But was the comparison about difference or similarity, divergent fates or convergent ones? Here the scholar encounters an indeterminacy that cannot be overcome, because Weinreich himself, at the climax of this excursus, perversely disclaimed any clear answer: "How far this 'Negroization' [*negrizirung*—a deeply disturbing term to which I will return below] [. . .] applies to *Eastern* European Jews, I will not analyze here. My concern here is simply to bring out that the situation of being [a] wronged [community] has not only legal and material but also *psychological* results."[32]

One way of imagining Weinreich's intent is to posit that his excursus on the African American situation was meant to mark not similarity but *difference*—not between African Americans and Polish Jews, but between Jews *of a certain type,* on the one hand, and *both* African Americans and Jews of *another* type, on the other. On this reading, suggested by Kamil Kijek, Weinreich's intention was ideological: to use African American woes to indict assimilationism among Polish Jews for rendering Jews more vulnerable to the wounds of social rejection—by contrast, evidently, to his own Yiddishist program, which presumably could help Polish Jews bear up by sustaining a separate value world of Jews' own.[33] We can see this impulse in Weinreich's most lamentably reductionist account of African American youth experience: "Often [. . .] the discovery of his 'racial' separateness comes to the Negro child as a shock" because, Weinreich averred, "the large mass" of African Americans had "neither their own genuinely specific forms of life nor aspirations toward their own [separate] culture. The standard to which they aspire is white America, their language is English; thus, when they become conscious that only blue eyes and smooth brown hair offer the key to paradise, it strikes them like thunder." It is no defense of this ignorant claim but merely clarification to underscore that

Weinreich's point was to indict not African American youth but Polonizing Jewish parents. Weinreich's follow-up to the account of the young African American woman's first encounter with raw racism was to compare her case with that of *Polonized* Jews specifically by invoking "Murzyn Warszawski" (The Warsaw Negro), a vicious 1928 satire of assimilated Jewish social and cultural climbing by the Polish writer (of Jewish origin) Antoni Słonimski: "One must admit that there is indeed an intersection between the Negroes of America and the 'Warsaw Negroes' to use the term that Antoni Słonimski introduced in his Polish play to describe recently assimilated Jews."[34] Concomitantly, Weinreich connected the same young African American woman's experience to the genuinely parallel case of Georg Brandes, the famed Danish literary critic who had only discovered his Jewish background through exposure to an antisemitic epithet and his mother's nonchalant revelation.[35]

Finally, returning to Polish Jews, Weinreich clearly did want to believe that there was a special connection between assimilation and greater psychic suffering. Thus, a section on Jewish experience in Polish-language mixed public schools contended that exposure to a climate of antisemitism among fellow students and sometimes teachers could substantially "hurry" the onset of the "second attack of Jewishness." Here too, Weinreich allowed his countervailing Yiddishist convictions free rein: the child should "see his Jewishness not by accident a la Georg Brandes, but through the fact that one speaks Yiddish at home, through a Yiddish plaque on the door. Then the child will grow with the consciousness that there are *various* groups of people in the world, and we are one of them, neither better nor worse than the others. When he later grows conscious that his community is oppressed, this will not call forth in him the feeling of inferiority; it will be an injustice against which one should fight."[36]

Yet though clearly there was some Yiddishist and antiassimilationist polemic at work in *Veg*, there are many other aspects of Weinreich's comparisons of Polish Jewish and African American experience that trouble this reading of the comparison as a calculated polemic. These suggest, rather, that for Weinreich, the force of the comparison of Polish Jews to African Americans was more unsettling to his ideological outlook than it was convenient: they suggest a fraught sense of *convergence* between the African American experience (as he understood it) of debilitating psychic misery and the trajectory of Polish Jewish youth as a *whole*, including his own nationally committed circles. Thus, at a juncture in *Veg* devoted largely to methodological ground clearing about race as a category and about how one might analyze national identity without violating methodological individualism, Weinreich remarked: "For us only one thing is important: whatever the root of national differences might be, they are a reality [. . .]. Generally, the matter is quite transparent, let us say, in the case of the American Negro, whose entire existence is determined by the color of his skin. Also quite clear is the situation of the Jew in an array of European lands, where his appearance, his way of speaking, and ultimately his birth certificate determine to a substantial degree his fate." Here European Jews as such—and particularly those who *are* different culturally from the majority—are presented as converging on the "African American" mode of minority experience, in which ascriptive identifications by the majority and world around them "determine to a substantial degree [one's] fate" and in turn create specific "national psychic forms."[37]

Other sources that Weinreich produced around *Veg* bespeak deepening worry about strong convergences between the African American experience and that of contemporary Polish Jewry *without* distinction between the assimilated and the unassimilated. The 1933 working notes for *Veg* place African Americans and Jews close together on a single spectrum rather than separating them into unhealthy and healthy forms of minority subjectivity:

> *Specific point of interest: belonging to a downtrodden community:*
> [. . .] every child feels uncertain in the world due to his being a child
> in the face of the overweening power of adults. The way the child
> moves past these child-adult conflicts decides to great degree his
> personality. Belonging to an exceptional group (for instance an il
> legitimate child) [produces] a double uncertainty which works
> constantly on his personality. The same is true of belonging to a
> minority collective (Catholics in a purely Protestant region; much
> sharper among Jews, sharper still among Negroes).
> *First intrusion*[38] *of the problem:* the infant feels no aspect of his
> Jewishness; if it does have an effect on him, this expresses itself in
> the relationship to him of those around him, and above all his par
> ents. It seems for instance that the marked pampering of children,
> the giving of special loving pity to them that one sees in Jewish
> mothers (and in Negro mothers as well) stems from the sensibility
> (perhaps an unconscious one): he will undergo much suffering later,
> let him at least have some joy now.[39]

Even more definitive on this score, finally, is a Wilno press report brought to light by scholar Leila Zenderland regarding a talk that Weinreich gave to a Yiddishist audience in Wilno right before the appearance of *Veg*. Actually, Weinreich delivered a *pair* of talks: one on his Jewish youth research project and the second on what he called "the race problem in America." Weinreich's explanation at the event for a topic that had seemed "a bit strange" to the audience, as the report's author put it, was that "it is precisely by orienting ourselves in the non-Jewish world that we gain, [Weinreich] contended, the possibility of understanding and conceptualizing our Jewish life." Significantly, Weinreich's talk laid out a much more encompassing sociological account of African American life than that which appeared in *Veg*. He dilated on the physical and psychic impacts of racism, African American politics, and African American popular religiosity. The reporter for the *Vilner Tog*, writing under the pseudonym Lux, came away with a strong sense of having heard a talk not about the African American "assimilationist" elite but, quite the contrary, about the African American popular masses. And the nub of what Lux took Weinreich to have demonstrated was not about the "shock of recognition" foregrounded in *Veg* but about something different: that the popular mass of African Americans "make do with little, are very patient and accept their bitter fate, waiting [passively] for redemption. Their way in the world is more similar to the medieval Jewish way" à la Ecclesiastes's cynical vision: "better a live dog than a dead lion."[40]

We may doubt that Weinreich's actual talk was wholly reducible to this crude claim—after all, he also addressed the topic of African American politics and was clearly aware of both the Tuskegee model and its alternatives (which had been discussed in East European Jewish letters before). But a larger point is clear: the reporter understood Weinreich to be speaking not about the possible bad fate of *assimilationist* Polish Jews but about a trajectory on which *all* Polish Jews, his Yiddishist-Diasporist audience included, might be embarked unless they marshaled their inner resources to avoid it. Thus, Lux elaborated on Weinreich's urgency: "And by the way, America has something of a connection to us, and even more certainly, American 'racism'—Hitler's laws against Jews are virtually a faithful copy of the anti-Negro legal structure in America." If here Lux invoked an identification between African Americans and the Jews of *Germany*—at a moment when Polish Jews across the board were suddenly in the position of worrying acutely about the political fate of their brethren to the west[41]—he or she clearly had Polish Jews in mind as well.

For those who might have missed this comparative dimension, Lux spelled it out unambiguously at the article's close: "The lecture, which lasted about two hours, was heard in a state of acute tension. For everyone, it opened up a new world in which we saw our own difficult fate, which seeks its resolution in general human redemption."

In *Veg* and around it, then, Weinreich pushed his audience—which was precisely *not* a Polonized, assimilationist audience but by definition a Yiddishist one—to see their own situation in relation to the African American experience of "the race-problem in America." Weinreich clearly took the African American experience itself to be a singularly painful one, and nowhere was this clearer than at the juncture where he informed readers that he would "not analyze here" precisely "how far" the African American condition "applies to *Eastern* European Jews." The full sentence reads thus: "How far this 'Negroization' [*negrizirung*]—whose sign is suffering without recompense [*fargitikung*]—applies to *Eastern* European Jews, I will not analyze here." Once we accommodate the shock of Weinreich's term *negrizirung*, with its brutalizing objectification of a particular community's afflictions as a "condition" others should seek to avoid, we gain an essential clue as to where his line of thought was trending—not in relation to "*negrizirung*" but in relation to *fargitikung*, the making good of a debt owed for injury, restitution, compensation. "Suffering without recompense" (*fargitikung*) was unhealthy and destructive for the person (and people) who thus suffered. It was, in Weinreich's view, the dominant fact of African American life, community, and personality. Did he think this was true—or *becoming* true—of Polish Jews? It is when we look beyond Weinreich's intriguing preoccupation with the African American experience to a different locus of his analysis of the Polish Jewish present that we see most clearly how deeply Weinreich was concerned that this was indeed the case—that "suffering without recompense," and its debilitating psychic consequences, was the horizon toward which a substantial swath of Polish Jewish youth was being driven. This second locus of analysis turned on *fargitikung*'s more scientific sibling: "*kompensatyes*" (compensations).[42]

Immediately following his declaration that he would not stake a clear claim about how far "negrizirung" applied to Polish Jewry, Weinreich launched into a comparative-historical discussion of "compensations." Though elsewhere in *Veg* he used the term in specifically psychoanalytic terms, here Weinreich meant a public cultural form: collective narratives of group distinction and other symbolic "resources" that a particular historical collective could provide to "arm its members" against internalizing hatred directed toward them. Weinreich's comparative argument about "compensations" began with yet another assertion of *difference* between various minorities: "Just as there are differences in the degree of oppression, and thus too also the psychic traumas that the oppression brings, so too there is quite a substantial difference in the compensations that a community possesses and with which it can arm its members. The compensations do not simply hang in the air, one cannot simply think up prettier ones. They stem from the past of the community, from its achievements in the present-day, and from its aspirations in the future." Weinreich then invoked a series of historical cases in which, clearly, a healthy (as it were) national tradition had served to provide highly effective compensations for communal setbacks and woes over a long period of time. Poles under Russian and Habsburg rule had steeled their children with stories of past national martyrs. Greeks under Ottoman rule had drawn strength from the Hellenic past. In both cases, the compensations had achieved "a deep psychological reality." To this he contrasted the situation of African American parents, averring that they had far fewer resources, far fewer commonly believed and already culturally ramified stories of past glories, to provide to their embattled children. And here, Weinreich placed the Jewish case alongside the Greek and Polish cases and (again) in contradistinction to the African American one: for traditional Jews, he claimed, rabbinic Judaism's ramified ideology of Jewish chosenness, linked to a rich past still present for traditional Jews, had functioned powerfully and effectively to make the insults of exile bearable.[43]

Yet for Weinreich, this reiteration of a nationalist confidence that East European Jews had long been, by dint of some kind of glorious history, better armored than many other groups against psychic wounds soon gave way to a much grimmer double claim about the present. First, he averred, it was an observable fact that the traditional Jewish theodicy of suffering as a mark of divine chosenness had *ceased* to offer effective compensation for most Jews. Without elaborating fully, Weinreich framed this as a deep shift, an effect of modernity that obviously could not be reversed simply by wishing it: "One of the marks of our era and one of the marks of the deep division among Jews today consists precisely in this fact: while the burden of being a Jew has persisted in one or another form for *all* Jews, the old compensation only obtains for some." This in itself was not necessarily a communal disaster; after all, what was stopping modern Jews from drawing on the same secular mythology that seemed perfectly adequate to Polish or Greek needs? And indeed, it seemed that modern Jews had produced a rich range of compensations rooted in various veins of Jewish experience:

> Instead there have arisen a variety of other compensations. We suffer because we are the bearers of truth and justice in the world, and for truth one gets beaten. Or: everyone is against us because we have no home; and so we're building our old–new home in the Land of Israel, and that will bring an end to our sufferings. Or: the current situation is the result of the capitalist order, and socialism will redeem us together with the whole world. Or: in every single land we truly are a minority [*minderhayt*] and we suffer persecutions, but because of this we are a world-people [*veltfolk*] with a broad outlook and with a degree of immortality. Or: who cares about these blows? From the Prophets through Einstein, the greatest persons have always been Jews. And the conclusion that flows from that: tell those evildoers to go to hell, you just show what you can do; we [Jews] with our abilities will outdo them nicely.[44]

But here the other shoe dropped: Weinreich made it clear that his actual findings about depth, extent, and unavoidability of future despair among Polish Jews suggested that these *other* compensations were also now simply *ceasing* to work for many Polish Jews. If sending Jews to a Polish school might have the effect of "speeding up" the "second attack of Jewishness," the larger, grimmer truth disclosed by the autobiographies was that *no* sector of Polish Jewry was proving able to protect its youth from this "second attack"—"it cannot be avoided."[45] Thus, cutting against his triumphalist critique of Polish-language schooling's impact on the Jewish psyche, Weinreich acknowledged in multiple places in *Veg* his recognition that the *Yiddishist* school—the central and often only tool through which Diasporism could reach Polish Jewish children, and of course the kind of school to which he had sent his own sons—was losing its effectiveness as a shaping and stabilizing force.[46] Indeed, even within the bosom of the family, all of these compensations seemed to be losing their power for young Polish Jews. Weinreich declared this issue a pressing research question for Jewish social science going forward: "Scholarship must discover which families employ which compensations; whether the various formulations are mixed together and in what degree, and to what degree and under what conditions do these compensations actually have a psychological effect." But elsewhere, he declared more directly his sense of an affective crisis: a child's home life could "provide a certain rationalizing counterweight" to oppression as a condemned minority, but this "cannot be a full equivalent [counterweight] no matter how well and correctly the adults explain the reasons for the oppression; for the explanations they give speak primarily to the *mind* whereas [the child] *feels* the oppression."[47]

In analytical terms, we can see Weinreich trying to understand *how* a positive identity framed by either religious or national ideals might give way to a minorityhood defined by a debilitating sense of inferiority, stigma, and bad fate. His working measure of what the former involved turned on two questions: Could the subject encounter hatred without internalizing it, and did the subject's community have positive cultural compensations that worked psychologically to protect him or her? And here, Weinreich's willfully opaque excursus on African American social and psychological suffering reveals itself to be, as it were, the dependent clause in his larger claim, because what *Veg* made very clear about Jews in Poland was Weinreich's unhappy conclusion that whereas previously Jews had been able to mobilize a store of effective culture-specific compensations to cushion themselves against the psychic suffering that objective downtroddenness could generate, this was in fact—for whatever reason—ceasing to be the case.

The thicket of references to the African American experience in and around *Veg tsu unzer yugnt* is so clearly central to Weinreich's developing thought that it has to be addressed distinctly. But it is also constitutes the proverbial trees for which one misses the forest. When we look beyond this dimension of the text, we cannot escape the sense that Weinreich had come to believe that some kind of move toward "bad minorityhood" was already happening, and quite far along, in Polish Jewish life, that it was *not* confined to assimilated, Polonized Jews, and that there were good grounds to think that it could no longer be contained by "having one's own culture"—by Yiddishist or other positive forms of Jewish identity that might compensate for the sense of being widely disliked and unwanted. *Veg* breathes with a sense that Polish Jews were a living demonstration of a new kind of process: the breakdown of a long-standing positive national-minority identity and sense of self into something defined by psychic misery and its pathologies under the pressure of majoritarian exclusion. In this context, the whole excursus on African American "suffering without recompense" reveals itself to have been an unsettled meditation on where Polish Jewry seemed to Weinreich to be headed, for if Jews could no longer find psychological succor in their compensations, then indeed they would be "suffering without recompense." This meditation was coupled uneasily with and not fully contained by Weinreich's eroding hopes that the positive cultural ideals of national-Yiddishist Diasporism could yet avert this outcome. It was that same sense that so discomfited Lux and the others in the audience for Weinreich's lecture on the race question in the United States, to which they listened "in a state of acute tension" as Weinreich "opened up a new world in which we saw our own difficult fate."

The point of the foregoing dive into Weinreich's tarrying with the question of "minorityhood" is not to endorse his account of Polish Jewry's wounded subjectivity as correct—but neither can it be dismissed. Certainly, we can reject much about his deeply problematic account of African American subjectivity. Weinreich manifestly wrote in full political sympathy with African Americans—his analysis highlighted the perversity of white racism, mostly captured the dignity of his African American interlocutors as well as their woe, and asserted as self-evident that African Americans deserved rights for the same reasons that all Americans did: "250 to 300 years of Negro presence in America" was the only "ground" needed for "Negro demands for equal rights." But unquestionably, his analysis was polluted by common Central European prejudices about African American "culturelessness" and a readiness to adopt the scientistic discourse of damaged African American subjectivity that Daryl Michael Scott has identified as pervasive to American social science not only among "racial conservatives" but also among "racial liberal" circles.[48] And, of course, empirically Weinreich based his claims about African American experience on thin evidence. But the same cannot be said of his arguments about Polish Jews: it was, as he himself said, not only numerous youth autobiographies that authorized his grim suspicions, but also a decade of participant observation, focused not least on trying to work with youth ranging from his own two sons, coming of age in the 1930s, to the youth gathered around Bin.

At the very least, it seems clear that Weinreich was profoundly worried that he was witnessing the replacement of an East European Jewish sense of self rich in cultural resources by a sense of debasing powerlessness. Regardless of how true we deem this to be, Weinreich's analysis is also interesting as a double moment of rupture and rethinking in Jewish Diasporism. Weinreich was among those Diasporists who not only *accepted* as a matter of fact that East European Jews were fated to be a national minority spread across multiple states, but also *embraced* minority status as a positive good, an ideal. On this view, Jews were pioneers of a worldwide detaching of national communal life from the state, of equal collective rights for all ethnonational communities guaranteed by some sort of federal system above or—even better—in place of nation-states. As one indefatigable champion of this idea, Avrom Golomb, put it in 1933: "Jews are spread across the whole world [and] *they want to remain where they are,* and it is where they already are [*es iz do*] that they must seek out whatever forms of national life are achieveable."[49]

Even in the best of times, this view had demanded much idealism, Golomb admitted: "This [. . .] ideal is new, it has no prototypes among other peoples, it was not part of the Jewish psyche, and that is why it is so difficult for it to take root in consciousness, that is why it—like every idea that comes before its time—is wrapped in fog and only small circles can absorb it."[50] And by the early 1930s, this exalted vision of minority-hood as a positive good had become an object of outright mockery in some quarters. In September 1934, *Haynt* carried a blistering satirical essay by the Zionist activist Yehoshua Gotlib titled "Minority-Complex," which argued that with Poland's renunciation of the Minorities Treaty, all the Jewish hopes invested in "minority rights, minority protections, Minorities' Treaties" and the "triumph of the minorities-principle" over the nation-state order stood exposed as a kind of psychopathological mania— the *real* "minority complex." Diasporism's idealistic celebration of Jews' minority status as an avant-garde instantiation of a coming world was now exposed as a ridiculous variant of Jews' old chosenness theology: our "unique minoritarian 'You God have chosen us' prayer."[51]

In relation to the wishful Diasporist vision found in Golomb, Weinreich's work marked an analytical watershed in Diasporist thought. If hitherto the Jewish national intelligentsia had thought about Jewish minorityhood primarily in political and legal terms, Weinreich assayed how it might also be a social-psychological condition—one that needed to be studied comparatively and historically and situated at the center of thinking about Diaspora itself. But it was also the beginning of a reckoning: if Weinreich remained very far from accepting the Zionist critique of minorityhood, clearly his sense of what *kind* of minorityhood Polish Jews could reasonably expect, short of some profound intervention, was rapidly growing grimmer.

Perhaps tellingly, Weinreich ultimately stepped back from this entire line of analysis and instead devoted the rest of *Veg* to a psychological analysis-cum-indictment of Polish Jewish culture itself. Marshaling an array of social-psychological categories drawn from the work of Charlotte Buehler and Lev Vygotsky, much of the rest of *Veg* elaborated a complex typology of all the ways that Polish Jewish youth were (ostensibly) seeking "compensations" (here meant purely in terms of the easing of psychological woe when the actual problem cannot be solved) rather than facing up to the realities of their situation. Ultimately he pinned much of the blame for this ostensible escapism less on internalized prejudice than on an ostensible flaw in Jewish culture itself: a "Jewish [psychological] specificity" according to which "Jewish youth does not feel *at home in its home.*" This self-image of oneself as a stranger rather than a native, he ultimately thundered, comprised not only "a fundamental question of the Jewish personality" but "also a fundamental question—one might say *the* fundamental question—of Jewish communal existence."[52]

Poetry as Psychic First Aid

At the center of the Diasporist project stood the ideal of a Yiddish *Kultur,* and at the center of the idea of *Kultur* stood an exalted conception of poetry as the most fundamental site for the realization of the self. Yet whatever readers found in the Polish Yiddish poetry of the 1928–1935 era, on the face of it this was not a poetry that offered much sense of plenitude, or even succor. With painful honesty, Poland's leading Yiddish poets made contemporary catastrophe, looming danger, and woundedness central themes in the early 1930s. It is perhaps unsurprising that a Zionist Yiddish poet like Shmuel Zaromb, who traveled across Poland preaching socialist-Zionist solutions to the youth, would write in 1929 a raw pronouncement on the futurelessness of Diaspora life—"To Nobody"—in which a hopeless Jewish patriarch curses God or Poland or modernity with whom he has "shared my bed/shared my wife/shared my child" and which has in return flung him "like a stone/that whines through the air/[. . .] a fright for others/and for myself as well." But such bitter ruminations on Polish Jewry's situation also appeared from the pens of figures more wedded to the Diasporist vision, or at least to the Yiddishist one. In 1933, responding presumably to the Nazi victory in Germany, Warsaw Yiddish poet Arn Tsaytlin offered a dread vision of coming Jewish extermination and the happy, forgetful world that would rebuild itself after Jewry's demise. Warning his readers that they should understand themselves as already doomed ("Who is guilty of the fact that we are dying?"), he imagined how the hands that today "lift the bayonets" would tomorrow offer generosity ("*hent vos shenken*")—but only after the world had rid itself of Jews. Invoking the remorseless discourse of fascism and race war ("He who dies is guilty, dying out is guilt./And guilt is punishment, and punishment will not pass over us"), Tsaytlin concluded:

> They'll choke us with gases. We'll lie under ash,
> Dead cities will yield to the village green.
> Young rains will give old earth a wash,
> And objects will speak in unknown tongues,
> Children will laugh, God will come on down.

Ideologically, Tsaytlin was something of a skeptic, unwilling to accept Zionism yet ever more doubtful about the Jewish future in the Diaspora. But by this time, even Polish Yiddish poets more solidly connected to the Diasporist vision than Tsaytlin were producing a corpus of poetry marked above all by ugliness, grotesquerie, and nightmarish visions; this applies mutatis mutandis to Warsaw's Meylekh Ravitsh, Yisroel Rabon of Łódź, and Wilno's Leyzer Volf.[53]

That said, there were at least a few cases in which Diasporist poets wedded such painful representations to a poetics that offered some redemption or defense of the Jewish subject. We have already seen one such case: the Bundist poet Gutgeshtalt with his bloody and confident offer to his readers of Marxism's most vital subject position: the foot soldier of revolution. And in the early 1930s, those with an eye on Poland's Yiddish literary scene might have expected something similar from a younger and greater literary figure, Chaim Grade.

Among a cadre of talented young poets in Wilno who came to local and soon global attention in Yiddishist circles in the 1930s, Grade emerged as early as 1931 as primus inter pares. At the center of Grade's youthful poetics, as Justin Cammy demonstrates, was, precisely, a burning sense that Polish Jews—and especially youth—were suffering an inner psychic "catastrophe" (one of Grade's keywords) and that this inner catastrophe was the product of larger "world-catastrophes" (*velt-katastrofn*) unfolding around them.[54] From the first, Grade was a deeply political poet, not only in the general sense that his early poetry is centrally concerned with the human condition as determined by the actions and inactions of other humans in society, but also in the more literal sense that he often wrote in direct reaction to political events. As Avraham Nowersztern has shown, Grade's star began to rise in the early 1930s precisely because of how he communicated in powerful high-prophetic fashion a horrifying vision of the political, economic, and moral situation unfolding in Europe and around the world, around Jews, and around the whole of humanity—and did so moreover in ways unmistakably in sympathy with the socialist worldview.[55] Grade's early poetry figured forth a world in which Cains of every sort murdered Abels as diverse as enslaved Africans, Parisian Communards, Viennese socialists, peasant cannon fodder in World War I, Communist political prisoners in Poland, and the pogromized Jews of the revolutionary borderlands.[56] The poem "World in Nineteen Thirty-Four," which got Grade into trouble with the police, directly addressed the recent victories of Nazism in Germany and the Right in Austria and linked them not just to biblical Sodom but also to recent events central to the imagination of the European Left: the crushing of the Paris Commune and Russia's abortive 1905 Revolution. Elsewhere, Grade took on the Polish state through images of prisons, jailers, and gendarmes and savaged the extrusionary ideal at the heart of Endek as well as Nazi ideology ("Poland for the Poles," "Germany for the Germans," etc.) with the parodic slogan "Sodom for the Sodomites." So, too, several of his early poems focused on what Grade figured as the everyday violence of capitalism: women forced by need into some sort of prostitution or concubinage was a repeated focus, as was the grueling poverty that dehumanized the poet's own mother and to which he attributed his father's early death. Throughout, Grade insisted that human evil, though ancient, was not rooted in nature but in society and economy, that political and moral evil was intertwined at the root with economic exploitation, and that both the suicidal violence of World War I and the current spate of Rightist victories were linked in some way to the daily violations of human dignity by greed and want.[57]

But if Grade's poetry yoked a sense of Jewish subjectivity in tatters to socialist ideals, not a shred of Gutgeshtalt's Marxian-cum-Sorelian optimism about Polish Jewish self-restoration through revolutionary agency can be found in his work. As Nowersztern and Cammy have observed, nearly all the poems with which the young Grade won attention between 1932 and 1936 were organized around a deep tension between the aforementioned socialism-infused representation of the "world-catastrophes" under way and a pained insistence on *helplessness* in the face of these catastrophes—helplessness not only of the poet but importantly, as Nowersztern notes, all of Wilno's and Poland's Jews. Thus, in "Vienna," three Jewish young men in Wilno rage at their complete helplessness in the face of news of the rightist victory over Red Vienna in Feburary 1934. The first rebukes himself for not giving his own life on the barricades, but the second remorselessly observes that even had he done so, it would have been a useless death—Vienna's socialists had had no shortage of bodies, only guns. The third wonders whether the telegraph pole by which he's standing is the gallows on which fascism will eventually hang him or the transmitter of the international news that Wilno Jews must hear.

Nor was Grade's doubt about Jewish political capacities a pose. Cammy notes that he rejected calls to join the Communist Party and even openly declared this refusal in the early parodic poem "Hey Comrade Grade." He seems indeed not to have embraced any clear party affiliation at all.[58]

But if politics offered no solution to an unbearable sense of helplessness (whether as effective action or at least mythic compensation), was the Yiddish poet simply to force already-suffering Jewish subjects to recognize their abjection? There was, as I noted, much Yiddish poetry from the period that did just that. And indeed, some of Grade's poetry did send readers down that stony path, particularly his grueling 1934 *poema* "Ezekiel."

However, one of the features that render Grade distinctive in his milieu—and historically interesting for us—is that he at least *sought* to do otherwise: throughout his first years of poetic emergence, Grade sought in conscious fashion to produce a poetry that would directly counter Jewish despair and instead lead his readers to affirmation and resilience. As Cammy suggests in a pioneering insight, Grade consciously sought to find his way to a poetry that could function not only as "a form of collective metaphysical questioning" but also as a form of "healing." Over the five years of poetic creation that eventuated in his first book, Yo (Yes), completed at the close of 1935, Grade deemed himself called to move his readers (and himself) to (as Cammy puts its) "active embrace of what the world has to offer." Cammy, for his part, questions the salience of this healing endeavor in Grade's actual poetry. Noting that Grade's private letters are permeated with doubt about his undertaking, Cammy argues that "the pessimistic mood" of most of the poetry Grade gathered in the collection Yo rendered the book less "a confident generational clarion call" than a "reflect[ion of] Grade's own conflicting identities."[59]

Undoubtedly, Cammy is right that we can hardly deem Grade's poems of affirmation an unqualified success; how could they have been? But Grade actually did produce a set of poems, albeit only a trio, that articulated a distinctive vision of how culture and aesthetic experience themselves might be refashioned as effective psychic tools. Tellingly, Grade closed the "Yo" poem-cycle with these three poems of affirmation placed together: "Ikh zing fun shney badektn barg arunter" (From mountains snow-covered I sing down), "Baym shayn fun der levone" (By the moon's illumination), and the titular "Yo." Grade's distinctive effort deserves historical attention for what it discloses about Polish Jewish thought regarding art's powers to shore up the self—but also for its strict sense of the *limits* of culture's capacities.

The fundamental move of affirmation in Grade's poetry consists in learning to *see* reality differently and, in thus changing one's relation to the world and to experience, to rescue one's subjectivity from despair. Each of the three poems with which Grade closed the "Yo" cycle centers on a lyric "I" breaking through to an affirming relationship to the world and his own fate not as he might wish them to be but as they are, complete with all the political and social "catastrophes" that have inflicted "woe" (*veytog*). Differing in each poem is the degree to which this attainment is presented as a state the poet-subject has definitely (if perhaps only temporarily) achieved or merely something the speaker is enjoining himself to *try* to achieve; so too does the content and ground of the affirmative relationship differ. But in all of the poems, we are made to understand that this new affirming relationship to the world is not something achievable passively through some kind of emptying or negation of the subject. There was ample precedent for exalting passivity in East European Jewish religious praxis, not least in the religious Musar subculture in which Grade had long been immersed, so it is all the more notable that Grade specifically rejected such praxis. Rather, the subject had to actively and repeatedly perform some kind of work on itself. At the same time, one limit is common to each of the poems: this affirmation of the world, even if achieved, cannot in any way change the world outside, which, the poet warns, will remain just as politically and socially catastrophic in "coming days." Whatever this affirmation is, it involves only a transformation of the subject's relationship—intellectual or affective or both—to the world and to experience.[60]

The first (and least) of these poems, "Ikh zing fun shney badektn barg arunter," yoked its affirmation to hackneyed Romantic tropes: a speaker ascending a snow-covered mountain, poised between the "abyss that gazes up with hungry eyes" and the heights. Amid the objective correlative we hear the speaker's inner address to his own heart at a moment of true transformation. The speaker, we learn, has sought "more than once be-fore" to command "you, my heart" to "prepare yourself to live through your own fall." But now he can speak with a new kind of authority, vouchsafed by something revealed or reordered by his ascent: "O, to my heights I have to clamber like a worm—/ be brave, my burning heart, this path is good." Here the speaker offers Grade's first concrete representa-tion of what the new affirmative subjectivity might involve: coming to see one's own painful personal history as having been "good" in an objec-tive, ontological sense, however experientially painful it has been. Thus, "it is good" that "my virtue once demanded:/ Old age should cast its shadow on my brow." So too, referring outward to several poems placed just before this one in the "Yo" cycle, the speaker affirms as "good" his painful personal history of loves lost to the pressures of poverty.[61] This centering of affirmation on a new attitude toward one's own past seems poised to slide into a mere wish that "my birth should not remain an evil accident." But the close of the poem offers something stronger. The mountain-climber, who now stands at the "highest heights," which he ex-periences as "a mighty temple cold and strict," finds himself "glowing and courageous, full of strength." A suggestion of some new creative power born out of "nights beclouded" in which the speaker "learned how to hope" takes definitive form in the last line: "*hob ikh a himl ful mit shtern oysgebenkt.*" The word *oysgebenkt* can mean "longed-for," but here Grade activates a rarer usage as a verb of completed action: "A heaven full of stars I've longed into existence."[62]

"Ikh zing" offered readers an especially narrow bridge of affirmation. The poet-speaker's new relationship to the world here consists only in having attained a new outlook on his own fate, based on nothing except the active intervention of the poet-speaker's own "virtue." The two poems with which Grade followed this one and ended the "Yo" cycle are more formally original, particularly in their imaginative elaboration of an idio-syncratic "revelation," to use Cammy's apt term, on which their accounts of affirmation turn. More apposite here, these two poems also offer more fulsome visions of affirmation: forthright assertions that behind all the suf-fering, the world itself is intrinsically, ontologically good and that the poet Grade can share with readers this "revelation." Grade's surprising poetic-mythic assertion of the world's essential goodness pivoted around an unlikely axis: in both poems, the raw fact of *evolution* in the basic bio-logical sense of the development of ever more complex forms of life over time becomes "proof" that nature and existence itself are moving toward the good and have an innately good telos. In both poems, the affirmation comes (in "Baym shayn") or is to come (in the more complex "Yo") by way of a new understanding of oneself not as a fallen creature but as (by definition) the pinnacle of a development toward which nature has been working all along via evolution, and which, we can presume, will continue on its upward course. "Baym shayn," the penultimate poem in the "Yo" cycle, narrates a revelation turned affirmation fully achieved:

By moon's illumination in my tiny chamber,
I gaze raptly at my nakedness—
Stripped completely of my garments,
I read my body like hieroglyphic script.

As every epoch leaves in stone its marking,
So has my origin inscribed on me its trace.
From the very chimpanzee it's been my path
to reach through nature to humanity.

My body is the dream of the gorilla,
Who lived for ages in the ancient wood.
Smiling, I paint myself the idyll
When I was still as yet orangutan.

For those who encountered this poem in *Yo,* the specifics of its account of revelation would have resonated powerfully in cumulative relation to the grim poems that precede it. The setting of "Baym shayn's" revelation is familiar from earlier poems, which repeatedly take place in the poet-persona's little bedroom, as he tosses in torment or lies frozen on his bed—a fitting image of confinement and fruitlessness for poetry that repeatedly dramatizes helplessness. So too, the moon had appeared before as a central figure in Grade's poetic universe, and indeed brought revelations in several earlier poems. But these had been terrifying revelations. In "Blessing upon the Moon," the moon appears as "a drowned, naked girl"; is driven mad as her light reveals the miserable poverty of a Wilno courtyard and "rotting" families; gives off a light that a mangy cat takes for "milk" but is actually "like poison"; and finally grants a "vision" to the poet in his room—but only a baleful one of a "moss-covered stone" in a "moonlit field" that "like the petrified heart of the world / keeps silent like me in my room alone." In another poem, moonlight "playing" over the "strings" of prison bars drives a political prisoner so mad that he begs his guards to save him. In a third poem, the moon returns with a (literally) edgy sort of positivity, cutting through the clouds like a "factory's circular saw." But if this symbolizes some sort of revolutionary potential, it doesn't yet offer the poet any redemption: he merely stands "like a golem, crazed in the middle of the street—/a telegraph-pole eaten away by political madness."[63]

By contrast, in "Baym shayn," all is redeemed by the moon's light, now pure, which lets the poet-speaker read a hitherto hidden truth inscribed by nature itself on his own body (in hieroglyphs, associated with hidden truths in the European imagination since the Renaissance).[64] Whereas in "Ikh zing," revelation had turned merely on coming to see one's life course as somehow providential, here the speaker discovers a redeeming truth about the cosmos itself:

> From jungle-dark—through milky way—to a new world,
> My blood-drops now like stars rise up.
> Man is still too animal to become as yet a god—
> With this song, I climb up from eternity.

With existence itself "revealed" to be an essentially good form of becoming, the poem concludes:

> What I have been is now so unimportant,
> What matters now is what I will be yet!—
> Just as at noon this room's illuminated,
> So gleaming are my words in the moon's light.

The new affirming relation to the world that the subject seems to have achieved here redeems not only the past, as in "Ikh zing," but also the *future*. A movement toward the better is unfolding in nature through evolution—and thus life is fundamentally struggling toward the Good behind all the obvious human misery.

The last of Grade's three poems of affirmation, the titular "Yo," reaffirms this strange myth of evolution in still more confident form: "A bridge of eons becomes a rainbow, thrown from my window to the Woods./The animals—my forefathers—with amazed eyes/sniff carefully my new-found form./They caress me with hot teeth and sharp claws;/For generations we struggled that you should come to be;/The jungle now makes a pilgrimage to me/whilst I climb higher to the shining stars." To this, Grade added a moment of existential vitalism. The speaker—who in "Yo" is not moving through time as in the previous poems but speaks the whole poem in a single moment while standing at his window at dawn—declares that "all that has a name or none,/fights in me against destruction."[65]

Placed within the historical context this chapter has reconstructed, the terms of Grade's endeavor lose whatever veneer of hermeticism they might have to the contemporary reader and become altogether understandable: this was an effort at psychic first aid. Granted, they also invite a question of intention, expectation, and reception: What could Grade have been thinking to predicate a poetic project aimed at "healing" his fellow Polish Jews on an idiosyncratic myth that readers could see him *making up* before their very eyes, and that they had no particular reason to *believe*? Cammy puts the point acutely: Grade's myth of evolution as vouchsafement of a kindly Nature was a "willed faith." Metaphysically, there is no compelling reason why the mere fact of evolution should be taken as evidence of the Good; it could just as well authorize a Schopenhauerian disgust with the blind will pulsing through life (elsewhere in the "Yo" cycle, Grade pointedly repudiates "that old bachelor Schopenhauer").

But clearly, Grade did not imagine his poetry as philosophy—as a vehicle to transmit a metaphysics that readers would accept as true of the world out there—nor would he have thought that his actual readers would construe his myth as a revelation of theological truths. As Cammy and Nowersztern demonstrate, Grade—like the other poets of Yung-Vilne— had an especially intimate relationship with an enthusiastic audience, the subculture of Vilna Yiddishism; and he knew full well that he was speaking to a highly secular audience. Grade's poetry itself thematized the difficulty of achieving the affirmation he enjoined. "Ikh zing" and even more so "Yo" are full of rhetorical *instruction* by the poet-speaker to his heart, enjoining it to believe and recognizing, too, that this is hardly an easy process. Indeed, as Cammy notes, in "Yo" the speaker recognizes in advance that his own heart will need such instruction repeatedly in coming days.

Yet in thematizing this, Grade also offered his reader the key: he could not offer belief, only a regimen of work on the self, a kind of spiritual exercise, in which everything turned on aesthetic experience. The historically appropriate question to Grade's poetry of affirmation is not how he could have imagined that anyone would *believe* this myth, but rather how he might have thought that his plainly idiosyncratic but beautifully imagined myth of evolution—with its smile-inducing orangutans, rainbow bridges, reverse pilgrimages, and filmic images of the moonlight picking out hieroglyphs on his own naked body or animals caressing him lovingly with their claws—*could* possibly work on the "heart" of his secular-modern reader. Here it is important to note that explicit thinking about myth, art, and how both might work on the modern secular subject were present in the discourse of Diasporist circles in the 1930s. In 1934, readers of the Lwów journal *Przegląd Społeczny* could read an essay by the Polish-Yiddish writer Debora Vogel assessing recent Polish and French children's books in relation to what she called "the 'legend' of modernity." "Legend," she wrote, had to be produced wherever some reality "haphazardly realized in life" has come to seem banal, opaque, or alienating; speaking in terms reminiscent of Russian Formalism's concern for "defamiliarization" as a kind of cleansing of perception, she hailed particular books for "rehabilitating" the "wondrousness" of simple everyday work, and others for instantiating compellingly "the legend of pacifism," meaning leading child-readers to the "conviction" that they were more like "distant Indian, Black, or Arab children" than unlike them.[66]

Clearly Grade deemed his task to be something more urgent than what Vogel had in mind: not providing children with the chance to experience the modern world around them as fantastic and humane, but rather helping young adults relate to a world of "catastrophe" as something other than soul crushing. But Vogel's linking of her theorization of modernity's will to "legend" to a specification of how exactly such legend might work on modern consciousness is suggestive in our context. For Vogel, it is through aesthetic experience more than intellection that the reader could "arrive," say, "at the conviction of the similarity of life, and thus of human closeness, everywhere." A good children's book did not transmit a finished message but "pull[ed]" the child "into concrete cooperation." It did so not by "suggesting the idea" it wished the child to absorb, but by "exemplification" of that idea in concrete aesthetic form.

Grade's poetry of affirmation makes considerably more sense read in this light: as a series of efforts to provide a poetically compelling representation of an idea—idea as myth, that is—in such a way as to operate on the reader's *imagination* of the world. Here, a further element of Cammy's work on Wilno Yiddishism in the 1930s is striking: his demonstration that evolution as a topos had already come to play a surprisingly significant role in the thought and poetry of the intimate milieu in which Grade moved. The topic of Wilno salon discussions, it was also a multivalent motif in the poetry of Grade's older contemporary, competitor, and friend Leyzer Volf, for instance. To try to "heal" the outlook of Wilno

Yiddish readers through a poetic myth of evolution was, then, not quite as idiosyncratic as it sounds. And though we can hardly prove that Grade's poetry worked on readers in precisely this fashion, it is striking that looking back at the distance of fifty years, one of Grade's friends, Shloyme Belis, recalled the impact of Grade's poems of affirmation "Yo" and "Ikh zing" with special warmth.[67]

Here we might also point to contemporaneous poems of a friend of Grade's who was then in his shadow but would soon emerge as the greatest Yiddish poet of the postwar era—and precisely as the Yiddish poet least willing to give up on affirmation of the self and its creative capacity: Avrom Sutzkever. Several of Sutzkever's early poems of the mid-1930s take up Grade's terms so directly that they can only be read as a response to Grade's attempted intervention. Thus a poem about the coming of spring, "Marts" (March), begins in the same small room in which Grade's poet-figure had fought to find an affirming relation to the world:[68]

> Today my little room burst into bloom white-budded,
> There's a knocking on my window, a blue-eyed love.
> From the deepest depths, from distances unsounded,
> Waters silver-hued sprang forth and heaved,
> A single word came gushing in my heart:
> Believe!

Can the poet do more than enjoin himself to such belief? In his 1935 "Heymishe Felder" (Fields of Home), Sutzkever invoked Grade's affirming project directly once again: "The fields of home breathe with the honey of youth/White birches recall early days and nights./Shining simplicity of earth! My fate's enough./Clamorous, steel sorrow: you I'll forget." He acknowledged the possibility that this was all just talk: "I don't know if I am sunrise or a fading sunset/maybe—a windmill that mills only its own hours." But Sutzkever closed by declaring a far more unalloyed faith than Grade in his own capacity to transform his readers' relation to the world through poetry alone. In a passage reminiscent of Goethe's claim that the very capacity of the human eye to see beauty testifies to a loving telos behind nature, Sutzkever closed that same poem with defiant confidence that the world's beauty could remake human consciousness: "Now, when I wash my eyes in the blue Viliya [river]/With your radiance they grow blue once again."[69]

Read as a communication and intervention directed not only to himself but to his fellow young Jews, Grade's poetry of affirmation (and

Sutzkever's) was supposed to work by helping readers see their fate as full of virtue rather than shame. For Grade, the ground of affirmation is our lowest common denominator: our naked humanity and the fact of life itself. In this sense, we might see Grade and Sutzkever starting down a path of twentieth-century thought about imagination's sovereign powers captured by Cora Diamond's remarks on Socrates via Martha Nussbaum:

> The notion of improvisation signals an entirely different view of what is involved in moral life, in life *simpliciter,* in which possibility and the exercise of creativity are linked. What is possible in [the story of Socrates's death] is something unthought of by his friends, and depends on his creative response to the elements of his situation, his capacity to transform it by the exercise of creative imagination, and thus to bring what he does into connection with what has happened in his life [. . .]. The possibilities are not lying about on the surface of things. Seeing the possibilities in things is a matter of a kind of transforming perception of them.[70]

On this view, our experience of the world is not fully determined by some objective set of circumstances, but is substantially determined by the "creative response" we can mobilize—"a transforming perception." It's fair to say that that is one of the things Max Weinreich would have wanted Polish Jewish youth to embrace, so that they could work to improve Jewish life despite their incapacity to change Polish Jewish political fate.

But if we should take seriously Grade's project of creating a poetry that would offer the secular Jewish subject a kind of affirmation of existence as the 1930s darkened, we cannot overlook the painful limit Grade set. Where "Yo" deepened Grade's strange myth of evolution as vouchsafing life's goodness, it also made more explicit a painful *sacrifice* that building a subjectivity on the basis of this cosmic-evolutionary myth entailed: the subject would have to recognize that *freedom* itself was mere illusion. Nature's telos was working through each individual; to recognize that one was part of an ongoing process of "ascent" *was* the recognition that made life something that could be affirmed rather than experienced as an "evil accident." But this meant recognizing that one's life was as *determined* as everything else in the universe: "The bird in his springtime flight" might feel free, but this was illusion; Grade, "grandson of the gorilla," could see "the entire world in its *tsuzamenhang*," the way everything hung together. Embracing the evolutionary process that ennobled life behind the scenes of human-made catastrophe did not offer any sort of power to *change* one's life—only one's outlook: "Yes!—that means: my destiny's my virtue." Grade ultimately renounced not just politics but the illusion of freedom. He simultaneously foregrounded the omnipresence of catastrophe in contemporary life, sought a poetics that would allow the Jewish subject some capacity to live with some sort of inner composure despite that catastrophe, and stoically accepted that central to the East European Jewish experience would be powerlessness to change much of anything.

Coda: Minorityhood, the Left, and Zionism

Diasporists like Weinreich and Lux were not the only ones to turn to the African American experience to try to comprehend East European Jewish trajectories. In August 1934, Poland's leading Yiddish newspaper *Haynt* reviewed a Russian-language anthology of African American poetry. A Communist production, it was hardly the sort of work that the Zionist *Haynt* normally praised.[71] But the review, by the Yiddishist intellectual Zeev Latski-Bertoldi, opened with effusion: "In whatever language these poems might appear, they will dispel indifference and awaken a burning interest. They give voice to the Negro tragedy, and that voice flows from an ancient source, from the Negro poets who were driven from African jungles to the banks of the Mississippi and who know well that life and death is in their tongue." Lamenting that the anthology focused on agitational poetry, Latski called for an edition "reflecting the entirety of Negro poetry in all its forms and hues." And he called for translations into Yiddish.[72]

What was this "entirety of Negro poetry" and why were Yiddish-speaking Jews called to encounter it? African American poetry demanded attention of all "lovers of literature" because it was great human culture—"a new country in the world-republic of poetry" in its own right. "Langston Hughes, [Claude] McKay, Sterling Brown, Countee Cullen, and the poetess Helen Johnson" were talents "who need not fear comparison to the greatest poets of world literature."

Yet this poetry also embodied a collective experience that Jews particularly needed to encounter. Unlike Weinreich or Lux, Latski presented African Americans as a *nation;* to speak of African American poetry as expressing the inner life of a people was to invoke the exalted Herderian terms that European nationalists usually reserved for their own peoples. But like Weinreich or Lux, Latski engaged African American experience in relation to his own rising fears about Jewish life. A Yiddish edition of this poetry "would be a great act of justice" because "we Jews are more prepared than other peoples to encounter the soul of Negro poetry. For we too are afflicted by race-hatred, we too have sung through the mouths of our greatest poets songs of 'woe and rage' [*tsaar un tsorn*] and we ourselves well know that our fate too is bound up in the liberation of humanity."

Here Latski signaled that he was embarked on a very different political evolution than those of his erstwhile Yiddishist-Diasporist comrades. Latski had long been a man of the Left, and remained sympathetic. He did not criticize the poets' pro-Soviet sympathies; it was understandable that African Americans should be inspired by "Soviet Russia," and "interpret the slogans of the Communist Revolution in their own way, for their freedom, for their redemption." Latski signaled his abiding allieg-ance to universal human liberation by invoking the "the great French Revolution," declaring African American poets the newest bearers of its ideals of "freedom and equality."

But by 1934, Latski was also a Zionist. He had embraced Zionism, indeed Ben-Gurion's brand of unapologetically nationalist Labor Zionism, by 1930.[73] It was for this reason he was welcomed at *Haynt*. And he sig-naled his orientation clearly in his review: to speak of "songs of *tsaar un tsorn*" was to invoke, unmistakably, Zionism's 'National Poet' Chaim Nahman Bialik, whose great pogrom poems were known in Yiddish under that collective title.[74]

Why was a proper Yiddish anthology of African American poetry so important for Latski the Zionist? The answer, it seems, turned on a spe-cial identification between African Americans and Jews as sharers not in "*Kultur*" but in woe. Latski had once been a true believer in the idea that East European Jewry could recreate itself as a modern, normal nation in the Diaspora.[75] But by 1934, he had qualified his former faith. Jews and African Americans, he was suggesting, lived in a state of oppression and therefore their cultures, though no less ingenious than others, pivoted on a special national "tragedy." The universals of love, nature, and labor were thematized in African American poetry, but so were "sadness and holy protest." At its heart, this was poetry about "the tragedy of Negro fate"; this was what the Jewish soul needed to hear.

Latski's vision of a special minority condition converged with the worries of Weinreich and Lux, but the moral-political thrust was the op-posite. The point of encountering the African American experience was not to "inoculate" Polish Jews against fallen subjectivity, but to help East European Jews recognize something already true of them: they were an oppressed people. Such peoples had their own distinct character, born of tragic fate. Latski's choice to connect African American poetry to one of the most compelling lines of the Jewish Bible, "life and death is in the tongue [Proverbs 18:21]," may be read as embodying this sense of shared fate.

Thus too, Latski's stance diverged from the sort of psychic rescue Grade and Sutzkever were attempting. He, too, wanted to reshape Jewish subjectivity through poetry. But this meant not restoring Jews' capacity for *amor mundi* but helping them recognize the political truth of their situation. Latski himself, once a believer in Jewish cultural agency, was taking a path framed by this recognition. A year after he wrote this review, Latski left Eastern Europe for Palestine, where he joined Ben-Gurion's Mapai.[76]

4

Antisemitism, Nationalism, Eliminationism

In mid-1934, Zeev-Volf Latski-Bertoldi wrote to Yankev Lestschinsky. Disturbed by an impasse in Jewish social thought, he thanked Lestschinsky as the exception: "Without 'impressionists' like you, we wouldn't learn anything from life. You have taken upon yourself a difficult task: to teach our bench-sitters, who know only how to look in a canonical book or a party-pamphlet, how to look at real life too." The particular sphere of "real life" that concerned Latski was the changing political situation in Europe—the "Hitlerist earthquakes." The impasse was the inability of his and Lestschinsky's comrades on the left to recognize that these "Hitlerist earthquakes" demanded Jews rethink their categories of political analysis. Unprecedented events "changed nothing in their daily outlook"; instead, they "hold on tightly to the petrified words [. . .] formulate[d] several decades ago."[1]

Actually, Lestschinsky was of two minds about how to approach the Polish Jewish situation. With Diasporists like his close interlocutor Max Weinreich, Lestschinsky shared the worry that pessimism among Jews was itself destructive: he closed his yearlong 1930 study of the Polish Jewish situation by remonstrating that despite the dreadful circumstances, Polish Jews had to overcome their "panic-mood, [their] opinion that the situation is utterly hopeless!"[2] But whereas Weinreich tarried with the view that diagnosing and combatting this "panic-mood" should itself be the primary focus of the Jewish intelligentsia's remediation efforts—that the fundamental task facing the Jewish intelligentsia was to find ways to help Jews "adapt" to conditions they could not change[3]—Lestschinsky could not embrace that internalism. Unlike Weinreich and *most* Diasporist thinkers, Lestschinsky set himself two parallel tasks of social inquiry as the 1920s gave way to the 1930s. He sought not only to grasp what was happening within Polish Jewry's communal and psychological life, but

Figure 4.1 "Jakob Lestschinsky (second from right) [. . .] and other delegates to the YIVO Conference pose at the grave of Tsemaḥ Szabad, a physician, leader of the Folkist party, and founder of YIVO, Vilna, 1935." YIVO Encyclopedia of Jews in Eastern Europe Online, ed. Gershon Hundert. Archives of the YIVO Institute for Jewish Research, YE 0555i1.

also—with growing urgency—to grasp where Polish (and European) society and state were headed, and where the nation-state as a global form was headed in an age of capitalist crisis, populism, and rising extremism.

A Marxist (albeit a heterodox one) since his youth, Lestschinsky had grown close to the Marxist Bund in the mid-1920s.[4] And on these matters, the Bund offered its supporters *certainty* even in the face of devastating events; the victories of the radical Right in Germany in 1933 and in Austria in 1934 simply redoubled the Bundist leader Henryk Erlikh's faith that class struggle would bring imminent redemption.[5] Lestschinsky could not abide in certainty: instead, as Latski recognized, he seemed compelled to struggle toward new understandings of the relationship among economic, political, and cultural crises. What this yielded was a notable transformation in Lestschinsky's thought between 1932 and 1934. In his wrenching 1930 sociological examination of the Polish Jewish economic situation, Lestschinsky still framed the question of Polish Jewry's future as an essentially economic one: whether the Jews as a population and community would be able to hold out materially against state economic-nationalist pressure and the conjunctural crisis of the Depression long

155

enough that when the Depression ended, Jews as a community would be able to recover their footing.[6]

But this sequestering began to give way between 1932 and 1934 as Lestschinsky wrestled with a growing sense that deep structural factors were driving Central and Eastern Europe polities toward "the rejection and extrusion of Jews," with widening support from key parts of "the surrounding non-Jewish society," as he put it in August 1933.[7] An essay from late 1932 confronted readers with alarming accounts of violent antisemitism in Poland's most educated strata, of police and government collusion or at best indifference, and of growing exclusion of Jews from state posts and jobs in municipalities.[8] But actually, in Lestschinsky's view, all this was only complexly related to antisemitism as a free-standing ideology. He did not fully abandon Marxian assumptions about the determinative power of economic conjuncture. Rather, he groped toward a model of how greater state readiness to exert control over the economy since World War I intersected with the crisis of global capitalism to impel state and social elites toward ever more consequential efforts to nationalize the economy and extrude "aliens."[9]

Lestschinsky was not the only Jewish intellectual to turn urgently toward investigating events in the polities in which European Jewry lived. He was not the only one who began to rethink long-standing assumptions about how modern societies worked and what forces shaped politics. And he was not the only one who began to draw disturbing conclusions about what was likely to happen in the near future, and with what intensity, duration, and effect. But neither was he typical. We do not have to embrace Latski's claim that Lestschinsky stood alone to recognize that indeed relatively few Jewish intellectuals so keenly sought for new concepts to comprehend what was happening around them.

This chapter is a history of some exceptions. It traces the disparate efforts of some half-dozen Jewish national intellectuals who sought, like Lestschinsky, to look with new eyes at "real life" in the 1928–1935 period—to make better sense of antisemitism and majoritarian nationalism, the workings of "rationality" and "irrationality" in society and state, and questions of how state and society were becoming conjoined in new ways in the framework of nationalism. The figures who command chief attention are a motley bunch: the Polish Zionist leader Yitshok Grinboym and the permanently uncompromising Diasporist Avrom Golomb, the minor Zionist-socialist activist and Polish politician Avraham Levinson, the Warsaw Zionist publicist Ludwik Oberlaender, the erstwhile Diasporist and heterodox socialist Lestschinsky, and an old comrade fitting the same description, Avrom Rozin (Ben-Adir). Readers familiar with East European Jewish intellectual life and how it is usually treated by historians may find this list peculiar in three ways. First, I focus equally on both Diasporist and Zionist analysts despite the fact that they themselves were ever less open to dialogue with one another. Second, many significant intellectuals of both camps are missing, while those who stand at the center of my analysis include minor figures alongside major ones. Third, although the works of analysis I attend to span the entire 1928–1935 period, I focus particularly on analyses produced in 1931–1932, *before* the Nazi accession to power in neighboring Germany.

My choices, far from being willful, embody a series of research findings and propound several arguments about a question central to this study: the question of what Polish Jews and their expatriate comrades could, and could *not*, see and articulate about their own situation. My exclusion of many intellectuals we might consider leading figures in the Jewish national intelligentsia both Diasporist and Zionist reflects my conclusion, arrived at with some surprise in the course of this research, that a great many Jewish national intellectuals did *not* change the tenor of their thought much in the face of what Latski called the "Hitlerist earthquakes." In turn, I have concluded that one of the powerful *limiting* factors in the Jewish social thought of this era was the enduring power of deep Marxist and progressive assumptions about the relationship between economics and politics. Latski was not the only erstwhile socialist-minded Diasporist to conclude that Diasporist analysis of the Jewish Question was crippled by an incapacity to think beyond the socioeconomic dimensions of East European Jewry's situation. In 1934, the longtime Yiddishist-Diasporist stalwart Rozin commented, "It seems to me that the general belief that a solution to *social* questions will perforce and mechanically bring a solution for the Question of the Jews [*yidn-frage*] is beginning to disappear. Until not too long ago, this conviction was altogether dominant in the broad circles of our socialist intelligentsia; with regard to *this*, there were no doubts or debates."[10] Rozin may have had in mind analyses like that made in 1932 by Avrom Menes, then close to the Bund, who reasoned via Kondratieff cycles that because antisemitism in the long nineteenth century seemed to have correlated to economic conditions, Jews could be relatively sure that the *current* wave of antisemitism would decline in direct correlation to economic recovery. The key assumption in Menes's argument was that there had been no fundamental change in the relationship of economy, culture, and politics since the nineteenth century.[11] This was precisely the assumption that Lestschinsky was starting to doubt.

Menes's adherence to such base-superstructure sensibilities seems to have been more the norm than the exception particularly in the Diasporist camp. That said, there were also some intellectuals in the opposing Zionist camp in Poland who bore the impress of this materialist common sense, including some I engage here. Thus, also in 1932, the Polish Zionist leader Grinboym interpreted the recrudescence of antisemitic student riots in some of Poland's cities primarily in terms of the students' material motivations. Facing a limited job market in the white-collar professions, they were seizing on antisemitic slogans to exclude potential competitors. Beneath all the talk of Jews as a moral threat to the nation, perhaps what was really going on was a rational pursuit of economic closure? In that same year, the socialist-Zionist publicist Levinson published an examination of antisemitism that at times embraced Marxian tropes: perhaps antisemitism was a "bluff" by "the owners of industrial capital and big agriculture" to obscure the "opposing economic interests of the owning class and the working masses."[12] But as we will see, both Grinboym and Levinson were drawn to think beyond the certainties of commonsense materialism and ended up pursuing intuitions little in evidence in Diasporist social thought. This was even truer of Zionist figures standing outside the socialist tradition, like Oberlaender, a perspicacious analyst of nationalism as a form of culture and affect. To study Zionists and Diasporists comparatively thus suggests that adherents of those two camps had not just different ideological commitments but different intellectual repertoires, with real implications for what they could (and could not) readily apprehend about the world around them.

But all of these arguments about what we might call the sociology of Jewish political knowledge in the early 1930s can only be made suggestively here, and they are ultimately subsidiary to the main point: to reconstruct some interesting developments in the political-analytical thought of the Jewish national intelligentsia as it engaged the question of what the Jewish future in Poland and Europe as a whole was likely to entail. Focusing on a handful of intellectual inquirers selected because they sought to think *beyond* long-standing intellectual orthodoxies, I take particular interest in three lines of new political-analytical thought.

First, some of those addressed here wrestled with the question of whether and how political enmities like antisemitism might be functioning as cultural *drivers* of politics and perception rather than merely decorating "underlying rational interests"; some of these looked to the burgeoning psychological sciences for orientation. Second, others—Lestschinsky was one—pursued unsettling intuitions about how new societal expectations directed toward the state by newly active and nationally conscious elements of the *majority* population made a turn toward new forms of antiminority policies likely in moments of crisis—and seemed likely to render such extrusionary tendencies strong and prolonged. Finally, I examine what was, perhaps surprisingly, the least common line of inquiry: inquiry into the workings of illiberal nationalism as an ideological project and the way that nationalists' quests across Europe to forge an obedient yet pathos-driven national community were powering new kinds of assaults against the Jews and against critical reason itself.

Through this investigation I hope to shed some light not only on the legacies of historical materialism in Jewish social thought and on the differential history of Diasporist and Zionist political perception, but also on two further questions of equal significance. One of these concerns the problem of explanation as against prediction. Stated thus, it seems bloodless, but it was nothing of the sort for Jewish national intellectuals who felt charged to guide Polish Jewry. Many of the sources we will encounter breathe with a tension between trying to explain complex phenomena—a slow process by its nature—and the need to offer purchase on what tomorrow would bring. Lestschinsky's writings, for instance, suggest a figure pulled between two recognitions. On the one hand, he himself did not yet have a satisfactory account of how exactly capitalist crisis, new forms of corporatism, youth extremism, radical rightism, and antiminority politics really fit together. But on the other, he was coming to believe that it *had* to be assumed, based on what one could see, that these hazy phenomena were not mere reflections but forces in their own right, that they would not pass away anytime soon, and that they would continue to amplify one another in ways almost certainly detrimental to Jewish well-being. This chapter's positive intellectual history is also, then, an attempt to tease out a particular kind of problem in the social-analytical thought of intellectuals who feel themselves to be speaking for and to a threatened community, and a particular kind of posture wherein the explanatory impulse competes with a futurity-laden sense of the need to predict in order to guide.

Finally, there is a more concrete question that must haunt any history of Jewish political analysis in the 1930s and does so with special force in Polish Jewish history: *When,* exactly, to put it crudely, did Jews begin to develop substantial analytical accounts of new kinds and intensities of danger to them? Put most crudely: Were there substantial accounts of a dangerous swerve in Polish political culture *before* Piłsudski's death in 1935 and the declared shift toward ethnonationalism by the OZON regime that succeeded him? This chapter should leave little doubt that the answer is yes. By early 1934 at the latest, there were robust articulations of where matters were going that proved to have pretty good predictive traction. And 1934 was only an *end* point in a process of growing understanding, as we will see by focusing primarily on emerging political-analytical thought that took shape even before the Nazi victory in 1933.

Charting "the Jewish Problem" in Poland circa 1930

We encountered Samuel Hirszhorn in Chapter 1 as a kind of representative Polish Jewish voice. His claim in the 1 January 1930 issue of *Nasz Przegląd* articulated the common sense of Polish and Polish Jewish liberals entering the 1930s: that the Jewish Question in Poland was basically a question of how strong the Endeks were and whether they could be kept in check. But Hirszhorn deviated from this script a bit. Polish Jewry was not facing ruination by the Right—but it *was* facing ruination, and this was due not least to the *policies* of the very Sanacja government that the Endeks attacked as "pro-Jewish." Indicting the Sanacja's directionless "etatism" as destructive in general, Hirszhorn suggested a worrisome irony that other Jewish observers would treat in a more sustained fashion. The Sanacja state was refusing to change policies ruinous to Jews for fear of being seen as "pro-Jewish," which meant that although the Endeks were out of power, their antisemitic campaign was shaping state policy.

This incipient sense that danger might be located not only on the antisemitic Right but also in the nature of democracy itself in a nationalist age was echoed elsewhere. Rokhl Faygenberg, reporting for Palestinian Jewish audiences shortly after Poland's 1930 Sejm elections, captured a sense of rapidly diminishing expectations among Polish Jews regarding the Sanacja regime. Jews had delivered their votes, but this was less out of any expectation that "salvation will soon come from the hands of the Sanacja" than "fear lest the petty nobles and the clerics who call themselves National Democracy come to power, for they would certainly bathe all the foundations of Poland in Jewish blood." Piłsudski's regime would "endeavor to maintain order" and "public attacks on Jewish towns will not be allowed"; on the other hand, "the government ministries will choke the Jews with new and renewed taxes."[13]

Capturing a widespread sense of Jewish relief that the Right had been balked for now, both of these essays wrestled with a different fear: a sense that the Sanacja regime was in its own way bound to a nationalist logic that dictated a social politics of rendering permanent the declassing that the Depression was inflicting on Jews. The emergent questions were of intent and extent. Hirszhorn recognized that the economic woes afflicting Polish Jewry derived not only from structural problems (the Jewish professional structure, Poland's agrarian economy) but also from policies pursued by the Polish state. Where he attributed the latter to inertia and pressure from the Right, other observers saw a more intentional policy of extrusion. Writing in 1929, the Jewish migration analyst Il'ya Dizhur argued that it could hardly be an accident that Jewish workers were "being pushed out systematically from the monopolistic state endeavors" and that Polish Jewry's commercial class was being crushed by tax policy.[14]

Vectors and Force: Antisemitism and Its Powers on the Polish Right—and Beyond?

Taken together, these texts capture key analytical assumptions in Jewish national intelligentsia treatments of Poland's Jewish Question circa 1930. They share a rough-and-ready sense that this was a drama played by three actors: the Right, the Sanacja regime, and "Polish society." Where Hirszhorn, Faygenberg, and Dizhur alike focused much of their concern on the second of these actors, other analysts focused increased scrutiny and concern on the first and third. They wrestled especially with two kinds of questions concerning antisemitism itself. First, would the virus on the right spread beyond its presumed bounds to other parts of Polish society and culture? Second, what precisely was antisemitism's content, character, and ideological *force* in rightist ideology, and were those features in transition to something new?

These questions took on new urgency in Jewish national intelligentsia thought over the course of 1931–1932 despite the fact that on the surface of high politics, little had changed. If anything, the Sanacja was still more firmly in power, having embraced more openly authoritarian means to disrupt its political competitors left and right. But the Endek Right had not been defanged, and unsettling notes of optimism were issuing from its leadership. This moved several observers to wrestle with old progressive assumptions.

In 1932, the former parliamentarian, vice mayor, and Zionist activist Avraham Levinson published a booklet on antisemitism, structured as a sort of exhaustive encyclopedia article. Levinson combined his Zionism with both socialism and internationalist progressivism, and as I noted earlier, his account of antisemitism ran in part along Marxian and progressive tracks. "The reactionary parties" reached a broad base of "clerks and bureaucrats, the small businessmen, the urban intelligentsia, student youth and many of the workers," he granted, but they were "run by the owners of industrial capital and big agriculture." Their "chauvinist-religious slogans of antisemitism are brought to conceal the opposing economic interests of the owning class and the working masses." Political antisemitism was primarily a subsidiary dimension of a general "Bourbon" reaction against Progress and democracy ("political antisemitism is the chief weapon of the reactionary parties in their quest to undermine the democratic and republican governments") and the Endek struggle against "the government of Piłsudski."[15]

Concomitantly, Levinson shared with Hirszhorn a reassuring sense that there was much good in Polish culture. At the heart of his book, written in Hebrew for socialist-Zionist comrades by a figure who had come to Polish culture only after deep investment in Hebrew, Yiddish, and indeed Russian, we find an unalloyed paean to Polish literature's humanism. A section titled "Literary Antisemitism" was actually a wide-ranging tour of modern Polish literature that, far from imputing overriding antisemitism, traced throughout its modern history a "doubleness" with regard to Jews, and treated it with analytical breadth: not simply praising writers who offered manifestly philosemitic portraits (Mickiewicz's Jankiel), he found much to like in writers whose representations of Jews were considerably more complicated. Depictions of Jews by the recently deceased novelist Stefan Żeromski, which seem jarringly ugly to some contemporary readers, struck Levinson as the product of an "honest and deep eye." More generally, he endorsed Polish literature's own exalted accounts of its history, task, and achievements ("the literature of Young Poland, which declared the slogan of pure art, free of social and political tendencies, generally remained faithful to its principles") and hailed Polish Romanticism as a model of liberal, humanist nationalism: "longing for freedom," it "transcended national differences and boundaries and spread over them the wings of peace and love."

Beyond the redoubt of Polish cultural humanism, Levinson was also happily aware that there were genuinely tolerant elements in the Sanacja state itself. Two years before writing *Antishemiut,* Levinson had resumed his Polish political career by serving as vice magistrate of the municipal government of the important central-eastern regional center Brześć nad Bugiem (Yid. and Heb.: Brisk d'Lita; Bel.: Brest), known in the West as Brest-Litovsk. In that context, Levinson had worked closely with the town's new non-Jewish magistrate, Tomasz Całuń. Całuń was a Sanacja man of impeccable Piłsudskite credentials who devoted much of his interwar activity to municipal politics before his death in 1936.[16] In Całuń, it seems, Levinson found a model of what Polish Jews hoped the Sanacja as a whole would be. In August 1931, representatives of the Jewish communal board of another mixed town, Ostrowiec-Świętokrzyski in the Kielce region (Yid.: Ostrovtse), wrote a letter to Levinson marked "urgent-confidential." Całuń, having served as chief magistrate of Brześć (and before that Radom), was now seeking the same in Ostrowiec, for which he had "the support of government elements." This moved the Jews of the town to ask Levinson urgently and confidentially for "exhaustive information about the candidate, his attitude to the Jewish population, etc" as promptly as possible. Levinson offered an unambiguous endorsement. Całuń was a man of "absolute honesty, objective," and "in his relations to the Jewish population he has shown tolerance and kindness."[17] A final document rounds out this picture: among Levinson's papers is a letter from Całuń thanking Levinson for a card he had sent, discussing what seem to have been local political matters in a friendly tone, and closing: "My wife and I send our greetings."[18]

Yet if Levinson's government service in Brześć offered hope that decency would hold the line in Polish civil society, it provided ample counterevidence too. Like so many other heavily Jewish towns across Poland, from Prużana and Kleck (Yid.: Kletsk) in the east to Błonie in the west, Brześć was a place where ethnic difference between "Poles" and "Jews" was a social fact inscribed in hearts and in a pervasive doubleness of institutions along ethnonational lines. Though Jews were a majority in Brześć, those who appealed to Levinson to take on the role of vice mayor in 1928 clearly felt that they needed a champion against discrimination; as one newspaper openly opined, "The question of a Jewish vice-magistrate was for the Jewish population a life-and-death one."[19] Levinson thus stepped, quite consciously, into a role fraught with ethnonational tension. His two years in Brześć became a kind of laboratory, apparently, for testing the trajectories of the Polish state where the rubber met the road. If work with Całuń inspired hope, Levinson's time in Brześć was also clearly fraught. He later recalled a politics of "strengthening the Polish foundation, of imposing the tax burden on the Jewish population, of linguistic Polonization aimed at the Jewish high schools, of the sidelining of Jewish clerks, of distancing Jews from state funding, of separation from the Jews through the erecting of modern Polish neighborhoods."[20] And in practice, sources suggest that Levinson was thrust into the role he had been expected to fill: rear-guard defender of Jewish interests against such nationalizing policies.[21]

Levinson's personal experience of Polish political society and the Sanacja regime between 1928 and 1930 clearly deepened rather than resolved uncertainty. The 1932 *Antishemiut* can be read as an effort to make sense out of this uncertainty, yet also as a text fissured by it. Most essentially, though it reiterated the progressive view of antisemitism as a smokescreen rather than an important driver of political life with its own logic, it also showed striking signs of worried reconsideration.

Some of this worry expressed itself around the disturbing career of a text published only a year earlier, *Świat powojenny i Polska,* by the Endecja's leader Dmowski. Levinson's *Antishemiut* devoted substantial attention to this restatement of Dmowski's long-standing account of worldwide Jewish-Masonic conspiracy operating at Poland's expense. On one level, Levinson's treatment stayed within the parameters of the progressive account. Placing Dmowski's text in the context of the tradition of antisemitic conspiracy theory from fifteenth-century Spain to nineteenth-century France, Levinson noted Dmowski's unoriginality: "The Bourbons of our time have learned nothing and forgotten nothing. Dmowski's system is a faithful copy of the system of [the nineteenth century conspiracists] Gougenot or Chabauty."[22]

But if Dmowski could be mocked as a regurgitator, the book showed two disturbing new features. First, Dmowski was far more upbeat than "his more original comrades": whereas earlier antisemitic conspiracists had stood "in fear of the Jewish-Masonic monster," Dmowski optimistically "prophesies its death in the near future." Dmowski's optimism extended to the struggle against the other lobe of the conspiracy, the Freemasons: their "secret efforts" to "enslave the societies of Asia" had been frustrated by the "fruit of their loins," the Bolsheviks; the Protestant states, "chief locus of Masonic power," were tottering; and parliamentary democracy itself, "another Masonic invention," was on its last legs. Second, Levinson was deeply unsettled by the book's reception. Though based on articles published in the right-wing press, Levinson remarked, Dmowski's new book had been taken up seriously by the mainstream press and those "government circles" marked by "tendencies toward convergence with the Endecja." Dmowski's rehashing of conspiracy theories more than half a century old had "made a serious impression throughout the whole of Poland's publicistic literature."[23]

With this last turn, Levinson directly confronted one of the great questions that haunted the edges of many Jewish analyses of the Right's antisemitism: whether it was spreading to other parts of Polish society to become political common sense. In his darkest moments, Levinson allowed (to socialist readers, let us recall) that he perceived cause for worry even regarding the Left. For all Levinson's talk of a unified Left-progressive front against a clerical-reactionary-capitalist Right ("the leaders of socialism and the leaders of democracy in all lands have always fought against antisemitism in all its forms"), Levinson perceived antisemitism as a real presence across the Polish Left, or at the very least a kind of objective weight hobbling its willingness to fight as it should. Granted, the worst offenders were the *least* formally socialist: those "labor parties that do not belong to the international workers' league," like the Polish Christian Democrats, the National Workers Party, and "the 'revolutionary fraction.'" But worrisome tendencies were also visible in the socialist party that mattered: "The PPS too [. . .] is in practice filled with a spirit of a-semitism," an unwillingness to confront antisemitism. Levinson linked this tendency in the PPS to disparate factors. The primary factor was a worsening sociopolitical reality that acted as a brake on the party. Competition between Jews and non-Jewish Polish workers who were the party's real and imagined base discouraged robust anti-antisemitic preachments:

> The struggle against antisemitism, despite the great moral powers that drive it, has encountered many difficulties that obstruct and weaken it. Social morality in its encounter with bitter reality is capitulating. On the one hand: the strengthening of the political impulse in socialism and of its [feeling of] responsibility for the fate of the state and the people are forcing it to strengthen the national foundation of the state and to protect it [. . .]. On the other hand,

among the workers themselves the struggle for [control over] the labor market grows ever stronger. And from here [proceed] the demands of the workers to nationalize labor, to shut the gates of the land to immigration by foreign workers and to shut the gates of industry against the entry of the Jewish worker. That is what closed the gates of the US, Canada, South Africa, Argentina [. . .]. We also find this opposition among Christian workers in relation to Jewish workers of their own country. Thus we see in Poland that factory workers (Łódź, Białystok) strongly oppose entry of Jewish workers into factories.

Then, too, there were "public-psychological factors, namely: the strong national coloring of Polish socialism, reckoning with the antisemitic spirit of the working masses, and fear that active struggle on behalf of the Jews would render 'treyf' its national kosherness in the eyes of the reactionary parties."[24]

These observations sat ill with the "party of humanity" ideal that progressives like Levinson embraced, but they could not be avoided. In another locus of the discussion Levinson noted that a program of "progressive antisemitism" had already been proposed by a circle of Polish writers around Andrzej Niemojewski, Iza Moszczeńska, and Aleksander Świętochowski shortly before the war. Readers who wanted to find a less worrisome account of the trajectory of all this could take succor from his impression that this particular effort had borne little fruit; but could one be so sure that the etiology of prewar antisemitism remained predictive of the phenomenon's reach and hold in the near future of 1930s Poland?[25]

Levinson's concern with the phenomenon of antisemitism among Polish progressives reflected a larger sense of an emerging problem among Polish Jews attuned to Polish intellectual life. In 1928, four years before *Antishemiut* appeared, a letter in *Ewa,* a feminist, Zionist-minded Polish-language journal for Jewish women, indicted the aforementioned Moszczeńska for yoking her feminism to antisemitism. Significantly, like Levinson, the *Ewa* correspondent took for granted the ostensible *abnormality* of this fusion of feminism and antisemitism: "In contrast to the rest of the world, the Polish women's movement is not free of antisemitism."[26] But was this abnormality reassuring or worrisome?

As was the case for Hirszhorn, Levinson's rising worries about antisemitism were largely defined in terms of the model of "spread" and "resistance." But in passing, he began to frame a different kind of question that stood in perhaps even more tension with his Left-progressive sensibilities and hopes: What if antisemitism itself was not a smokescreen or a tool, but an idea with real power to shape perception and politics? Levinson could not quite bring himself to offer a clear answer. But in a strange section of his book that tarried with the political-theological thought of the German cultural critic Oskar Schmitz, he revealed a half-articulated sense that antisemitism might be less a tool that rightists used instrumentally and more a powerful myth that drove them.

In 1924, Schmitz had attained bad odor in Jewish circles for an essay in the German Jewish journal *Der Jude* that seemed to reject the possibility of Jewish integration into Christian societies—and to suggest that Judaism itself might be to blame. Yet as Franziska Krah notes, by 1931 Schmitz had become a defender of Weimar against radical Right impulses and come to see antisemitism as a dangerous psychosis intrinsic to Christian culture. Perhaps it was in this light that in 1932 Levinson recognized in Schmitz "one of the better of the German people" and was able to revisit Schmitz's earlier essay with greater charity. There, Schmitz had stated his case about the Jewish condition in perfervid terms drawn from the German Romantic tradition. Each "nation" had its own "Daemon"—which meant, according to Levinson, "an exaggerated particularity which manifests itself with the force of a psychological law." Born in each case "as a reaction against the feeling of low self-worth," these cultural-psychological peculiarities "render difficult friendly and peaceful relations with [each nation's] neighbors. From the German standpoint, the hindrance to the unity and peace of Germany is France's aspiration to power and glory, and from the French standpoint, the obstacle to the unity of Europe is German Protestantism; Puritan England is the 'daemon' of capitalism and mechanization [as regards] continental Europe," and so forth.

And the Jews? What had discomfited Jewish readers back in 1924 was Schmitz's suggestion that the "daemon" specific to Judaism was something that European civilization intrinsically could not abide. In one of Schmitz's formulations, this was the idea of chosenness itself, "which elevates Israel over all the other nations of the world." In a more psychologically sophisticated variant, "the daemon of the Jews" (here Levinson quoted Schmitz) was a "Pharisaic" "negation of the world" that turned on a permanent deferral of Messianic deliverance: exilic Judaism declared "hope in the Messiah's coming, but at one and the same time it ensures that no Messiah will come. The Messiah must remain unreal, he must not come."

Christian civilization, sunk in a "Sadduceeic" this-worldliness it could not recognize, could not abide this "unique and dangerous structure of the Jewish negation of the world."

Levinson was well aware that this was hardly a well-developed social theory: Schmitz clothed his argument in "the garb of an apocalyptic outlook with which it is difficult to agree or disagree on logical grounds." But there was an insight at work in Schmitz's cultural-psychological argument that Levinson found compelling, and it had to do with finding a conceptual language better suited to making sense of the phenomenon that was staring European Jews in the face: the manifest fact that "the Jewish people appears to many in a demonic form" and indeed a variety of demonic forms. "From an economic standpoint, a people of Rothschilds; from a political standpoint, a people of Trotskys; from a moral standpoint, a people of Shylocks, etc." If Levinson's own Zionist convictions about Jewish "abnormality" inclined him too readily to deem "correct" Schmitz's earlier allegation that Judaism's own myths of "chosenness" were co-responsible for antisemitism, Schmitz's more complex formulations about European "Sadduceeism" helped Levinson redirect his analytical gaze toward something in European culture itself that could not abide what it understood Jews to be. "The scattered and dispersed People Israel appears in the form of various demons, namely, the demon of world conquest, the demon of financial control, the demon of Bolshevism, etc. in accordance with the various Jewish communities and their classes."[27]

Levinson was not the only analyst growing worried about antisemitism's virality. In that same year 1932, his far more prominent compatriot in Polish Zionist circles, Grinboym, took up the question too. Grinboym engaged more directly with a second concern only hinted at in Levinson: a sense that the Right's antisemitism was more complex, potent, and protean than the progressive temperament was wont to assume—and might be undergoing a fateful transformation. A December 1932 essay opened with an analysis of the student-led antisemitic riots that had played out in Poland's university towns over the preceding two months. It developed into a wide-ranging consideration of the antisemitic movement in Poland as a whole that broached the sources of its attraction, the character of its ideology and practice, resistance to it in Polish public life, and the critical question of whether it was drawing in elements beyond the organized student Right.[28]

The late 1932 university riots were, Grinboym averred, in large measure an intentional repetition by Endek activists of a phenomenon that had first manifested a year before. This time, the "spontaneous" riots were planned in advance and intended not least as an attack on the *government's* authority. Given that all of this had the feel of planned reiteration, there had been good reason, Grinboym continued, to assume that this time there would be *less* actual violence and a more ritualized pro forma set of consequences: the state would shut down the universities for a few days, and when they reopened, things would be quiet. Many factors should have ensured this. The police had responded robustly to the student rioters, as had the student Left. The government had threatened to strip universities of their autonomy if the violence resumed. Polish American organizations had demanded order lest Poland's international image be further harmed. More "adult" elements on the right had called on the students to desist from violence.

But alarmingly, the expected ratcheting down had *not* in fact occurred. Reopening had brought *more* violent behavior. This unexpected development formed the nub of Grinboym's first key argument: that the Endek-student violence would continue because these attacks were a *winning* strategy no matter how the process played out. Either the sight of Polish police beating Polish youth in defense of Jews would attract mass support to the Endek cause or the police would discover themselves unwilling to suppress the violence beyond a certain point. Both would be victories for the Endeks. Even if neither was to happen and the government enforced order, that too would only substantiate the Endek claims the riots were *designed* to make: that the Sanacja put Jewish interests over Polish ones and the Endeks were the only real opposition to the Sanacja regime. Also alarming, Grinboym contended, was that efforts by the Sanacja's critics from the Left—the socialists and peasant-party circles—had not awoken mass interest, but the 1931 student attacks in Wilno *had* succeeded in "drawing the masses after the students, and the attacks on the Jews turned into a small pogrom."[29]

Grinboym was attendant to complexity in all this. Thus, having noted how the Wilno attacks had turned into a genuinely popular anti-Jewish riot (this was the riot in which Max Weinreich lost sight in one eye), Grinboym carefully anatomized the differences among the attacks in Warsaw, Wilno, and Lwów over the past two years. The 1931 events in Wilno had been an exception that year. "In other cities, the mass has only followed the students in small measure. In Warsaw, no one followed the lead of those students who headed out into the streets. By themselves they could hardly do much, and they were also beaten by the Jews, who protected themselves." But conversely, there were also signal differences between the attacks in 1931 and the ones that had just now occurred in autumn 1932. If "this year too, nothing changed in Warsaw," this was not true in Lwów. There Endek elements were successfully using the stabbing death of a rightist student during a fight with Jewish workers to transform student attacks into a real ethnic riot. And there were worrying signs as well among the servitors of the state:

> In Lwów, the influence of this faction is great and this time it succeeded in drawing elements from the masses. It's come to a pogrom. The Jews have been beaten in the street, and at this moment the number of injured has reached as many as one hundred; windows of Jewish warehouses have been broken, [. . .] a fire was set in the building of the *Hashmonai* organization. This is reminiscent of the 1919 pogrom in Lwów, when they entered into Jewish apartments and beat them. [The recent] attacks lasted a whole day and the police didn't muster the strength to suppress the students and the masses who accompanied them [. . .]. If this were a matter involving Communists, or Ukrainians [. . .] the [police] would have "quieted" them already and restored order. But when the demonstrators are student youth whose anger has been ignited by the killing of a comrade, when a mass of [other] Poles accompany them, and when they are beating Jews—will the hearts of the policemen and the authorities allow them to use those means that they would use if faced with Communists or Ukrainians?

At the heart of the unexpectedly intensified student violence, Grinboym discerned a double rationality. The students were fighting "their own war, the war of their competition with their Jewish fellow students"—their effort to force a large subsection of the student population out of the universities in the context of an ever-contracting white-collar job market could be construed as a textbook case of rational market closure à la Max Weber. And the Endeks' strategy of using the students to gather a mass following against the government was equally rational, in that it could not fail: it would "drown the government in the tears of the Jews [that is, force the Sanacja to lose legitimacy by defending Jews] or in their blood." Furthermore, there were disturbing grounds to suggest that both gambits were working well. An ever-widening array of white-collar professions were closed to Jews for all intents and purposes; even Jewish-owned factories often refused to hire Jewish engineers so as not to lose government favor and aid. And the government's hesitations suggested that the Endecja's calculus was well founded: "Certainly, [the Sanacja government] knows the real feelings of the police and its bureaucrats and is being very careful not to overstep the line. In Lwów, the mayoralty demanded that the Jewish community board openly and clearly denounce the killing of the Polish student [. . . .] Doesn't this remind you of days of yore under Tsarism?"

Analytically, this essay propounded a kind of divided picture of antisemitism. On one level, antisemitism was a weapon deployed in a disciplined fashion by rational actors seeking perfectly rational—if ugly—goals: economic advantage or political traction. Yet at another level, Grinboym cast what we might call an anthropological eye on the violence itself: he was attentive to the way violence was bound by certain kinds of unspoken rules yet could "evolve" from street fighting to the more unbounded violence that ensued when Jewish homes became legitimate targets.

In a follow-up essay in early 1933, Grinboym turned to a topic that had also preoccupied Levinson: the Polish Right's readiness to propound ever more grandiose and absurd claims about Jewish plots against Poland. Grinboym addressed a wave of antisemitic claims by Endek representatives in the Sejm that Jews in Poland were actually a fifth column—not in the usual metaphorical sense of being bearers of moral dissolution, but in a straightforward military-cum-geopolitical sense. Jews, the Endeks charged, were developing armed paramilitaries in the guise of sports leagues. Another speaker, Grinboym recorded, demanded attention to the role of Jewish individuals as army suppliers, on the grounds that said Jews would throw their resources into the service of invaders in the event of a war. Although Sanacja ministers dismissed this claim in the context of budget negotiations, the army was indeed moving to reduce reliance on private provisioners.[30]

Second and most worrisome to Grinboym was his sense that these sorts of claims seemed to be resonating beyond Endek circles, as embodied by a bizarre set of recent events in Warsaw. In a speech at a Jewish public event protesting Nazism, Gershon Levin, a well-known doctor and public figure in Warsaw Jewish public life, had invoked the Purim story. An Endek publicist had seized on Levin's reference as a kind of coded declaration of Jewish desire to undertake violence against Gentiles, and this had spiraled into the assertion that Levin was head of an illegal secret armed Jewish force. All this, along with the threat on Levin's life by Endek youth activists, was internal to the discourse of the antisemitic Right. But more alarming, and significant, was that police investigators in Warsaw had felt a "duty to send [their] people to search [Levin's] house to see if any weapons were there." In the event, the search had been called off when colleagues of Levin's on a city health commission intervened with the authorities. But the very fact that an Endek claim of secret Jewish militia activity run out of the home of a public figure was deemed credible enough by police—by the state—to demand investigation suggested that the ground had shifted as to "what can be believed in Warsaw not only by the mass of extremist youth, but also by the authorities."[31]

The writings of figures like Hirszhorn and Faygenberg, Grinboym and Levinson radiated uncertainty above all regarding where Poland's political culture was headed. Yet this was not uncertainty in stasis; the texts by Grinboym and Levinson, both from 1932, registered both a new degree of worry and a focusing of analytical attention on three kinds of troubling phenomena. The first and most obvious worry concerned antisemitic ideology: that it was proving to be less tightly moored to the Right, more supple and protean, and more "viral" and catchable beyond the Right—even (or perhaps especially) its more extravagant, irrational, far-reaching forms. A second worry fastened on a more structural problem: whether antisemitism's spread, if indeed such was under way, might substantially shape the actions of parts of the Polish polity and the Sanacja state even if many political actors did not themselves embrace the antisemitic program. And this invoked a third dimension of thinking already evident in Levinson's comment above about factories and professions closed to Jews by the state and by Polish workers themselves: perhaps there was a range of serious dangers to the Jewish future that stemmed less from antisemitism per se than from some larger formation of nationalism in an age of new political expectations, new social strains, and mass democracy. Maybe Jews had to ask not only where antisemitism would go but also about nationalism's lines of force generally: about the expectations of key elements in Polish society and the state regarding not so much "the Jews" but the future they wanted for *Poles,* for themselves. Each of these questions drew Jewish analytical attention, albeit in ways that tell us as much by their silences, limits, and relative *disconnection* from one another as by their positive claims.

Antisemitism as Irrationality? The Psychological Turn

One site of analysis that registered growing Jewish worries about the power of antisemitism in its most irrational forms was budding Polish Jewish engagement with Freudian and other emerging traditions of psychological thought. In the interwar period, it seemed to growing numbers of thinkers that attention to the irrational in human cognition might offer a new Archimedean point from which to understand and ameliorate conflicts of multiple sorts. The Marxian and liberal models inherited from the nineteenth century assumed a tight linkage between intent, ideology, and rational calculative interest. But what if it was true, as Freud and others had begun to argue, that all people were prey to prerational drives largely opaque to them, and that affective "economies" that did not line up with economic rationality were at work in all of us? If ideology and political behavior were essentially determined by prerational needs, frustrations, desires, and fears, redressing political pathologies would demand redress of psychological pathologies first.

Europe's psychoanalytic revolution began to manifest in Polish Jewish letters in the 1920s. The year 1928 saw the publication in Warsaw of a Yiddish translation of Freud's 1921 *Massenpsychologie und Ich-Analyse*. Though the Yiddish translation faithfully reproduced Freud's footnotes and diagrams, its crude format, low price, and front matter marked it as a work intended for a wide readership.[32] The *Massenpsychologie* seems a telling choice as Freud's first Yiddish translation: it was the work wherein Freud for the first time applied psychoanalytic theory to the mystery of group identity. *Massenpsychologie* argued that the groups that mattered most, like families, religious communities, and nations, were precisely *not* merely "communities of interest" (as per liberal thought) but rather dependent on sublimated forms of love powerful enough to overcome the narcissism of self-interest. Concomitantly, *Massenpsychologie* offered a grim view of intergroup enmities as deeply rooted in human nature. Every human relationship contains "a sediment of feelings of aversion and hostility, which only escapes perception as a result of repression," and this relationship only scaled up as human difference grew greater. Even "closely related races keep one another at arms' length," and "greater differences" generated "almost insuperable repugnance such as the Gallic people feel for the German, the Aryan for the Semite, and the white races for the colored." Significantly, Freud maintained that such dislike was not a "prejudice" (that is, culture) but a *natural* expression of individual narcissism that "works for the preservation of the individual, and behaves as though the occurrence of any divergence from his own particular lines of development involves a criticism of them and a demand for their alteration." Hatred of Others was terrifyingly *natural*: "In this whole connection men give evidence of a readiness for hatred, an aggressiveness, the source of which is unknown, and to which one is tempted to ascribe an elementary character."[33]

Whether this aspect of Freud's analysis is what specifically attracted his first Polish Yiddish translator is unclear, though the editorial front matter did note that Freud's "supremely original theory" allowed analysis of every aspect of both "the individual and the masses." Other precincts of Polish Jewish thought certainly engaged with the prospect that enmity toward out-groups had its own psychic physiognomy. Already in 1924, the Warsaw Bnai Brith lodge—a gathering place for Polonized but Jewishly engaged elites—hosted a lecture titled "The Psychology of Antisemitism." In 1932, the lodge revisited the question in a talk titled "Antisemitism in Light of Psychoanalysis," by Gustav Bychowski.[34] Trained in Zurich and in Vienna under Freud, Bychowski wrote original work on schizophrenia, translated Freud into Polish, and pioneered the application of psychoanalysis to Polish literary creativity in his 1930 study of the Polish Romantic Slowacki. Apart from the 1932 talk at Bnai Brith, Bychowski's itinerary suggests a man with little interest in Jewish matters, and indeed, Bychowski had always been and remained deeply identified with Polishness (he gave the echt Polish name Jan Ryszard to his son, who during World War II would serve—and fall—in the Polish wing of Britain's RAF Bomber Command). Thus, this turn in Bychowski's thought suggests growing concerns about antisemitism among Poland's most Polonized Jews by 1932. I have not found the 1932 text itself, but further data suggest that this engagement with antisemitism came just as Bychowski was turning toward an enduring interest in the broader psychology of hatred and political extremism.[35] Clearly, he was thinking about hatred as a key vector of the larger problem of political psychopathology when, in 1935, he visited Freud in Vienna to ask what sort of "prognosis" Freud offered for human civilization in an era when "waves of hatred shake the foundation of the human world"—and what psychoanalysis could do about it.[36]

More to the point for our purposes, figures across Poland's Jewish *national* intelligentsia—those writing as ethnic Jews for ethnic Jews—also began in this period to explore psychological science's intuition that anti-semitism was something irreducible to calculative reason. Weinreich's 1935 *Veg* included a terse suggestion that antisemitism in Europe among lower-class elements—and also hatred of African Americans among poorer white Americans—served as psychic "compensation" where economic and political equality were denied:

> Anyone a bit familiar with America knows [. . .] [that] the person-ality of the "100%" American is quite determined by the fact he is surrounded by Blacks and immigrants to whom he does not belong. To this not-belonging to a stigmatized community there sometimes accrues a very real value. Take for instance the "poor whites" in the American South. There are Negroes who are richer and more educated than some whites; but the "poor whites" nevertheless re-gard themselves as a thousand times better than *every* Negro. [. . .] The same thing applies today in Germany, where many "pure Aryans" have the satisfaction at least that they feel themselves to be better than Jews. These are national elements that come from *non*-belonging to a community, and these elements must be quite important if they can for a time compensate even for the depriva-tion of this-worldly satisfactions.[37]

Here, the fantastic element was only a pacifying force, a compensa-tory benefit. Other analysts went considerably further in imagining imag-ination as a *motor* of antisemitism, and antisemitism itself as something that pervasively shaped cognition and experience. In 1932, *Miesięcznik Żydowski* carried a translation of the conclusion to Fritz Bernstein's 1926 study *Antisemitismus als Gruppenerscheinung,* widely regarded as the first sustained effort to theorize antisemitism through psychological theory.[38] Bernstein argued that the suffering attendant on the human condition in-evitably generated in all individuals some complex of inadequacy and frustration, and thus also a deep need for a compensatory outlet of blame. At the same time, a variety of factors operated to restrict application of that natural need to blame others so that it would not (generally) be ap-plied to family and other primary social groups whom the individual needed. Concomitantly, the ideal *natural* target of need-driven enmity pro-jection was the nearest outsider group—"neighbors" who are not part of a familial group but whose copresence is thick enough that one can at-tach meaningful pretexts of guilt to justify the projected hatred. Bernstein's was a social psychology that took the social seriously and, disturbingly, suggested that regular intergroup contact *facilitated* pathological projection. Real contact, what Bernstein called "border contact," was key: a particular stranger group was a more "useful" target the *more* common and reiterated one's encounters with it. The ideal condition for intense and continuous group enmity was one in which a minority was widely dispersed among and in frequent contact with the majority group—precisely the Jewish situation.[39]

Bernstein was a Zionist, and *Miesięcznik Żydowski* identified with Zionism. But it was not only Zionists within Poland's Jewish national intelligentsia who began to explore the possibility that antisemitism was a psychic structure of need, desire, and belief that did not simply hide or serve economic calculus. In 1932, the Diasporist Golomb, then still a leading pedagogue in Wilno's Yiddishist school system, wrote three jarring essays about the "psychology of anger" in Poland's leading Yiddish scholarly journal, the *YIVO-Bleter*. Marshaling wide psychological literature, he argued first that aggression was a deeply rooted part of the psyche that operated prerationally and was "more important for the formation of character than all elements of conscious understanding combined." Second, Golomb averred, the development of human civilization had actually greatly *increased* the stimuli to anger and given us greater capacity to feel anger toward *abstractions*—toward, say, imagined enemies. Third, he warned, any given formation of social "environment" and "educational" practice *trains* its young people to direct their anger in some way, and where there were established forms of group prejudice in a given culture, children were "trained" by all sorts of environmental factors to react to certain kinds of people with anger and hate at a *precognitive, embodied* level. Golomb drew a piquant comparison: "In America they used to inculcate in dogs anger toward Negroes. [. . .] It is in this sort of trained form that [the] entire social orientation affects certain strata of the population [in Eastern Europe] toward Jews. In everyday antisemitism there is without question such an unconscious trained anger, instilled through tradition, law-like norms both written and even more so unwritten, which nevertheless are quite consistently applied through social relations generally." Golomb was vectoring on a theory in which antisemitic imagination was not a *rhetoric* laid over interests, or mere compensation, but something embodied and compelling.[40]

Beyond Antisemitism: State Rationality, Nationalism, and State Capture

Even as some within the national intelligentsia began to analyze the Jewish Question in terms of affect rather than interest, others of equally diverse affiliation turned in a different direction: toward the political-*structural* question of how the antisemitism of *some* in the society might affect state actors regardless of where they stood personally on the matter. These questions took shape against the continuing pull of happier assumptions, indebted to both Marxian and liberal traditions, that ultimately policy makers and bureaucracies in modern states were ruled by economistic rationality and that therefore, eventually, policy makers both in the international community and in Poland would come around to full-fledged support of Jewish economic reconstruction (rather than letting Jewish immiseration fester). Such ideas were particularly cherished by Jewish intellectuals with at least one foot in the world of practical social work directed at helping Polish Jews weather the Depression. Moyshe Zilberfarb, a Marxist in ideology but in practice a productivization activist who led the Warsaw branch of the ORT industrial-training organization, captured this outlook in 1930, in this surprisingly optimistic formulation: among those who were "beginning to correctly construe the Jewish national problems and to understand how to peel [them] back to their social-economic core," one could "also find today men of the state [policy makers] who are beginning to grasp that one must not allow the declassing-process to lead to a complete economic ruination of the Jewish population [and] that it is in the interests of the state that it should work against this process with all of its powers." Outside of the USSR, admittedly, the number of such policy makers was not great, but "tomorrow it will grow larger and the day after tomorrow regime-men will sit down and consider plans for the colonization or industrialization of the Jewish population which they are currently allowing to bang its head against the wall."[41] The assumptions here were twofold. First, East European policy makers would seek to solve social problems in a utility-maximizing fashion. Second, this rationality would ultimately dictate a fair shake for Jews if they recast themselves as laborers.

But a very different line of analysis was beginning to vie with this one. In late 1932, Lestschinsky, based in Berlin for some time, returned to Warsaw in the immediate wake of the latest round of antisemitic student riots. This inspired an essay that combined a complex analysis of the character, locations, and trajectories of antisemitism in Poland with attention to the mediations acting on the Sanacja state.[42]

Though in some ways less worried than Levinson or Grinboym that deep changes might be afoot in the nature and reach of antisemitism, Lestschinsky did discern four sites where antisemitism was exerting powerful shaping effects: the recent riots of course, but also the so-called cold pogrom of antisemitic attitudes and unequal treatment in universities, technical schools, professional apprenticeships, and the like; the practices of various state bodies toward Jews; and attitudes gaining ground in the national movement of Poland's most important minority, the Ukrainians, who made up a majority in Poland's southeast. Regarding Polish society at large, Lestschinsky found one "great consolation" amid recent events: the social composition of the recent pogroms indicated to him that while the "broad masses of the Polish people" and even the "working class" were not free of antisemitism, they remained resistant to the Right's ongoing calls for violence. This "great consolation" had its limits: Lestschinsky charged that Poland's socialists had decided to ignore popular anti-Jewish feeling rather than conduct active anti-antisemitic education, that this was gradually "strengthening antisemitism among the worker-masses," and that this "snake will someday repay the sin of Polish socialists with its poison." Yet for now, he concluded, violent antisemitism among Poles remained limited to the middle class and to the "sons of the priests and petty nobility."[43]

But much of Lestschinsky's concern focused not so much on society as on what this unevenly textured and distributed set of anti-Jewish attitudes and political aspirations might do to the state and its policy. Lestschinsky here took a strongly intentionalist view of state policy toward Jews, arguing that multiple levels of the regime were pursuing what he called a "hunger principle": bringing a plethora of statistics about Jewish exclusion from municipal jobs and from state-run or state-backed industries like the tobacco trade, he concluded that the Sanacja regime was intentionally working to exclude Jews from all state-administered industries and institutions, from forestry to teaching in the state schools, even as state involvement in all these branches was growing rapidly. Most damning, he alleged that there could be no doubt based on the most recent events in Lwów that "the regime *wanted,* genuinely *wanted* a pogrom."[44]

Yet strikingly, this was *not* an argument about antisemitism in the state apparatus, but something else. Regarding the state's willful failure to suppress the recent student attacks, he reported two alternative accounts circulating among Polish Jews, neither of which rested on charging the state's ranks with antisemitism per se. One account suggested that those in "the high spheres of Warsaw" felt it expedient to let the "sons of the priests and petty nobility" vent their anger so that it would not be directed at the regime. Another account held that the highest municipal officials in Lwów refused to use force to suppress the riots because they were too closely tied to the students by family and ethnic ties.[45]

In taking these accounts seriously as hypotheses, Lestschinsky's analysis opened up the possibility that even if state elites were indeed making "rational decisions" (rather than, say, acting on personal antisemitism), this would not necessarily dictate a policy of reconstructive aid to Poland's Jews as per Zilberfarb's 1930 hopes. Lestschinsky was vectoring on a different kind of analysis of state rationality that thought in more structural terms about what might be called "state capture," and asked further what that might have to do with mass politics, democracy, and nationalism in an era of scarcity. Here we can see Lestschinsky the erstwhile Marxian Diasporist vectoring on the same insights as Grinboym the Zionist leader—and more generally on a line of thought pronounced in Zionist circles. As we saw in Chapter 1, Alter Druyanov heard the same argument sotto voce in Polish Zionist circles in late 1931. Even as he dramatized the debate between Warsaw and Galician Zionists as to whether Sanacja officials were antisemitic, Druyanov had put his finger on an arguably more important point: it might not matter what the Sanacja officials really felt, because the real point was that Jews were "unwanted" by substantial parts of the larger society, and so the regime had to treat them that way regardless.[46]

Two further analytical specifications of this argument emerged in contemporaries' analyses. One argument was that regime policy toward Jews had been *captured* because, by dint of mass enmity against Jews by a plurality of "real Poles," the regime could not take the *risk* of being seen to "serve" them. This was what Giterman of the Joint Distribution Committee saw to be the new reality in February 1934.[47]

Another version of this argument sidelined antisemitism altogether to ask a different kind of question: Was there something intrinsic to the nation-state and national-*majority* politics in the age of mass democracy and the social state that pushed any regime structurally toward extruding middleman minorities? One especially early articulation of this view appeared from an unlikely source. Avrom Rozin was a typical member of the Yiddishist-Diasporist intelligentsia: early flirtations with Zionism and Territorialism had been pushed aside circa 1905 by a conviction that the future of the Jewish nation would unfold in Eastern Europe and the task of the national intelligentsia was to midwife the necessary recasting of economic, political, and cultural life for this rebirth. Rozin, like Zilberfarb, became a leading activist in productivization work in the 1920s, serving as editor of the ORT-affiliated journal *Virtshaft un lebn* (Economy and Life). In this capacity, he sometimes expressed the same faith as Zilberfarb and other ORT activists: eventually, "men of the state" in Eastern Europe would be moved by "reason" to take up the cause of recasting Jews as a proletarian element, if only because neglecting or actively worsening the Jews' situation would be bad for the larger economy.[48]

But a more worrisome view flickered in and out of Rozin's analyses. In marginal notes written already in 1928, Rozin argued that the new states in Eastern Europe were all converging on policies that, if realized, would bring general misery to East European Jews: "*the economic politics which is being more or less systematically carried out in these lands* [. . .] nationalization, standardization, [. . .] state monopolies, state favoring [. . .] of urban and rural cooperatives." Rather than endorsing an antisemitism thesis, however, Rozin groped toward the possibility that the new East European nation-states were impelled to such measures *regardless* of policy makers' attitudes owing to an intersection of economic-structural factors and a fundamental postwar shift in the relationship of state and society. An underdeveloped agrarian economy ensured a "struggle between village and city." The deeper shift was *democratization* and its effect even in authoritarian states: "The active entry of the broad strata into the social arena, the gathering together of the folk-masses who strive to realize their organized will, protect their collective interests [. . .]— all of this now forces the state to actively involve itself in the struggle of social powers."[49]

In this context, Rozin suggested two dark possibilities regarding state policy. First, a state-capture thesis: even a non-antisemitic regime like Piłsudski's Sanacja might be *made captive* to a national public unwilling to see "their" state help Jews: "Traditions and prejudices [of anti-Jewish sentiment] have much deeper roots [in Poland] and [. . .] the ruling power, even when it is not particularly against us, is at any rate in the best case certainly not for us." Second, Rozin suggested that there was a new structure of social change operating regionally, perhaps globally, that had little to do with antisemitism yet would just as surely devastate

East European Jewry (and any middleman minority): regimes presiding over modern nation-states *had* to meet the demands of the national majority, and regimes presiding over impoverished agrarian economies *had* to squeeze the urban population, which meant "first of all the entirely urban Jewish population." Extrusion of urban "middleman minorities" was built into the nature of a state founded on service to the nation-as-demos just as it was built into the demands of belated capitalist development.[50]

This line of analysis sidelined the question of "how much antisemitism" to focus on how an ensemble of new societal expectations directed toward the state both expanded and constrained the policies it could pursue, especially where some concept of popular democracy was accepted by all and especially in settings where nationalism informed the expectations of social groups and regimes alike. Here, in a mode that could be said to presage postwar analyses like that of Etienne Balibar, the problem of a minority in the age of mass democracy coupled with nationalism, need, and fear is not so much the process of its "othering" per se as the process by which the majority comes to see the state as the protector of *its* communal future (and the future of its children) over that of "strangers" when the chips are down.[51]

The Question of Nationalism

In 1932, *Miesięcznik Żydowski* published "Współczesne ruchy nacjonalistyczne a antysemityzm," a quietly innovative essay on nationalism and the transformation of Polish political culture by Ludwik Oberlaender. Oberlaender's analysis had something to say about the problems that troubled Levinson and Grinboym—how seriously to take antisemitic belief and affect as social powers in their own right, and the question of what precisely gave antisemitism momentum and attraction. And, like Levinson (and Hertz and Kipowa), he also assayed the specifically "Polish Question" of whether antisemitism was moving to the center of Polish political culture. But Oberlaender foregrounded a problematic largely absent from those analyses: the role of European nationalism as a distinctive ideology and machinery that, in its drive to ethnonational unification and mobilization, *naturally* inclined to mobilize and weaponize the deep reservoir of Judeophobia in Christian Europe—and in so doing, was successfully transforming essentially pre-political Judeophobia into a core commitment of mass political culture and consciousness.[52]

The essay took as its framing problem what Oberlaender presented as the unforeseen worsening of antisemitism in recent years. Speaking in terms still redolent of the old Polish liberal tradition, Oberlaender laid some of the blame on the "instincts and urges of the masses"; later in the essay, he extended this claim in a specific indictment of Polish (Catholic) mass culture as "completely uncritical and capable of believing in anything when it comes to Jews. Knowledge about Jews and Jewish matters in Poland is so minimal, the hearts and minds of Poles are filled with so much prejudice and the whole attitude in this issue is so laden with magical thinking that even the wildest, most bizarre, and stupidest idea wins belief without encountering the slightest internal resistance." Here, Oberlaender's analysis was less innovative than that of Levinson and Grinboym: where they hazarded the question of openness to mytho-political antisemitism among Poland's men of letters and governing elites, Oberlaender remained wedded to the traditional progressive and Polish Positivist account; namely, that the problem was the masses' *ignorance:* "Like a man who sees a Chinese or a Black person for the first time in his life and cannot see individual differences in their facial features, so the concept of Jewry in Poland is still uncritically undifferentiated. That is why it is so easy to use the 'Jewish argument' and the Jewish symbol in demagoguery and political rhetoric." Equally indebted to the progressive canon was Oberlaender's conviction that under the right circumstances, instinct could be overcome by "criticism," by reasoned discourse.[53]

But several more unsettled lines of analysis carried the essay beyond these familiar tropes and converged with concerns particularly, if dimly, visible in the analyses of other Zionist observers like Levinson and Grinboym. With regard to antisemitism itself, Oberlaender complicated his own progressive ascription of anti-Jewish sentiment to ignorance by proposing a more complicated historical-anthropological model of why European culture was so prone to antisemitic sentiment. Where a thoroughgoing progressive and socialist like Levinson could confidently aver that in the modern age "religious" antisemitism was actually religious in name only and in fact a mask for secular-rational animus, Oberlaender entertained the darker possibility that the specific Christian vision of Jewish malignity born in an earlier religious age retained much power to shape thought and emotion despite the changes modernity had brought. "We emphasize the concept of a special divergence, because there is such a strong memory of our historical divergence in the consciousness of the nations around us that it acts with its own magical effect and [. . .] traditions on the fantasies and consciousness of the surrounding [cultures]." Perhaps the felt sense of profound Jewish difference had been born initially of theological conflict, but it had inscribed itself so deeply in European culture and habitus that it had become a free-standing intellectual and affectual ("fantastic") cultural reality.[54]

Thinking thus in less reductionist cultural-historical terms about Judeophobia, Oberlaender also diverged from progressives like Levinson in theorizing nationalism as a distinctly *new* structure of intentions and desires in its own right—and as the prime *agent* of antisemitism's transformation into a political power in the 1930s. Nationalism as a term and problem barely made an appearance in Levinson; when it was not liberating in character (as was, in his view, Zionism), it was presumably something indexed to the "Bourbon" reaction against which progressive forces continued to struggle. Oberlaender, by contrast, represented nationalism as an ideology with a new logic of its own: an affect-driven desire to create a unity of will. "Militant nationalism is derived from the instincts and appeals to the instincts. It endeavors to create unity and unanimity in the nation, to absolutely remove differences of opinion."[55]

For Oberlaender the real agents of antisemitism's apotheosis were integral nationalists whose primary concern was to excite national feeling and mobilize the masses who composed the putative nation. Europe's integral nationalists from Hitler to Dmowski focused their ire on Jews not only because they themselves were antisemitic but also with two other expedients in mind. First, the drive to generate a form of affective unity and excitation in the masses demanded an assault on the critical faculty itself. Indeed, the present interwar moment saw a generation of nationalists across the continent working assiduously to suppress the forms of critical thought that alone could counteract historically sedimented prejudice. And Jews were deeply identified with the critical imagination in modernity.

Second, and more concretely, integral nationalists striving for national unity seized on anti-Jewish sentiment because of the fateful historical *accident* of popular Judeophobia. The preaching of antisemitism was a powerful tool of national mobilization because the construction of Jews as the nation's enemy made intuitive sense to so many already, because, in turn, Jewish difference and malignity were already self-evident and deeply felt truths for many Europeans. Nationalists desperate to mobilize the putative nation used antisemitism because it was "easier than any other form of effort and struggle—it attracts the mass, giving them a surrogate for ideals and national goals."[56]

Between Explanation and Prediction before 1935—and Even before 1933

Running through some of these analytic texts was a current of predictive urgency—a sense that matters were changing too fast and becoming too dangerous to allow for the slow social-scientific work of iteratively aligning evidence and explanation. If such predictive urgency was implicit in the strange chronotopic sensibility of Burshtin's representation of antisemitism in his 1931 *Ployne* (see Chapter 1), it was rendered explicit in a text like Lestschinsky's aforementioned essay from late 1932. Alongside his account of how antisemitism and nationalism might intersect in days to come in the dominant Polish political culture, Lestschinsky manifested this extrapolative concern when he turned to the simmering conflict between representatives of the Polish nation-state and insurgent Ukrainian peasants in the kresy. Grimly, Lestschinsky predicted outright ethnic civil war there that would also inevitably target the region's Jews:

> And if you inquire further into the political conflagration now burning around a large part of Polish Jewry, you feel even worse. We mean the conflagration burning across eastern Galicia, Wołyń, and the Minsk region. Yes, it is a real conflagration there and no matter how many hundreds of peasants they shoot and how many dozens of villages they wipe out, they won't manage to put out the national conflagration. [. . .] There will come a time when the struggle will take the form of an open war and open uprisings. Rivers of Polish, Ukrainian, White Russian, and Russian blood will be spilled, and everyone will know why. But it is also certain that Jewish blood will be spilled more than that of anyone else, and no one will know why.[57]

Actually, Lestschinsky offered a twofold take on why the kresy's Jews would likely be targeted despite their essential irrelevance to the conflict. He drew a distinction between the killing that Poles and Ukrainians would inflict on one another and that which all sides would direct at Jews: whereas in the first case "everyone will know what [the killing] is for"— that is, the violence would be a form of political rationality in the terrible sense that ethnic cleansing is a rational politics given zero-sum ethnonationalist assumptions—in the second it would be violence with no coherent political end. However, even as Lestschinsky flirted with an account that would see irrational antisemitism as an independent political driver, he also adduced a different argument: that Jews in the kresy were in fact objectively Polonizers, that the Ukrainians knew and resented this, and that there was thus an objective factor in Jewish behavior that would ensure Ukrainian nationalist violence against them. The indecision in Lestschinsky's account marked a theoretical uncertainty typical of an entire generation of broadly Marxian thinkers about how to construe the causal significance, if any, of ideology independent of interest. But alongside the indecision, there was also a terrifying growing certainty—the niceties of satisfactory explanation aside, too much observational evidence pointed toward danger for one to dismiss it just because one's models could not explain it.

Lestschinsky did not abandon his commitment to causal explanation as, over the next two years. he sought clearer understanding of where Poland, East Central Europe, and the world were headed politically, and what it all meant for Jews. In mid-1934, he sat down to try to draw his observations together systematically, and the text this yielded, "In the Grip of a Transitional Era," anticipated certain lines of revisionist Marxist thought concerning the state and nationalism as non-negligible factors in how capitalism shapes society and polity. Thus, acknowledging that recent decades had given birth to a new kind of professional-managerial middle class that classical Marxism had failed to predict, Lestschinsky suggested that this new class was a key factor explaining why so many states were moving toward fascist forms: in league with the old falling commercial bourgeoisie, this new managerial class was seizing power directly or indirectly in state after state and improvising mixed capitalist-socialist economies in a desperate effort to rescue private property itself. Lestschinsky also gestured to an explanation of why this rescue of capitalism seemed to involve the demonization of some national "Other" in the political realm: seeking to save capitalism within the bounds of this or that state, regimes felt compelled to try to foster cross-class harmony despite real class-interest divides, and one obvious means to do so in a world of national divisions was to gin up competitive antagonisms toward other communities (though *why* weaponizing ethnic difference was an effective strategy, Lestschinsky did not explain).[58]

But Lestschinsky's social-scientific urge toward a satisfactory theory of nationalist political metastasization that would retain materialist insights was shadowed by a different kind of question, an essentially *predictive* one: Where was the Jewish situation in Eastern Europe headed, how far would things go, how long would the new status quo—whatever it would be—remain in place, and what would become of Jews in the process? Lestschinsky signaled this different concern in his very title, "In the Grip of a Transitional Era." Here the question of *time* was made manifest in a double sense: When were already-visible pathologies likely to *crest,* and how long they would last—and what would become of Jews in the meantime? Lestschinsky's essay is shot through with tension between the urge to explain and a drive to take stock of real-life trajectories that he could not yet explain but that he could no longer ignore. It was not only the case that Jews had already been driven into an economic "abyss" far deeper than anything they had seen before, but also that the regimes running Poland, Lithuania, and Latvia were already moving consequentially toward convergent programs of extrusion essentially aimed at rendering this Jewish pauperization permanent and irreversible. In all three countries (to say nothing of Romania), he saw the regimes turning toward policies that aimed not only at "economic isolation and extrusion," with the goal of driving as many Jews to leave as possible, but also minimization of Jewish role in all branches of life that had "spiritual influence on the population" and a cultural politics of extruding Jews from the nation's civic and cultural life (while at same time destroying their separate national life so that they did not affront the nation with their difference).

To this he added a series of sharp observations about Polish and Baltic political societies. Jews had now been abandoned by most of the various freedom-fighters that had fought the old Russian autocracy alongside them. Only the "pure-proletarian wing" of the old "army" continued to adhere to the "old freedom-ideals." The peasantry had turned rightward, while the victory of the "middle classes and of the middle-classes' ideology"—by which he meant the very fact that the intelligentsia, middle-class, and aristocracy leadership of the liberation movements had managed to build independent states—had "even more fully torn away the petit-bourgeois masses from the proletarian wing." If at least the socialist Left had not abandoned its humanist opposition to ethnic hate, this was small consolation, because the Left was not powerful enough to make a difference. It was relatively small in Eastern Europe for developmental reasons, had been subjected to distressingly effective repressions in all three states, and had not yet found any effective means to win the struggle for political hegemony in "the newly arisen postwar situation." Finally, there was the dread fact, which could not easily be explained but certainly could not be ignored, that the rising generation poised to take power in Eastern

Europe was "in its fundamental makeup" given to "national egotism [. . .], chauvinism and cruelty."[59]

In the final analysis, there was no *time* for a final analysis. Lestschinsky clearly hoped to help chart the way to a new political sociology of capitalist society. He seems to have retained his socialist faith that the brutal rescue-effort on behalf of capitalism would ultimately fail. But in the meantime? Amid all the confusion, three things seemed overwhelmingly likely. First, the worsening of the Jewish situation in Europe was not some accident or blip but itself a result of deep conjunctural processes. Second, highly interventionist states manned by fearful, desperate, and increasingly depraved elites would continue to seek to reorder society, not only with the consent of dominant parts of those societies but indeed in response to their demands. The final likelihood was that this would not end tomorrow and, hence, that East European Jewry would not emerge unscathed from this situation's prolonged "grip."

Lestschinsky was groping toward extrapolative thinking—risk thinking—alongside or in place of social-scientific explanation. And he was not the only one. In May 1934, Mojżesz Kleinbaum (later Moshe Sneh), a young Warsaw-trained medical doctor and emerging left-leaning Zionist publicist and activist, offered a concise but penetrating analysis of a large-scale outbreak of anti-Jewish violence in Białystok and several other towns, which he took as a revelation both for Jews and for the Polish state:

> The recent attacks against Jews in various parts of Poland show clearly how large and powerful is the wave of anti-Semitism which is flooding virtually the entire land. Not only we Jews were surprised at the great strength possessed by extreme Polish nationalism and which has suddenly manifested itself before our eyes, casting upon us a fear for tomorrow. The security services too, which are after all best able to assess the actual composition of the significant political forces in our society, have only now in the face of these anti-Semitic excesses discovered, for example, that there is such a large national-extremist youth (NARA) organization in Bialystok.

In particular, the events revealed just how powerful antisemitic currents were among Polish youth. They also bespoke the influence of the Nazi example. Among the young, "the Hitlerist regime [. . .] calls forth wonder and excitement." Across the Polish political scene as a whole, the influence of the German case was not surprising because "the Jewish question is in truth much sharper and weightier [here in Poland] than in Germany."[60]

Kleinbaum was arguing that the treatment of Poland's Jews as a *problem*—an approach long since normalized in Polish political life—had made it inevitable that substantial parts of the Polish public should take interest in Nazi Germany's consequential answers to its Jewish Question. And here Kleinbaum shifted into a predictive mode. It had been revealed that substantial numbers of Polish youth found the Nazi example inspiring. In general, fascism was emerging victorious around the world. Did it make any sense to bet that it would *not* have ever-greater influence in Poland too?

The threat embodied in a rising generation of youth imbued with antisemitic ideals was on the horizon, and there was also a more immediate coming reality with which Jews would have to deal. The antisemitic "plague" had now "altogether overspilled the boundaries of the Endecja. It has seized the United Peasant Party." In a larger sense, "the ever-growing woes of the impoverished Polish masses on the one hand and the influence of the so-called 'spirit of the times' on the other have now suddenly placed the leaders of the Sanacja face-to-face with the accomplished fact of strongly developed anti-Semitic sensibilities in the village and in the cities."

In these circumstances, antisemitism's further spread was no longer the only danger; the reach already achieved had now produced a structural change in political life. Now, even many elements still opposed and immune would recognize that fighting it was ill advised: "We have to recognize that no one in Poland [. . .] is willing to take upon himself the thankless struggle against anti-Semitism." Kleinbaum saw little hope that the organized Left would do much, leaving aside the question of whether it could even if it wanted. Granted, "the PPS is itself a victim of the antisemitic mood that is pulling workers from its ranks, because it will not collaborate with the antisemitic agitation," but "it is too weak and lacks the courage to begin a counteroffensive against that agitation. The PPS has responded with passivity to all direct attacks on it—how then can one demand of it activism regarding, of all things, the Jewish question which touches it only indirectly?"[61]

The only power in Polish society that *could* do anything to repress antisemitism as a force was "the government and the government camp." But, Kleinbaum continued, "here there has been a small misunderstanding:

the Sanacja has no desire to open an internal war against anti-Semitism. It is afraid that it will be accused of love for the Jews." Here Kleinbaum moved toward a theory of state capture as the chief danger facing Jews rather than antisemitism's spread per se. The Sanacja, Jews had to understand, faced a difficult choice of its own. "The accomplished fact of strongly developed anti-Semitic sensibilities in the village and in the cities" forced the Sanacja to recognize that antisemitism might give the Endecja "the street," and this it could not allow. It faced a stark choice: "Either begin a vast enlightenment campaign against anti-Semitism in Polish society and—after a full eight-year delay—begin to educate the Polish masses in the spirit of justice, human equality, and friendship between nations, or itself take over anti-Semitism, take over the antisemitic sensibilities and bring them within the loose boundaries of the large and motley May Camp." And indeed, Kleinbaum noted, there are already "large and influential" parts of the regime "that are inclined to go [the latter] route." The evidence thereof included Bogusław Miedziński's "famous speech" in which this head of the Sanacja fraction in the Sejm proclaimed that the Sanacja's tolerant relationship to the Jews stemmed only from "political necessity"; a new industrial law excluding Jewish bus lines although Jews had developed that industry; "antisemitic slogans of the Sanacja in many municipal elections"; "the sharpened antisemitic tone of the Sanacja Youth Legion youth"; and "enthusiastic articles" in the regime-affiliated *Gazeta polska* regarding Endek youth.[62] This last was the most significant, Kleinbaum reasoned. The Sanacja could never make peace with the Endecja, it might not be willing to let rioters beat Jews in the streets of Białystok, but it *had* to meet the youth where it was. If it had to choose between winning the (real) nation's youth and protecting Poland's Jews, the choice was obvious and inevitable.

Kleinbaum did not accuse the Sanacja as a whole of having already fully embraced this cynical path, but the salient fact—and here again he shifted into predictive mode—was that the latter path was far easier and far more expedient for a regime already stretched beyond its powers, and all the more so when something as vital as the youth of the nation—the *real* nation—was at stake. The apposite case was not that of Nazi victory in Germany but the more recent case of Austria in February, where the clerical-nationalist Dollfuss had recognized that the only way to beat the rising Austrian Nazi Right in the internecine struggle for support from "patriotic" Austrians was to steal Nazi thunder by crushing the "Bolsheviks and Jews" and embracing ultranationalism. In Poland, the Endek

Right was not necessarily fated to win; the Sanacja might still outflank it. But if it could only do so by meeting rising antisemitism halfway, it would; if the path of least resistance was adopting anti-Jewish rhetorics and policies rather than trying to uproot the sentiments that made such policies seem commonsensical, that was the path the Sanacja would take.

Kleinbaum ended by insisting that regardless of the grim situation, Polish Jews had to mobilize politically to fight for their position through politics, in the Sejm and in public opinion. There were suggestions in his article that he shared the worry that Polish Jews might be so overwhelmed by the situation he was laying bare that they would give up on struggling for a better future in Poland with what tools they had. But Kleinbaum did not pull punches; Jews had to expect a "true antisemitic flood."[63]

Importantly, some Polish Jewish analysts came to similar conclusions before 1933 or 1934 as well. Oberlaender's 1932 analysis culminated, with a certain progressive brio and irony, in a surprisingly optimistic vision: antisemitism would actually prove, he was sure, painfully counterproductive for all those Polish, German, and other nationalists who sought to put it to use. One could "organize the mass with antisemitism for a time," but antisemitism's appeal to the basest instincts, its immediate gratification of greed and violent desires, its enjoining of all involved to incessant falsehood would "reduce the effective and long-term level of the political and social culture of the masses" by accustoming them to the pursuit of primitive desires. A mere surrogate for real national values, antisemitism would undermine the masses' capacity to make real sacrifices or attain to national creativity.

But this happy vision of antisemitic nationalism's self-immolation via success did not lead Oberlaender to an optimistic conclusion regarding *Jewish* fate. Oberlaender too was thinking about time. Strategies of mobilization around antisemitism undertaken by Europe's Hitlers and Dmowskis might backfire, but only eventually. In the meantime, what would Polish Jewry's fate be? Oberlaender, like Levinson, wrote with respect for the Polish national tradition: "There was a time in Poland when anti-Semitism was doomed to staying on the farthest outskirts of the culture. It simply could not get through the wall of Polish humanism." But two things had changed, with grave consequences. First, political and cultural life was now being democratized—the masses were now entering politics—and would inevitably mean the rapid transformation of Polish cultural life: "They are starting to create—and they will create—their own new culture." Second, at that very moment, organized, confident anti-semitic nationalist propagandists were working assiduously to "break the wall, and insert anti-Semitism into Polish cultural and everyday life [. . .] to strike consciously on this new front of Polish culture." The antisemitic project would eventually collapse under the weight of its own empty promises; but in the meantime, there was no reason to think that assiduous nationalist efforts to weaponize antisemitism would let up soon, or that these would not succeed in creating a toxic environment for East European Jewish life, albeit of as yet indeterminable toxicity.[64]

Two notes of conclusion are in order. First, one way to understand the especially strong extrapolative and predictive drive of figures like Oberlaender, Kleinbaum, and Lestschinsky is to understand it as an emanation of something contemporary historians generally regard as a pathology in itself, namely their own nationalism. These were intellectuals who felt obligated to guide "the Jewish people," and guidance meant trying to help one's people understand what was coming. Latski recognized this about Lestschinsky when he noted that the latter's "difficult calling" was to teach this intelligentsia to think from reality rather than theory. For this, "of course they will curse you, but pay it no heed—you bear in your heart a higher tribunal, before which you will be called to give an account." That higher tribunal was, of course, "the Jewish nation" and its needs.[65]

Second, in establishing both the contents of a new Jewish critical analysis and its extrapolative urgency, this chapter throws a different light on Chapters 1 and 2 and on Chapters 5, 6, and 7, because although the thought and work of sociological thinkers is hardly typical, the trajectories of these intellectuals were *not* foreign to the rest of Polish Jewry. As we can see in the case of young people already encountered, like Astour, Binyomen R., and Forget-Me-Not, not only worry but also searching *thought* about growing antisemitism, illiberal nationalism, and extrusion politics could be found among "ordinary people." Furthermore, as we can see from the figures highlighted in Chapter 1, not only the analytical impulse but also the extrapolative one was ambient. Chapter 5 turns our attention back to the grass roots, and especially to young people, to develop a clearer picture of a turn in Polish Jewish political sensibility from the certainties of ideology to skepticism and urgent inquiry. In a larger sense, this multilayered awareness of the political dangers threatening Polish Jewish well-being was a framing condition of the kinds of thought about what was to be done that will concern us in Chapters 6 and 7.

The history of analysis and extrapolation elaborated here helps clarify that this search for practical answers in culture or politics was driven not only by a developing understanding of the dangers already visible around Jews but also by a probabilistic calculus that compelled some to ask questions like: How much time remained in which to act? What resources and options did one really have? and What might one have to abandon in order to salvage anything?

5

From Ideology to Inquiry

As she traversed Jewish Poland between 1928 and 1930 for Palestine's socialist-Zionist newspaper *Davar,* Rokhl Faygenberg observed a voluble discussion on the Warsaw–Otwock train line. "A young man wearing a *kashketl* grew heated amongst his Jewish listeners and did a bit of accounting: if the Bund's war for Jewish proletarianization continues to bear fruit at the current rate, it will take (given the number of Jews in Poland) 46,000 years. And couldn't a Jewish majority in Palestine also be achieved in the course of 46,000 years?" The young man's Hasidic garb reveals someone from the traditional sector, certainly neither a Zionist "New Jew" nor a Bundist "conscious worker." Yet his challenge—delivered, undoubtedly, to an audience that included other traditional Jews, given Otwock's popularity as a Hasidic resort town—bespoke clear understanding of core Bundist and Zionist arguments about how the Jewish problem could be solved. For the Bund, the solution would come in two stages. Ultimately, Marxist revolution would build a socialist society free of prejudice, but in the meantime, Polish Jewry would be pushed into the proletariat by the self-overcoming logic of capitalism itself, and would thus take part in the revolution and merit its fruits. The young man in the *kashketl* parried this vision by invoking the still-dominant Zionist argument for how Jews could win sovereignty in Mandate Palestine: mass colonization under British auspices would produce a Jewish majority in Palestine, which would then be able to demand Jewish sovereignty on democratic-majoritarian grounds.[1]

Perhaps literary license was involved in this vignette; no doubt Faygenberg did not choose at random to record this pro-Zionist argument for readers in Palestine. But no less relevant is something that she was far from alone in registering: in unlikely sites of Polish Jewish life, old ideological certainties were coming into question and a new posture of skeptical inquiry was emerging. Faygenberg's miniature also speaks to a question that consumed contemporaries: Were Polish Jews, gripped by a sense of crisis, being driven toward irrationality, escapism, and fantasy? Or were they being driven toward skepticism and critical inquiry? Max Weinreich, having recognized that Polish Jewish youth were consumed by the sense that Polish Jews would be denied a decent future, spent the last third of his *Der veg tsu unzer yugnt* marshaling Austrian and American social psychology to argue the former. As we saw in Chapter 3, Weinreich's study of the emerging culture of doubt among Jewish youth offered real insight into how felt futurelessness could recast the consciousness of members of a targeted minority. But as to *why* so many Polish Jewish young people saw their only hope in a politics of exit, Weinreich turned to reductionist psychologism: an extended assertion that Polish Jewish youths' mass turn to Zionist and (to a much lesser degree) Communist politics derived from a prerational need for *compensations* in a situation where real solutions were unavailable. As one group of scholars puts it: "Weinreich's diagnosis of the situation facing Jewish youth in Poland was psychological immaturity: they were simply running away from their problems."[2]

Weinreich did not take this stance because he thought Polish Jews faced no real problems. Nor did he believe that there *were* clear political solutions the youth were overlooking. Though Weinreich had been a Bundist since his youth, by the 1930s he clearly saw little hope of revolutionary salvation. Instead, he sought amelioration. He grew interested in the ideas of Booker T. Washington, which he seems to have read as an argument about why embattled minorities might do better to prioritize communal economic self-help over political contestation with a majority bent on maintaining political supremacy through violence. So, too, he hailed the late-life preachments of the Bundist Arkady Kahan-Virgily that Jewish youth should turn to agriculture—heterodox notions for Marxists suspicious of "voluntarism" and anxious to see Jews become urban proletarians. But Weinreich had no illusions that a turn to agriculture was a cure-all. Rather, recognizing that there *weren't* any sweeping fixes to the Jewish Problem *was* maturity.[3]

For those who were coming to share the sense that Polish Jews really had few resources with which to address their problems, old questions of Jewish political reason took new form. Two questions of reason now loomed large. The more far-reaching one intertwined prediction, political sociology, and ethics: How should Jews direct whatever resources and energies they could muster? What was the best use of their limited collective powers? What Faygenberg's vignette and Weinreich's condemnatory account of Polish Jewish irrationality in *Veg* demonstrate is that a second, more narrowly empirical question accompanied this one: Were Polish Jews *thinking* rationally in the sense of thinking about means and ends, asking sensible questions, and seeking clear answers? Or were they taking flight into realms of fantasy or the wish for a deus ex machina? As we saw in Chapter 3, Weinreich was not the only observer convinced that Polish Jews were in the grip of irrational thinking; figures as various as the Diasporist Golomb and the Zionist Perelman shared his concern.

But other observers were pulled toward a different view. Though Weinreich's interlocutor Lestschinsky also sometimes remonstrated against Polish Jewish "panic," he increasingly registered the *opposite* sense: that much of what Yiddishist intellectuals like himself were wont to condemn as panic actually expressed realism and rationality at the grass roots. In early 1933, the Warsaw weekly *Literarishe Bleter,* Poland's leading journal of Yiddish letters, invited a frank debate about the state of secular Yiddish culture. No doubt the *Bleter*'s editor, literary critic Nakhman Mazyl, hoped to elicit practical suggestions about how to shore up the Yiddish cultural sphere, for even as secular Yiddish culture was blooming aesthetically, signs of its failure to secure a stable mass base of devotees had grown too strong to ignore. But actually, Lestschinsky's response in the journal shunted these questions of culture aside. His essay "More Open and More Honest" did sound standard nationalist worries about the death of the Jewish national spirit. But threaded throughout the essay and forcefully stated at its close was a different argument: that the Polish Jewish masses' indifference to Yiddish culture and readiness to assimilate was a manifestation of desperate practical *rationality*.

Lestschinsky's account of what was transpiring in European societies in the era of nationalism and capitalist crisis, examined in Chapter 4, was also reconfiguring his assessment of Polish Jews' individual choices. If "assimilation, or more accurately the flight from our own culture, our own language, our own forms of life" was "proceeding with giant steps" in Poland or Romania, it was not because new opportunities were opening up before Jews as they had a century ago in Western Europe. On the contrary, "rejection and extrusion of Jews from the surrounding society" had "never been so powerful" as now. But this made for a cruel "irony of our epoch": the growing economic-cum-communitarian nationalism and anti-Jewish sentiment throughout Eastern and Central Europe compelled each individual Jew to maximize whatever slim chance each might have to "fool the world around us, dissolve into it and disappear."[4]

And as his account of what was going wrong in central European societies grew more ramified, Lestschinsky was also pulled toward seeing the other lobe of Polish Jewish "pathology"—mass conviction that there was no good future to be hoped for in Poland and concomitant interest in exit—as sociologically informed, if perhaps only "felt," rationality:

> And do the Jewish masses not feel that with the passing of the current "humane" generation [of state-men, the ruling stratum] [. . .] and with the rise of a new younger generation [. . .] for whom personal and national egoism, chauvinism and cruelty constitute its fundamental makeup—do the Jewish masses not feel instinctively that with the rise of this new generation there must come even harder and darker times? Is it therefore surprising that the Jewish masses are quite disappointed in their past hopes which so tragically and so quickly expired, and that they are so pessimistic and so dark in their outlook on the near future in the diaspora?[5]

The inner oscillation in how these observers assessed political reason at the grass roots remains visible also in our historiography. The past few years have brought a wave of revisionist histories of Polish Jewish political culture in the 1930s that upend old models of a Polish Jewry stably divided into socialist, Zionist, Orthodox, and assimilationist camps. This work, embodied with particular force in the studies of Kamil Kijek, Irith Cherniavsky, Daniel Heller, and Rona Yona, demonstrates clearly that for a growing mass of Polish Jews, particularly youth, the old ideological faiths of the 1920s lost their hold and a search for new moorings became essential. But this work also leaves open the question as to what began to replace those old faiths—or rather, it suggests two very different answers.

On the one hand, this new work collectively foregrounds a picture of Polish Jewish youth culture as permeated by *fantasies* of self- and world-transformation. Heir to the late Ezra Mendelsohn's insistence on searching as the central feature of interwar Polish Jewish politics, this work in some ways recapitulates his "suggest[ion]" that in the 1930s "the appeal of modern Jewish politics" increasingly became a matter of *myth,* to be tapped by competing movements' "promotion of heroic models of activism." In the hothouse environment of wrenching economic collapse (Yona) or out of the intolerable psychic-cum-political impasse experienced by a generation of Jewish youth ever more deeply Polonized but thus ever more wounded by hateful rejection (Kijek and Heller), Polish Jews on this model were driven from ideology to myth. Thus, in his account of the explosive growth of Revisionist Zionism's Betar youth movement in Poland, Heller argues that beneath the familiar slogans calling for the immediate creation of a Jewish state and mass aliyah, Betar youth culture pulsed with a deep attraction to Polish nationalism's cult of heroism, vitalism, and martial valor and with a frustrated aspiration to share in that cult. Like all these works, Kijek's uniquely encompassing sociology of Polish Jewish youth in the 1930s, based especially on the corpus of YIVO autobiographies that constituted Weinreich's source base, is far too complex to be reduced to any one conclusion, but certainly one of his emphases (visible in his very title "The Children of Modernism") is that 1930s Polish Jewish youth—like other youth cohorts around the globe—were drawn to visions of transformation through radical direct action.[6]

Yet the powerful revisions of these scholars also point in a different direction as they move us past old movement-and-ideology histories toward a different feature of the newly emergent postideological Polish Jewish political culture: the emergence of what we might call a culture of skepticism, inquiry, and judgment. In his 1933 essay cited in the Introduction, Mikhl Astour disagreed with those who charged that his generation was falling into unreasoning "panic." He insisted that his generation understood its situation more realistically than the adults: "We are already living in the catastrophe, but the older generation of the Jewish intelligentsia cannot adequately grasp this—it is too immersed in ideological-theoretical problems. It is much easier for the youth to orient itself amidst the confusion: that which for the older generation is even now still just theory has become for us reality." Freed of old ideological certainties (however unhappily), Astour's Jewish youth were not instead dupes of compensatory drives or a search for new myths. They were not fantasists but inquirers.[7]

The rest of this chapter analyzes a range of ethnographically rich sources that bespeak new intensities of skepticism, open-ended argument, and critical inquiry among some Polish Jews at least sometimes, though certainly not all or all the time. All of these sources concern the experience of young Jews on the cusp of their twenties, if not still younger. This may suggest some real generational differences, and this view has loomed large in much recent work; but I suspect that there is a great deal of mere accident to this. We happen to have a uniquely rich corpus of material about the recasting of political sensibility among young Polish Jews, but this is because a whole series of competing actors, from the Yiddishist-Diasporist YIVO to the Zionist Hehalutz organization, took "the youth" as a central focus of concern and inquiry for the obvious reason that, as Weinreich acknowledged in his 1935 *Veg,* "he who has the youth, has the future." The sources that command my attention here are indeed for the most part either connected to the YIVO youth research project or are reports by Zionist emissaries from Palestine who, amid repetition of socialist-Zionist boilerplate, reported insightfully on aspects of Polish Jewish youth culture they found surprising and unsettling. But the absence of similar sustained data collection about older Polish Jews hardly suggests that most remained cheerfully certain about previously held views. Certainly, sources like those surveyed in Chapters 1, 2, 4, and soon Chapters 6 and 7 strongly suggest otherwise. The sources on the thinking of young people examined in this chapter placed alongside those we have seen and those yet to come suggest a transformation in Polish Jewish political culture that we have too long underplayed: a large-scale shift toward skepticism about all existing ideologies and an urgent desire for real information about the world's trajectory, about the situation in Poland and Palestine, and about what real options one had, if any.

A Generation of Inquirers:
Binyomen R.'s Auto-anthropology

We have already had several occasions to engage the commentary on Weinreich's *Veg tsu unzer yugnt* by the young Jewish man calling himself Binyomen R. from the provincial town of Bielsk-Podlaski. It offers, as I noted, powerful confirmation from below that many Polish Jews were gripped by deepening doubts about their future in Poland, that those doubts were driven by political woes as much as by economic ones, and that those doubts drove many of his peers—and Binyomen himself—to make new political choices. Here we will see that Binyomen's commentary offers more still. When read contrapuntally with his especially rich YIVO autobiography of the previous year to sort out where the author spoke from ideology and where from experience, Binyomen's testimony offers us access to a quiet transformation in *how* he and many of his peers sought to arrive at political understanding and judgment. Some did so, it demonstrates, not as convinced adherents of an ideology or devotees of a myth, or as psychological automatons driven by raw, prerational needs they could not comprehend, or again as people making a panicked, thoughtless leap, but as people ever hungrier for real information and critical insight even as they became more desperate to find some way forward.[8]

One thing of which Binyomen was sure was that Weinreich's insistent effort to reduce *all* youth political thought to a story of an irrational search for psychological "compensations" was wrong. Binyomen did not dismiss psychological argumentation outright, nor rule out the possibility that the declared motivations for a course of action might actually be less significant causes of behavior than occluded motives invisible to the actor. Speaking observationally, Binyomen agreed with Weinreich, for instance, that when younger adolescents joined youth organizations with ramified ideological programs—organizations like Ha-Shomer ha-Tsair in particular—they did so much less because they had processed and embraced this ideology than because of a desire to belong, connections with friends, or homosocial attraction.

Yet Binyomen dissented sharply from Weinreich's sweeping claim that psychological factors fully explained the youths' mass turn to political organizations—that the mass influx of youth into such organizations reflected the workings of psychological needs ("libido") over both ideological suasion and calculated choices (both of which Weinreich lumped under the term "logic"). Binyomen countered that this did not apply to "organizations that recruit in late adolescence"—by which he meant Hehalutz, the Zionist elephant in the room.

In the case of Hehalutz, he contended, neither psychological motivations nor ideological attractions were primary: "One has to search in order to find those who enter the organization due to an abstract ideal." Rather, most of those who joined Hehalutz did so "because of bad conditions." Binyomen adduced specifics from his own experience. He outlined, for instance, a complex sociology of the interactions of gender and ideology. Whereas young women who joined the Marxian-Freudian Ha-Shomer ha-Tsair movement were full of "temperament" and sought the intense self-fashioning demanded by the movement, "90%" of the young women who joined the less ideologically baroque Hehalutz movement did so in sober hopes of escaping their "bad conditions." Among young men, the situation was somewhat different; Binyomen granted that a higher proportion of the young men joining Hehalutz seemed motivated by ideological enthusiasm than was the case among the young women thinking overwhelmingly in practical terms. But, he added, this was only a difference of proportion: "One can say the same about the boys too, though in a much lower [dis]proportion." That is, among the young male joiners too, *most* were driven by desperation to leave Poland and practical calculation that Hehalutz was the most promising vehicle thereto: the "shared logic here is not the program [ideology], but rather the bad conditions which drive them to a sociopolitical reaction." Binyomen went on to grant that once one joined, less rational and more compensatory (or "libidinous") factors could come into play. He agreed with Weinreich's charge that the intoxications of hora dancing and Hebrew group song culture in Hehalutz played a role for many members. But he remained convinced that in Hehalutz Zionism and indeed in Communism and Revisionism, the primary drive to join was "dissatisfaction" with one's lot, and "psychological feeling and sentiments only point the way toward *which* [group] of dissatisfied [people] one should join."[9]

Significantly, Binyomen's dissent from Weinreich's psychologism was not the end point of his critique. Binyomen also argued that when Weinreich did think seriously about youth politics, the older scholar misunderstood the essential trajectory thereof. It was not just that Weinreich failed to see that the old four-camp model of equally convinced and equally siloed Zionists, Diasporist-socialists, Orthodox Jews, and integrationists no longer held for most Polish Jewish youth. Rather, Weinreich did not understand that ideological thinking *itself* was on the decline. Perhaps at one time young Jews had chosen an ideology and followed its dictates, but now what was more common was an open-eyed relationship to all of the ideological visions bequeathed by the 1920s: the Jewish young person today "quickly becomes independent in his thinking." Binyomen suggested that Weinreich's very choice to call Jewish youths' mass influx into movement-affiliated youth organizations a form of "politics" overstated the role of ideology in Polish Jewish youth culture. Actually, none of the youth organizations young Jews were joining in large numbers could really be called "political organizations," with the exception of the Bund's Tsukunft organization on the left and the *partial* exception of the Revisionist Betar on the right. What Binyomen meant by this peculiar claim was rendered clearer by the latter case. True, Betar preached an ideology (which he deemed "fascist"). But in fact, many of those who joined Betar did so only in the hopes of getting an aliyah Certificate. And this was even truer of those joining Hehalutz: "Is the struggle between the League for a Laboring Land of Israel and the Revisionist movement a class-struggle? It's a 'secret' that absolutely everyone knows that it is first and foremost a struggle for Certificates."

Furthermore, Binyomen reported that the past two years or so had brought a fundamental transformation in how his peers related to political-ideological argument of *any* sort. "About a year and a half ago" (that is, mid to late 1933), the youth of Bielsk had undergone a double process of political upheaval. At the time, there had been a massive shift of youth support to either Communist or Zionist affiliation, marked by the fact that "a large part of the Bund went over to the Reds [or] ran over to Hehalutz." Initially, this shift had been accompanied by a notable upswing in the intensity with which the young Jews of the town wrestled with the movements' competing claims: "that was a time of large *masuvkes* [Yiddish/Polish: mass meetings] by the [Communists] and large *asifot* [Hebrew: mass meetings] by [Hehalutz]." But "today, interest in that has died out."

What did it mean to say that that interest had died out? One thing Binyomen deemed clear was that Jewish young people's faith in the ideological promises and predictions of the various movements was collapsing. This was especially obvious regarding the Communists: "A year and a half ago, I often heard from devotees of *Unzer veg* that quite soon the Red banner will flutter over the municipal council building ('today, when the world is pregnant with the social revolution, Jewish youth concerns itself with Zionism [. . .] and other such nonsense,'—that for example is what Yoelke Naymark said to me then). Today, even among [the Communists] such 'Hasidic' deep faith has grown much weaker."

And what was emerging in this space left by the evaporation of faith in the capacity of the old political ideologies to serve as a guide? First, Binyomen insisted that the chief factor "driving" the youth was neither "compensation" nor ideology but a search for some—for any—better future. Weinreich's bitter thoughts regarding "individualistic" motivations for joining parties (by which he meant joining Zionist movements that afforded some possibility of actual exit) led Binyomen to reflect once again on the centrality of *thinking about the future* among his peers. In Bielsk, he reiterated, both the choice of Communism and the choice of (Hehalutz) Zionism had everything to do with the sense of a foreclosed future. Interestingly, perhaps surprisingly, these varieties of future thinking varied somewhat because, on the whole, the Communist youth were in a better economic situation than most of those who were choosing Hehalutz:

I can say with certainty that our Reds around here are for the most part in a good material situation, at any rate by contemporary standards. They have work and earn something—granted, the earnings are only enough for one person and there is no way to get married with such earnings. Fear about the future expresses itself in their case in their hopes for the social revolution. On the other hand, the largest part of Hehalutz right now consists of an element which cannot wait long, suffers from chronic unemployment, and they cannot be lulled with future-music, they are ready to emigrate now.

Bielsk Communist youth could locate and even quantify their foreclosed futures: they earned enough to live but not to marry. For many of Binyomen's fellow halutzim, the foreclosure of the future was more total: their futurelessness had no discernible horizon. The masses of youth attracted to Zionism included the most materially desperate and in a larger sense those "who are dissatisfied with their situation, those who have no future here before them, who don't believe that they have any prospect here of a better life."

Second, Weinreich's reflections about what factors could account for the common phenomenon of young Jews moving restlessly from one political camp to another provoked Binyomen to reflect on a notable divide in the *degree* of political consciousness or interest among those who did so. "I think that among those who change parties, one has to distinguish two types: typical careerists and those who are truly searching for a path in life and go through much psychic wrestling [. . .]. I am not speaking here about simple 'dark masses' of Bundists and Reds who ran over to Hehalutz because of material motives. I think that the [YIVO] youth-research [project] must do much more to shed light on those who change parties because they are honestly and truly seeking a path." Readers might see something self-regarding in this distinction, but that is not entirely fair: Binyomen himself wrestled openly with the question of whether by Weinreich's or indeed his own standards he was a "careerist" too. More importantly, this differentiation between those who changed parties for "careerist" reasons (that is, pragmatic, individualistic reasons) and those for whom this reflected intense political searching should not obscure a commonality between them: both the "careerists" and "those who change parties because they are honestly and truly seeking a path" were neither followers of an ideology nor creatures of their urges and compensatory drives, but people seeking in some basic sense to think rationally, calculatively, and practically about what might help them.

Once again, the unique doubleness of the records Binyomen left us—the 1935 reflections inspired by Weinreich's *Veg* but also a 1934 autobiography-diary—is essential: here, too, the evidence of the 1934 autobiography both resonates with and empirically grounds the analytical claims of the 1935 text.[10] This is true of Binyomen's claims about the reach of exitism; as the reader will recall, the 1934 text records without adornment the sudden growth of Bielsk's Hehalutz branch from thirty to seventy members in 1933 and its more recent decline to fifty, as well as the virtual collapse of the local Bundist Tsukunft youth group as members left en masse for either Hehalutz or the Communists. But as regards the question at hand here, in a sense, the most striking evidence the autobiography brings lies in its silences. Nowhere in the autobiography does Binyomen express any sort of quiddity about the motivations of most of his peers moving in either of those directions. It was self-evident to him as he wrote in 1934 (and thus before he was moved to respond to Weinreich) that the majority of his peers who were turning to Zionism were driven not by Zionist ideals but by a pained search for something that might help them. Thus it makes sense, further, that whereas Binyomen was moved at times to discuss real ideological commitments in a few of his Communist and Revisionist acquaintances (impressing him as idealism in the former case and disgusting him as fascism in the latter), he had little to say about parallel phenomena in the socialist-Zionist Hehalutz, the very movement he ultimately chose to join. In essence, there was little to say about ideology within Hehalutz because what drove people like Binyomen to join it was overwhelmingly exitism, whether driven by raw despair or by considered judgment about the situation in Europe.

Binyomen's 1934 autobiography attests in equally pervasive fashion that among his wide circle of acquaintances, there were few who fully embraced the postulates of any of the competing ideological systems that ostensibly so permeated East European Jewish life. Binyomen had a special term for those few, whatever their ideological confession: "idealists" or "activists." What is clear from his autobiography is that they were the smallest "group." He found them more among the Communists than anywhere else.

The vast majority of Bielsk youth were not idealists but rather of two other types in Binyomen's experience. The majority simply cast about for a chance at a future through some sort of "exit." A minority—but not a vanishingly small minority like that of the idealists—were politically "conscious" but not ideologically convinced. They were, like Binyomen, "searchers." The 1934 autobiography demonstrates a trajectory of ever-multiplying contacts with such searchers, whom Binyomen found in every political camp and, even more so, moving restlessly *among* those camps like himself. What characterized his multiplying circles of "conscious" acquaintances was a shared impulse toward political inquiry and desire for intellectually serious discussion outside bounds of party affiliation.

Unless we assume that Jewish life in Bielsk was some freak exception, Binyomen's 1934 combined autobiography-diary suggests powerfully that, in the 1930–1934 period, substantial numbers of Polish Jewish young people were engaged in an intellectually searching and serious effort to comprehend their political situation. As the autobiography makes clear, Binyomen's own political education from early adolescence through writing the autobiography at age nineteen or twenty involved both much reading of political journals and newspapers of widely disparate outlook in Yiddish, Hebrew, and Polish and much sustained discussion with many other young Jewish interlocutors belonging to multiple camps or moving between them. It was through schoolmates with whom Binyomen had been connected from earliest childhood that he first encountered both politics as such and political dissensus. In the autobiography, a discussion of *heder* education gives way to this aside: "Of these school-mates, Shoylke, Itshe, and Yisrolik are members of Ha-Shomer ha-Tsair; and the last is now on *hakhsharah* in Grodno [Bel.: Hrodna]. Shmuelke left several weeks ago for the Land of Israel as a halutz. Yoelke and Shaye are activists for the 'Reds'. Only I am for the meantime 'homeless.'" As the autobiography unfolds, it becomes clear that these and other young people he had known since childhood had engaged in political discussion and argument for *years,* and continued to do so even when political choices made them opponents.

The autobiography chronicles, in turn, how a growing accumulation of new political interlocutors joined the old, thus multiplying rather than narrowing the range of Binyomen's sustained engagement with clashing political views. In early 1931, a young woman who was tutoring him for his application to gymnasium instead spent much of her time in wide-ranging discussion "about politics, about Zionism, Territorialism, Yiddishism, and Hebraism" with a third person (also significantly older than Binyomen). Binyomen found these discussions more compelling than his studies. In turn, this third person, Volf Kaplansky, remained a presence in Binyomen's political life—not as a model or guide but as someone who came to represent in articulate fashion a political stance that Binyomen did *not* embrace but about which he clearly thought. Kaplansky became a "*Shteynbergist,*" a Territorialist, who published some essays, Binyomen recorded, in the Wilno socialist journal *Baginen.*

This ever-widening circle of political discussions narrowed briefly during Binyomen's half year away at the Grodno Tarbut Hebrew high school beginning in late 1931. There he found himself for the first—and only—time in an institution with a strong ideological identity and ideologically selected cohort. There, disputes narrowed to intra-Zionist ones. But his return to Bielsk in early 1932 (because his parents could no longer afford tuition) ensured that Binyomen's simultaneous engagement with clashing political ideals resumed in earnest. Unable to afford schooling as his family spiraled into debt, but left to his own devices for nearly a year, Binyomen read voraciously at a Bielsk library. At the same time, he was plied with Communist journals both Polish and Yiddish ("*Tribune, Unzer veg, Miesięcznik literacki, Nowy przegląd*") by a newly Communist acquaintance named Toli; he relates that he read the journals seriously. Meanwhile, his older brother was becoming a committed activist in the non-Marxist Labor Zionist Frayhayt organization. Binyomen's continued engagement by proxy with Zionist ideas was magnified from late 1932 through late 1933 when the reopening of aliyah possibilities to Palestine and the intense politicking of competing Zionist camps around the Eighteenth Zionist Congress produced an explosion of enthusiasm and debate among Bielsk's youth and adults alike.

When the furor of the Zionist Congress elections died down, only the "activists and the conscious" (*di tuer un di bavustzinike*) remained deeply engaged, Binyomen's autobiography recorded. This distinction is significant. Binyomen was not one of the former but one of the latter, "the conscious," and he clearly did not lack for others of the same sort. Although his older brother's departure for a Hehalutz training kibbutz in 1933 forced Binyomen to take his place in the failing family shop and brought an end to his year of undisturbed reading, he did not cease to inquire. In the course of writing his autobiography over much of 1934, he engaged in intense political discussions about "everything under the sun: socialism, communism, fascism, Zionism, Revisionism, Kakowski, Goebbels [. . .]" with two young "proletarians" from a nearby town who had come to Bielsk for army service matters. Strikingly, what attracted Binyomen to Velvl (a locksmith) and Meir (a carpenter) was not shared *ideology* but shared *seriousness* of thought. Velvl was "revolutionary-socialist inclined, almost Communist," whereas Meir belonged to the Zionist Frayhayt. What drew him to them (within the space of a broadly shared socialist sympathy) was that both were "conscious, independent guys" (*bavustzinike eygene yatn*).

A number of other such "conscious" young people of different political persuasions figure in the final diaristic part of Binyomen's autobiography, against the backdrop of continued triangular conflict among Left Zionists, Revisionists, and the Diasporist Left in Bielsk's Jewish public life throughout 1934. Another new friend, Sane Nalevke, was still pious but "thirsted for knowledge," sought to "swallow the whole library in one gulp," and had joined the Zionist-socialist Frayhayt. Yet another, Ezriel Aronovitsh, had completed "all seven grades" of the Yiddishist TsYShO school and was "altogether conscious"—meaning, as we can now understand, striving seriously to comprehend the situation. But like Binyomen himself, he was a "non-party type" pulled between "the Reds" and "Hehalutz." Too much a "pessimist" and ironist to embrace simple answers, he would, Binyomen predicted, "ultimately [. . .] enter Hehalutz like his brother Hershl, who is also a similar type," and both would follow their "oldest brother [. . .] already in the Land of Israel."[11]

Finally, in its closing present-focused pages, Binyomen's autobiography-diary fastens on two further interlocutors, both Communists, to whom Binyomen related in a tellingly divided fashion. One, a former yeshiva student who had moved through Frayhayt Zionism to Communism, won Binyomen's unalloyed respect as a "true idealist"—something more common in Communist circles, Binyomen averred, than in the Zionist ones toward which Binyomen himself was moving. The other commanded his attention solely because of his intelligence—their relationship played out in part over sharp debates about the role of ideological judgment in assessing literary texts—even as he earned Binyomen's contempt for having moved serially from the Bundist Tsukunft to the Zionist Frayhayt and now to the Communists for reasons Binyomen adjudged cynical.[12]

To sum up, reading Binyomen's detailed narrative of his political education between 1929 and 1934 alongside his 1935 commentary on Weinreich's *Veg* demonstrates two vital facts about Binyomen's generation of Polish Jews: first, there was at least a substantial minority who eschewed ideological certainty for prolonged and serious inquiry, and second, what characterized such "conscious" youth was keen readiness to engage in inquiry and argument beyond the bounds of party. Of course, this pattern of serious argument had its ideological limits; admitting that he himself had been briefly interested in Bielsk's newly created chapter of the Revisionist Betar movement some years earlier, by 1934 Binyomen viewed Betar's sanctification of violence with disgust. But neither was political argument *limited* to those with whom Binyomen was emotionally close. Actually, Binyomen's portrait of political discourse among Bielsk youth is one of intimacy *without* friendship—of young men (and in a few cases women) who recognized one another as people trying seriously to find some answers to shared and pressing questions about their era, their fate, and their choices, if any.

Two specifically textual elements of Binyomen's autobiography capture the social actuality of this subset of "searchers" across political lines. First is that Binyomen calls them by a distinct set of terms that he does not bother to explain to his reader, most particularly "conscious." He uses this term to name not a particular politics but rather intellectual seriousness about political inquiry. Thus, although Binyomen credited his childhood acquaintance Yoelke with having been the first to make him "conscious in political matters" (*bavustzinik in politik*), Binyomen's use of the term does *not* mean that Yoelke had shown him the *truth* of an ideology. On the contrary, Yoelke is one of several Communist acquaintances who had repeatedly tried and failed to persuade him to adopt their views; thus, Binyomen comments sourly at one point that Yoelke had attempted to convince him of the merit of "a superficial, empty [Communist] pamphlet" that "could only persuade dummies."[13]

Second, even where he does not employ terms like "conscious," Binyomen repeatedly registers that intellectual seriousness—or lack thereof—could be recognized *across* ideological lines. Though he had a sharply negative view of the adult Zionist "establishment" in Bielsk, he was evidently impressed by the director of the Grodno Hebrew gymnasium and by the history teacher, Shabtai Kolbe, despite the fact that the latter's affiliation with Ben-Gurion's Poale Tsion Right put him among those whom Binyomen elsewhere denounced with the revolutionary epithet "reformists." Concomitantly, although Binyomen found little to like about Ha-Shomer ha-Tsair, the Białystok "shoymerte," Chava Lapin earned his respect for her learned engagement with Yiddish literary culture. And the converse also held. Although Binyomen was attracted to the "idealism" that he found much more often among Communists than among Zionists, he easily recognized shallowness in Communist interlocutors where he found it; after spending time with Bass, a former halutz who had become Communist, he concluded that Bass knew little ("he's been caught by the [Communist] pamphlet *To those caught by Zionism*") and had nothing to offer intellectually.

Thus, within the bounds set by a general leftism, both Binyomen and a number of interlocutors who were, variously, members of the Zionist-socialist Frayhayt, Communists, products of the Yiddishist-Bundist TsYShO, or members of Frayland-Lige Territorialism explored political questions with real seriousness. This, moreover, was outside any discernible party-institutional setting. At formal party-linked events, it seems, there was no space for serious discussion, and attendees assumed much starker political positions; thus, Binyomen describes with evident distaste the ritualized political "combat," complete with catcalls, that surrounded a talk in Bielsk by visiting Labor Zionist activist Beyle Zlotnicka. Rather, serious discussion happened in private, and "conscious" searchers sought each other out precisely so that they could have serious discussions—because they recognized in one another people trying to understand what was happening around them. They were "honestly and truly seeking a path."

From Ideology to Inquiry

If no other sources I have found come close to the rich detail of Binyomen R.'s sociology of "searchers," many sources do attest to an emerging subculture—or at least a common practice—of inquiry over ideology. Sustained exposure to journals preaching worldviews sharply at odds with one's own or that of one's parents was, as many scholars have observed, clearly common. In one 1934 YIVO autobiography, a young man raised in a religious home and educated in *heder* recorded how he was nonetheless exposed to Zionist and Marxist texts and arguments as early as age ten: even as one older brother studying in a yeshiva sent him texts of religious reproof, another was growing active in the Labor Zionist Poalei Tsion Right and an older sister was involved in the Marxist-Zionist Poalei Tsion Left. Simultaneously, little supervised at school, the autobiographer and his friends interspersed Talmud study with daily reading of Warsaw's *Moment* newspaper, where a mainly non-socialist Diaspora-nationalist line jostled with helpings of Revisionist Zionism.[14]

Evidence of serious discussion across even the sharpest ideological divides is also not hard to find. Raised in poverty in Warsaw, Avrom Meirkevitsh joined a branch of the non-Marxist socialist-Zionist Frayhayt at a young age. Looking back years later, he describes its impact on him as profound; he was, in Binyomen's terms, closer to an "idealist" than a "conscious independent guy," in the sense that he took Frayhayt's ideological teachings seriously, even attending its summer instructional retreat. But Meirkevitsh's political education was not confined to that setting. In many other spaces—at home, at work, in personal life—he also engaged with the radically anti-Zionist and Diasporist socialisms of the Communists and even more so the Bund. Meirkevitsh's home offered sustained contact with both of those even before his discovery of Frayhayt. His older brother subscribed to the Communist daily *Fraynd* and later the "very serious journal of the Bund, the *Folkstsaytung*," which Meirkevitsh read from a young age. The world of work was also a site of political discussion. Becoming an apprentice purse maker after *heder,* Meirkevitsh was by age fourteen "already a full member of the leatherworkers' union." That union was, like many, "under the full influence of the Bund," and Meirkevitsh's union youth section was in the hands of a Bundist activist, Koyfman. Meirkevitsh, already an active Zionist himself, and "a few of my comrades" would "jostle" with Koyfman about politics. But he also recalls Koyfman with evident respect as "a very devoted and able activist in the leatherworkers' union" and a "devoted leader of the youth section." Thus, Meirkevitsh was exposed to Bundist ideals both at home and at work by older youth who commanded his respect, just as the older youth of the Zionist Frayhayt did. Finally, he also encountered Bundist and Diasporist ideals through affiliations of his own choosing. He joined the Bundist sports organization on Nalewki Street. And as he went on to join Frayhayt, he remained connected to friends who enrolled at the Yiddishist "school at 51 Mila St." Precisely at the moment in mid-adolescence when Meirkevitsh began to immerse himself in Frayhayt Zionism, his exposure to the most vigorous forms of countervailing Diasporist-Marxist, anti-Zionist, and Yiddishist discourse on the Polish Jewish street not only did not dwindle but actually grew more multistranded.[15]

Meirkevitsh remained committed to the movement he had first chosen. Other young Polish Jews traced more complicated paths. In some cases, this was a path that ultimately led to ideological certainty. But plenty of others, as we can already see from the cases of Binyomen and Forget-Me-Not among others, moved not from one certainty to another but from certainty to doubt. A 1934 YIVO autobiography by a Łódź youth calling himself Jezik Tomszow traces a political path from open-minded inquiry to ideological commitment and back again. Jezik's engagement with political thinking began circa 1930 when, as a new employee in a workshop, he listened in on discussions between a journeyman with Zionist sympathies and the shop's union delegate. Strikingly, the two debaters, noting Jezik's interest, jointly urged him to begin to attend political meetings of various parties to form his own opinion. Thereafter, his story initially seems as though it will fit the narrative that this chapter seeks to trouble: a movement toward ideological certainty. Night classes for workers run by the Marxist-Zionist Poalei Tsion Left party exposed him for the first time to serious Yiddish belles lettres while also convincing him of the truth of Marxist class analysis. In a turn common enough in that milieu, he moved from the Poalei Tsion Left's scholastic Marxist-Zionist fusion to Communism: "Every minute of free time was calculated with an eye to the goal. To read stories was senseless; one should only read works with factual reports and concrete arguments that could be put to further use."

Caught by a police inspector and beaten bloody for "Jew-Communism," he was sent to prison, where he had the chance to interact with Polish political prisoners. As we learned in Chapter 3 from a different 1934 autobiography by a Communist, that of "Greyno," such prison-time exposure to ethnic Poles sharing radical ideologies could serve as the ultimate confirmation of Communism's potential to create a society free of ethnic hatred. But for Jezik, exposure produced the opposite effect: struck by the distance between the Communist Party's claims about the character of "the workers and popular masses" and the reality of deep differences between himself and the Polish prisoners, he felt growing doubts about Communism's social analysis. Leaving prison, he also left the Communist Party. Crucially, this exit was not a leap into another ideology but rather a return toward more open-ended inquiry that simultaneously involved intensive reading in a recognizably anarchist vein, rejoining the Poalei Tsion night classes not as a Communist infiltrator but as a student hungry for "history and sociology," joining a reading circle for those who "remained Communist not in deed but in thought," and ultimately organizing his own study circle. None of this entailed a total break with Marxist ways of comprehending the world—the rhetoric through which the autobiography is narrated is replete with Marxist tropes and certainties—but it is far from the earlier Communist enthusiasm that he himself could objectify by 1934 as "romantic feeling."[16]

Beyond the YIVO autobiographies and such memoirs, a third, very different trove of sources sheds further light on these same phenomena. This third trove does so somewhat inadvertently, even to some degree against the will of the sources' authors—but this is a great merit in methodological terms. I refer to the vast archive of reports sent to headquarters by the numerous Hehalutz emissaries (*shlihim*) dispatched from both Palestine and Poland to "get a handle" on the mass of youth spontaneously flowing into the organization and its affiliated youth movement in streams between 1928 and 1932 and in a flood between 1932 and 1936. The shlihim were avowedly *not* hoping to find skeptical young people— quite the opposite. And they were primed by their ramified socialist-Zionist ideals to impose judgmental categories that obscure as much as they reveal. But the archive they left reveals that at least some of them were serious sociological observers. Many of them registered the tremendous variety of youth sensibilities that they found on their travels. And within that variety, some of these participant-observers were repeatedly struck, and disquieted, by the evidence of skeptical inquiry, hard questions, and ongoing searching they encountered within some of the Hehalutz branches.

One of the shlihim we have already encountered, Haim Ben-Asher, spent the last months of 1930 traversing Poland's northeast from Smorgonie (Yid.: Smorgon; Bel.: Smarhon) to Kleck to Prużana and points south. His task was to visit some of the numerous newly emergent branch organizations (*snifim*) of Hehalutz ha-Tsair and to report back. The reports he submitted display a keen awareness of great variety among these snifim: "Just as the faces of people are never alike, thus too our branches."[17] In Lebiedziew (Yid.: Lebedeve; Heb.: Lebedovah; now Liebiedzieva in Belarus), he encountered the sort of branch that Hehalutz shlihim always hoped to find: all thirteen members knew Hebrew, and its leader, Tsukerman, was "a girl of very clear ability." But Lebiedziew was the stark exception. In Smorgonie he found "a branch of very simple and uneducated [youth], a few individuals who know Hebrew." In Kleck the local Hehalutz ha-Tsair—"the main youth group in the town"—was drawn from the "laboring [classes] and from the street" and Hebrew was not studied. In Turef, Hehalutz ha-Tsair was the only pioneer organization in town; the leadership was enthusiastic but ignorant of things that Ben-Asher deemed basic to informed Zionism and socialism. In Stołpce (Yid.: Stoybts; Bel.: Stowbtsy), he found twenty-eight members, most between the ages of fifteen and sixteen, almost all of whom were "workers" with only three students among them. Finally, in Prużana, as we have seen, the situation was more complicated: within Prużana's far larger Hehalutz ha-Tsair organization, numbering some 130 members, around 30 percent knew Hebrew and embraced a recognizable Zionist agenda. But many others lacked even the most basic grounding in Hehalutz-related concepts.

Had Ben-Asher's reports stopped at this crudely binary division between snifim where the members fit a recognizably Zionist-Hebraist mold and snifim where they did not, they would simply serve as further evidence of a point emphasized in Chapter 2: the degree to which young people without a Zionist background were flowing en masse into Zionist frameworks. But having engaged in intense discussion with these young people—in Prużana, for example, he spent two days and nights meeting with the rank and file, conducted intense discussions with the organization's leaders, and took part in a large "general gathering of the youth"—Ben-Asher discerned a more complex political culture taking shape. His reports offer a portrait of a Hehalutz scene in which searching intellectual engagement with the sociopolitical realities of the Yishuv and of Poland, and with the problems and possibilities presented by both, was widespread and substantially unmoored from Zionist myths and ideals. The young man who headed Prużana's Hehalutz ha-Tsair worried "a bit too much," as Ben-Asher saw it, about whether Hehalutz was too focused on emigration to Palestine and too little concerned with "the reality and activity in the diaspora." Participants in a general meeting of the youth— it is unclear whether this refers specifically to Zionist youth or (as in other places that Ben-Asher visited) a meeting open to the whole of the local youth—pressed Ben-Asher on "the political situation that is taking shape." One young woman, a member of Ha-Shomer ha-Tsair, asked whether under current conditions it made sense to join a training kibbutz. A young man who had left Ha-Shomer ha-Tsair "began to argue for an idea [. . .] of adjusting the pioneering movement to work in the Diaspora, and to direct the 'cultural' activity to that end in a period of lack of aliyah."

Thus, amid the dizzying variety of Hehalutz ha-Tsair local cultures that Ben-Asher found, we can discern a sociologically variegated population of young people whose affiliation with a Zionist organization meant neither a full-fledged ideological investment in a vision of Jewish self-reinvention along socialist, secular, and Hebraist lines nor a simple, unthinking search for exit, but a searching political engagement with the real situation in the Yishuv in relation to that in Poland. Reports by other shlihim after the unstoppering of aliyah possibilities in 1932, while they differ in categories, emphasis, and level of detail, repeatedly register phenomena akin to those Ben-Asher described. They bespeak forms of engagement with the Zionist project that were neither "properly" Zionist nor merely emigrationist, neither ideological enthusiasm nor unthinking affiliation. They betray surprising indifference to core concerns of the Zionist vision and tradition yet deep interest in the decisive questions bearing on Jewish society building in Palestine. They show a deep hunger to understand the world around them and readiness to transgress party lines in the quest for that understanding.

Moshe Kliger's reports in August 1933 from deep in the southeastern Wołyń region, based on meetings with a wide variety of Zionist groups in the area including Hehalutz, the Hehalutz ha-Tsair youth group, and the adult artisans' group Ha-Oved, reflect a dizzying range similar to what Ben-Asher had found. On the one hand, like his predecessors, Kliger found that hope for a Certificate was essentially the *only* motivating factor driving many or even most of those affiliating with the area's Zionist organizations. Meeting in Równe with the executive committee of a chapter of Ha-Oved—a Zionist organization directed at artisanal elements already out of school and working (or, more likely, seeking work)—he found that they "think that in a few days they will be given Certificates." Even more dispiriting, the organization had at its height attracted some fifty-five members, but most had concluded that it was a waste of time and only fifteen remained.

Yet sometimes, Kliger found something quite different. Like his predecessors, he was struck, and appalled, by rank ignorance of Zionist ideology, socialist ideology, and cultural matters among many of the young people joining the movement. But in some places he found that this ignorance coexisted with a powerful hunger to understand the political world. In Kowel (Ukr.: Kovel'), Kliger found young people who, though students well along in their studies at the Tarbut gymnasium, were "simply ignoramuses (I'm not exaggerating—maybe this is the general level of studies and information in the Tarbut gymnasia?)." And further, "[they are] so crude in their relations with friends, cynical and with a very ugly relationship to everyday issues in life." But Kliger also discovered that the general ignorance and widespread crudeness common among the young men (as Lova Levita had four years earlier, Kliger found the young women generally more impressive) *coexisted* with a different impulse. Over the course of a weeklong meeting of Hehalutz ha-Tsair youth from Kowel, Luck (now Lutsk in Ukraine), and other area towns, Kliger remarked "a wakefulness in the discussions whose like I have never yet met in any meeting in which I've participated":

> People sat with mouths and minds open [to] concentrated thought and their eyes lit up at every idea that was raised. As though new, wide horizons opened before them. I talked with them about socialism and education, first principles in sociology. Over the last week, the work was intense—four discussions each day, each lasting two hours, and the two hours flew by, the people simply didn't feel the time.[18]

At a nearby site, apparently the village of Zielona, Kliger recorded an even more striking version of this disjuncture. He was truly appalled by the cultural sensibilities and behaviors he found among the young people attending a youth movement meeting there: petty thievery and, even worse, a profound indifference to cultural life as such. One young man could "play the violin with great talent," and one young woman showed great talent for "declamation," but "to get them to do something of this sort is a backbreaking undertaking" because "there is no fitting understanding of these things—poetry, music, declamation—among the comrades" and "no concern among any of them to create here [. . .] a rich [cultural] life." Kliger was "flummoxed—to find alienation from such things in Wołyń?!" Yet, once again, one matter aroused great interest: "On the other hand, there is here an awareness and interest the likes of which I've not yet encountered for discussions, the study side of things. [. . .] Among all of them there is a *desire* to study, to know." Kliger himself, it is worth noting, was not an emissary from Palestine but someone from the area; given his local roots, his sense that all this was a "new phenomenon" should be taken seriously. Something was changing.

Other shlihim active in the Fifth Aliyah years registered still more clearly the centrality of the sort of expressly political questions that Ben-Asher had encountered in 1930. Working his way across the Łomża region in north-central Poland circa 1934, Yisrolik Kopit registered the same sociological quiddities that Kliger had found. Like all shlihim, Kopit hoped to find snifim marked by dedication to kibbutz-movement ideology in all its demanding particulars and to a larger myth-saturated Zionist enthusiasm. He found one such in Piątnica, a small town outside Łomża: "The comrades are in the hall all day, reading, discussing, singing, dancing; there is enthusiasm [. . .]. The cultural work is also more directed." But mostly, the snifim did not fit this bill. Kopit found far more raw desire to leave than enthusiastic singing and dancing. He complained of meeting "dozens (no exaggeration) of comrades" on this leg of his tour "who have been sitting at home for months and years doing nothing" beyond waiting for a Certificate—and who "when they meet a representative" like himself "surround him and raise questions with great contempt and cynicism."[19]

Crucially, however, Kopit's report on the snif in the important Jewish center of Łomża itself recorded a third sort of milieu irreducible to *either* of these poles of ideological commitment versus unengaged emigrationism. The Łomża snif was far from ideal: though "fairly large," it was "empty of Pioneer content." Yet when Kopit varied his own standard practice, he found that there was more to be said of these lackluster halutzim. Having tired of the "cliched form" that his visits had begun to take, in which he delivered lectures about "the situation in the movement," he instead organized "an evening of questions and answers." The Łomża halutzim asked him "interesting questions regarding the kibbutz here, the kibbutz in the Land of Israel, aliyah. And of course there were also a few political questions."

The emergence of a political culture of inquiry marked by skepticism and searching rather than ideological conviction is made manifest in a series of discerning reports by emissary Miriam Shlimovits (later Shalev). By the time Shlimovits arrived in the Równe region in late 1933 or early 1934, she had already seen many faces of Polish Jewish youth culture and relations to Zionism. Shlimovits herself was a devoted adherent of constructivist-socialist Zionism in its most far-reaching forms: the obligation of every Jewish individual to settle in Palestine, the importance of psychosocial regeneration through communalism and manual labor, the importance of such revolution in Jewish women's lives no less than in that of men, and the centrality of personal cultural revolution through uncompromising Hebraism. Arriving in Palestine in the early 1920s, she had thrown herself into some of the experiments that exerted a strong attraction on the youth of the Third Aliyah, those children of World War I and the Russian Revolution. She joined the experimental women's farm at Nahalat Yehudah in the Jezreel Valley, where, tellingly, she eventually took over from the storied Hebraist activists Sarah Rubinstein and Brakha Habas as the teacher of Hebrew "language and literature" to the other female pioneers.[20] She then joined Kibbutz Ein Harod.

In short, Shlimovits too came to Poland not as a sociologist but as a committed ideologue. But as with those of Ben-Asher in 1930, Kliger in 1933, and Kopit in 1934, the numerous reports Shlimovits sent as she

Figure 5.1   Gathering of Hehalutz activists, Nowostaw, 1 March 1934, Miriam Shlimovits (Shalev) among them. Ghetto Fighters' House Museum Archive, catalog no. 1954.

moved through Galicia and up into the Polish Ukraine over the course of 1933 are marked by insightful attention to the differences among the local political cultures of the kibbutzim, snifim, and communities she visited—and by a capacity to register complexity. Thus, in her first visits to Hehalutz training kibbutzim, she found (and lamented) environments marked by needlessly grueling primitive communism (and "sadistic" ritual hazing of newcomers with cynical questions and forced "collectivization" of the clothes, razors, and soap they'd brought).[21] But a report on the kibbutz labor battalion at Wieliczka outside Kraków, written only a day after the aforementioned report, registered a mix of disconcerted surprise with grudging respect. Discomfitingly, most of the twenty members were "altogether indifferent" to "cultural work" of any sort, ranging from "study of Hebrew" to "the literature and interests of the movement." But Shlimovits was deeply impressed by how fully these same members strove to meet the demands of communal work and communal living. Both aspects, she reasoned, might owe something to the advanced age of some of the group members—men (and a handful of women) who were "27-28-30" years old. More to the point, for our purposes, is how this second report registered Shlimovits's capacity to appreciate *seriousness* of purpose even when it diverged from her vision of proper Zionism.[22]

Most apposite, when she turned from the training kibbutzim to local Hehalutz organizations, Shlimovits found essentially the same "searcher" sociology and culture that Binyomen described. In the small Wołyń towns of Kolki (Ukr.: Kolky) and Osowa Wyszka (Yid.: Osove; Ukr.: Osova), she discovered environments in which the young halutzim were engaged in a sustained, critical, and urgent effort to make sense of their *political* moment globally and assess the political claims and promises made on all sides.

Kolki's Hehalutz branch lacked "a Pioneer environment." But despite this "sin," Shlimovits was moved to acknowledge the members' intellectual intensity: they "seek an answer for their many questions; [they] research and argue." Attributing this in part to the presence of a strong Betar chapter with which the snif was locked in struggle, Shlimovits wavered over how seriously to take these political engagements. She wondered whether these young people were asking so many political questions "not out of a desire to know" but for polemical reasons, "to know how to answer their opponents," which brought a certain "superficial clamorousness." But this oscillated with a much more sympathetic impression: "In general one feels here activity, wakefulness, and vitality."

More importantly, Shlimovits's description of the actual questions being asked by her young interlocutors does not square with a portrait of superficiality. Rather, it bespeaks critical inquiry regarding key questions. Questions bearing on Palestine included "doubts about the socialist kosherness of the struggle for Hebrew labor" and whether "the fundament of Hehalutz [was] Zionism or socialism." Larger questions bearing on Poland, Europe, and the world included, tellingly, "What is the source of antisemitism?" The range and character of the questions suggest that the internal debate in this Hehalutz chapter was wide-ranging, unregulated, and irreducible to ritual affirmations and denunciations. The Kolki youths' concern for the "kosherness of the struggle for Hebrew labor" tells against Shlimovits's suspicion that argument in the snif was oriented toward polemic with Revisionism, which had no problem with the demand that Jewish employers in Palestine hire Jewish laborers. The questions about socialism, nationalism, and antisemitism bespeak the embeddedness of the Palestine question in a larger concern for the reemergent Jewish Question locally and globally.[23]

In turn, in the "unusually impoverished" townlet Osowa Wyszka, Shlimovits found a youth scene marked by searching engagement with the political questions facing Polish Jewry in ways that reached beyond Zionism altogether. Osowa Wyszka's Hehalutz chapter was caught up in an intense three-way intra-Jewish struggle-cum-dialogue with a strong Betar organization and also with "the Jewish Workers' Party (YAP)," which evidently stood somewhere on the Communist-to-Bundist spectrum, and was certainly Diasporist and anti-Zionist. But what appeared to be organizational confrontation on one level was actually a hothouse environment of intense political searching. In a manner that disquieted Shlimovits, the young people of the town interacted with little regard for the boundaries between what were in principle utterly opposed ideologies: "Members of YAP come often to Hehalutz. Take part in meetings [. . .]. Members of Betar can also always be found in the hall, and many members of Hehalutz visit YAP, read the newspaper there, take part in meetings."

A certain tendency in the historiography of Polish Jewish youth culture suggests we might read this porousness as a sign of the limits of politics, a world of nonintellectual youth sociability underneath the supposed party splits. But Shlimovits's description signals something very different: a shared urgency of concern, doubt, and political purpose across movement lines. The Osowa Wyszka Hehalutz youth were consumed by "doubts regarding the correctness of [our] path" and particularly "doubt regarding whether we have the ability and possibility to solve the question of the masses [*sheelat ha-hamonim*]." I will return to the special import of this specific locus of doubt—the same that Ben-Asher had deemed especially noteworthy in his report from Prużana three and a half years earlier. For now, what is notable is the seriousness of the political debate for the young people themselves. Here, movement back and forth between Zionist and Diasporist frameworks bespoke an urgent search for answers.

One further remarkable feature of these emissary accounts is how *little* they encountered full-fledged investment in socialist-Zionist ideology or the kind of myth-infused relationship to the Yishuv and its achievements of the sort that Zionist publications propounded and Bundists and Communists eagerly attacked. The "idealists" (to use Binyomen R.'s term) in the local Zionist youth scenes they visited across the length and breadth of Poland seem to have been substantially outnumbered by the two other "types" that Binyomen and others identified in parallel ways: by a large group of young people driven by a raw desire for exit, and by a smaller but far from negligible subset of searchers pulled toward urgent critical inquiry regarding the realities and potentialities of the Yishuv and Poland alike.

From Ready Answers to Hard Questions

Among the varied responses that doubt about the future provoked in Polish Jews, not least was a turn toward critical inquiry moving restlessly beyond any of the ready-made ideological certainties on offer in Jewish life. But what was the *content* of the questions being asked? Amid the sources that capture the emergence, and felt newness, of the skeptical "searcher" posture itself, we find some indications.

First, both Faygenberg's report from Warsaw in 1929 and Shlimovits's report from Kolki in late 1933 or early 1934 show a readiness to pose hard questions about the core claims and myths of *all* the competing movements in Polish Jewish life: Bundist, Zionist, or otherwise. Second, many of the sources from at least nominally Zionist circles, from Ben-Asher in 1930 to, again, Shlimovits in 1933–1934, capture a growing insistence on thinking about prospects in Poland and in Palestine in the same frame.

Third, clearly many people at the grass roots—not just Binyomen R. or Forget-Me-Not, encountered in Chapter 1—were trying to get some analytical traction on the same larger questions about the shape and trajectory of illiberal politics in Poland, in Europe, and around the globe that preoccupied intellectuals like Oberlaender or Lestschinsky. Thus, Shlimovits's interlocutors asked themselves, "What are the sources of antisemitism?" Y. Kosoy, reporting on his travels through Galicia in what seems early 1933, found that "in many places, the activity of the branches focuses on discussions of 'the political situation in the world,' the Popular Front, and other matters of that sort."[24]

Fourth, one common enough feature was lack of faith, or indeed loss of faith, in the imminence of socialist Revolution, whether from abroad or from within. Binyomen R. put it lucidly: "If I believed that the social revolution was going to break out tomorrow, I would of course chuck all of my Zionist 'petty bourgeois illusions,' as would 90% of today's halutzim" and all of the "*halutsishe*, Poalei-Tsion, and Bundist leaders." But "for now," he concluded, "we stand in a fascist era."[25]

Finally, clearly Binyomen was not alone in thinking concretely about his situation in terms of categories of risk and likelihood. When Astour insisted in 1933 that Polish Jewish youth actually understood the reality of the Jewish situation far better than older intellectuals, one of the key dimensions of this superior capacity for judgment was the readiness to think extrapolatively: "The youth [. . .] knows that however dark the present may be, the future will be even darker."[26]

As we saw in the introduction, Astour's essay gave precise expression to how Polish Jewish political thought was being reorganized by the three-fold conviction of political harm likely to hit, hit soon, and hit hard; the cruel limits of Polish Jewish capacities to blunt or avert that harm; and skepticism that any outside force or underlying historical process would ride to the rescue. In Astour's analysis, we can see the operation of the chastened and questing posture of inquiry that the shlihim observed and to which Binyomen attested. In his consequential reasoning that one had therefore to seek another path that did *not* rest on lingering hopes that Jews could improve Jewish life in the Diaspora if they but found the right "levers," Astour embodied a new triage-politics welling up in Jewish life, to several further faces of which we now turn.

6

Palestine as Possibility

Zionism as an organized force in Polish Jewish life suffered a massive
setback in 1926–1927, when the Fourth Aliyah—the first mass migration
of Polish Jews to Palestine—ended in economic crisis. The number of
Polish Jews who annually declared their Zionism by "buying the shekel"
fell from 110,000 in 1927 to 10,670 in 1928. Returnees to Poland aired
their grievances. Opponents of Zionism wrote postmortems.[1]

But the proverbial ink was still drying on those postmortems when,
already in late 1928, large numbers of Jewish youth, particularly in Poland's eastern reaches and smaller towns, began to turn spontaneously to
youth Zionist activism and Hehalutz.[2] A far larger watershed came in
mid-1932, to reiterate, when the British Mandatory reopened Palestine
to unprecedented if still sharply limited Jewish immigration. Over the
next four years, tens of thousands of Polish Jews left for Palestine: Irith
Cherniavsky calculates that of the roughly 100,000 Polish Jewish immigrants to Palestine between 1929 and 1939, 65,000–70,000 came between 1929 and 1936. This was a mixed group cutting across all class
lines of Polish Jewry: by Cherniavsky's count, of the 100,000, 35,000
came as family members, 22,000 as halutzim, 18,000 as "middle class
and artisans," and 10,000 with the modicum of resources that qualified
them as "capitalists."[3]

And this population was just part of a larger Polish Jewish reorientation
toward Palestine as a possibility. Considering Hehalutz, the sharply opposed Betar, and other Zionist youth groups together, the number of young
people in Poland formally affiliated with Zionism every year between 1932
and 1935 hovered close to 100,000. And this was not a fixed population,
but one drained by aliyah, on the one hand, and people leaving the organizations, on the other. The number of adults who expressed interest in
Palestine in various ways is harder to count, but it evidently numbered

hundreds of thousands. In 1933, nearly 500,000 Polish Jews "bought the shekel." Of these individuals, 215,000 cast votes in the 1933 elections to the international Zionist movement's Eighteenth Congress. Some sources suggest that the Revisionist Zionist movement that broke away from the Zionist organization thereafter commanded as many as 450,000 supporters in Poland by 1934–1935; whatever the real number, that support was certainly less connected to Revisionism's militaristic Zionism than to its well-publicized petition campaigns demanding that Palestine be opened to unlimited Jewish immigration. As many as several hundred thousand Polish Jews investigated the possibility of direct family emigration under the mandate's "small capitalist" rules: as noted, Cherniavsky made the telling discovery that by 1939 the Land of Israel Office in Warsaw, which handled inquiries about Palestine by Polish Jews, had a card file of some 200,000 names—a number that, in turn, clearly does not encompass untold thousands of people who "took steps toward aliyah" but did not register with the office.[4]

Where Chapters 1 and 2 introduced us to the scope and paradox-ridden character of this massive turn toward the Yishuv, this chapter focuses on one particular stream in the torrent of discourse around the Zionist project in Palestine that inundated Polish Jewish life between 1928 and 1935. During his six-month tour for the Jewish National Fund in 1931–1932, Alter Druyanov offered numerous talks about the Yishuv in the towns that hosted him. Druyanov found that any lecture on life in Palestine aroused intense interest. But he also found that audience responses displayed a strange duality: a marked bifurcation between uncritical enthusiasm and searching inquiry. Reflecting on his lectures to small-town audiences, made up evidently of mostly middle-of-the-road General Zionists, he underscored that such audiences yearned for some sort of exalted representation of the Yishuv's achievements—even *needed* it psychologically amid otherwise depressing circumstances. But in travel notes taken at the time, he also recorded a hunger for accurate information in those same audiences: "special importance that the representative of Zionism should be specifically a person who comes from the Land of Israel. [. . .] *Especially* good if the emissary knows the ins and outs of all aspects of life in the Land of Israel even if these are not relevant to his task. They will ask him for guidance, and he must offer a correct answer."[5]

This bifurcation between a desire for celebratory propaganda and acute interest in the reality of the Jewish situation in Palestine was just as pronounced in the Jewish schools Druyanov visited. One Hebrew school principal complained to Druyanov that the students "were addicted to thoughts about Palestine [*mahshavot al Paleshtinah*]." Druyanov's school talks on the progress of the Yishuv commanded rapt attention—but also called forth a flood of questions. Some of these questions manifested what Druyanov called "romanticism" and led him to conclude that the Yishuv was for many students "a living ideal, from which [flows] power and strength to struggle in the diaspora as well." Yet if these sorts of questions, "sometimes naïve," betrayed a myth-infused relationship to Jewish life in Palestine, other questions posed by gymnasium students were "sharp and penetrating to such a degree that it was difficult for me to respond." Even in Hebraist-Zionist schools, investment in Zionist myths of Jewish rebirth in the Land of Israel coexisted with a much more analytical hunger for concrete knowledge about Palestine and the Yishuv.

Druyanov wrote in early 1932, after several years in which Palestine was nearly closed to Jewish immigration. Later that same year, Palestine reopened to Jewish immigration at unprecedented levels. In this context, the sort of open-eyed interest in the Yishuv's real potential and limits that Druyanov had found in Zionist circles became a stance that made sense for far wider swaths of Polish Jewry. Zionist emissaries who came between 1932 and 1936 would find the same mix of desperate excitement and searching inquiry among both longtime Zionists and Polish Jews previously distant from Zionism. Observers of this turn in Polish Jewish life described it variously, but all agreed that Polish Jews of all backgrounds were keenly interested in making sense of the rapidly changing Yishuv as a real community—and potential home—in comparison with Poland.

This chapter investigates how Polish Jews of many varieties negotiated a new relationship to Palestine and the Yishuv in ways determined less by Zionist or anti-Zionist images than by the fact of the Yishuv as a rapidly growing, partially open, and perhaps substantially different kind of Jewish community that might meaningfully improve a sizable number of Polish Jewish lives. To center the discussion on a relationship to Palestine defined less by credulous acceptance of Zionist myths and more by a relationship of information seeking is to engage in a partial history. Here we rejoin the debate regarding the degree to which we should think of Polish Jewish political-cultural transformations in the 1930s as a crisis-driven flight toward fantasy and myth. Everything I noted in Chapter 5 regarding the crucial revisionist work of Kijek, Heller, Yona, and Cherniavsky, among others, applies not least to Zionism, of course. Cherniavsky's survey of 1930s coverage of Palestine in the pro-Zionist *Nasz*

Przegląd finds plenty of Zionist mythemes: tropes of the preternatural dynamism of the Yishuv, the physical and psychological vitality of the New Jew, the "primitive" Palestinian Arab peasantry that was nonetheless amenable to peaceful coexistence, and so forth.[6] Yona's recent work on Hehalutz at the grass roots demonstrates that even passing encounters with halutzim engaged in manual labor could inspire powerful fascination in other young Polish Jews living through the collapse of the old Jewish commercial niche.[7] Heller's argument that Betar youth were attracted to images of Jewish militancy and armed strength out of an overdetermined mixture of deep attraction to Polish nationhood and felt rejection by it fits well with models of Zionism that emphasize its masculinist and militarist dimensions.[8] Clearly, these scholars are right that some Polish Jewish relations to Zionism in the 1930s partook of such ideological fantasies.

But we need to be no less attentive to the very different set of relationships widely remarked by contemporaries: forms of engagement with Zionism marked by hunger for *accurate* understanding of the Yishuv and Palestine, indifference or skepticism toward Zionist ideological pretensions, and (yet) deep interest in the possibilities that the Yishuv might offer to Jews individually and collectively. In this chapter, I first investigate some of the means by which less-curated information circulated: newspapers, personal letters, personal contact, tourism, and travel writing. Then I examine a striking phenomenon: serious consideration of the Yishuv as an actual society, its achievements as well as its problems, by non-Zionists and even anti-Zionists. I focus on two especially rich cases: travelogues by the Territorialist-turned-Diasporist-turned-Territorialist Yoysef Tshernikhov and by the inveterate Diasporist Max Weinreich in which open-eyed reportage turned into unexpectedly serious engagement with Zionism's *political* claims—above all the claim that the Yishuv offered better future prospects to Jews who could get to it than did the Diaspora. Finally, I bring these two foci together to capture some of the ways that Polish Jews of various sorts began to articulate to themselves how the Yishuv might really be different from Poland and what significance that difference might bear for (some) Jews' lives.

Seeking Information about Palestine's Yishuv

The Hehalutz emissary Ben-Asher's reports from the kresy in late 1930 reveal a Hehalutz milieu in which an ideologically "correct" relationship to the Yishuv seems to have been surprisingly lacking. Rather, Ben-Asher encountered repeated critical inquiry regarding the realities and challenges of life in the Yishuv. Thus, at the large meeting he conducted in Prużana, with its 130 Hehalutz ha-Tsair members, he was plied with not only penetrating questions about the situation in the Diaspora and whether Zionism offered any answers, but also pointed questions about life on the kibbutz. Young women in particular confronted him with questions about the "insecurity of family life" in the kibbutz environment. Another interlocutor pressed him to address corruption in kibbutz life as reflected in the use of private money by individuals and the securing of extra work hours (to meet individual needs) through personal connections. This last question was based on both "rumors" and "letters": by 1930, Polish Jews had sources of direct information about life in Palestine not under any movement's control.

Still sharper questions about Palestine faced Ben-Asher in his visit to a group of ten members of the Shahariah training kibbutz stationed in nearby Ludin. To his comrades, Ben-Asher reported his sense of a merely practical "emigrationist" discontent at work—hints that members would leave Hehalutz if aliyah Certificates were not forthcoming. But he also recorded an uncomfortable exchange that pointed in a very different direction: "In the conversation, there was a need for elementary conceptual clarification regarding the right of the Hebrew worker to work in the Jewish economy in the Land. There were comrades who saw in the conquest of labor a contradiction to the socialist conscience, an illegitimate taking away of another's livelihood, etc." Ben-Asher seems not to have noticed the contradiction between his allegation of nonideological escapism in the Ludin group and the evidence he himself provided of the members' moral-political struggle with a problem at the heart of the socialist-Zionist project: the fact that in order to realize its ideal of a Jewish people regenerated as a "working nation," socialist Zionism demanded that Zionist institutions and Jewish entrepreneurs in Palestine hire only Jewish laborers.

Thus, Ben-Asher—like Druyanov—found a culture of hard questions at the heart of organized youth Zionism in the saddle years between the Fourth and Fifth Aliyot. The rapid swelling of youth Zionism's ranks after the reopening of aliyah in 1932 only served to feed this culture of inquiry over ideology. As they traversed central Poland, Galicia, and Wołyń over 1933–1934, Yisroel Kopit and Miriam Shlimovits/Shalev—two other shlihim we have met—encountered the same mix of ignorance and intellectual seriousness, at the heart of which lay hard questions about both the Jewish situation in the Diaspora ("What is the source of antisemi-tism?" and so forth) and penetrating questions about the realities of Jewish life in Palestine. Alongside "interesting questions regarding the kib-butz here, the kibbutz in the Land of Israel, aliyah," Kopit faced ("of course") a few "political questions." Shlimovits confronted discomfiting questions about Arab and Jewish labor competition embedded in a larger context of searching discussion about Poland and Palestine, nationalism, socialism, and the causes of antisemitism. Importantly, she also noted an-other material factor that fed this culture of searching beyond the private letter. One of the ways in which the Hehalutz youth of Osova traversed the supposedly high-walled boundary between Zionism and Diasporist so-cialism was by reading the newspaper of an opposing movement at the Jewish Workers' Party clubhouse. Whether the Bundist *Folkstsaytung* or something closer to Communism or Anarchism, said newspaper would undoubtedly have been packed full of information about the limits, fail-ures, and weaknesses of the Zionist project in Palestine. To insist on reading both Zionist and anti-Zionist newspapers simultaneously was the practice of people hungering for understanding rather than party-line certainties.[9]

These and many other sources by shlihim point to two understudied dimensions of the Polish Jewish relationship to Palestine. First, plenty of information about Palestine circulated among Polish Jews, and not all of it by any stretch of the imagination came from Zionist sources. Second, as the content of the questions addressed to the emissaries attests, a non-negligible number of people of varied ideological backgrounds not only could but *did* seek to actually comprehend the real character of life in Palestine's rapidly changing Yishuv.

Many sources bear out this impression that Polish Jewish life was sat-urated with information about Palestine from multiple perspectives. The consistently anti-Zionist Weinreich prefaced a travelogue of his 1935 visit to Palestine (to which we will turn extensively below) with a double-edged comment. On the one hand, he highlighted the orienting power of preex-isting ideological commitment even as he acknowledged that "everyone" now had a view of the Yishuv: "*Erets-Yisroel* is after all a point of con-flict in Jewish life, everyone comes to it with his own theory and conclu-sions in advance." But on the other, he also noted that he himself—a man with long-standing Bundist allegiances whose personal archive demon-strates that until the 1930s he had only the most dismissive relationship to the Yishuv—could not help but know "quite a lot prior to my trip."[10]

Elsewhere in the same travelogue, as he described his journey, he prefaced some comments about the nonsocialist planned town of Afula with the telling comment that "everybody knows about Afula."[11] It is fair to say that today almost *nobody* outside Israel has any associations with Afula, much less that they self-evidently "know [something] about" it. The same information saturation was registered already in 1933 by the other non-Zionist "inquirer" into Palestine to whom we will soon turn, the Wilno Jewish communal leader turned Territorialist Tshernikhov, as he listened to a young Palestinian Jew discussing various coastal settlements on a bus ride: "The young man talks ceaselessly about every Jewish settlement we pass through. But nothing about it sounds new. How much we have already heard and read about all this."[12]

Such contemporary comments help orient us toward some of the more material and institutional dimensions of this knowledge saturation—dimensions that made it possible for large numbers of Polish Jews to negotiate their own understanding of the Yishuv outside any movement's interpretive grid. Most obvious was the role of the Jewish press in all three of its languages, and even the non-Jewish Polish press. Not only Zionist publications but newspapers outside any of Poland's several Zionist subcultures devoted massive coverage to every aspect of life in the rapidly expanding Yishuv. Over the course of 1931, the politically neutral Warsaw Yiddish boulevard daily *Unzer ekspres* carried at least 428 articles dealing with "Palestine" or the "Land of Israel"; over 1935, that number reached 845. The number of articles matching that description was quite a bit larger in Zionist journals like Poland's leading Zionist daily *Haynt,* but the coverage grew at a faster clip in *Unzer ekspres.* Though it is not yet possible to cleanly quantify coverage in the rest of the Polish Jewish press even at this primitive level, a similar explosion in Palestine coverage undoubtedly characterized other non-Zionist publications.[13]

Much of what circulated was marked by ideological predispositions for or against Zionist ideas. But expansion of discourse about the Yishuv also served to expand ideologically unregulated knowledge about it. Thus, as noted, Cherniavsky's survey of 1930s Palestine coverage in the pro-Zionist *Nasz Przegląd* reveals plenty of Zionist mythemes. But as Cherniavsky notes, these jostled on the page with two very different sorts of information-cum-representation: attention to problems and attention to practicalities. "From the abundance of writings and reports published in the Polish-Jewish press, it can be inferred that the *olim* were exposed to a great deal of information about what was happening in [Palestine]. [. . .]

Despite the fact that most of the information published in the press emphasized the positive and optimistic face of what was going on in [Palestine], readers could inform themselves about the darker sides of life there: the difficulties of making a living, price inflation, the negative relationship to new *olim*."[14]

Nor was the press simply a site of representations positive and negative. Cherniavsky makes the important observation that as the Fifth Aliyah got under way, papers like *Nasz Przegląd* offered increasing amounts of practical information about how an individual might actually construct a new life in Palestine. Through the mid-1930s, it carried a column by Miriam Vohlman offering practical advice about aliyah, with particular attention to issues relevant to white-collar professionals, students, and educated young women—not appropriately Zionist types like halutzim but unreconstructedly urban and middle-class Polish Jews.[15] My own less systematic but more wide-ranging survey of Polish Jewish press coverage of Palestine supports the view that the incredible amount of Yishuv coverage across the political spectrum made it ever harder for readers to avoid exposure to clashing representations and multiple sources of information.

Thus, Polish Jews could learn quite a bit about Palestine from the press. But did they? Here, acid comments by the *shaliah* Lova Levita in 1929 offer a striking testimony that presages what Shlimovits would find as well four years later. Levita complained that many young people he was meeting "draw their knowledge of the Land" from the Polish-Yiddish daily press, particularly "from *Haynt, Moment,* and the *Folkstsaytung.*" This extraordinary lineup tells us something that Levita conceals. *Haynt* was a Zionist daily, whereas *Moment* was not (yet); what both had in common was massive and variegated daily coverage of life in Palestine—indeed, one could learn a tremendous amount about Yishuv life from *Moment*'s regular Palestine correspondents like the aforementioned Rokhl Faygenberg and Yehudah Leyb Vohlman, a Polish Jewish journalist who had settled in Palestine in 1925. No less remarkable was the spectacle of young people hoping for aliyah with copies of the *Folkstsaytung* as their guide. The *Folkstsaytung* was a Bundist daily committed to relentless attacks on Zionism; one could indeed learn about the Yishuv from its coverage—but exclusively negative things. If these young halutzim were ignorant by Levita's lights, they were by his own admission reading about the Yishuv and drawing conclusions that certainly contravened the intentions of the *Folkstsaytung*'s writers and might have surprised *Moment*'s measured writers too. They were using the Polish Jewish *non-* and even *anti*-Zionist press to inquire about the Yishuv outside the terms of both Zionism and its opponents.[16]

Beyond the press, the Fifth Aliyah period saw the rapid development of other sites where ideologically unregulated information circulated. As Ben-Asher's remarks demonstrate, a second conduit of unregulated information was the flow of personal letters from Jews in Palestine to family and friends in Poland. The first mass settlement of Polish Jewish immigrants in Palestine in 1924–1925 ended under a cloud of crisis, but actually most of the Polish Jewish immigrants who came in those years stayed. This can only have made for a tremendous increase in the amount of personal correspondence—and unregulated information—flowing from Palestine to Poland. The massive upswing in aliyah beginning in 1932 could only have produced yet another sharp rise. Moreover, because the population that came to Palestine in these *aliyot* was socially diverse, its correspondence mediated Palestine to an equivalently diverse cross section of Polish Jewry reaching well beyond Zionist subcultures.

All this is attested in Marcin Kula's history and anthologization of 445 personal letters sent between 1926 and 1939 from a Warsaw Jewish family to their son and brother Moniek, who had emigrated to Palestine in 1925 at age twenty-six. Although we only have the Poland-to-Palestine half, those letters exemplify how an emigrant's reports about his life in Palestine—and the very fact of his building a life there (he married, a son was born in 1932; his setting down of roots is exactly coterminous with our time frame)—rendered Jewish life in Palestine concrete for a Polish Jewish family that had entered the mid-1920s harboring a range of attitudes toward Zionism. Moniek's father related to his son's choice through a thick weave of Zionist myth; himself a small businessman, he was pleased that Moniek found work as a road paver (an icon of Zionist manual labor since the Third Aliyah), and hoped Moniek would marry a Yishuv-raised woman unmarred by "diaspora psychology." By contrast, Moniek's brother Dolek was "not an enthusiast of the Zionist project." Yet Moniek's letters spoke to him too, and by 1926 Dolek hoped to visit Palestine "for 4–6 weeks" if he could find the money. In late 1928 he told Moniek that the Palestine letters offered a departure from "this gray everyday life and bring some light to our dark apartment."[17]

These letters show further how personal Poland-to-Palestine connections could grow ever thicker over our time frame. As Kula notes, growing numbers of Jewish families like Moniek's lived in an environment in which emigration to Palestine became a common occurrence after 1924, and (again) after 1932. This created a feedback loop: an ever-expanding net-work of contacts in Palestine oriented Polish Jews ever further toward the Yishuv as a reality and possibility. In December 1932, Moniek's father wrote to inform him that "the brother-in-law of Moyshe Kuropacki from Lublin, a Gerer Hasid with a lot of capital, is preparing for a trip to Israel" and that "Blas' younger brother" was coming to study at "the Mikve Yisrael agricultural school." Where the former piece of information testi-fies to networks that kept Polish Jews informed of other Polish Jews' en-gagement with Palestine—and reminds us that Hasidim too were among those growing more interested in moving there—the latter testifies to deep-ening familiarity with what Palestine might offer the *next* generation.[18]

A family member's successful transition in Palestine could be the most convincing argument of all. In one of the 1934 YIVO youth autobiogra-phies, we hear from a young woman who had come to share the wide-spread conviction that Palestine offered a better future than Poland. Having joined a Zionist organization, the young autobiographer remarks that in her little spare time from seamstress work she does indeed read the newspaper and "political books." But such engagement with Zionism was the product rather than the cause of her choice to try for a Certifi-cate and a life in Palestine. She attributes the chief source of her decision, and of her newfound sense of hope ("I foresee a better future"), to letters from an older sister who had recently gained a Certificate (through what seems to have been a marriage of convenience) and settled on a kibbutz. The sister's "very good letters from there" not only gave the young woman the "courage" to pursue a Zionist path but also convinced her parents that this was the correct choice: "I also see the satisfaction of my parents that they have done well as regards the oldest daughter." Here, turning to Palestine was a considered act by someone informed about some real possibilities for a different and better life there.[19]

Personal contacts via visit or letter could of course serve as vectors of Zionist or Yishuvist myth and affect, but they could also cut sharply *against* ideologically romantic accounts. Thus, in 1930 one kibbutz movement emissary bitterly lamented "the great 'effectiveness' of private correspondence" in sowing doubts about kibbutz life.[20] Yet such disen-chanting letters did not necessarily undermine interest in emigrating to Palestine. In fact, they could serve to intensify correspondents' interest pre-cisely by bypassing ideological representations to offer more useful infor-mation regarding how to make a life there. Traveling through the Pinsk region in 1930, the *shaliah* Hershl Pinski discovered that a recent *oleh* from a local training kibbutz had been in touch privately with his former comrades to offer practical advice about where to settle in Palestine. This ran counter to the settlement goals of the United Kibbutz movement, which wanted halutzim to join the kibbutz movement and settle where they were told. But it ran counter precisely because it facilitated alternative settlement choices once one had gotten to Palestine under kibbutz-movement auspices.[21]

Beyond newspapers and letters, the Fifth Aliyah period saw the rapid expansion of secular-national Polish Jewish tourism to Palestine—visitors coming with no firm intent to stay and with itineraries that included not only traditional pilgrimage sites but also New Yishuv destinations. As masses of Jews turned their attention to Palestine, markets responded by rendering travel between Poland and Palestine substantially easier. Trip organizers offered help completing Polish and British paperwork.[22] As one observer put it in 1934: "The Land of Israel is still a land of wonder, but it is no longer a distant land. [. . .] A trip to the Land of Israel is now an easy and pleasant journey." He meant this in the most material sense: the Gdynia-America shipping line's 15,000-ton cruise ship *Polonia,* which began regular trips back and forth to Palestine in 1932, made extra efforts to ensure that the ship was comfortable for typical Polish Jews—down to a kosher kitchen. And the cost of the trip had fallen to levels comparable to the cost of a trip to the Carlsbad spa.[23]

Significantly, the rapid expansion of Palestine tourism for Polish Jews reached well beyond any sort of organized Zionism. There were some Zionist efforts to shape tourists' experiences. In Palestine, organized efforts to foster a network of Jewish tour guides got under way in the mid-1920s.[24] In Poland, various Zionist fractions worked to organize trips, as when in April 1934, the Warsaw Tourism Office of the Jewish State Party organized a trip to Tel Aviv's Levant Fair—itself a centerpiece of Yishuv propaganda aimed at world Jewry well beyond Zionist ranks.[25] And tourism could also be folded back into intra-Jewish ideological struggle, as when a group of Zionist women activists from Bełchatów (Yid.: Belkhatov) near Łódź, returning from "*Erets Yisroel,*" reached out to local "Jewish women and girls" to counter local anti-Zionist messages.[26]

But clearly many Jewish tourists to Palestine set their own agendas with little Zionist input; by the mid-1930s, Zionist tourism coordination efforts were still trying to "catch up" to the massive influx.[27] And such tourism was driven by more than a desire for enjoyment. Per a 1935 article in *Moment,* the Polish Jewish tourists coming to Palestine wanted to see "the colonies, the kibbutzim, the new cities, [Jewish settlement in] the Emek, the Dead Sea" because "they have read so much about this, [. . .] and it is no wonder that they want to be convinced that everything they have heard is really correct."[28]

In early 1934, the popular correspondent B. Yeushzohn treated readers to his take on the already familiar genre of the Palestine travelogue. What renders his account interesting is his depiction of several new types of Polish Jews now traveling en masse to Palestine alongside committed Zionists, on the one hand, and religious pilgrims, on the other. Reflecting on his own experience on the *Polonia,* Yeushzohn related that his fellow Jewish passengers in first and second class consisted mainly of non-Zionists. Further, within that framework he mapped three distinct types of Polish-Jewish non-Zionist relations to the Yishuv—and, by the same token, to Poland.[29]

On the one hand, half of the second-class berths and a good many of the first class were taken up by a type that Yeushzohn dismissed as "half-assimilated pseudo-intellectual *arriviste* well-off ignoramuses" but whom we might simply describe as tourists: men and women who treated the cruise as a vacation to be spent in "smoking rooms" playing cards, who talked about the same things while en route to Palestine as on a trip to "resorts in Otwock," and who were excited that the entertainer Hanka Ordonówna was on board.

As against this, Yeushzohn described a second, smaller group of educated professionals of "the assimilationist camp." These had for many years been "distant and alienated from us"—that is, *Haynt*'s pro-Zionist Jewish-national readership—but had recently become interested in Zionism's "new world." They now came to Palestine driven by deep "curiosity and surprise" and displayed a special interest in the halutzim (traveling in third class), their "Land of Israel songs," and "*hora*-dances." But these "assimilated camp" elements also came driven by deep worry, under the pressure of "Hitlerism" in Germany or "other, more home-grown reasons."

Third was a substantial group of "simple Jews of the mercantile world"—"Nalewki Jews"—coming to see for themselves whether Palestine offered good possibilities for "setting oneself up decently in life, both for themselves and even more so for their children." This third group was sociologically distant from the Polonized professional group. But they shared an interest in the Yishuv defined by serious inquiry. Here, "tourism" meant to see for oneself whether Zionist promises of a better life for Jews in Palestine than in Poland were hot air, or something more.

Wrestling with Zion Not as Idea but as Fact

It is no surprise that growing numbers of those sympathetic to Zionism were keen to visit in the 1928–1935 period. More surprising is the ever-growing list of committed *critics* of Zionism drawn to see Palestine for themselves. Some, like the writers Leyb Malakh and Yoysef Opatoshu, came with anti-Zionist agendas and sent back exposes of Zionist aggression, Hebraist oppression of Yiddish, or Yishuv brittleness little different from those that had attended the crisis of the Fourth Aliyah in 1926.[30] Others, like the Communist Yiddish pedagogue and children's nonfiction writer Helena Khatskels, settled on a second mode of non-Zionist writing about the Yishuv: focusing on avowedly apolitical dimensions of everyday life. In Khatskels's case, long-standing radical sentiments—in the early 1920s she had participated in openly Communist politics in the new Lithuanian state—were trumped by professional and personal ties. In Lithuania, she had cofounded an experimental Jewish orphanage with a most unlikely partner, the German-Jewish Zionist educator Siegfried Lehmann. Lehmann had left for Palestine and founded a related institution in 1927, the Ben-Shemen Youth Village orphanage-cum-boarding-school.[31] It was to Ben-Shemen that Khatskels traveled in 1930, and in a 1931 travelogue for children published in Wilno she combined a sympathetic description of life there with reticence about politics.[32]

But alongside these two already familiar modes of non-Zionist writing about the Yishuv, the situation of the early 1930s moved several critics of Zionism toward a third sort of investigation: grappling seriously with Zionism's core claims about the Yishuv as an answer to the Jewish Question. In the spring of 1932, Wilno's much-loved communal leader and public health activist Tsemakh Shabad, long a measured but resolute critic of Zionism on Diasporist grounds, traveled to Palestine. He "returned full of impressions," in the words of his son-in-law, who was none other than Weinreich, still a far more absolute anti-Zionist.[33] Shabad, it seems clear, was in the midst of rethinking his own Diasporist hopes; whether his encounter with the Yishuv was cause or confirmation, by the end of his life in 1935 he was turning away from Diasporism to Territorialism. This, according to Shabad's longtime Folkist-Diasporist comrade Tshernikhov, who himself was on a complex path vis-à-vis the Yishuv. A Zionist in his youth, Tshernikhov had broken with the movement before World War I and had (like Shabad) embraced Yiddishist-Diasporist ideals. But by the early 1930s, Tshernikhov too was losing his Diasporist faith and turning toward the Territorialist idea.[34]

Shortly after Shabad's trip, the rising complexities of the Polish and European Jewish situation impelled these two intimate witnesses to Shabad's Yishuv-mediated turn away from Diasporist faith to negotiate a new relationship to the Yishuv themselves. In 1933 and in 1935, respectively, the moderate anti-Zionist Tshernikhov and the sharply anti-Zionist Weinreich were moved to visit Palestine—Tshernikhov for the first time in twenty-three years, Weinreich for the first time ever. And both followed with reflective travelogues that sidelined perennial points of polemic between Zionists and Diasporists (the language question, most notably) to seek to understand what kind of Jewish society was actually taking shape in Palestine. Where other Yiddishists simply dismissed Zionism's claims that Jewish settlement in Palestine would yield substantially new and better forms of Jewish life, these travelogues confronted those claims seriously in the mirror of reality and possibility, and compelled readers to do the same.

In the travelogue he published in the Zionist daily *Haynt*—itself a notable choice—Tshernikhov's overriding claim was that, in ways both compelling and unsettling, the Yishuv had indeed become a substantial Jewish society of a genuinely new sort and effected genuine changes for the better in Jewish lives. As Tshernikhov emphasized, he could appreciate the scope of this change by direct comparison with his own previous visit in 1910. That first visit had come several years after Tshernikhov had broken with Zionism. It had confirmed his sense that Zionism could not bring about any of the demographic, social, or cultural transformations he and his fellow progressive nationalists deemed so important for East European Jewry. Conversely, his 1933 travelogue was permeated by the recognition that, although not all of Zionism's hopes had been or likely would be fulfilled, what had transpired in the interim was a process of growth, transformation, and consolidation that far exceeded his earlier skeptical expectations.[35]

Some of Tshernikhov's metrics were typical. He emphasized the rapidly growing demographic and political significance of a Jewish laboring class in Palestine—something that impressed him both relative to what he had seen in 1910 ("little Jewish lords" presiding over exclusively Arab labor) and relative to the chronic unemployment and prospectlessness among "our youth at home" in contemporary Poland. He also noted the extraordinary growth of Tel Aviv. Though he still saw relatively little to like about that hodge-podge city—which contrasted poorly, in his view, to the clean modernity of Alexandria and Cairo—what mattered was the contrast with Jewish Poland: "Especially in contrast to what goes on in the dying Vilna, Tel Aviv seems a city with many more residents than the statistics suggest."[36]

Tshernikhov laid equal emphasis on what he deemed a remarkable transformation of Jewish consciousness. His encounters with youth and with Jewish laborers moved him to effusions about health and regeneration; but he insisted, in ways that must have been striking for readers, that for all the romanticism of the rhetoric, not only the outlook of young Jews in Palestine but also their habitus really were altogether different than among young Jews "at home." His encounters with Jewish children convinced him that the Yishuv was raising "a strong, healthy generation." Encounters with laboring youth left him pleasantly surprised by the capacity of the new society to integrate quite disparate sorts of immigrants, including a German Jewish arrival of Communist background. Unlike some non-Zionist visitors, he found Yishuv Jews mostly pleasant, though this was not true in the Revisionist stronghold Petah Tikvah. More to the point, they were for the most part confident and seemed to feel profoundly at home; he noted an encounter with a friendly young mother who could not imagine living in "the Exile." This, too, was utterly at odds with the situation he saw in Poland, a point he made repeatedly.

Tshernikhov did not conclude that all his earlier doubts had been misplaced. His travelogue gave substantial space to voices skeptical of the Zionist project—more so, strikingly, than the far more unambiguously anti-Zionist Weinreich would, as we will see. These included an aging farmer in Nes Tsiona, originally from Białystok, who had come to an *anti*-Zionist position on Jewish labor, immigration, and state building and was markedly more at home with his Palestinian Arab laborers than with Yishuv Jews. Other voices included two young disillusioned halutzim whom Tshernikhov allowed to articulate a sharp leftist class-warfare position. Against the Labor Zionist Mapai Party's "constructivist socialism," which dictated that Jewish labor and Jewish employers cooperate in a corporatist arrangement long enough to create a self-sufficient Jewish society, these young workers expressed doubts about the Jewish labor ideal, fulminated against cooperation with "kulak" citrus growers, and propounded instead the possibility of common cause between Jewish and Arab workers. Asked by Tshernikhov, "How, then—I ask—will a Jewish state be built?" one answered pointedly: "Nobody said it would be." This interlocutor went on to suggest that if only the Bund could overcome its reflexive "hatred of Zionism," it would find that its politics of internal Jewish class struggle made more sense in Palestine than anywhere else.

Beyond according space to such critical voices, Tshernikhov openly communicated his own sense of high obstacles to Zionism's further development. He was struck by the depth of real class tension within Palestine's Jewish society. And—again, more than Weinreich would—he devoted substantial attention to Jewish-Palestinian tensions. He conducted a series of sustained discussions with Jewish farmers in Nes Tsiona and Rehovot regarding their more compromising (or was it self-interested?) take on the Jewish labor/Arab labor question. He noted substantial social modernization under way in Palestinian Arab life. In Nes Tsiona/Wadi Hunayn, he noted that the houses of the halutzim faced a counterpart Palestinian section composed not only of Bedouin tents but well-built houses and cafés with gramophones playing popular music from around the Arab world. And Tshernikhov did not confuse this sort of social development with interethnic rapprochement. As against the confident outlook of many of his interlocutors, Tshernikhov allowed the aforementioned Nes Tsiona grower to give voice to a sense of profound Jewish vulnerability in Palestine: the grower's anti-Zionist stance, it turned out, was driven largely by a desperate sense that if Jews continued with the Zionist program, they would be massacred—that (here Tshernikhov quoted the grower) "the events of 1921 and 1929 are a plaything in comparison to what awaits us in this land." Tshernikhov did not endorse this apocalyptic view, but he did observe that for all their sense of being at home, Jews did not feel safe walking the five kilometers between Mikve Israel and Tel Aviv at night.[37]

But a different fact loomed larger for Tshernikhov: his overall impression was that Palestine's Jews for the most part possessed a confidence about their future and their capacity to shape it that could not be found in the Diaspora. This was not all to the good, as Tshernikhov saw it. He was evidently deeply disturbed by what he found to be widespread aggressive, essentially expulsionist sensibilities toward Palestinians among many Jews. His standard question of whether "a Jewish state" would be founded in Palestine elicited a confident "of course" from a Jewish shopkeeper in Petah Tikvah; his follow-up question regarding Palestine's Arabs was met by a nonchalant declaration that "it wouldn't be a terrible thing if they left." Tshernikhov noted that the eleven-year-old son of one of his friends had offered the same "solution": "The Arabs? They'll go to the Hejaz, Syria, Yemen [. . .]" Tshernikhov was moved to remark pointedly, although his own travelogue did not bear it out, that "in essence, this is what everything thinks in Erets Yisrael"—and to wonder to the reader how the shopkeeper, a relative newcomer, had developed such "aggressiveness" so quickly.

Tshernikhov thus allowed readers to see his own uncertainty about what the future would bring. But at the same time, he complicated this dissent from Zionist certainties by acknowledging in multiple ways that he and other non-, ex-, or anti-Zionists had themselves profoundly underestimated the capacities of the Yishuv to alter the terms of its own situation. To a fellow visitor's comment about the fragility of the Yishuv's water resources, Tshernikhov acknowledged the counterclaim that new sources of water were already being found, and noted that new irrigation equipment once imported from Germany was now being produced locally.

And in the meantime, the attainments were real and distinctive. It was not just subjective feeling, though the "elemental joy [in Tel Aviv]" led Tshernikhov to pronounce with sad definitiveness that "in all matters what is going on here is unlike what is going on in other Jewish communities." He sounded more analytical notes too. First, he wrestled with the possibility that seemingly subjective factors like "confidence" and "joy" should actually be reckoned as objective factors—as fonts of energy that enhanced Palestinian Jewry's capacity to shape a new kind of Jewish life. Tshernikhov treated seriously the claims by his interlocutors that investment in the Zionist project produced heightened effort and a "constant acceleration of the tempo from the Jewish side."

In a more down-to-earth sense, Tshernikhov paid attention to how the transformation of the Yishuv involved not only demographic and communal consolidation but also the extension of partial but real Jewish dominance over particular stretches of territory and space. Struck by the remarkable growth of Tel Aviv and other once-anemic centers like Petah Tikvah, Tshernikhov also pinpointed a subtler but significant infrastructural-political development: the way the constant movement of Jewish trade and transport bound once-isolated Jewish communities in the coastal plain—Tel Aviv, Ramat Gan, Bnei Brak, Petah Tikvah—into a single domain. In turn, he noted that this was not just an inadvertent effect of development but a product of intentional, strategic Jewish collective effort to turn the infrastructure of British empire to Jewish needs. Palestine's railroad infrastructure was unalterably structured by British imperial visions of regional control, but the Yishuv had turned the British road system to its own advantage by creating a cooperative bus system controlled by the Labor Zionist movement's Histadrut, and thus not by the market's dictates but by Zionist strategic-territorial needs. The Jews of the Yishuv were proving able to accumulate and use forms of what sociologists of the state like Anthony Giddens and Michael Mann have called "infrastructural power" to win control over *space*. "Everything aside," Tshernikhov concluded, "regardless they've managed to get a sort of Jewish 'canton' in the Land of Israel." If this was no state—something Tshernikhov treated as the self-evident goal of Zionism—it was still quite different from minorityhood in Poland defined not least by lack of Jewish access to any sort of state-like power.

Tshernikhov's 1933 trip was a double return: a second visit to Palestine and a return to grappling seriously with Zionism's claims to be able to create a better form of Jewish life. By contrast, Weinreich's encounter with Palestine in November 1935 was his first in both senses. Unlike Tshernikhov, Lestschinsky, and a fair number of other Yiddishists who now turned urgent attention to Palestine, Weinreich had never even flirted with Zionism before. Though Weinreich grew steadily more interested in Zionism as an ideological force in the early 1930s, that interest had nothing to do with sympathy. On the contrary, his relationship to Zionism as expressed in *Veg* had been the thoroughly antagonistic one of a Diasporist watching with mounting frustration as the competing ideology gained adherents on what he deemed false pretenses. Nor did his choice to visit in 1935, or to write a travelogue, stem purely from curiosity. As with all of his travels, he went in part to raise money and support for the YIVO Institute.[38] Similar practical concerns were also involved in his choice to write at length about his trip: though he placed a first essay from the trip in the Wilno *Tog*, the other twelve installments of his "letters from a journey" were published in the New York *Forverts*, for which he, like many other European Yiddishist intellectuals, wrote when he could because the *Forverts* paid dollars.

That Weinreich certainly remained ready to puncture Zionist myths in Palestine was evident in the first of his *Forverts* essays, which began, as so many accounts of arrival in Palestine did, with a description of the physical travails of disembarking in Jaffa's crowded port and moved on to a comparison of Tel Aviv and Jaffa. At first, Weinreich's telling seems another iteration of a standard Orientalist trope: brought to shore by shouting Arab porters, Weinreich discovered a dirty old city of Jaffa sitting side by side with a strikingly new Tel Aviv. Yet having invoked the ready-made contrast of new versus old, clean versus dirty, European versus Arab, Weinreich sharply undercut it. The shouting Palestinians turned out to be shouting good-natured instructions about where to sit in the boats, and Weinreich noted further that he soon discovered that Arab Jaffa included neighborhoods of nice new houses inhabited by cultivated Palestinians, while parts of Tel Aviv turned out to be wild and ill constructed.[39]

Such an opening might seem to signal a typical choice of Yiddishist Palestine travelogues, already a genre of its own. Rather than celebrate Zionism's achievements (the kibbutz, Tel Aviv, the revival of Hebrew), the Yiddishist or otherwise anti-Zionist traveler would seek out Jewish life standing outside Zionism: plucky secular Yiddishists at the edge of the Zionist Left or beyond it working to publish a journal despite Hebraist pressures or Yiddish-speaking Hasidim in Jerusalem or Tiberias maintaining a rich traditional life and living (perhaps) harmoniously with their Arab neighbors.

But Weinreich did not take this path at all. He showed shockingly little interest in Palestine's Yiddish cultural scene (despite the fact that he clearly spent time in those circles fund-raising for YIVO), only a passing interest in Hasidic Yiddish, and surprisingly limited attention to the topic that so dominated most Yiddishist travelogues about Palestine—namely, Hebraist persecution of Yiddish. Although Weinreich reiterated standard criticisms on that matter, he actually displayed deeper interest in Hebraist sociolinguistic achievements themselves. More importantly, he subordinated the entire question of language and culture to discussion of social, economic, and political features of Jewish life in Palestine. Readers used to Yiddishist reportage on Palestine framed by the Hebraist-Yiddishist *Kulturkampf* would have to wait until Weinreich's eighth installment for any sustained discussion of the language question, and the ninth for anything of substance about Yiddish per se. And Weinreich not only postponed this discussion until he had completed searching essays on Yishuv society and on Jewish-Arab relations in Palestine. He also chose to conclude the series by once again shifting attention away from the language question to the socialist-Zionist workers' organization the Histadrut, to the state of

Palestine's Jewish economy, and finally to the core political question of what Palestine could actually offer European Jews.[40]

In other words, even more than Tshernikhov, Weinreich chose to focus overwhelmingly on precisely those things hailed by Zionists as the defining achievements of Zionism in Palestine: the Histadrut, the kibbutz (in its most moderate form at Deganiah), Jewish self-defense efforts, and Tel Aviv as an experiment in Jewish self-organization and national space making ostensibly unlike anything existing in the Diaspora. The travelogue he produced is distinctive not only for its open-ended and precise engagement with the Yishuv's most substantial achievements. Also striking is that, at key junctures, Weinreich wrestled seriously with the most fraught question of all: crudely, whether Zionism—or something(s) about Palestine and the Yishuv themselves—was actually allowing Jews to produce a life in Palestine that was in some senses substantially *better*, by Weinreich's own standards, than that which they could attain in Poland or the Diaspora in general.

Why did Weinreich take the bull by the horns? I have not been able to find any direct evidence about Weinreich's intentions, other than a tight-lipped note in 1933 regarding his father-in-law's return from Palestine "full of impressions" and his own declaration of proper social-scientific intent at the opening of his travelogue: "I [. . .] resolved that I would not travel as a tourist who gets a taste of a specially dolled-up institution or situation and thinks that he has seen the Land. [. . .] I wanted specifically to see not the decoration, but the everyday reality [*vokhedikayt*]."[41] But no external compulsions can explain the intensity of Weinreich's grappling with Zionism's political claims. Given the increasingly pro-Zionist sympathies of the *Forverts* editor Ab. Cahan, Weinreich likely could not have published a sharp attack on the Yishuv in the *Forverts* even had he wanted to. But he *could* have done what many other travelers (like his fellow Wilno Yiddishist Khatskels) did: write an anodyne human-interest travelogue with political questions left out. Or he might have focused exclusively on the parapolitical dimensions of the Zionist project for which many on the non-Zionist Left, from Cahan to Emma Goldman, felt some sympathy even if they thought political Zionism was misguided: the kibbutz experiment in collectivism and the formation of a Jewish working class.

But Weinreich chose to engage with a range of Zionism's most distinctive attainments in the Yishuv and to wrestle openly with the significance of those attainments for readers seeking clarity on the claims that swirled around Zion and Diaspora alike. Thus, the series' eleventh and penulti-mate essay, "The Histadrut—the Jewish Labor Organization in *Erets-Yisroel,*" was marked by a deep interest in the organization's workings and a careful weighing of the obstacles to its development, on the one hand, and the factors it had going for it, on the other. Weinreich offered a perspicacious analysis of the problems facing the Histadrut in the con-text of both the emerging economic downturn in mid-1930s Palestine and the fundamentally structural problem of whether the Histadrut's effort to build a socialist economy and egalitarian Jewish society within the frame-work of capitalist market relations could succeed (about a third key question, that of whether to prefer Jewish labor over Palestinian labor, he had much less to say than Tshernikhov). He noted worker anger over the Histadrut's expenditures on the well-appointed Beit Brenner building in Tel Aviv when the money might have been used for unemployment sup-port. More fundamentally, he clearly outlined two fundamental prob-lems facing the Histadrut's effort to engineer socialism through monopo-listic control over labor: the resentment that naturally arises among newly arrived work seekers in the face of such monopolistic control, and the more complicated question of whether workers' cooperatives under the Histadrut's umbrella might inevitably become joint-ownership capitalist enterprises given that they involved an initial set of worker-owner-investors operating in a market system.[42]

But even as he outlined the Histadrut's problems in detail, he regis-tered his genuine wonder at its institutional achievements: its creation of a working medical service on a mass scale, its provision of banking ser-vices, its newspaper *Davar.* Regarding *Davar*—a newspaper with which Weinreich himself developed a complicated but respectful relationship during his stay—Weinreich related that its editors aspired to raise its sub-scriptions from the already impressive 20,000 to 30,000, and opined, "And I am sure that they will succeed; they are very efficient people and know how to get work done." Turning to the question of the organi-zation's relationship to Jewish workers themselves, Weinreich acknowl-edged a line of critique pertaining to the Histadrut's labor monopoly: Did not such a monopoly mean that the Histadrut as a mass organization was founded not on choice but rather on compulsion? Speaking in the careful tones of the sociologist, Weinreich granted that it is in some sense impos-sible to know what mix of free will and compulsion is involved in the choice of an individual to join the Histadrut, given that, indeed, an organi-zation "with such broad reach," serving 100,000 people, "is almost like a state, and a state has a thousand tools with which to work." I will return in passing to this insightful comment by a longtime antistatist on the unique infrastructural power embodied in states. Here I want to draw out what proved to be a central analytical leitmotif in Weinreich's essays: his fascination with the objective power and significance of subjective commitment and belief. "But I do not conclude from this, as others do, that insofar as the Histadrut holds its members in part by compulsion, it follows that its accomplishment is a smaller one. I don't hold this view because the fact remains: this 'compulsion' is built entirely on free will."

Specifying elsewhere that he meant in particular veteran Jewish workers rather than new arrivals, Weinreich related his impression that the mass of Histadrut workers were willing to accept the decisions of the Histadrut because of a deep "love" for the organization's leadership founded on the awareness that those leaders had themselves "stood behind the plow." In turn, Weinreich concluded that the qualities of Histadrut leadership, and its ability to sustain the organization through good times and bad, were predicated not only on the "excellent human material" of which the leadership consisted for the most part, but on the fact that "their strong faith in the Zionist ideal gave them strength to bear everything." Lest the reader miss the connection between Zionist commitment and Jewish socialist success in Palestine, Weinreich clarified: "There are no more hundred-percent Zionists than the leaders of the working class."

Visible here was one of the larger interests that had emerged from Weinreich's youth research: a reluctant fascination with the power of Zionist ideas, however wrongheaded or fantastic he deemed them, to power far-reaching Jewish action and self-transformation. The anti-Zionist outlook that Weinreich had brought with him to his early 1930s youth research had grown more complicated: if *Veg* mostly framed Zionism as *escapist* fantasy, merely compensatory, at other junctures Weinreich had wrestled with the very different impression, both scandalizing and fascinating, that Zionism was somehow managing to summon new energies in its youthful adherents in ways that Diasporism could not. In *Veg*, Weinreich viewed it as cold, hard fact that thousands of "middle class" halutzim were proving able to embrace self-proletarianization and commit themselves to unrewarding manual labor while even those Diasporist youth who had gone through socialist-minded Yiddishist schools could not. The only explanation, as he saw it, was cognitive: the fantasy (or prospect) of a new life in Palestine was endowing Polish

Jewish adherents with the psychic wherewithal to *actually* transform their lives.

Now in late 1935, some parts of Weinreich's Palestine travelogue continued in this "psychoenergetics" vein, as he turned his attention to achievements and institutions that seemed to him to bespeak the effective power of Zionist idealism to allow its adherents to sustain their commitment despite grave hardships (and countervailing facts). The series' ninth essay, "Hebrew and Yiddish," is a careful sociolinguistic investigation that began with the acknowledgment that "the Hebraists have succeeded in making Hebrew a living language" and allowed that this in itself, certainly born of Zionist-Hebraist idealism, was impressive. In the middle of the essay, Weinreich lent substance and enthusiasm to this grudging congratulation in a vignette about a meeting with an amateur agronomist on a bus trip from Tiberias to Tel Aviv. Noting that the man had a storied family (he "comes from a family whose name has a lovely ring [because] several of his brothers and sisters died in [Jewish] self-defense [activity]"), Weinreich related without sarcasm the agronomist's efforts to transplant a particular sort of nut grown in America to Palestine because the species in question could grow on rocky and hilly land. Weinreich concluded with a portrait of the agronomist, almost certainly Baruch Chizhik, that foregrounded the effective power of Zionist faith: "This practical farmer and theoretical botanist spoke with tremendous enthusiasm about the Hebrew terminology of botanical science. He explained to me that the word 'group' can be translated in Hebrew in certain cases by the word *kavod* because one encounters such a use of the word in kabbalistic works and perhaps earlier too. And from the inspired manner with which he talked about this, I recognized that the stony earth of *Erets Yisroel* and the self-defense and his botanical experiments and his Hebrew are all various aspects of one ideal."[43]

Laying aside the ambiguity of *Veg,* here Weinreich presented Zionist faith as a power to release new energies to transform place, language, and political condition. Still more explicit—though also more agonistic—was a discussion of the question early in the series, in the first essay on the kibbutzim, where Weinreich allowed Zionist claims to confront his own cherished Diasporist hopes:

Near the Kinneret Sea lie scattered other *kevutsot,* and I saw some of them. Local people took me around, showed me the holdings. [. . .] They enjoy not only the satisfaction of people who began small and gained through hard work. [. . .] That which binds them all together is the ideal of building up *Erets-Yisroel*. [. . .] Whether *Erets-Yisroel* will truly become a Jewish country [*a idish land*], and whether it will be with their *kvutsah* methods, is an altogether different question. But they are deeply convinced that the answer is yes. And in this resides their great strength and their great happiness. A new hen-house for a Jewish farmer in New Jersey is just a hen-house; for a Jewish *kibbutznik* in Deganiah, it is a step in the upbuilding of the Jewish people.[44]

Weinreich did not accept his interlocutors' faith in the national significance of their actions uncritically. Yet he underscored the *practical* power of this faith to generate and sustain institutions that he regarded as genuinely worthwhile. And there was a reflexive dimension here that would have been shocking to any fellow Diasporist: Weinreich's comparison of the Deganiah and New Jersey farms to the detriment of the latter. The anarchist chicken farms of south Jersey were precisely what a Diasporist-socialist like Weinreich was supposed to aspire to sites of autonomous Jewish economic and cultural life carved out locally wherever Jews lived, with no grand emigration schemes, no aspirations to statehood, and no accession to the notion that Jews were not "at home" in the Diaspora.

Ultimately, this dimension of Weinreich's thought remained within the bounds of the psychologistic mode that had permeated *Veg*—a matter of understanding the hidden wellsprings of national and individual will, staying power, and creativity. But the most analytically significant moments in Weinreich's analysis proceeded from the *opposite* move more typical of a Diasporist travelogue: from the demolition of Zionist myths. Two myths in particular came in for critical analysis. The first was the notion that Jews in Palestine were more secure than Jews elsewhere because "return to the Land" endowed them with a sense of agency and pride ostensibly missing among Diaspora Jewry. The second was the celebratory discourse about Tel Aviv, "the first Jewish city," which resonated with the semimystical view that the city's creation and rapid growth demonstrated Zionism's unique productive vitality or the unique transforming and vitalizing powers of the Land of Israel itself as opposed to the supposed incapacity of Diaspora Jews to build anything lasting.

However, something strange happened as Weinreich subjected these myths to critical comparative scrutiny: as he laid bare their falsity, he ended up elaborating ways in which the Yishuv was actually different institutionally and materially—different in ways that gave it real advantages over Jewish life in Poland regarding both self-determination and security. Thus, Weinreich's sixth essay, titled "Jews in *Erets-Yisroel* Feel Safer Than Elsewhere—Why Is This So?," reported with admiration the resolute commitment to armed self-defense among kibbutz youth when faced with reports of violent Palestinian demonstrations in nearby Balad ash Sheikh following the November 1935 funeral of Izz ad-Din al-Qassam, leader of an organization that had killed Jews in the Haifa area beginning in 1931. While Weinreich admired the readiness of young Jews to take up arms against such dangers, he sharply disputed the Zionist explanation for it, evidently made to him repeatedly: "When you talk to a Zionist, you have a ready answer for it: this is *Erets-Yisroel*. In no other land is this possible." Weinreich exploded this Zionist myth by offering readers a capsule history of how Jews in Eastern Europe had in fact organized self-defense efforts in the face of the pogroms years earlier. Moreover, Weinreich continued, recent attacks on Jews in Eastern Europe were everywhere accompanied by signs of self-defense, demonstrating that "the will and the ability" of Jews to resist violence with violence was growing stronger outside Palestine (and outside Zionist circles) too.

Had Weinreich stopped at this point, he would have had in hand a well-crafted Diasporist polemic exposing Zionist myths about weak East European Jews and strong Palestinian New Hebrews to the light of reasoned empirical counterargument. But significantly, Weinreich did not allow himself the easy route of pretending that Zionism's claims about the political significance of Palestine for Jews were reducible to the myths that accompanied them. Instead, he grappled directly with the question that followed: If indeed there was nothing specific to "the Land" or the psychology it bred that could explain Palestinian Jewry's commitment to self-defense, why was it that East European Jewish self-defense efforts were concretely so much less developed than those the Yishuv had been preparing? The answer, Weinreich recognized, lay in differences of political and legal regime. In Palestine, Jews had a recognized right of self-defense and the British themselves allowed Jewish settlements weapons for emergency use. In Eastern Europe, by contrast, governments or police actively undermined Jewish self-defense organization: "This means that Jewish self-defense can only be underground, and necessarily has facing it both the hooligans and the police." Even more important, he argued later, was that Jewish youth in Eastern Europe did not possess equal rights to carry and use weapons, and this, coupled with the fact that Jews were generally not allowed into the various national officer corps, also worked against the kinds of organizational and material factors necessary for self-defense. To underscore his point that *Erets-Yisroel* in no way intrinsically bred braver Jews or better self-defense, and that everything depended on the legal regime in place, Weinreich suggested further that in places where Jews possessed full legal equality, like the United States and the USSR, one might expect Jewish self-defense efforts to be on the same level as those in Palestine should the need arise.

In making this eminently rational institutionalist case, however, Weinreich swept aside a Zionist myth only to foreground one of Zionism's most compelling *rational* arguments: differences in legal regime, in the behavior of the police, in government policy—in short, differences in the *state*—were fundamental determinants of such matters as whether Jews could defend themselves effectively. Given the notable uptick in violent incidents directed against Jews by Polish rightists in 1931–1934—and Weinreich, we should remember, had lost sight in one eye in one of those attacks—Weinreich's argument had uncomfortable implications: Palestine really *was* a place that afforded Jews unparalleled opportunity to organize communal self-defense. It might be true that the key factor was a racialized British colonial policy rather than the vitalizing power of the land, but the result was no small thing under the global circumstances—something Weinreich was perhaps acknowledging when he ended with this lame sentiment: "We hope that in other lands, these conditions will change for the better."

Elsewhere in the travelogue, Weinreich allowed compelling articulation of a second dimension of Zionism's claims on behalf of the Yishuv's superiority as a site of Jewish national life. The framework of this articulation was the question of whether the building of Tel Aviv merited the excitement that so many visitors felt about "the first Jewish city." Weinreich thought little of Tel Aviv concretely: in his first essay, he dilated on its dirtiness, its poor planning, and the inferiority of its phone system to Wilno's. But he acknowledged that such factors were irrelevant to the real reason that Tel Aviv generated excitement in others. What excited others was what Tel Aviv suggested about replenished Jewish-national capacities to create something significant. Weinreich introduced readers to a "friend of mine, a thoroughgoing leftist who considers himself an 'internationalist' and regards me as a 'nationalist'" who nevertheless regarded Tel Aviv with great pleasure because "Jewish hands had built up such a great city" on what had been, as the friend himself had seen before the war, "nothing but sand." Weinreich averred directly to readers: "I must admit that I do not find this compelling. That Jews are capable not only of building a city but also of building even greater things I do not doubt, and I do not need any evidence of it. The entire question is whether they give us a chance to show what we can do." Thus, Weinreich turned an internationalist friend's astonishment at the fact of a Jewish city into an occasion for an avowedly Diaspora-*nationalist* avowal of Jewish capacities merely awaiting the right chance.

But here again his thought took a striking turn:

[But] someone might say: look, isn't *Erets-Yisroel* the only land in the world where Jews *are* given such a chance to develop themselves? Where they wish to, they can build their own villages and establish a socialist life-style there. If they want to, they are allowed to build whole city quarters for themselves in Haifa and Jerusalem, and thus they are both more secure in their life and property and in their culture. When they wanted to, they were even allowed to build their own city. Where else do Jews have such opportunities for development?

Were someone to speak to me thus, using the existence of Tel Aviv as evidence to support Zionism, I could accept it or not, but I would certainly understand it, because the argument has a lot of logic and a lot of demonstrability [*bavayzikayt*]. In general, it is this that constitutes the great power of Zionism as opposed to other Jewish programs: the fact that others must appeal more to theory, while Zionism has much to show.[45]

Although the last sentence is once again a narrow focus on motivation—that is, not which of the competing ideologies is more correct, but (merely) which compels its followers more successfully—the rest of the argument operated on a different plane far more challenging to Weinreich's own Diasporism. Weinreich here invented an interlocutor whom he allowed to elaborate both the positive claim on behalf of Mandatory Palestine's provision of opportunities for Jewish collective action and national life, and the accompanying challenge to Diasporist hopes about Eastern European Jewry: "Where else do Jews have such opportunities for development?" Moreover, Weinreich allowed his invented interlocutor to lay out Zionist claims in ramified fashion. Palestine's greater opportunities applied across the board to everything that ought to matter to someone who cared about Jewish well-being collectively and individually: to lifestyle, to culture, to Jewish power to shape the space around them, and also, crucially, to enhanced capacities to protect their own "life and property."

There was a still sharper self-critique embedded in this part of the discussion. Weinreich allowed his imaginary Zionist interlocutor to articulate a further claim that struck at the theoretical heart of Diasporism: the argument, shared by Zionists and Territorialists of all stripes, that the *concentration* of Jews in compact territories was a more nationally productive and physically *secure* mode of organizing Jewish national life than the situation of universal minorityhood in which East European Jews found themselves. Some Diasporist theorists had long argued that minority status was a positive condition, and some—like Golomb—still did. But Weinreich here not only avoided this political-moral argument. He actually acknowledged the empirical force (the *bavayzikayt*) of the territorialist-cum-nation-statist claim as realized (only) by Zionism.

Weinreich did not leave matters on this note of surprising accession to Zionist arguments. In particular, he proved ready to investigate the Jewish-Palestinian conflict in ways that challenged Zionist discourse and found complexities where Zionism preferred simplicity. (I will return to Weinreich's confrontations with this question in Chapter 7.) For now it suffices to say that in his attention to the Palestinian-Jewish imbroglio, Weinreich broached a different kind of question, which also marked the limit of his newfound sense of the Yishuv's advantages: the question of whether the Yishuv had much of a future at all, or might be consumed by interethnic war. On a less apocalyptic but equally deflating note, Weinreich was also attentive to signs of renewed economic crisis in Palestine's Jewish sector, heralding *perhaps* the same sort of housing-bubble collapse that had ended the Fourth Aliyah. In short, Weinreich's willingness to reckon seriously with what the Yishuv demonstrated regarding Zionism's claims about the practical superiority of ethnic concentration over dispersion and minorityhood was shadowed by a second decisive political question: What could Zionism actually offer Diaspora Jews at the present moment, and what might it reasonably be expected to offer in the near future? On this score, too, his answers were surprisingly complex; we will return to them (and to Tshernikhov's thoughts about the same question) in Chapter 7.

What I wish to underscore here is how his analytical comparison of Yishuv and Polish Jewish circumstances moved this inveterate Diasporist toward a surprisingly humbling argument about Diasporism itself. Throughout the first essays in the series, Weinreich had voiced fierce resistance to the common Yishuv conviction that East European Jewry was in a state of terminal crisis. He acknowledged that many of his interlocutors in the Yishuv were very well informed about what was happening in the Diaspora, and further acknowledged that the Yishuv's Hebrew press carried a great deal of reliable news about Jewish life abroad. But he complained that the Yishuv ignored or dismissed positive news from Poland; in one of the few instances of genuinely confident Diasporist rhetoric in the Palestine reportage, he complained of his interlocutors' ignorance of the "800 free-loan societies" in Poland that were keeping "thousands" of Jews on their feet, and all due to the efficient work of "local forces." But in the later essays on Tel Aviv and self-defense, Weinreich robbed his own protests of much of their power by essentially acknowledging that both in terms of the extent of true national autonomy and in terms of quality of life, the Jews in Palestine were in a substantially better situation than those in Eastern Europe, and that furthermore this had something to do with institutions of self-determination and the degree of Jewish concentration in a territory.

Between Vernacular Zionism and Negotiated Yishuvism

Thus, in the early 1930s, Polish Jews of all varieties who had previously had little or no relationship to the Zionist project in Palestine began to think about it urgently. This chapter can only begin the work of reconstructing the concrete thinking that began to take shape in this still largely unmapped space, but some lines of thought emerge. Concretely, the Yishuv increasingly seemed to many Polish Jews to be a place where where the Jewish *individual* could make a decent life. The 1934 autobiography by "Rex" declared unabashedly the young author's conviction that in the Yishuv, a Jew, "whether he is a worker or a merchant or a clerk, can realize himself." Rex himself had trained as an engineer but saw no prospects of employment in Poland. Palestine could be a "solution to the Jewish Problem" *and* a chance at individual self-realization.[46]

There were also more directly political intuitions taking shape that stood in complex relation to the various official Zionism formulations of how the Yishuv was supposed to work. Jewish experience in *Poland* seems to have bred at least two distinct kinds of interest in the distinctive character of the Yishuv as a *national* space. As Weinreich observed acidly, some Polish Jewish youth seemed to be attracted to the trappings of ethnonational state power: "The Land of Israel offers the promise of one's own nation-state life, with Hebrew letters on the stamps, with Hebrew labels on the factory blueprints, with Jewish policemen even."[47]

But the actual *experience* of the Yishuv as fundamentally different from Poland points to another different phenomenon too. The "vernacular Zionism" of some Polish Jews turned on the distinct view that the Yishuv allowed one to live free of forms of degradation associated with life in Poland. We have seen sources from the period that suggest how changing views of antisemitism's hold in Poland could make for a Yishuvist "leap" even among young people with little political consciousness and no Zionist engagement whatsoever; this seems to have been the case with the young Hasidic autobiographer we encountered in Chapter 2, whose sudden desire to go to Palestine despite his own Agudah affiliation was "awakened," as he puts it, largely by infuriating encounters with youth antisemitism.[48] As Weinreich put it in *Veg*, Polish Jews imagined life in the Yishuv as a unique situation of "not being among strangers."

More pointedly, there are signs of a growing and spreading intuition among Polish Jews that life in the Yishuv was actually more physically *secure* than Jewish life elsewhere—that Jews in the Yishuv could defend themselves in a way that other Jewries could not. Ironically, the power of the idea that the Yishuv offered a unique kind of safety for Jews could also work against Zionism. One of the deepest worries for Zionist observers of the Diaspora in 1929 and again in 1936 was that the appearance of Jewish vulnerability in Palestine upset Diaspora Jews deeply and sapped support. In 1936, the emissary A. Gershom would warn the Histadrut that the Yishuv's initial policy of avoiding organized Jewish counterviolence was dangerous because "many see in this a weakness on our part." The appearance of dependence on the British was equally dangerous: "It has much influence here, and weakens [us]." Seven years earlier, Levita had come to Poland immediately after the 1929 attacks and made the disturbing discovery that while the attacks had initially awoken "a great people's movement" of "enthusiasm" for the Yishuv among Poland's Jews, this was giving way among many to despairing worry that the Yishuv could not survive against what his Polish Jewish informants called the "wild Arabs." He had also registered, as we saw, the way the attacks intersected with Jewish consciousness of anti-Jewish sentiment in Poland.[49] But between 1929 and 1936, the pendulum swung in the other direction. In 1935 Weinreich cited a recent story he had heard about a mother who had told her son to be careful in Tel Aviv, to which he had answered, "Of whom do I have to be afraid here?" Such sentiments could arise in unlikely subjects. In autumn 1932, the unyieldingly Diasporist and (then) anti-Zionist Golomb was forced to leave Poland on suspicion of Communism; finding teaching work in Palestine, of all places, he found much to dislike about the Yishuv. But soon he and his wife perceived a different side of concentrated Jewish settlement, as he later acknowledged: "It was good to wander the streets of Tel Aviv after midnight and not have any fear—not for dogs and not for two-legged attackers."[50]

If these intuitions might be called a "vernacular Zionism" in the making, a cobbling together of information, myth, and hope for better, there are also sources that point to still more coolly considered forms of thinking about the Yishuv as a space of different and better possibility for Jews who could get there. In February 1936, the veteran Polish Zionist politician and Sejm deputy Apollinary Hartglas wrote a furious essay titled "Palestinism: A New Creature on the Jewish Street." Hartglas wrote to anathematize this "Palestinism" in the name of proper Zionism: whereas Zionism properly understood involved a national "renaissance" of essential socioeconomic, political-cultural, and cultural transformations of Jews themselves, Palestinism "means simply the transplanting of diaspora Jews as they are, with all of their merits and flaws, to the Land of Israel [. . .] an escape from the Exile in order to create a new Exile in the land of Israel." The latter, he thundered, was a "cancer growing on the body of Zionism." At one level, Hartglas was reiterating a stance familiar from numerous writings by his more prominent colleague Grinboym and others in the *Al ha-Mishmar* faction in Polish General Zionism. According to this view, the upbuilding of a worthwhile Jewish national community in Palestine presupposed a thorough process of Zionist ideological and cultural recasting in the Diaspora; the Yishuv had to forge strong Zionist and Hebraist institutions before it could assimilate less selective Jewish migration on a large scale; and therefore Zionist activity had to remain bipolar, propounding Jewish national identity and interests in the Diaspora even as it sped up the tempo of creating an "economically healthy [. . .] politically independent Jewish majority community in our historical homeland."[51]

But if the piece was nothing more than representative *ideologically*, it offers us striking *sociological* indications regarding changing Polish Jewish attitudes toward the Zionist project. Hartglas's account was marked, first, by a sense of the sheer size and scope of the "Palestinism" he was decrying. Indeed, this was the express grounds of his worry. If "Palestinism" were simply a phenomenon among some hitherto distant assimilationist circles and a few businessmen, he wrote, it would be small cause for worry—but it had become a "Palestinism of the Jewish masses" as well. Second, Hartglas was particularly disturbed by a phenomenon of special interest to us: his sense that the Palestinist sensibility was taking on more assertive, expressly political forms. He found the "most striking example" of this in recent declarations by an assimilationist Jewish veterans' organization. "Already two or three years ago," he wrote, assimilationists of this sort "had begun to chatter, to demand Certificates, but they did not yet dare to assert their own view about what Zionism ought to be. But now we have arrived at that point."

Hartglas's observations, made in anger, resonate powerfully with the whole body of sources adduced in this chapter. His article suggests in content and timing the consolidation on a "mass" scale over several years of a whole gamut of new ways of thinking about the Yishuv as a realistic and attractive possibility by ever-deepening contrast to Poland.

And Hartglas's piece is not the only one to articulate how an emergent culture of sober exploration of the Palestine option could metamorphose into an inchoate politics marked by a willingness to *negotiate* a relationship to Zionism and even make demands on it in the name of Polish Jewish need. This development can be traced in the aforementioned 1934 text by Yeushzohn, for instance, with its striking specification of two distinctive formations of considered engagement with the Yishuv in light of a sense of danger in Poland. Both his second and third "groups" (his Polonized white-collar professionals and his Nalewki merchants, respectively) were driven in the first instance by a sort of "exitism" in which the catalyzing factor was a sense of foreclosed possibilities in Poland. This sense of foreclosure was expressly political-cum-cultural in the first case; the second case was murkier, a general sense that it had become both reasonable and imperative to find out if the Yishuv might actually be a "*takhles,*" a practical choice. But in *both* cases, this "push" intersected with the much-advertised and discussed fact of the Yishuv's massive growth and concretization over the past few years to birth new kinds of reflective engagement with Zionism.[52] Thus, if it was the mainstreaming of extrusionary antisemitism that pushed Yeushzohn's Polonized professionals to look for an alternative to their integrationist aspirations, it was the fact of a vibrant, actually existing Yishuv that allowed them to take the Zionist alternative seriously for the first time. In parallel, if the simple "mercantile Jews" were driven in part by a sense of foreclosed economic possibilities, they were also asking whether Palestine offered them—

and their children—a better chance at a *"takhles,"* a decent life in the "bourgeois" sense of health, happiness, and safety. This, too, was political thinking about the Jewish future.

Finally, similar sensibilities can be reconstructed from the previously cited frank letter from the Joint Distribution Committee's Giterman to the Jewish Agency's Werner Senator about the suddenly almost-unlimited prospects of interesting Polish Jews in "Palestinist work." Giterman, we recall, relayed from his uniquely informed vantage his sense that "the Jewish intelligentsia" and "the money-aristocracy" of Polish Jewry were suddenly open to work in Palestine—and not only "closely [aligned]" elements already sympathetic to Zionism but many who were "yesterday distant or even antagonistic" toward Zionism. The cause of this deep shift was twofold: if "the expanded absorptive capacities of Palestine" served as the "pull-factor," the "push" was "the rise of open and hidden Nazism."[53]

These three sources suggest in complementary ways how new relations to Palestine were crystallizing into a distinctive *politics:* a reflective, critical rethinking of Jewish individual and collective future prospects in Palestine as opposed to Poland (or in the Diaspora as such), powered by a sense that in *fact*—not merely or primarily in principle—the Yishuv might indeed be both different and (for Jews who could get there) *better* in concrete ways than Poland, however much one deemed the latter home. In Hartglas's view, such a Polish Jewish relationship to Palestine was a threat to real Zionism. For Yeushzohn, it testified to Zionism's prescience. For Giterman the Diasporist, it was tragic but understandable and, under the circumstances emerging in Poland and across Europe, inevitable.

7

Reason, Exit, and Postcommunal Triage

In mid-1934, the American Yiddish poet Yankev Glatshteyn returned to his native Lublin to see his dying mother. He stayed to spend time among a Polish Jewry he had left twenty years earlier. That same year, he began to produce an account of his trip; installments published over the next few years later appeared, apparently without substantial changes, as the 1938 and 1940 works *Ven Yash iz geforn* and *Ven Yash iz gekumen*. For all their modernist complexity, these works were manifestly autobiographical; the narrator's moniker "Yash" was Glatshteyn's real-life nickname.[1]

A late chapter of the second volume recounts Yash's excursion to the beautiful Renaissance-era town of Kazimierz-Dolny (Yid.: Kuzmir). Yash is accompanied by a Polish Jew called Nayfeld, a lawyer who has done so well "out of Jewish troubles, Jewish fears, and Jewish helplessness," as he puts it sadly, that he has retired at forty-three. Nayfeld's extended monologue during their transit is the chapter's focus.[2]

Nayfeld's is an unsettlingly double discourse. He begins by effusing about the joy of encountering Kazimierz-Dolny: "something you feel in the marrow of your bones." But upon learning of Yash's roots in Poland, Nayfeld shifts, with the phrase "politically speaking," into an extended meditation on the Polish Jewish crisis. Polish Jewry, he tells Yash, is now living in fear of violence sure to come. The patriotic love that Nayfeld and many other Polish Jews felt instinctively for Poland has been undone: "Poland was not liberated for us." Jews have "been so terrorized by all sorts of persecution, and our economic life has been so undermined by every kind of official and unofficial discrimination, by boycotts open and hidden, that our youth is haunted by the specter of poverty as never before." The youth was, moreover, right to be hopeless: "What makes it so bad is that our children have no future here."

Then Nayfeld interrupts himself again as their carriage enters the woods: "Take deep breaths," Nayfeld instructs Yash. "Polish woods can cure the sickest heart." Hearing the nightingale beloved of Polish Romanticism, Nayfeld commands the carter to stop so that they may listen. But then once again, a reversal: as the carriage passes a knot of Jews whose "sad eyes" hungrily assess what gains might be gotten from trade with the riders, the reverie is undone. The Jewish Question reasserts itself. These impoverished Jews, "our international bankers" and "dairyman-Rothschilds," Nayfeld remarks, are being "driven out of the villages systematically—not with laws, but with terror: their houses, which were just waiting to go up in smoke anyway, are being burned down. The peasants are being 'stirred up,' and quite often they greet those quiet Jews with sticks and rods." This is in turn part of a macropolitical process, "an ongoing war [. . .] against us, a starvation-siege" waged by some Polish collective actor, undefined but clearly the state, that keeps "a complete account" of "how many Jewish businesses have now fallen into Polish hands." Less open than the Nazi anti-Jewish campaign in neighboring Germany, the "Polish approach," Nayfeld avers, is more effective: "The Poles are doing it a lot more intelligently than Hitler. They don't babble or scream, they don't make a big deal of it," and yet the Jewish situation made untenable by the Depression is being kept that way by "siege."

Nayfeld's diagnosis culminates in a grim vision of *exit* as Polish Jews' last hope—or what would be a hope, if it were available. Omitting mention of Palestine, Birobidzhan, or any particular territory, Nayfeld looks to mass emigration as such as the only thing that might give a substantial number of Polish Jews a decent life. Its continued foreclosure is thus disastrous: "Once, we saved ourselves through emigration [. . .]. But now we have to stare collapse right in its Angel-of-Death eyes." Polish Jews find "no exit and no entrance" because they are deemed undesirables— "the countries of the world have armed themselves against us." The only bit of hope left—a policy prescription—is to approach this closure as what later observers would call an "image problem" that concerted "propaganda" by Polish Jews themselves might partially rectify:

"And all across the world, they've given Polish Jews a bad name"— now he spoke with Hasidic intensity—"We should sound the alarm! We ought to explain to the world that Polish Jews have an inner fire, we're believers, we have a wealth of faith that the big world out there can't imagine. We're smart, we still have God in our hearts and we have true faith and confidence, a wonderful, optimistic faith—not merely a religious faith, but the sort of faith that nourishes the soul and prevents it from departing the gaunt, starved body."[3]

Glatshteyn's Nayfeld figure concatenates a politics at the limits of politics: an assault on the whole community is ongoing, driven by structural factors that will not be reversed, and exit anywhere is the *only* hope that *some* Jews might avoid the community's ugly fate. Obviously, it is epistemologically easier to attribute this argument to its author, the American Jewish Glatshteyn, than to "the Polish Jew Nayfeld." Whether or not Glatshteyn actually spoke with a real figure who articulated Nayfeld's views in the summer of 1934, clearly the Nayfeld figure is carefully constructed to do literary work.[4] More generally, undoubtedly Glatshteyn meant the Nayfeld episode (as he did every episode in the narrative) to speak not only to the Jewish Question but to many questions. Thus, the song of the nightingale moves Yash to reflections not about Poland's Jews but about art.[5]

But whether or not the Nayfeld figure embodies an actual individual with whom Glatshteyn spoke in the summer of 1934, Nayfeld's particular analysis cleanly distills many of the new lines of Polish Jewish social and political thought we have been investigating. And this is no accident: Glatshteyn returned from his trip gripped by urgency to relay what he had seen.[6] Whatever else it was meant to be, the Yash narrative was meant as serious reportage of what he had found.

Nayfeld proves representative of actual Polish Jewish thinking, as we will now see, in his unhappy but resolute vectoring on the view that *exit for some* might be the only genuine solution for *any*. This chapter aims in part to recover figures in opposing Polish Jewish national circles whose thinking began to recenter, unhappily, on the idea of exit for some as a kind of communal triage. This thought was increasingly distant from any of the organized political agendas still grinding along in Polish Jewish life.

The Nayfeld character also embodies a second key dimension of the Polish Jewish political thinking investigated below. The structure of self-interruption that Glatshteyn weaves into this episode about Yash's journey with Nayfeld is itself an argument: that there can no longer be a relationship between the realm of Jewish *identity* (and culture, affect, longing, loves) and Jewish political *reason*. Glatshteyn takes great pains to communicate that Nayfeld is deeply, fundamentally Polish. It is not simply that Nayfeld is objectively Polonized, his success as a lawyer indicating comfort in Polish language and civic life. Nor is it merely a matter of ideology, as when Nayfeld relates that "believe it or not, I was once an ardent Polish patriot." It is more than this: Nayfeld, we are given to understand, fully *feels* Poland to be his home. Escorting Yash through Kazimierz-Dolny, Nayfeld relishes the chance to show him an old castle deemed the site of a mythic love affair between the Polish king Casimir and a "beautiful Jewess" called Esterke. Like her biblical namesake, the Polish Jewish Esterke resonated in Jewish folklore—despite the sinful character of her entanglement (or perhaps because of it)—as a central symbol of Jewish-Polish intimacy. Glatshteyn's text emphasizes that this "transborder [*tsvishngrenets*] legend" of Jews' connection to the central strands of Poland's history resonates deeply for the Nayfeld character even "now."[7]

And beyond the Jewish-Polish synthesis, Nayfeld also manifests a profound, enchanted relationship to Poland's natural beauty. Poland's woods have a curative effect on Nayfeld's Jewish body no less than on a Polish one ("Take deep breaths"). He is no less one with Poland's woods and animals than a "true Pole."

But Glatshteyn's point is that although Nayfeld's Polishness is soul-deep, it is *politically* irrelevant. The whole structure of the episode encodes an insistence that belonging, love, and identity simply cannot bear any longer on how Jews should assess their situation or what they have to do—which is to leave if they can. Nayfeld, at home only in Poland, embodies a way of thinking at odds with Poland-centered Jewish Diasporism and Polish Jewish assimilationism alike, both of which sought to parlay at-homeness into a politics.

To contend that Jews had to sever their politics from their deepest identity commitments flew in the face of every major Jewish ideology born in Eastern Europe. In East European Zionism, Diasporism, Orthodoxy, and integrationism alike, political action was inextricable from the cultivation of the right sort of identity; indeed, the latter was often the chief concern, the *raison d'etre*, of the former. Of course, it is even more obviously the case that this argument, embedded in the narrative's structure, is Glatshteyn's rather than Nayfeld's. But here, too, Glatshteyn captured an unsettling shift in real Polish Jewish political thinking: a sense that the need for clarity about ever-worsening problems demanded that one sever analysis from sentiment, ideals, even the most cherished aspects of one's own identity.

Those real historical actors in and around Poland who groped along the two paths of thought embodied in the figure of Nayfeld were moved to do so by a shared sense that the Polish and European Jewish situation was growing very bad. In different ways and to different degrees, it was this sense of crisis (and of Jews' profoundly limited capacities to redress it) that forced the actors examined here toward a focus on strategies of exit and toward a sense that ideology and ideals had to be put aside in favor of clear-eyed understanding. In a larger sense, it pushed to the center of their thinking the most concrete question: What (if anything) might actually improve the life chances of some Polish Jews?

Separating this question from the various bundles of political commitments, hopes, and ideals that Jews bore opened a space for forms of political thinking that we might call "rationalizations"—not in the negative sense but in the precise Weberian sense of affording oneself a greater capacity to think simultaneously and reciprocally about the relationship between one's desired ends and what could actually be achieved with the means really at one's disposal. Such a question could take a kind of inchoately quantitative form about resources and return: How *many* Jews could be helped by one or another program, how *much* help would be provided, and how *much* did the program cost, in terms of Jews' collective quantum of resources? To think in those terms did not mean, of course, that one fully escaped ideology. But to posit a quantum of total communal resources (or, as some did, the more abstract concept of total communal "energies") opened a space to imagine the Jewish commonweal not from the standpoint of what *ought* to be but from the reality of that population's capacities to shape its own fate under determinate conditions.

Given the global conditions that obtained in the early 1930s, this kind of thinking took shape with special force around the question of Palestine, and thus Palestine and the Yishuv return to the center of our discussion. One of the first stops on Max Weinreich's Palestine itinerary was Kibbutz Degania (Aleph), and his arrival coincided with a celebration: Degania, one of the Yishuv's first experiments in collectivist settlement, was celebrating its thirty-fifth anniversary. Narrating this visit in the travelogue he began to publish shortly thereafter, Weinreich acknowledged that the place and its people, with their joy in achievements that had come hard, had made a deep impression. But he also posed a set of penetrating questions: "We Jews are justified in thinking, when we see a corner of the Land of Israel: how much has that bit of happy pride [*nakhes*] in real achievements cost the Jewish people? And what significance does that bit of *nakhes* have in comparison with the sea of troubles in which Jews are being soaked? And doesn't this bit of *nakhes* draw off an entire stream of social-communal [*gezelshaftlekh*] energy from possibilities which in truth bring much more [use]? Every conscious Jew [. . .] must ask many and more such questions."[8] As we saw in Chapter 6, Weinreich's first encounter with Palestine's Yishuv compelled him to grapple seriously for the first time with concrete Zionist political claims about the communal benefits of territorial concentration as against dispersion, and of real if intermittent access to state power (even if the "state" in question was the fickle British Empire and not one's own) as against its lack.[9] But with this early barrage of questions Weinreich also signaled that he would take up a further decisive question: What was Zionism actually giving Jews in the Diaspora at the present moment, and what would it give them in the near future?

At one level, Weinreich's questions simply repeated what had long been the most fundamental critique of Zionism made by those who took as their primary concern the commonweal of the whole Jewish people.[10] Among those who had made that critique not so long ago was Weinreich's father-in-law, the noted Wilno physician and communal leader Shabad. In 1927, as the promises of Zionism's Fourth Aliyah seemed to be collapsing, Shabad had reflected angrily that if "the huge mass of energy and resources which had been devoted to Palestine were [instead] focused here in the so-called Exile, the results would be greater and more fruitful."[11] As the 1920s gave way to the 1930s, the same critique of Zionism from a Jewish-communalist standpoint was mounted by some in the revived Territorialist movement: Zionism claimed to be redeeming the exiled Jewish nation, but true concern for embattled European Jews demanded that all efforts and resources be turned toward seeking a territory that could (ostensibly) accommodate far larger numbers of Jews with less conflict (see below).

Yet by 1935, Weinreich was no longer launching a confident critique. A return to other dimensions of his Palestine travelogue will show that he meant these questions not as polemic but *as* questions. In keeping with his readiness throughout his Palestine travelogue to put aside old certainties in favor of real investigation, Weinreich closed with an essay that confronted the question of how much Palestine was actually helping and might further help Polish Jews as individuals seeking a better life. How much emphasis should be given to seeking paths of Jewish exit, at what cost to other commitments and projects; what is the proper relationship of ideals, empiricism, and analytical reason in Jewish political choice-making; and what is the actual value of Palestine and the Yishuv for Polish Jews?

And finally, for Weinreich and for others we will encounter in this chapter, the unfolding situation and the limits of Jews' capacity to redress it called into question the very category of community and communal loyalty itself. In place of community, a figure like Binyomen R. gave voice to the prerogatives of the desperate individual. Still others acted in service of a category hovering uneasily between community and individual, between selflessness and "selfishness": the family. These were ideas of partial rescue, of politics as a kind of triage.

Ideals and Exigencies

In late 1934, the preeminent analytical voice of the national intelligentsia Yankev Lestschinsky published an essay in a Łódź Labor Zionist newspaper explaining why he, of all people, would not throw his support behind a newly revived Jewish Territorialist movement and would instead support Zionism. Lestschinsky's argument offers a first iteration of how perception of looming crisis and time running out could force this practical question to the center of what had been seamlessly ideological debates, with surprising effects.[12]

Lestschinsky wrote in response to the reemergence of the old Territorialist idea in the form of a newly constituted movement calling itself Frayland. Created in 1934 (though with deeper roots) by mostly Polish Jewish intellectuals, students, and professionals who shared Lestschinsky's view of unprecedented danger to European Jewish well-being, Frayland aimed to (somehow) acquire a "large and empty" territory in which masses of desperate Jews might resettle and create a new life. The founders of Frayland expected Lestschinsky to join them, with good reason. Not only did their analysis of the Jewish situation fit his, but they saw Lestschinsky himself as a spiritual godfather of their movement. Years earlier, he had broken with Zionism to become a leading theorist-activist for a Jewish politics that would aid "the great masses of the nation" in a way that Zionism with its Palestinocentrism and Hebraist obsessions could not, and that Bundism with its narrow Kautskian class-politics orthodoxies refused to. Circa 1905 Lestschinsky had begun to articulate a politics simultaneously revolutionary socialist, cultural nationalist, and open to the idea that territorial concentration might be an essential part of the solution to the Jewish Problem. Thereafter, Lestschinsky had traversed the political spectrum and by the 1920s had grown close to the Bund, as noted; but by 1930 his disillusionment with the Bund was under way. Under these circumstances, those declaring for Territorialism in 1934 (many of whom knew Lestschinsky personally) expected his full-throated support.[13]

Instead, Lestschinsky released a position paper as to why he could not support the renewal of the Territorialist program in Frayland—and why instead he now felt compelled to align with Zionism. He began by impugning Territorialist hopes that organized Zionism would actually support the new movement rather than see it as a competitor for scant Jewish resources. The Territorialists argued thus: "The Zionists themselves admit that Palestine is not for the millions, only for the thousands—not for the Jewish body, but [only] for the Jewish spirit. And with a light heart, they draw the conclusion: it follows that the Zionists will not obstruct us, and perhaps even aid us!" But, Lestschinsky remonstrated, the Zionists would do no such thing. On one level, Zionists would not support Territorialism's supersessionist vision for obvious subjective reasons: they had spent their whole lives building the Yishuv. At another level, he suggested, many Zionists apparently believed that Palestine could eventually absorb millions of Jews. Lestschinsky's own views on this claim as of mid to late 1934 are unclear; other pieces from the same year suggest that he was considerably more skeptical. But clearly he was also reassessing his own skepticism in light of the extraordinary expansion of the Yishuv in the past two years, which he had not predicted. And Lestschinsky saw another reason to reconsider his earlier dismissal of Zionism's obstinate Palestinocentrism. Zionists would reject the Territorialist logic not least because they believed that it was *only* for "the Land of Israel" that Jews would be willing to mobilize extraordinary energies and resources. This might be adjudged irrational, but—Lestschinsky anticipated the Zionist argument—culture and prejudice were also social facts, and did not a social fact on a mass scale have to be taken into account as an objective determinant of what communal "policies" could succeed?

Having ventriloquized the Territorialist-Zionist debate as one over communal reason and policy priorities, Lestschinsky declared for the Zionists. His explanation as to his own position was tangled (as one of his Territorialist friends turned critics, Avrom Rozin, would thunder in immediate response), but the three strands just noted were distinctly visible, as was an interesting fourth.[14] It was simply a political fact that the Zionist movement would not yield to Territorialism now of all times, when the Yishuv was growing rapidly and Zionism was full of confidence. Of course, this in itself could be read merely as observation about entrenched commitments; the very same point could be made by Zionism's critics. But Lestschinsky also endorsed the "objectivity of the subjective" argument that the Zionist project and the Land of Israel, with their uniquely powerful affective influence over Jews of many backgrounds, were the only factors that could in fact move large numbers to sacrifice for something that could improve a substantial number of Jewish lives. No such mass sacrifice would materialize even if Territorialists managed to secure the promise of some new "empty land." Actually, some leading Territorialists acknowledged this to be an accurate characterization of the "folk's" sensibilities. Whereas Lestschinsky's old friend turned critic Rozin aspired to overcome this "romanticism" and reeducate Jews toward more rational investments of their energies, Lestschinsky was moving toward the view that Jewish communal policy had to work with the cultural material it had.[15]

Lestschinsky's late embrace of Zionism over Territorialism was not free of ideology. Another strand of his argument betrayed nationalist romanticism: "Where are the guarantees that in the new land 'gifted' to us, they will allow us Jews not only to do the hard work of pioneering, but thereafter to grow and grow and bring the ideal of a homeland to its highest level?" Jews "needed" to be regenerated, and Zionism was actually doing it.

But Lestschinsky also sounded an argument bespeaking a terrifying *new* sense of crisis, limited Jewish resources, and of time running out. "As far as its own conscience goes, it is now a thousand times more difficult for Territorialism than it was years ago to justify its rejection of the concrete territory called Palestine, which has not only performed miracles with regard to the psychic transformation of the Jewish soul, but has also performed the miracle of miracles: *made possible the migration of 50,000 Jews in a single year.*" If Lestschinsky the nationalist could not give up on the "transformation of the Jewish soul," he now nonetheless deemed the highest "miracle" of all the capacity of organized Jewish effort to facilitate emigration for two hundred thousand desperate Jews. This "miracle" was made possible by the concrete facts of the Yishuv and the modicum of power Zionism had carved out—concrete facts that Territorialism simply could not offer at this juncture.

In the context of Lestschinsky's other writings, the essay breathes a sharp sense of time having run out. It is in this context that Territorialism's demand to start over had to be rejected in favor of uniting communal effort behind Zionism's bird in hand. "*We must not restart the experiment*" not least "precisely because the abyss has opened so much wider; precisely because life itself has shown so clearly and so sharply that the fundamental source of all troubles lies in landlessness, in homelessness."[16]

Emigration as Communal Evacuation

As figures like Lestschinsky rethought their relationship to Zionism under the pressure of the sense of time running out, the same sense of crisis was recasting how others—across political lines—were conceiving the scope, purpose, and urgency of Polish Jewish mass exit as such. Poland's Jewish Central Emigration Society, generally known in Yiddish as YEAS, was one of a network of relief organizations created by East European Jewish activists under the sign of international progressivism. Created in 1924 with a leadership from across the Polish Jewish political spectrum, it cast itself as an apolitical organization in multiple senses: it sought to bring order and rationality into Jewish emigration work, it brought together non-Zionist and Zionist elements, it advertised good working relations with the relevant Polish state ministries, and it framed the need for re-newed substantial Jewish emigration itself in purely socioeconomic terms, as an outlet for impoverished elements in Polish Jewry. Of course, YEAS's activists were driven by a growing sense that Polish Jews faced problems to which emigration was one part of the solution. At the YEAS's founding conference in 1924, one of the resolutions adopted underscored "the des-perate situation of the Jewish masses in Eastern Europe." By the time of its second major conference in 1931, the tone had grown darker still, with the organization declaring the limited opportunities for Jewish immigra-tion "a grave danger and terrible catastrophe for tens and hundreds of thousands" of Jews across Poland. But as to what *problem* emigration was the solution, the organization's answer underwent a telling change between 1924 and 1934.[17]

At the 1924 and 1931 conferences, YEAS conferees had framed the problem in purely structural-*economic* terms with no hint of a political analysis. But by 1934, the YEAS leadership had forthrightly revised its analysis of the problem to which emigration was an essential solution in terms familiar to us from the political-sociological analyses of incipiently post-Diasporist analysts like Rozin and Lestschinsky. The question of Jewish emigration had to be thought about not merely in relation to "the general phenomena and laws of life that induce mass migration among many peoples," but in relation to the politics of the nation-state, Polish and otherwise:

> The burden of taxation presses primarily on the urban popula-
> tion. Mighty and capital-rich non-Jewish cooperative movements are
> developing, doing grave damage to Jewish traders and shopkeepers.
> The ruling peoples are developing a native commercial class at a
> truly rapid pace. It receives state support and this helps it push out
> the Jewish trader. Emergent cartels are pursuing a forthright policy
> of connecting directly with the consumer and freeing themselves of
> middleman petty commerce, which lies in Jewish hands. And fi-
> nally, state capitalism, etatism, is becoming a decisive factor in the
> economic life of the country, commanding as it does the power and
> influence of the state itself, access to credit, etc.; in the monopoly
> enterprises created or supported by state capitalism, there is no
> place for Jewish labor or for Jewish professionals.
>
> This all, taken together, leads to a situation in which every shock,
> crisis, and transition produces the greatest damage among Jews.
> Whole swaths are being uprooted from their economic soil and
> being impoverished.[18]

Jews as a national minority and middleman minority had to assume that for *political*-structural as well as economic-structural reasons, many or even most of them could not reasonably expect a viable future in situ. By 1934, YEAS activists were declaring the ever-tightening limits on Jewish immigration around the world to be "the central problem" of contemporary Polish Jewish life because the facts pointed to extrusion as the horizon Polish Jews had to face. Mass emigration might be the only solution to a political problem.

This was not the only evolution imposed on the thinking of the Polish Jewish activists who devoted their time to YEAS. One of YEAS's more prominent leaders, Leon Alter, was a committed Polonizer, having even served in the new Polish state's Emigration Office until "new reactionary winds" pushed him out in 1923; he remained fiercely "anti-Zionist and anti-Bundist."[19] Yet he was the exception. Actually, YEAS was dominated by men who were, crudely put, Jewish nationalists—who identified as servant-administrators of a posited Jewish nation. Many were supporters of Zionism. Founders included the Zionist leader Ignacy Schipper and Moyshe Shalit, who combined intense commitment to East European Jewish culture in a national vein with support for Labor Zionism. Thereafter, YEAS's board of delegates became increasingly dominated by out-spoken Zionists like the sociologist Aryeh Tartakover, his lieutenant Natan Meltzer, and others.[20] This itself set up an interesting tension within the organization. Emigration was of course a deeply individual-cum-familial act; its implications for "the national community" were quite mixed, a fact about which Jewish nationalists, like other East European national-ists, worried greatly. As Tara Zahra has shown, emigration in the interwar period was something that nationalists from Poland to Czechoslovakia worked to bring under control and reshape in ways that would "serve the nation" rather than "robbing it" of "resources."[21] The elements that came to dominate the YEAS shared in this outlook and nearly succeeded in committing YEAS to it. Yet the unfolding of YEAS's history suggests how an organization dominated by committed Jewish nationalists, and indeed Zionists, was pushed to sideline cherished visions of disciplining Jewish emigration for the sake of the Jewish "national good," and instead to throw its support behind objectively assimilationist efforts to aid the Jewish emigrant as he or she tried to get out to anywhere, under any conditions.

On a quotidian level, YEAS's practice was virtually unmarked by any expression of the nationalist ideals held by a majority of its stakeholders. Mostly it worked to smooth the path for would-be individual emigrants without conditions: information about conditions in potential receiving countries and ways that access might be won, juridical help with formal administrative requirements, mediation services at an emigration transit point in the Gdańsk-Pomerania region, maintaining a hostel in Warsaw that served some 20,000 migrants over the course of the 1924–1934 pe-riod, and the provision of tiny loans to individual migrants. As against this, YEAS did next to nothing to "discipline" the emigrants in ways that would preserve—much less enhance—national identity. The 13,000 zlotys it spent on "agricultural training" for emigrants in 1929 was dwarfed by 370,000 zlotys of direct financial support to individuals. YEAS indeed sought to facilitate emigrants' integration into their new societies; in 1928 it began to offer language courses in English, French, and Spanish.[22]

Events at the lively YEAS national conference in 1931 demonstrated that this disjuncture was both visible and bothersome to many dele-gates. Zionist elements took the floor to demand that YEAS reorient its work from simply helping individual emigrants to reshaping the migra-tion process and the emigrants themselves. Tartakover demanded that YEAS acknowledge "the importance of the ideological moment in the emigration-movement" and reorganize itself around the view that "the emigration-question in its entirety is a national-social problem." Others demanded "large-scale enlightenment work among the working-class emigrants," the maintaining of "closer contact with the emigrants in the receiving lands," and active efforts to direct emigrants toward "compact" Jewish settlement rather than allowing individuals to make settlement choices based on market opportunity (as of course most immigrants did). Demands for additional emphasis on "productivizing" job training and agrarian settlement were voiced by figures associated with Labor Zionism, who invoked Hehalutz as an exemplar. And this antiassimilationist vision of emigration organizing won the day, with a resolution calling on senior partners in Jewish emigration work in France and the United States, avowedly *integrationist* organizations, to "undertake activity with the goal of rooting the Jewish emigrants in the receiving lands through pro-ductivization and by settling them in colonies that will constitute a con-centrated force and will strengthen their social and economic position."[23]

But even as these nationalists won the discursive debate, the deep-ening plight of Polish Jewry was pushing others in the organization toward the view that all this was a distraction, a luxury. Their démarche provoked "heated arguments" at the 1931 conference. Most interestingly, a leading voice among the opponents, Yitshok Valk, was himself one of the nation-alists. Active in YEAS on the ground in Wilno, Valk was a longtime Zionist, active in Tseirei Tsion and later Poalei Tsion.[24] Yet at the 1931 meeting, he pushed back against the "social-national" vision. Against the demand for "an active emigration-politics" inspired by Hehalutz, Valk in-sisted that YEAS had to approach emigrant aid "in purely practical terms." Instead of seeking to direct emigrants into "compact" Jewish com-munal settlement, the YEAS had to work harder to seek out underex-ploited migration opportunities: "Great emigration opportunities like for instance to France are being neglected." Instead of trying to remake the Polish Jewish emigrant socially and culturally, the YEAS ought to "take into account the healthy instinct of the immigrant herself who carves out new paths."[25] Valk continued to argue that Jewish emigration policy should focus simply and solely on maximizing Jewish exit until the very end.[26]

And in *practice*, Valk's minority view seems to have won out between 1931 and 1934. By 1934, in tandem with its open declaration that mass emigration was a necessary response to the slow-motion political assault on the Polish Jewish future, YEAS seems to have dropped talk of colonization in favor of a full-on embrace of individual and familial emigration as such. Any talk of emigration as a mixed blessing due to national dispersion and indiscipline fell by the wayside. Emigration simply had "colossal positive influence" on the Jewish situation: "Emigration has rescued from collapse great masses of Jews and given them the chance to lay a foundation in their new lands and create for themselves better life-conditions." No less tellingly, sometime in the months that followed the 1934 publication, YEAS dispatched longtime member Dr. Peker to the Soviet Union to investigate whether there really was "the possibility of Polish Jewish emigration to Birobidzhan." Thus, an organization dominated by Zionists but pledged to aid Jewish emigrants as such was driven by emergency to actually investigate Jewish settlement possibilities in a Soviet territorial project created not least to undermine Zionism.[27]

But of course, the activists of YEAS were well aware of the same grim fact that gnawed at Glatshteyn's Nayfeld: the doors of the world were closing further, with the one partial exception of Palestine. The 1934 document noted that even countries that remained somewhat open were working to make entrance still harder.[28] From its beginnings in 1924, YEAS leaders had enjoined "the Jewish representatives of all lands to conduct a war against the limits on immigration and to conduct a broad propaganda campaign across the entire world for the rights of the Jewish people to free migratory movement." This idea—which would soon appear, as we saw, in the mouth of Glatshteyn's Nayfeld—would remain one of the straws at which emigration activists grasped. But in the meantime, there was only closure, with the one exception of Palestine. In these circumstances, as we saw in Chapter 6, even some non-Zionist intellectuals were moved to reevaluate earlier assumptions about Zionism and the Yishuv. But more than that, they were also driven to try to understand concretely how *much* succor Palestine was offering and might yet offer to some Polish Jews.

(Whom, How Many, How, and How Much) Can Palestine Actually Help?

The question Weinreich posed at the beginning of his travelogue regarding just how much use Palestine had been and might yet be for desperate Polish Jews was no intelligentsia parlor game. As we have seen, Zionist emissaries found it welling up from the grass roots, to their discomfort. Thus, in 1934, Miriam Shlimovits encountered Hehalutz youth in Osowa

Wyszka "consumed" by "doubt regarding whether we have the ability and possibility to solve the question of the mass of Polish Jews [*sheelat ha-hamonim*]."[29]

Others took a much more optimistic view: the YIVO autobiographer "Rex" declared in 1934 that "between four and six million Jews can easily find a place in Palestine."[30] Once again, the trope of prophecy must be resisted (at any rate, both the doubts of the Osowa Wyszka youth and Rex's optimism proved accurate in different ways). Relevant here, rather, is the *separation* of the question of Palestine's concrete significance for the Jewish Question from the ideological questions that had long swirled around it. The doubts Shlimovits encountered in small-town eastern Poland came not from local Communists or Bundists but from youth in Zionist ranks; they reflected both a collectivist moral urgency and an urgent concern for the quantitive-calculative question of how *many* Palestine could help. We may judge Rex's countervailing certainty Pollyannaish, but, as Bassok notes, it came amid an argument about Zionism marked by the same peeling away of ideological sentiment from a focus on how many Jews facing foreclosed futures could find a concretely different life in Palestine: "As regards a solution to the Jewish Problem, many compare it to a *perpetuum mobile* or a problem with no solution, but I do not share that view. Palestine is indeed a solution to the 'Jewish Problem,' though this doesn't mean that *all* Jews will live in Palestine. Between four and six million Jews can easily find a place in Palestine, and that will be enough. I mean Jews from Poland and parts of Romanian and Russian Jewry. And of course, for German Jews, Palestine is the last salvation, for they are living as though on a volcano."[31]

We can hardly imagine that these efforts to gain some concrete sense of how, how many, and how much Palestine could actually help were confined to educated Jewish youth in Warsaw and declassed youth in the eastern hamlet of Osowa Wyszka. Once again, unconnected sources turned up almost at random bespeak a discourse unfolding *sotto voce* but widely across Polish Jewish society.

In the midst of this, some sought to find ways out of the magic circle in which the Osowa Wyszka halutzim and Rex were trapped to attain more robust answers, or at least to better clarify the metrics by which this question might be answered. Some of the most arresting efforts in this regard are found in the searching travelogues of the non-Zionists Tshernikhov and Weinreich. One of the themes that Tshernikhov brought to the fore several times over the course of his 1933 travelogue was the question of *expectations*—and the fact, as he saw it, that the Yishuv's growth had repeatedly exceeded skeptical expectations, including his own. Thus, one travelogue installment related a discussion about water resources and the possibilities of large-scale agricultural development with another Zion-skeptical colleague. Relaying his colleague's observation about how scant Palestine's riverine water supply was, Tshernikhov also acknowledged apparently reliable reports of much more substantial sources of water being found in underground aquifers, relayed the confident claims of an American Jewish farmer in the Sharon region that Jewish agriculture would soon be able to feed the whole country and produce winter vegetables for export, and noted that new technical means of efficient irrigation were now being developed as a native Jewish industry in Palestine rather than being imported from Germany. These were of course Zionist talking points; but Tshernikhov also deemed them true, and the lesson he drew was that, once again, what had seemed like reasonable skepticism that Palestine could feed and house many more Jews might actually be ill founded.[32]

Beyond the question of agrarian development, Tshernikhov also allowed that his earlier general skepticism about the Yishuv's capacity to continue rapid growth as a society and economy (that is, to sustain a rapidly growing Jewish population) might also have been misplaced. By mid-1933, the Fifth Aliyah was in full swing: 30,207 Jewish immigrants arrived that year (and were largely absorbed by the cities), 42,359 would come the next year, and 61,854 the next, compared with 4,075 in 1931 and 4,944 in 1930.[33] The question thus became whether this level of growth could be sustained. Tshernikhov did not venture an answer, positive or negative; but he allowed the logic of the positive, optimistic argument to be heard in full force around the question of economic growth and global Jewish *investment* in Palestine.

Writing for readers who surely knew that the Fourth Aliyah had ended in crisis not least because suddenly heightened levels of small-scale private investment had dried up with equal suddenness, Tshernikhov addressed this renewed question through a discussion involving himself, another visitor from Poland, and two Yishuv interlocutors including an old friend and colleague Meirson. Tshernikhov's fellow visitor made the skeptics' case: once again, as in 1924–1925, the growth of Palestine's Jewish economy was an "artificial" product of resources being redirected to the Yishuv from the Jewish Diaspora, not something growing out of the Yishuv's exalted productivization of Jews. And this was the worst kind of investment: high cost, low return. The implication, of course, was that this tap would be turned off once again when more rational forms of investment reemerged. To this argument from recent history, however, Tshernikhov allowed his Yishuv interlocutors to counterpose the argument that grim horizons of threat to Jews in Europe had changed Jews' rational calculus profoundly and permanently: "It's as though they are saving [the money they're investing] from a conflagration [. . .]. You don't see what is happening in the world and see money with the eyes of yesteryear." Here again, arguments about rationality were not of course fully disentangled from ideological commitment. A comment by Tshernikhov's old acquaintance Meirson resounded both with persistent national collectivism and with the insight that Jews would be forced to turn to Palestine by political and economic pressure: "You know, I'm also not in agreement with how one often speaks and writes about the diaspora here, but answer honestly: now, in the atmosphere and perspective of our era—after the death of liberalism and the death-throes of humanist socialism (its ostensible antagonist but in actuality more its follower)—does the diaspora really have another choice, does it have a national idea, even a limited objective possibility of national creation?" In response to all this, Tshernikhov recorded his own insistence that the older generation of Jewish capitalists would regard investing in Palestine as madness. But he allowed that his interlocutors might have a point, and gave them the last word: "Worlds are collapsing; can [a transformation in investment rationality] be otherwise?"[34]

Where Tshernikhov's interlocutors in Palestine were thinking about the rationality of Jewish individuals with resources investing with at least some hope of return, many other Polish Jews gave charitable gifts to Zionism's so-called national funds. In his *Veg tsu unzer yugnt*, Weinreich presented this outflow of resources from a community sinking into ruin as a textbook example of irrational "love" prevailing over rational calculus. On this score as on others, his unlikely respondent-from-the-sticks Binyomen R. offered a different interpretation. Even as he granted the partial truth of Weinreich's claim that in all forms of political choice, "love" could be more powerfully operative than "*konsekvent*" thinking (thinking directed by reason), Binyomen saw this particular behavior otherwise:

Not only Zionists can be blinded by love; such a thing can be found in all of the parties without exception. I think, however, that with regard to that fact about the [Zionist] fund[-drive], this has nothing to do with it essentially. Each [such] fund is self-justifying, in that there are people who need it and [who] support it. Keren Kayemet and Keren ha-Yesod were created by the Zionist movement, Keren Tel-Hai by the Revisionists, Keren ha-Yishuv by the Agudah. It's hardly necessary to aver yet again that the money that people donate for Land of Israel fund-raising would never under any circumstance be given for diaspora needs, simply because idealism on that score is lacking [*poshet vayl s'iz nito der idealizm derbay*]. The guilt for this lies in our present circumstances, which we feel as yet [too] weak to change in any radical fashion.[35]

Weinreich's reduction of the *particular* choice of Jews to send money for Jewish settlement and society building (of different and even opposing sorts) in Palestine to the workings of mere "love" and "affect" rang false to Binyomen. Against it, he registered his sense that what was operative in such material support for Palestine settlement was also a reasoned view: that Jews had a capacity to reshape conditions in Palestine with the collective resources they could muster in a way they simply could not in Poland. We might note the eminent reasonability of such an assessment given the vast demographic differences between Poland with its 30 million inhabitants and Palestine with just a bit over a million total, of whom by late 1935 some 30 percent or so were Jewish (to say nothing of the fact that Jewish monies directed to Palestine went in good part to an internationally recognized, substantially autonomous Jewish *administration* that could direct it toward collective goals and goods). But objective reasonability aside, what is significant here is Binyomen's strong feeling that in such giving, serious reflection on what Jews did and did not have it in their *power* to do was in the mix, whatever other factors might be playing out.

For his part, Weinreich moved over the course of 1935 toward a far more complex weighing of the Yishuv's/Palestine's practical significance for Jews facing, as he had put it, "a sea of troubles." In the twelfth and concluding installment of his Palestine travelogue, Weinreich revisited the question he had posed so critically earlier: granted, Zionism was a "human" achievement, but was it more than that: a practical contribution to solving the problems of substantial numbers of Jews? His formulations mapped closely onto Lestschinsky's Janus-faced thinking.[36]

On the one hand, Weinreich briefly moved as close as he ever had, or would again, to a romantic appreciation of Zionism's effects on "the

Jewish soul": "There has arisen a Yishuv that is young, interesting, and unadorned in its humanity. A Yishuv that has taught broad strata of Jews how to work [. . .] where former yeshiva students have become leaders of great communes, where former bookbinders have become engineers on the railroads, where thousands from the Polish and Lithuanian townlets once forced to be idlers have found work and satisfaction."

Yet on the other hand, Weinreich was careful to short-circuit any romance of Zionism per se. He shrewdly suggested that capitalism no less than Zionist idealism was the motor of this change, remarking that the other place where East European Jews had also been "taught [. . .] how to work" was of course "America." He declared the kibbutz "a truly great accomplishment [. . .] in the human sense," but in so doing invoked the sharp question he had raised at the beginning of the series: Did Palestine help Jews in any concrete way, and how much did it "cost" the global Jewish community?

Here, in the final installment, Weinreich offered a clear answer to his own earlier questions: "And also from the standpoint of getting several hundred thousand Jews set up in life, this is no small thing when one recalls that the entire world has barred its gates to Jewish wanderers." Weinreich the inveterate Diasporist and anti-Zionist now declared Zionism a uniquely concrete success in his own communalist terms. In having provided better life chances for several hundred thousand Jews, Zionism had achieved something that no other Jewish movement had, and that any Jew concerned for the Jewish commonweal had to welcome regardless of ideology.

Ultimately, Weinreich concluded the essay and the series on a more guarded note (or rather more guarded about Palestine, though less so about Eastern Europe). To the ledger of Zionism's concrete achievement of giving several hundred thousand Jews a better life when no one else would, he added a surprisingly positive spin on what he had until only recently viewed as Zionism's "spiritual sleight of hand": "And it is also no small thing that the Land of Israel has become for millions of Jews not only a matter of pride, but also the land of their hopes." But were these hopes justified? "But here we need to think carefully. Is there a possibility that these hopes will be realized? Can the Land of Israel really save the millions-strong masses of Jews in the lands of the Hitlers and almost-Hitlers?" Weinreich offered neither a positive nor a negative answer: "One can answer: no. One can answer: there is no way to know. One can answer:

maybe [. . .]. One can answer with all sorts of such suppositions, but those are all matters that are not built on facts."

Yet though not willing to become a believer, Weinreich could not remain the same sort of convinced skeptic he had been. Events in Palestine and in Poland had moved Weinreich to assess Zionism for the first time not against the grid of ideology but on a ledger of resources sunk and individual Jews helped. The question now became what might Palestine yet be able to do for still other Jews in days to come, and by extension, how Jews in Poland and Europe should relate to it as a matter of communal focus, support, and policy. The last installment in the series did not simply leave this question of Palestine's/the Yishuv's future hanging in the rhetorical firmament, but grounded it by reflecting on the state of the Diaspora no less than that of the Yishuv and, extrapolatively, by thinking about the future in relation to evidence of the recent past rather than ideological first principles. Like Tshernikhov, Weinreich sought to reach some sort of concrete purchase by focusing on the question of whether the Yishuv's economic and infrastructural expansion (and thus its expanded absorptive power vis-à-vis masses of Jewish immigrants) could continue—which was in essence a question about whether the investment of Diaspora resources and energies that fueled it was likely to continue to flow or would rather evaporate, causing another 1926-style collapse.

Before turning to this lobe of Weinreich's argument, we should remind ourselves that this was not the first time his travelogue had struggled to gain clarity about the Yishuv's future. This same extrapolative sensibility had come to the fore in Weinreich's treatment of the Palestinian-Zionist or (as it increasingly was) the Palestinian-Jewish conflict. Weinreich's treatment of Jewish-Palestinian relations was careful, exploratory, drily critical, yet also at times self-critical. In ways that cut strikingly across our contemporary historiographical battle lines, Weinreich "promiscuously" drew comparisons to both imperial-colonial and ethnonational conflicts, all with particular attention to the postimperial East European scene.[37] Thus, in ways that resonated with the Bund's critique of Zionism as a colonial project dependent on Jewish service to the British Empire, Weinreich explained the inevitability of Palestinian "ungratefulness" via comparison to the recent denouement of centuries of German settlement in the Baltic. It was Baltic German settler nobles who had built Riga and Revel, but when Baltic independence came, they had "gotten it in the neck" regardless from Latvian and Estonian peasants turned nationalists. Notably, this latter conflict was one toward which Weinreich and his Jewish readers would have felt utterly neutral. Though Weinreich clearly sympathized with Palestine's Jews, he was not willing to let that sympathy paralyze analysis; maybe Palestine's Jews were in the same situation that once-dominant but now dispossessed Baltic Germans had faced. Indeed, Weinreich was willing to go further and indict Jewish aggression toward Palestinians in the most unsettling terms possible. Faced with his Labor Zionist interlocutors' protestations that their schools preached tolerance and were not responsible for rising anti-Arab hostility among younger Jews, Weinreich noted that such matters were not so simple, for "if Polish kids in Vilna or Grodne throw rocks at Jewish kids, it's not simply because their teachers told them to; it has to do with the whole atmosphere." Here, Palestine's *Jews* were the Endeks and their sympathizers, and the Palestinians were the Jews.

Thus, Weinreich could sympathize with the Palestinian point of view—elsewhere, he noted forms of social discrimination between educated middle-class Jews and Palestinians and laid the blame as much on the former as on the latter. But his ultimate question was not moral but practical: Where was all this going, and what would become of Palestine's Jews? Here, Weinreich allowed his readers to hear his Zionist interlocutors' realistic assessment of the Palestinian Arab stance: even the most "moderate" Palestinian elements would at most be willing to accept the current Jewish population, and only if Jews foreswore further immigration. Unlike Tshernikhov, Weinreich saw no widespread confidence among Palestine's Jews that they could "handle the Arab question" through transfer or forcible expulsion. On the contrary, he concluded, the disinclination of most Jews in Palestine to discuss "the Arab question" suggested fear and denial more than confidence. And well-informed Zionist interlocutors ("responsible people" without the "superficial arrogant relationship to the Arabs that you find among uninformed Jews in the diaspora") were still more worried. They saw, Weinreich reported, that Palestinian economic, educational, and political progress over the past fifteen years had been quick and knew that however much this was due to the influx of Jewish capital or British tax redistribution, this would hardly render Palestinians acquiescent toward further Zionist settlement.

What of the future, then? As he recorded himself putting the question to a Yishuv interlocutor, wasn't the Palestinian-Jewish balance of forces getting less advantageous—and more dangerous—for the Jews? Ultimately, Weinreich allowed his Jewish interlocutors' starkly clashing answers to stand and left his readers to decide for themselves. One interlocutor acknowledged dread that Palestinian hatred toward Jews was growing strong and that "someday, God forbid, we will also have to get on ships and leave." A second, however, offered a bit of grimly sober optimism à la Ben-Gurion. Palestinians and Jews were indeed in a race between the rapid modernization of the former and immigration by the latter. Jews had ten years to achieve a population of 1,000,000, at which point it would be possible to demand Palestinian recognition of the Zionist program. Whether this moment of confrontation would be relatively peaceful or necessarily bloody was left unsaid—though Weinreich quoted another interlocutor's remark that Palestinians were divided into three groups: those Jews could buy off, those who would come to an agreement out of fear, and those who would fight—and thus the answer to the question was "whoever is stronger will win." But Weinreich also allowed readers to hear a telling comment by this same third interlocutor about the perils of low expectations. Did Weinreich think it "impossible" that by the end of "ten years" the Jewish population could reach 1,000,000? Hadn't it seemed even more impossible that it should have grown from "80,000" (more or less) in 1914 to "400,000" in 1935?

If Weinreich's framing of the Jewish-Palestinian question betrayed uncertainty, his analysis of the Jewish Yishuv's economic prospects in the final installment of the travelogue was confident. Weinreich visited Palestine at a moment of substantial economic downturn after several years of gravity-defying "*prosperiti.*" Taking up the same theme Tshernikhov had in 1933, Weinreich acknowledged the force of the skeptical argument that the Yishuv was too heavily dependent on the influx of private, immigrant capital and hence subject to its speculative whims. But in a move that would have appalled Bundist colleagues who made much of the "unnatural" character of the Yishuv's economy, Weinreich suggested that precisely this "unnatural" mechanism had not only proved its ability to nearly triple the size of the Jewish population in Palestine in a decade's time, but might in fact be relied on to solve the Yishuv's economic crisis in the foreseeable future and support its economic growth in perpetuity. The past decades had proved that Jews around the world wanted to support Jewish settlement in Palestine and would continue to do so for the foreseeable future: "The conclusion to draw from this story is that one shouldn't compare *Erets-Yisroel* and its economy to normal lands, and one shouldn't focus too sharply on its balance of trade. As long as there is somebody who will invest, *Erets-Yisroel* can bloom, even with such an abnormal trade-balance of 4 million Pounds export against 18 million Pounds import." Here, Weinreich once again turned openly to the Jewish political condition in a grimly predictive mode: "As long as there are Jewish woes in other lands, rich Jews in those lands will perhaps desire to bring their capital to *Erets-Yisroel,* and given that we can be sure that in the near future there will be no lack of such woes, it may be that the stream of capital to *Erets-Yisroel* will continue to flow." What Tshernikhov had allowed a Zionist interlocutor to voice in 1933 was now acknowledged as fact by an inveterate Diasporist and onetime Bundist.[38]

And Weinreich wandered further in surprising directions. He noted that his Zionist interlocutors had long been "beside themselves" with worry that the flow of private investment was misdirected: money that should have gone to the movement instead flowed into speculative private building. But Weinreich's response marked one of his few divergences from the economic assumptions of his Labor Zionist interlocutors and a surprising appreciation of the workings of capitalism in general: "If you can't do what you want, you have to want according to what you can do. If agricultural and industrial economy is not being built on a large scale, one has to be satisfied with the housing construction, which led to prosperity for several years and brought the Jewish population of *Erets yis-roel* to nearly 400,000 people, when a decade ago it totaled 125,000."

Here, strangely, Weinreich's non-Zionism allowed him a *greater* optimism about Palestine's further absorptive capacity than most actual Zionists could sustain. For a Zionist, the question of absorptive capacity was inevitably wrapped up in more fraught questions about whether the particular kind of Jewish national society he or she wanted would be attainable. For Weinreich the question was simpler: Was there some reason to think that global conditions would continue to drive Jewish emigrationism and Palestine-investment and thus too the expansion of the Yishuv's absorptive capacity? The answer was yes.

Weinreich's painful transition from polemical certainties to real inquiry regarding Palestine was not the only transformation under way in his thinking. Two other metamorphoses were visible. First, Weinreich's very formulations signaled a new willingness—or compulsion—to separate *political* questions in Jewish life from *cultural* ones, existential questions from questions of identity. Weinreich had spent his life fighting for the Yiddishist vision of Jewish culture and identity; he was the sort of progressive cultural nationalist for whom the perpetuation of a distinct strain of human cultural creativity was both the highest goal of any nation's life and the only real justification for the perpetuation of nations as such. But by the close of 1935 he was sidelining the old questions of the Hebrew-Yiddish *Kulturkampf* and focusing on the sociopolitical realities of Jewish life in the Yishuv. The Jewish Problem against which Zionism now had to be judged was not the problem of how to reinvent Jewish peoplehood but "the sea of troubles in which Jews are being soaked." Second, in seriously displacing his own judgment of Zionism from the grid of identity and culture to the grid of the Jewish Question, Weinreich was helping to render conceptual rather than merely polemical the idea that Jewish politics had to answer to a reality of limited communal resources and the obligation to maximize concrete help to members of the nation.

Territorialism and Zionism between National Regeneration and Evacuation

As a Diasporist like Weinreich began to think seriously for the first time about what Palestine might offer his people, a few advocates of Jewish collective resettlement and territorial nation building, both Zionist and Territorialist, began to wrestle with the sort of purer evacuationist impulse that was finding expression in YEAS. Among Zionists, the worsening crisis in Europe provoked renewed debate about a question that had troubled the movement in various forms since the beginning: To what degree was Zionism a nation-building and nation-regenerating project, which entailed highly selective immigration and intensive "reeducative" work, and to what degree was it simply called to make a home for large numbers of Jews facing troubles? Asked in a variety of ways with varying degrees of abstraction and double-talk, the question seems to have imposed itself with new clarity on those in the movement who were particularly concerned with the Polish Jewish situation. In November 1934, Eliahu Dobkin, long the head of Hehalutz's efforts in Poland, registered a year of debate with the figure who until recently had been at the center of Polish Zionism, an increasingly alarmed Yitzhak Grinboym. Speaking within Zionist circles, Dobkin characterized Grinboym's stance thus:

> Grinboym said here that we have arrived at a situation in which the Land of Israel has become a country of refuge for the hounded [*eretz miklat la-nirdafim*], and that if there is a collision between

bringing to the Land of Israel an element which is important from the standpoint of the building of the Land as opposed to human material which is hounded by pogroms and by all sorts of state attacks and by the catastrophic economic situation, then we have come to the moment when the Land of Israel must choose the tormented Jews because it is the last refuge for those Jews—that at this stage of Zionism and in this situation of *aliyah,* we must [use] the Land of Israel to redress Jews' woes.[39]

Dobkin disagreed. He granted Grinboym's basic claim that the situation of the Diaspora had reached a point of crisis—or as he put it, that "the Jewish people is drowning in the sea." But nevertheless, he reaffirmed the position hegemonic in Labor Zionist circles since the Balfour Declaration, namely, that the realization of the Zionist project demanded a *selective* immigration policy in which "good human material"—defined by the demonstrable readiness and capacity to transform oneself into a secular, socialist, nationalist, Hebraist laborer and, if necessary, soldier—ought to be given immigration preference insofar as organized Zionism had anything to say about the character of Jewish immigration to Palestine. For Dobkin, the very fact of a worsening Jewish situation dictated a redoubling of stringency: "Friends: the Land of Israel is indeed a place of salvation, a life-boat for Jews, but it is truly a life-*boat*. The Jewish people is drowning in the sea. When you have a sinking ship and you have a life-boat, you have to be careful not to load up the life-boat with material that can overturn it."[40]

Historians remain unsure what to make of such arguments within the Zionist leadership. The cynical view is that views like Grinboym's were largely lip service and that the increasingly dominant Labor Zionist movement was in all events firmly committed to maximizing the influx of "good human material," as Ben-Gurion put it in terms that have become vaguely infamous. The defensive view is that Zionists actually had profoundly limited control over any aspect of immigration, that they knew this very well, and that views like Dobkin's bore only on the narrow question of what kind of policy the movement should adopt regarding the labor-migrant category (the "Certificates"), which was the only category over which the Zionist Jewish Agency actually had any say. To this, defenders add that even figures highly committed to "selective immigration" worked hard, if ineffectively, to find other ways of widening aliyah opportunities for "petit bourgeois" migrants (for instance, getting the British

Mandatory to lower the sums needed to qualify under the separate "individual capitalist" category, which was far out of reach for many Polish Jews). History seems to have split the difference; there is clear evidence supporting both characterizations, and when the dust settled, a good many of the actual migrants who made it to Palestine in the 1932–1936 period did not fit the Labor Zionist youth-socialist ideal. They were in essence refugees.[41]

However, not from the standpoint of the history of Zionism and its choices per se but from that of political thought in and around the Polish Jewish situation, it is worth noting a further remark of Dobkin's: that this was not only "an argument that I've been conducting with [Grinboym] for a good year"—since Grinboym's departure from Poland and also the Nazi accession to power—but also "before him with others day in, day out." The question of providing *refuge* was beginning to impose itself not only on individual Polish Zionists like Valk of the YEAS but within the Zionist leadership.

The much thinner archive of a movement that sought to compete with Zionism provides a striking parallel. One of the polemical "trump cards" of the Territorialist movement revived in Poland in 1934 under the moniker Frayland was the claim that it alone among Jewish ideologies placed the concrete rescue of the maximal number of Jews over less communally responsible ideological goals. Where Bundists clung to the conviction that galloping pauperization of Jews would lead dialectically—and soon—to proletarianization, and Diasporists in general refused to acknowledge that Jews might need to be evacuated from Eastern Europe no less than Germany, Territorialists (on this view) soberly considered the facts and set out to reorganize Jewish communal goals around them. Conversely, though Zionists sometimes spoke in such ostensibly sober terms, their romantic obsession with the Land of Israel compelled them (Territorialists argued) to mortgage East European Jews' future to a cruelly selective effort to colonize a territory that was not only contested but also (ostensibly) far too small and resource-poor to help most Jews under any circumstances.[42]

Yet Frayland Territorialism was actually just as entangled with ideological commitment and longing as were any of its antagonists on the Jewish street. Almost all of its leading figures seem to have cherished far-reaching visions of Jewish cultural and social reconstruction rather than simply resettlement. Figures ranging from young activists like Astour to older leaders like Yitshok Shteynberg and Rozin/Ben-Adir were fiercely committed to building a socialist society. Yiddishism was no less central for many of its most vocal supporters.[43] Even Frayland leaders more leery of social radicalism like Tshernikhov (who had seen the Soviet project up close as a defense lawyer between 1917 and 1923) cherished romantic anticapitalist ideals of "productivizing" Jews—ideals little different from those of Labor Zionism.[44]

More subtle but perhaps no less significant was how Territorialism spoke to those who identified strongly with Jewish nationhood, could no longer see hope for it in the Diaspora, but were also unable to identify with Zionism largely for Yiddishist reasons. In a private letter sent in 1934, the erstwhile Diasporist Kalmanovitsh (by then himself turning toward Territorialism) reported to his brother-in-law in America that the secular Yiddishist Jewish youth of Wilno had universally abandoned Diasporism and were now divided into two camps: "Palestinians" and "Birobidzhanians." Turning to his own experience, Kalmanovitsh gave an intimate account of how his son Sholem (later the Israeli scholar of Yiddish Shalom Luria), raised with impeccable Yiddishist education, had joined the wave of youth abandoning hope in Diasporist Yiddishism for Soviet-oriented Communism, and then how—and why—the reemergent Frayland Territorialist movement had rescued Sholem from Communism. Interesting is Kalmanovitsh's sense of why Territorialism had proved so compelling to his son and his circle: "There are national feelings [among the Yiddishist youth]—that's the tragedy—there is a natural Jewish pull" but for a growing number of young people like his son, these feelings could not overcome despair about prospects "here," in Poland. They needed either a revolutionary or a territorial else*where* in order to be enlivened. "Yiddishism pushed the children into a dark abyss" because it seemed hopeless; either Communism or "Territorialism pulls them out, awakens hopes."[45]

That Frayland Territorialism was actually suffused with extravagant collective-regenerationist visions was visible not just in retrospect but at the time, as evidenced by an internal warning note sounded in the *Frayland* journal in 1934. An essay by the Warsaw Yiddish poet and activist Meylekh Ravitsh expressed certainty that masses of Jews would embrace the Territorialist idea—but only insofar as Territorialism focused solely on finding "an empty land" for desperate Jews. Ravitsh cautioned his fellow Frayland intellectuals that Jews did not need another "ideal," only an "idea": "It is an excellent idea to create not a territorialist party, but a league." This was in part tactical advice: in a Polish Jewish political sphere marked by a "lust for narrow party sensibilities," Frayland should bill itself as a supraparty entity open to anyone who supported its mass evacuation/colonization goals regardless of what other particular politics they supported.[46]

But Ravitsh was not just talking tactics. He was rebuking his fellow Territorialists for forgetting that finding a land to which to evacuate a large mass of European Jews as soon as possible was truly the priority: "A party is a matter of the world to come and territorialism is a this-worldly matter from beginning to end. Or at least it *ought* to be. Should Jewish territorialism manage to find among the thousands of empty lands [. . .] a land adequate to concentrated mass immigration, *then* we can talk about culture-problems and also about socialism there. To speak about this now [however] means not only to be premature, but also, I think, to mislead ourselves with empty words." Read practically, Ravitsh was warning his fellow Territorialists that they would lose their chance at attracting a mass base if they insisted on socialism and Yiddishism. The prospect of a better life in a new land would appeal to a far larger base among desperate Polish Jews than socialism would, and even more so than Yiddishism. And his reminder of what Territorialism "ought" to be suggests a moral-political reading too: the need for maximal mass evacuation was simply so great that it outweighed any other commitments. In relation to this goal, any ideology about what sort of society Territorialism should aspire to build was utopian, a matter of the "world-to-come," and had to be subordinated to a single-minded focus on getting access to a territory.

Ravitsh's comments signal an inner debate in Territorialist circles the scope of which I cannot reconstruct for lack of sources. But a retrospective source, by movement insider Shoyl Gutman, resonates closely with this reading. Gutman suggests substantial tension within the leadership between those who saw territorialism as a cure for "*yidishkayt-noyt*" (the needs of Jewishness or Judaism) and those who saw it as a cure for "*yidn-noyt*" (the needs of Jews). Invoking the history of Zionism as a parallel, Gutman casts this as a tension between "Ahad-Ha'amist" principles that saw Territorialism's task as the cultural regeneration of Jewry by a self-selecting vanguard and what he calls "Herzlian" sensibilities that understood Territorialism as a response to the dangers of dispersion and minorityhood.[47]

In calling on Zionism and on Territorialism to elevate communal rescue over cherished visions of national regeneration, Grinboym and Ravitsh alike spoke as movement leaders to fellow movement leaders. There is tantalizing evidence that parallel evolutions were taking shape at the grass-roots level too. Examining the experiences of Hehalutz emissaries like Ben-Asher in 1930 and Shlimovits in 1933–1934 as they traversed the kresy, we discovered in Chapter 5 an emerging grassroots politics defined by a posture of inquiry over ideology and a hunger to actually understand the possibilities for Jewish life afforded by Palestine in contradistinction to Poland. Those same sources and others from the same time and place also point to a third striking phenomenon: a restless triangular movement among poles of raw exitist conviction that *any* destination was better than Poland, serious engagement with Zionism and with Palestine as offering prospects for a better Jewish life, and a continued search for ways of bettering the Jewish situation in Poland. This bundle of tensions could also, it seems, push those subjected to them toward an inchoate tripartite politics that sought to somehow bind together commitments associated with competing Zionist, emigrationist, and Diasporist outlooks.

We see indications of this in the memoirs of someone who was almost certainly a direct participant in the freewheeling 1930 Prużana Zionist meeting that Ben-Asher attended, one Zelig Geyar. Geyar was raised in the bosom of Prużana's robust Hebraist subculture, a product of its Tarbut school system. The natural next step, ideologically and socially, was to join Prużana's strong Ha-Shomer ha-Tsair group (which apparently remained solidly committed to the movement's classical Zionist-Hebraist ideals even at a moment, the late 1920s, when many other branches were turning to Communism). But for reasons Geyar links to class differences—he was one of many Tarbut students in Prużana who, contrary to the stock claims of the Bund, came from a poor home and had to seek artisanal work—this proved an unsatisfying step for him and for a whole cohort of Hebraist-educated "working youth" like him. "Most of the youth in our city was organized in the Ha-Shomer ha-Tsair movement. But among the members there were young men and women who did not continue in school, but rather started to work or learned a [artisanal] profession, and the educational [and] scouting activity of Ha-Shomer ha-Tsair did not speak to them." Of special interest was what *did* compel this post-Tarbut "working youth": "What interested them were work-questions and problems of emigration, because they saw that the opportunities to continue their lives in the town were very minimal." Committed to Zionism, they were also ready to explore other possibilities of leaving *and* simultaneously eager to find ways to fight "for better work conditions" in Poland. But compelled to "[seek] a framework that would integrate Zionist activity with struggles over work conditions," they could not find one among any of the existing political frameworks. The Zionist Ha-Shomer ha-Tsair and Hehalutz insisted that all energies be bent toward preparing oneself for aliyah, while Jewish union activity (such as it could possibly have been in a collapsing provincial economy like Prużana's) was firmly in the hands of anti-Zionists: "The activity of professional organizations that fought for better work conditions was of some importance, but those organizations were under the exclusive influence of the Bundists and the Communists." Instead, Geyar and his friends expressed their triangular political urge by establishing "after some debate [. . .] a youth organization [affiliated with] Poalei Tsion."[48]

Assuming they formally affiliated their group with the small Poalei Tsion Right movement, the umbrella organization with which they affiliated was the Frayhayt youth movement. Frayhayt was an unusually decentered youth movement connected with Poalei Tsion Right, the socialist-Zionist party in Poland aligned with the constructivist-socialist mainstream of Labor Zionism in Palestine. Formally affiliated with Hehalutz in the period with which we are concerned, the actual ideology of Frayhayt varied tremendously on the local level. Thus, sometimes Frayhayt was a bastion of an increasingly endangered ideological coupling between Zionism and genuine Yiddishism. Miriam Shlimovits encountered one such Frayhayt branch in Kobryń (Bel.: Kobryn) in 1933. But from the early 1930s onward, such Zionist Yiddishism grew rare (thus, Shlimovits deemed the Yiddishism of the Kobryń branch "the old type").[49] Instead, Frayhayt began to be associated with young people engaged with Zionism but concerned that it was not focusing intensely enough on general-socialist and Jewish-national *political* struggle in Poland.[50] This identification occurred to Ben-Asher when he was confronted by comments to that effect by the increasingly dissatisfied head of Prużana's Hehalutz ha-Tsair branch: "There was in these comments a turning of thought in the direction of Frayhayt, as though there are [separate] tasks [for Hehalutz, for Zionism] in times of *aliyah* and times of constriction thereof." In Kleck, he noted, the entirety of the town's Hehalutz ha-Tsair chapter had formally gone over to Frayhayt, and it seems no coincidence that it was there that Ben-Asher remarked a culture of discussion among the local youth across the threefold divide of socialist Zionism, Revisionism, and Diasporist-revolutionary socialism (just as Shlimovits would find in Osowa Wyszka four years later). Another Hehalutz *shaliah* recorded a similar shift in Lida in 1933 and lamented it in terms that suggest a similar ideological valence: "There is no branch of Hehalutz Ha-Tsair here at this point. Everyone left for Frayhayt a little while ago. The pain [must be] great indeed if our comrades are going over to them."[51]

The history of Frayhayt as a movement is of only secondary significance in our context. More important is the larger sensibility that seems to have sometimes found an "address" in Frayhayt but in other cases just as easily remained within a Hehalutz ha-Tsair framework. This was an ambient sensibility that, it seems, grew locally and spontaneously out of Zionists' uncertainties about their own Zionism, about exit in general, and yet still more powerful certainties that there was little to hope for in the Diaspora *whatever* one did.

And beyond Geyar's case, one fascinating source suggests that under the right circumstances, this threefold uncertainty could be welded together into a distinct politics. To some degree, Geyar's zigzagging line of thought was a product of the 1929 moment, when the prospects of Zionism and actual aliyah were dim. But this same restless triangulation could emerge even at the high point of Zionism's practical promise for Polish Jewry, in 1933, as demonstrated in the recollections of a member of the Frayhayt/Poalei Tsion Right club in Kraków. In 1933, David Ben-Gurion's demands that Poalei Tsion Right unify with Hitahdut, a second socialist-Zionist party strong in Galicia and more closely aligned with Ben-Gurion's Mapai, called forth hot debate in the Kraków club. Significantly, the memoirist relates, this was because "we didn't see ourselves as a movement whose only goal was to encourage aliyah to the Land of Israel, but also as a Jewish movement with local significance." The Kraków club had worked to "forge connections with institutions that had no direct connection to the Land of Israel," including YEAS. Thus, within Kraków's Frayhayt club as in backwoods Osowa Wyszka, Zionist ideas of Jewish self-transformation in and through Palestine were interwoven with a second view that one ought to participate fully in Polish Jewish communal life *and* a third interest in the possibility of ameliorating the Polish Jewish Problem through *non*-Zionist emigration. This can of course be seen as a fundamentally romantic effort to hold together opposing programs; but it can also be seen as a practical and responsible effort to avoid squandering any opportunity to better the actual lot of Polish Jews.[52]

On the Irrelevance of Culture and Identity

Glatshteyn's character Nayfeld embodied an especially painful form of work on the self: abandoning the things one loved and the things that defined one in order to focus all energies on some concrete improvement of the situation, at least for some. Such a sensibility can be seen in the calls by Ravitsh, a man wholly devoted to Yiddish culture, to sequester Yiddishism in favor of a pure rescue-Territorialism—even one that meant, potentially, "swamping" the movement and the new territory with people who had no truck with Yiddishism: Polonized and half-Polonized Jews, Orthodox and half-Orthodox Jews, and who knows what. It can be seen in Weinreich's readiness to suspend his own deep Yiddishist commitments to soberly assess what Palestine might offer Polish Jews. It can be seen in the readiness of the Zionist-minded Valk and the Yiddishist-nationalist Lestschinsky to embrace programs of exit that would not advance these ideals in any way. And it can be seen in Binyomen R. of Bielsk, whom we might call a "Yiddishist that wasn't."

Actually, Binyomen's leave-taking of his own culture and identity was a twofold if not a threefold process. Several years before Binyomen wrote his autobiography in 1934 and his response to Weinreich's *Veg* in 1935, he had broken decisively with a Zionist-Hebraist identity cultivated since his early youth. Though raised in a traditionalist home evidently distant from any sort of robust relationship to Zionism, he had received a better-than-average traditional education that afforded him excellent working Hebrew. He had of his own accord embarked on a well-worn path from traditionalism to a thickly cultural and romantic Zionist Hebraism. Consuming a diet of nationalist-romantic Hebraist-Zionist children's literature like the pseudo-biblical epic *Akhsah bat Kalev,* by Yisrael Shaf, then the earlier nineteenth-century romantic verse of Micha Yosef Lebenzon, he even tried some imitative pseudo-biblical poetry of his own (from which he cited a few lines in his 1934 autobiography). And this carried over into more serious engagements. In 1931, he briefly embarked on the distinctive path of interwar Poland's fading Hebraist "elite" by matriculating at the famed Grodno Hebrew teachers' institute (which demanded a high mark on the entrance exam). While at Grodno, he read only Hebrew literature in the local Hebraist library.[53]

Yet by 1935 Binyomen had come to see Hebraist and Zionist cultural visions as empty cant. In a multipage indictment, he painted the Hebrew school as culturally, even cognitively, harmful. "Hebraism and its educational world in the diaspora" inflicted "suffering" on "the Jewish child" by placing him in "linguistic chains [that] do not allow him his natural expression." The Hebrew school students he knew could not understand their science lessons or even write an essay about a Zionist icon like "Max Nordau."[54]

And by the time Binyomen R. wrote in 1934–1935, he had not only come to reject the Hebraist project but had been engaging for several years with its Yiddishist antipode. Indeed, many aspects of his writings suggest someone moving toward Yiddishism. It was not just his anti-Hebraism (coupled with rejection of his former religiosity) and his own supple Yiddish style (about which he boasted, reasonably, that it was better than that of the students in the Yiddishist school). More positively, he recalled how one young woman hired to tutor him in Polish instead let him read her fine collection of Yiddish literature. He noted his immersion at fifteen, at the home of a Grodno uncle, in landmarks of prewar Yiddishist high culture like the 1913 *Pinkes* and the literary omnibus *Di yudishe velt*. He cited Dovid Bergelson's difficult modernist triumph *Nokh alemen*. Most decisively, he declared Yiddish "our language."[55]

Yet even as Binyomen demonstrated his deep immersion in Yiddishist culture, he methodically disclaimed the *relevance* of Yiddishism's vision no less than Hebraism's. While professing that "the youth must aid the YIVO," he dismissed the idea that YIVO's work could have any practical effect: "Practical reforms of any significant dimension are [impossible] in the present order in general and in our diaspora-life in particular." Elsewhere, he attacked the hope at the heart of Weinreich's youth research even as he participated in it: "[more] knowledge and researching the situation will not brighten matters." Most striking of all, at the very moment that he wrote his shattering indictment of the Hebraist project, and even as his engagement with Yiddish culture deepened, Binyomen R. chose to affiliate formally with *Zionism*. In the summer of 1934, he joined Hehalutz.[56]

This was a political choice at odds with his cultural commitments. Moreover, Binyomen R. was conscious of this and articulated it. His 1934 autobiography shows him to have been moving toward this very sense of the need to separate the Question of Judaism from the Jewish Question, and to prioritize the latter in his own thinking, even before his final disillusionment with Hebraism. In December 1931, still at the Tarbut teachers' seminar in Grodno, he attended a lecture by Bialik, the living symbol of the Zionist-Hebraist cultural project.[57] Reconstructing the talk in a manner that convincingly approximates Bialik's stance and phraseology ("the very essence of our life is culture, and with the power of spirit will the many be vanquished by the few, the strong by the weak [veln bazigt vern *rabim be-yad me'atim, giburim be-yad halashim*]"), Binyomen R. recalled that "his speech did not please me at all. I was especially disappointed by his '*ein lanu esek be-politikah*' [we have no truck with politics]." At the time, he related, he was a "Grinboymist" and sided with the latter against Bialik regarding the need for a Zionist politics that would be as attentive to Jewish political needs as to "the Land of Israel" and "pure culture."[58]

Sometime between 1931 and 1934, Binyomen R. sundered his politics from his identity. A real-life version of Glatshteyn's Nayfeld, his cultural loves and his own identity had become irrelevant to the questions he had to ask and the choices he had to make. He was clearly not the only one.

No Cure for Everyone: On Reason and Self-Rescue

But why did Binyomen choose *Zionism* specifically? He offered two ramified arguments about why Zionism was the right choice despite his emancipation from Zionism's mythologies. One was elaborated organically in his 1934 autobiography, as an account of the conclusions at which he had arrived after years of reflection and argument. The second appeared a year later in his response to Weinreich's *Veg*. There, as we have seen, Weinreich had mobilized a battery of psychological theories to argue that those joining Hehalutz were not thinking rationally. Binyomen disagreed. But this was not just an empirical argument; it was also an argument about political choices and ethics.

Toward the close of his long 1934 diary-cum-autobiography, Binyomen offered a present-tense declaration of the political choice he had finally made. Having wavered for several years between revolutionary politics and Zionism, he had chosen the latter:

> Giving myself a true accounting of the soul regarding what I am doing, and seeing the two paths before Jewish youth—that of [the Communist] "Our Path" and that of Hehalutz—I choose the second. Simply because I cannot sit and wait, I cannot stand and gaze into the future when my feet are burning under me, when it's not ground under me but glowing coals. I cannot attack the idea that Zionism actually [represents], which I hold to be the striving

of the Jewish masses for their national liberation. I cannot sit and wait for a social revolution in a time when the conditions are not yet ripe for it, as [the revolutionaries] themselves admit. For my national liberation I'm supposed to wait, according to *Unzer veg* [a Communist journal], for the social liberation of the proletariat of all nations! Nowadays, in the current fascist epoch there is only one path for the Jewish youth, toward its productivization and proletarianization, and that is Zionism. That is Hehalutz. It's true that the exit is too narrow and can't meet the need of the millions of Jews. The Land of Israel can however be a partial solution for the Jews-question [*di yidn-frage*] and meet the need of hundreds of thousands. It's clear that only the social revolution can bring the full solution of the Jews'-question but in the meantime, let us use every means of salvation for thousands of Jews, especially given that the Land of Israel can solve the Jewish question at least in part. For the meantime, we don't have anything better than Zionism.[59]

He followed with a sheepish note: "I've written about my 'ideology' and completely forgotten about the autobiography." The embarrassment was doubtless unfeigned. Throughout his autobiography, Binyomen showed impatience for the ritual declarations of conviction that permeated Jewish public discourse; for him, as we saw in Chapter 5, real political thinking could only happen in a second sphere of intimate discussion with fellow "seekers."

But the autobiography also leaves no doubt that Binyomen had finally come to a decision about his own choice. When he began his autobiography (in diary form) in March 1934, Binyomen was politically "homeless," a member of no party, though acquaintances had sought to recruit him for Hehalutz, Ha-Shomer ha-Tsair, the Communists, and the Revisionists.[60] But as we have seen, this was not because he was unwilling to think seriously about the political future. Quite the contrary, his autobiography captures someone unable to stop. And it allows us to see what specific paths of thought carried Binyomen R. to Zionism instead of revolutionary socialism.

Clearly, this had nothing to do with some return to the Hebraist Zionism of his youth, as the 1935 indictment of Hebraism's romance of cultural and linguistic regeneration shows. Just as clearly, his growing sense of political threats taking shape around Polish Jewry—from the rightist politics becoming ever more dominant among educated Polish youth in Bielsk to the anti-Jewish instincts of the police to the triumphs of the Right in Germany and Austria—*was* a decisive factor. A second key factor that in turn transformed this sense of danger into the first principle of a new politics was the skepticism that most fundamentally set him apart from his socialist friends: his strong sense that the world was entering a "fascist epoch" and that no revolutionary deus ex machina would arrive anytime soon. Throughout both texts, Binyomen reiterated this hard skepticism multiple times and ways, in some senses identifying it as the ground of Jewish political realism. Looking back at the religious atmosphere of his childhood home, he wrote with bitter mockery of his naive reaction to the messianic speculations with which some religious leaders gilded the worsening Jewish situation in the late 1920s: "When I heard that the Hofets Haim was saying the Messiah would come quite soon, I was very happy."[61] Looking back at 1934 after a year of Zionist commitment, he wrote in 1935, "If I could have believed that tomorrow would bring social revolution, like some of my Red friends, perhaps I would have given up Hehalutz and jumped over to their camp [. . .] for I saw in their camp more true belief than in Hehalutz. But I did not possess such faith then and I do not have it now, though I'm no longer a Hebraist."[62]

Respecting the "idealists" among his revolutionary friends far more than the "careerists" and the desperate youth flocking to Hehalutz, Binyomen had nevertheless come to believe that the *latter* had the only realistic politics. But was his choice to join Hehalutz the act of reason Binyomen thought it was, and if so, what kind of reason was it? Weinreich for one challenged such claims to rationality aggressively, as we have seen. Not accidentally, Weinreich's general insistence that Jewish youths' political choices were driven by a prerational search for "compensations"— by which he meant psychic outlets that *feel* like "solutions" to problems but to which we are driven precisely because we cannot actually solve those problems—surfaced with particular force in his treatment of the mass turn to Zionism among the youth during the years of *Veg*'s composition. Thus, a key point in Weinreich's analysis is marked by his turn to a 1934 autobiography that declared, "'Save yourself, he who can,' cries Zionism—and we listen."[63] Weinreich acknowledged that that young man's declaration was meant "in the plain sense—saving oneself from the Diaspora." But plain sense, Weinreich continued, dictated the view that this informant himself did not know what was really driving him, and could not be acting reasonably:

Were it truly only a matter of the chance to leave the Diaspora, the disproportion between wanting to and being able to would be clear to [anyone]. Why does Zionism so strongly grasp large parts of the Jewish youth? Why is the Zionist not "grasped" by sober assessments of the absorptive capacity of the Land of Israel, about the growing power of the Arabs and so forth? Because the opponent [of Zionism] appeals to the Zionist's reason, [whereas] his own Zionism grows from much deeper psychological foundations. The Zionist has "saved" himself through his Zionism. Here he finds (perhaps only for a time, perhaps for his whole life) something that restores him even if the path to the Land of Israel is blocked to him. He is not saving himself by going to Palestine, he is saving himself through his Palestinism. Zionism is not a realistic way out for him but a *psychological* salvation.[64]

On one level, it would be unfair to read this turn in Weinreich's argument as merely a polemical attack on Zionism. Weinreich extended this same interpretive principle to *all* political choices on the part of Polish Jewish youth: "Of course, in just the same way, belonging to any other party can also be a psychological way out of specific conflict situations." But at another level, Weinreich clearly felt compelled to take special aim at Zionism. After many pages of more catholic argument, he returned to the attack:

In certain respects, the Land of Israel, as concerns its psychological radiance, is like the Soviet Union. At the moment, it offers work— no wonder it attracts. It offers the Jew the feeling of not being amongst strangers. It is far away from home and difficult to get there—that is a virtue. It is distant from home in linguistic terms, or at any rate aspirationally so—that is a virtue. The Land of Israel communicates [the possibility of] having one's own [nation-]state life [*an eygn melukhish lebn*], with Hebrew letters on the stamps, with Hebrew labels on the factory products, with Jewish policemen even. The entirety of it is quite small, but it awakens hopes for something greater, and I, Haim or Khane [archetypical Jewish names], can also take part. For something like that, it is worth expending one's powers.[65]

Binyomen R.'s 1935 riposte to Weinreich regarding Zionism began as an *empirical* argument with this characterization of what was actually going on in the minds of young people like himself who were drawn to Hehalutz. Responding directly to Weinreich's dismissive formulation that Zionist affiliation couldn't really be about actually trying to leave given the obvious "disproportion" of desire to leave the Diaspora and the difficulty of doing so, Binyomen insisted that improving one's chance of getting out was really at the heart of it. It was "certainly true," he agreed, that for "many young people, Zionism is a psychological salvation." But "most of the youth that has joined Hehalutz" had done so with the actual intent and desire to "emigrate to the Land of Israel." For them, no "psychological salvation alone can satisfy. They have seen that Moti, Meyshl, Yisrolik and Avner are actually leaving for Palestine, and they have become halutzim in hopes of emigrating as they have." The proof that psychological compensation, however real, was not the ultimate goal of such youth expressed itself in the conditionality of their membership: Binyomen noted (as did so many observers) that if and when such youth concluded that no aliyah Certificate was forthcoming, they left the organization. As for the rationality of joining Hehalutz in the first place, it was not disproven by the "disproportion" at all. Binyomen and his friends knew full well that it was hard for a halutz to get a Certificate—so hard that, he acknowledged, it had come to seem much like a "lottery," a "*mazl-zakh*," a matter of luck and fate. But if this verged on acknowledgment that it was irrational to hope for a Certificate, Binyomen drew a key distinction: winning a lottery was "blind accident," whereas the "main thing" involved in getting a Certificate was "personal characteristics"—meaning not that there was anything one could do to oneself to ensure access to a Certificate but that one *would* gain a chance at one if one became a halutz and engaged in the transformations enjoined by Hehalutz. Joining Hehalutz put one in some sort of line, however crowded, unruly, and unfair in its regulation; given the situation, it was one of the few actions a young person with no resources could actually take that could concretely improve his or her chance of getting out of Poland.[66]

In short, though deeply skeptical of the cultural and psychological pretensions of self-making so central to organized Zionism both right and left, and though attracted to Communism's "idealism," Binyomen chose instead an option that offered a concrete chance of changing his own situation. Just as he had counterposed Grinboym's insistence on "politics" to Bialik's prioritization of "culture" in 1931, Binyomen R. iterated the same distinction in 1934 and again in 1935 in more fundamental form: however attractive, Communist ideals must be rejected because they defer a solution for any Jews, whereas Zionism in the age of the actually existing

Yishuv offered a partial solution for tens of thousands, perhaps hundreds of thousands.

But there was another face of Weinreich's critique of Zionism in *Veg,* and so too of Binyomen's response: an essentially *moral* argument about what the individual Polish Jew owed—and did not owe—the embattled Jewish community. Though Weinreich wrote *Veg* in a scholarly tone, certain moments betray his deep worry over what he was finding. The most naked of these came at the close of *Veg*'s third section. Acknowledging, against his own psychologism, that much of the pull of both the Jewish Yishuv in Palestine and the Soviet Union was because both "at the present moment offer work" when Jews in Poland were undergoing headlong class free fall, Weinreich also acknowledged with frustration that Jewish youth seemed willing—even eager—to embrace such declassing when and *only* when this was part of a larger investment in the Zionist or the Communist project. By contrast, they bridled against it when such declassing marked their future in Poland: "One asks oneself: why [are they willing to] be a garbage-man in Tel Aviv or a road paver in Magnitogorsk, while in Vilna they wouldn't take on such work even if it were available?" Here, Weinreich's Diasporism burst the bonds of his tone of objectivity to become an accusation:

> This is a fundamental question bearing on the Jewish personality. But this is also a fundamental question—one can say, perhaps, *the* fundamental question of Jewish collective existence [*fun der yidisher klalisher eksistents*].
>
> It's a well-known fact that when one is in a new land and has no other choice, new powers [energies] manifest themselves. The history of the US shows that emigrants are more capable than those who stay at home, and we from our own short history in the US know this too. But among everyone else in the world, people manage to achieve something in their homelands too. Among us, the youth has to tear itself away from its home environment and its ties to be able to draw forth from itself greater quanta of energy [*kdey tsu kenen aroystsapn fun zikh gresere skhumen energye*]. Among us, even those who have found a solid footing in life want to leave. Among us, even those who could find something for themselves don't want to think about trying to make a life here. Among us, we don't even want to take a look at our way of living because each of us is already leaving, if not literally than psychologically.[67]

Read in this context, Binyomen's 1935 response to *Veg* was not only an articulate counterargument to Weinreich's dismissal of joining Hehalutz as objectively *irrational*. It also addressed the moral-political question Weinreich raised: Was not Binyomen's choice to devote all his energies to attempted self-rescue via aliyah a betrayal of the community at the moment when it needed every individual's energies to stay afloat? Binyomen's most open reflection on this question was incited, tellingly, by an earlier moment in *Veg* where Weinreich alleged that Polish Jewish youth eagerness to leave the Diaspora was a kind of psychological "complex." Citing the autobiography of a young man from the Lublin region ("now in Tel-Aviv") who pinned the difference between Jewish and Polish youth on the latter's possession of a home, Weinreich turned the tables. The problem was not that Jews were homeless, but that they had *convinced* themselves they were: "Does this [autobiographer's] explanation offer us anything? One thing is certain: it underscores the fact that the Jewish youth *does not feel at home in its home*. It uproots itself with a remarkable ease. More than that: when it leaves and goes elsewhere, it is capable of much greater efforts."[68]

Binyomen clearly felt the moral charge embedded in the social-psychological diagnosis. He began by appropriating Weinreich's own terms and explaining why he and his fellows were *right* to feel that Poland was no home: "A Jew is by nature given to faith [that things can work out], [but] here, the place he was born [yet] in which he encounters enemies at every step, he is already in utter despair and does not believe that one can build something here that will last." It was not unreason but reason to feel greater "hopes for the future" in "a new land" in contradistinction to what, in Binyomen's view, Poland was becoming. And here, finally, he turned to Palestine and the individual search for exit:

When a Jewish young person has faith that he is building a structure for the good of the entire people, he is capable of the greatest sacrifice and willing to make it, and can also utterly transform himself beyond recognition. From knowledge and research on the situation, things won't get any happier for us. And we won't find any real cures that way either, certainly not for the whole Jewish collective in this present order and in the sort of era in which we find ourselves today [*terufes veln mir derfun oykh nit gefinen, bfrat nokh farn gantsn yidishn klal in der itstiker ordenung un nokh in aza tekufe in velkher mir gefinen zikh haynt*].[69]

Here, within the space of a sentence, Binyomen moved from a pious insistence that Zionism was a service to "the entire people" to a very different statement about Polish Jewish political reason. There *was* no "cure" that could help the entire Jewish people, and no amount of thinking and research by Weinreich, socialist thinkers, or anyone else would turn one up. And in the context of a discussion of why Zionism, this statement was also a frank political claim: perhaps indeed throwing all one's energies into trying to get out was abandonment of the community, but given the irredeemable general Jewish situation, it was eminently rational for the *individual* to abandon sentiment and community alike to try to get out. Read in this light and in the larger context of Binyomen's otherwise relentlessly antiromantic writing, the sentence about how building a new Jewish society in Palestine was service to "the entire people" reads less as a residue of Zionist idealism than as sop to the conscience. But it was also a kind of terrible honesty that confronted *both* Diasporist *and* Zionist hopes, *any* Jewish communalist ideal, with the unsentimental assertion that in the absence of other realistic alternatives, the only sensible and perhaps even moral choice was that—as Binyomen's anonymous peer had put it a year before—"he who can" should "save himself." Binyomen gave voice to a disturbing conviction that was undoubtedly (as Weinreich charged) on many others' minds as well. He was making explicit something implicit in much of the thinking addressed in Chapter 6. If there was no way to genuinely improve collective Jewish prospects "in this present order," and if such "selfishness" could actually help some substantial number of individual Polish Jews find a better future in Palestine, then cold reason dictated rescue for those who could be "saved"—a politics of *triage.*

In turn, Weinreich's own belated serious engagement with the Yishuv at the close of 1935 bespoke an evolution in his own thought that almost, if not quite, acknowledged the harsh moral logic of postcommunal self-rescue. One of the later essays in his travelogue took up the experience of Palestine's newest immigrant subculture, the tens of thousands of *German* Jews flowing to Palestine as, above all, refugees. Weinreich's sympathetic treatment of their difficult experience brought a moment of especially sharp criticism toward the Yishuv itself. The German Jewish refugees, he reported, were regularly attacked for not being real Zionists. Many were doing tolerably well in Palestine economically, but faced aggressive Hebraist efforts to suppress even the most modest German-language culture.[70]

This portrait harked back to the first installment of the travelogue, or a prelude to it, which Weinreich had published early in his trip concerning his shipboard experience. The first half of that essay focused precisely on the emotional plight of the many German Jewish refugees on the ship for whom Palestine loomed not as a welcome salvation but as an estranging one. Among the 400 passengers, the majority were German Jews. They were, Weinreich related, people without the slightest shred of Jewish knowledge or identity whose choice to leave for Palestine had been a wholly practical one. Forcibly extruded from German life, "one decides that one has to look around in the world. So many Jews are traveling to the Land of Israel, why not us too? We might be able to rescue a few *Marks*." But these German Jews regarded their destination apprehensively not merely because of the many practical forms of displacement involved but also because of the intolerance of two others sorts of Jews, the veteran inhabitants of the Yishuv and confirmed Zionist youth from Eastern Europe with whom they shared the ship: "But here, on the ship, even before they have seen the mountains of *Erets Yisroel* from afar, they are already afraid. [. . .] Yes, a Lithuanian Jewish girl, perhaps 16 years old, remarked to them that when they arrive [. . .] the German Jews must remember their national duties." Weinreich drove the point home with an implied comparison between the young Zionist girl's talk of "national duties" and the semantically identical terminology of the Nazi regime these German Jews were fleeing: "It's these national duties they fear, because the poor things have no idea what it could mean. The Hitlerites talk constantly about national duties, and the result is Jews get it in the face."[71]

But if Weinreich here flirted with deploying one of the most explosive weapons in the anti-Zionist arsenal of the 1930s, the second half of his essay made a sharp about-face. Among the few non-Jewish passengers onboard was a *Sudetendeutsch* engineer whose visceral disgust at being asked whether he would need kosher meals revealed his antisemitism. He turned out to be "a hundred-percent Nazi." A true journalist, Weinreich took the opportunity to interview him and devoted the essay's second half to his findings. In conclusion, he underscored two troubling points. First, the engineer was deeply inspired by the Nazi ideal and related with easy conviction that the authority of the recently established Nazi regime was rooted not in tyrannical control but in popular support—not what progressives like Weinreich or his readers at the *Vilner Tog* wanted to hear.

Second, Weinreich took pains to communicate the power of the engineer's antisemitism and the ways it troubled his own sense of the world.

Describing the engineer's conspiracy theory about the (imaginary) Jewish origins of the Czech leader Tomáš Masaryk, the essay took a striking turn:

> Thus spoke the engineer, who is what you'd call an educated man. And I could only listen and be astonished. I felt as if a poisonous snake were crawling around me and there was no way I could avoid its bite. I have lived through that twice already—once in Russia and once in Germany, in the era of the Revolutions—how the anti-democratic propaganda used the wildest tricks one could imagine to stamp everyone a Jew. Miliukov, Kerensky, Chernov, Lenin—all of them were depicted as Jews in the venomous underground pro-paganda, against which there is no help because it never comes out into the light and thus one cannot deny it. It is apparently one of the best means to whisper in the ears of the ignorant masses: just look, the Jews are ruling over you!

Rhetorically, Weinreich's first essay staged a confrontation between an increasingly common internal critique of Zionism and a manifestly more existential issue—a matter of intra-Jewish cultural politics as against a looming danger that had nothing to do with what Jews wanted and could not be countered with words. Sympathetic to the critique of Zionism's ideological intolerance, Weinreich nevertheless confronted his readers—and himself—with the possibility that the seriousness of this charge paled against the danger of the new antisemitism. Significantly, in this same period Weinreich turned express analytical attention—for the first time really—to the anti-Jewish political vision of the *Polish* Right.[72]

In turn, Weinreich's subsequent essay on German Jews in the Yishuv activated these unsettling potentials. Weinreich's account of the travails of German Jewish adults in Palestine stood alongside a very different ac-count of Nazism's *younger* victims and their relationship to their new home. Part of the eighth essay offered a detailed reconstruction of Wein-reich's conversation with Hanoch Reinhold (later Rinot), a leading figure in the Youth Aliyah program that ultimately brought some 5,000 young Central European Jews to Palestine in the 1930s.[73] Remarkably, this was the only point in the entire series where Weinreich named his interlocutor, in a biography that was also a paean: "I had a long conversation about the Youth Aliyah with one of its leaders, Hanoch Reinhold, who now re-sides with a group of sixty young people in Ein Harod. He is a wonderful young man of about twenty-eight, with a healthy appearance, with intel-

ligent eyes, and with excellent theoretical grounding in Jewish matters."
With evident sympathy, Weinreich described Reinhold's efforts to persuade the German Jewish establishment to devote funds to the resettlement of German Jewish boys and girls in Palestine. And he understood
the agreement of the youths' parents to this effort in matter-of-fact terms
as born of the realization that "under National Socialism, their children
would have no future in Germany."

Here, Weinreich opened himself to a double acknowledgment of his
own. He was moving from the anti-Zionism of his own Bundist past
toward a considered selective pro-Zionism of a soberly political sort:
under present circumstances, perhaps there were indeed some Jewish
communities for whom a Jewish national-territorial project able to open
doors for some was the best alternative. And this was also an acknowledgment of a point like Binyomen's: under some circumstances, like those
in Germany, there could no longer be any responsible talk of "staying and
achieving something in one's homeland." Individual youth exit under
those circumstances was not betrayal but rationality, even when it was
undertaken by people of high capacities rather than simply the most desperate. It was a form of communal triage.

Of course, Weinreich could make this very different moral calculus
with regard to Germany not merely because things were clearly so much
worse for Jews there in 1935, but also because he felt no sentimental at-
tachment to German Jewish identity. The Jews of Eastern Europe had a
real culture to lose, as he saw it, and he was not willing to give it up. In
the years that followed his intense but brief grappling with the triangle of
Nazism's potentials, Zionism's concreteness, and Jewish need, he would
reaffirm his unshakeable devotion to Yiddish culture, lay bare his deeply
Romantic sense that Eastern Europe was preternaturally generative of
Jewish creativity, and turn back to psychological investigation, in the
hope, perhaps, of finding what he had called in _Veg_ the "mighty psychic
lever" to shore up Polish Jewry for the long haul.[74]

But in the meantime, his sympathetic portrait of the German Jewish
Youth Aliyah project brings to the fore a last question that unsettled Jewish
political thought in the 1930s. The heroes here were young people who
had found different lives in Palestine not simply thanks to their own initiative and that of the receiving society, but thanks too to the interven-
tions of their parents, who stayed behind. The question of leaving became
still more complicated when the dyad of individual and community was
complicated by this third category. Was thinking about exit in terms of

the fate of one's *children* selfishness vis-à-vis the community or true self-lessness, individual calculus or the only way to save something?

"And Even More So for Their Children"

In his 1934 shipboard anthropology of why various sorts of *non*-Zionist Polish Jews were traveling to Palestine, the Warsaw journalist Yeushzohn discerned three kinds of motivations, as we saw in Chapter 6. Some were going as tourists. Others, though, were asking whether they should seek a different future in Palestine. Of these, some—the most intellectual, professional, and Polonized—had previously been "distant and alienated from us" but were now driven by "Hitlerism" or "other, more home-grown reasons" to engage for the first time with Zionism's promise and project of an alternative national *identity*. But others, "simple merchants" whom Yeushzohn characterized as "Nalewki Jews" after the commercial thoroughfare of Jewish Warsaw, were traveling to Palestine to see for themselves whether the Yishuv really was a better place for "*takhles.*" This meant in part whether Palestine's rapidly expanding Jewish society in the making was a better place to refound lives and businesses. But Yeushzohn also underscored a second concern: these merchants were keen to investigate whether Palestine would afford better chances than Poland for a "*takhles* both for themselves and even more so for their children."[75]

In thinking about their children's prospects, in Yeushzohn's telling, they were thinking in *part* in terms of psychic-cultural regeneration; he noted as a kind of reported speech the merchants' attraction to the idea that their children would "become 'altogether different people' there." But in asking about a *takhles*, they were also asking whether one could make a "decent life" in the sense that more utopian contemporaries would have called petit bourgeois but that *we* mock only at peril of hypocrisy: *takhles* meant a decent and secure life. And they were thinking of a *takhles* not only for themselves but "even more so for their children": what was at stake was not their own happiness but their children's future.

Not only Polonized Jews, on the one hand, and Nalewki's ideologically indifferent commercial stratum, on the other, were thinking about their children. In early 1935, Shmuel Lakerman left for Palestine with his family. A photo in the archives of Kibbutz Lohamei ha-Getaot records that leading figures of Wilno's Yiddishist "scene" turned out to bid him farewell. And no wonder: Lakerman was a Yiddishist-Diasporist stalwart who had labored for years in service of what his wife, Basya, called "the building of Vilna's *yidishe gezelshaftlekhkayt*"—the bundle of social and cultural endeavors undertaken under the broad umbrella of the secular Yiddishist, progressive-to-socialist vision of Jewish national-communal flourishing in Eastern Europe.[76] He had been active in Yiddishist-Diasporist causes since the turn of the century. In the new Poland, he had thrown himself into the TOZ Jewish public health organization, the Wilno branch of the Diasporist Folkspartey, and Wilno's storied Yiddishist school movement as one of its "most devoted activists." And he had worked to pass this love of Yiddish along. His son Ezra studied in Wilno's Yiddishist schools, and testament to the depth of familial commitment to Yiddish culture shines through in Ezra's own life course. Coming to Palestine at age eighteen, replacing his "Exile-name" Lakerman with "Lahad," Ezra integrated: he made a professional career in the Israeli army and even edited a navy newsletter (in Hebrew of course). But he also became a serious amateur scholar of Yiddish theater and wrote about it extensively, not only in Hebrew but in a sophisticated Yiddish, despite the aggressive Hebraist monolingualism of Israel's early years.

Why did such a figure as Shmuel Lakerman leave for *Palestine,* of all places, with his family? It was certainly not because he embraced the Hebraist-Zionist vision embodied in the Yishuv. Indeed, shortly before he left, he joined the Territorialist-Yiddishist Frayland-Lige—something more understandable given his intense Yiddishism. In a polemical postwar history of the Frayland-Lige, Mikhl Astour insisted that Lakerman had remained a "true Fraylandist" and had moved to Palestine only out of material need.[77]

But Lakerman's intentions in taking his family to Palestine were a good deal more complicated than Astour wanted to believe. His path immediately following his emigration to Palestine was unlike that of other displaced Yiddishist-Diasporists—men like Avrom Golomb, who spent their years in Palestine waiting to leave for some other place where they could resume the cultural life around which they had built their identity. Upon arrival Lakerman turned energetically to studying the troubled land in which he found himself and the Jewish polity-cum-society he had joined. In July 1936 he returned to Wilno for a short visit some ten weeks into what was becoming a concerted multipronged Palestinian rebellion against British rule and war against the Yishuv—what Palestinians would name the Great Revolt of 1936–1939 and what world Jewry would experience as a fateful second closure of Palestine. Lakerman found himself offering

Figure 7.1 Farewell party for Shmuel Lakerman upon his emigration to Palestine, Wilno (Yid.: Vilna), 22 February 1935. Ghetto Fighters' House Museum Archive, catalog no. 31886.

a Yiddish-language lecture about the events at Wilno's Conservatory Hall. His lecture bespoke a multisided engagement with Palestine over the past year. He offered his listeners a detailed analysis of the Yishuv's strengths and vulnerabilities alike: its semiautarkic economic situation meant it depended little on Palestinian Arab production or labor, its well-developed system of buses allowed Jewish communities to remain connected, and it had the means to defend Tel Aviv and other core Jewish communal centers. At the same time, Lakerman showed that he had engaged in unusually serious discussions with a nationally conscious Palestinian interlocutor, an "Arab teacher who often discussed Arab-Jewish questions with [him], has learned Yiddish well, and sometimes even reads a Yiddish newspaper." Lakerman paraphrased the teacher's riposte to the Zionist talking point that Jewish settlement had brought great economic benefit to all in a way that bespoke serious engagement with the Palestinian national perspective: "'Have you ever seen a case wherein someone walks into your house and offers to do you a favor? And were he indeed to do so, wouldn't you suspect him of some hidden motive?'"[78]

If all this careful weighing showed a man trying to understand the new home he had chosen objectively, Lakerman also, strikingly, now aligned himself with one of Zionism's most fundamental arguments (to the manifest irritation of the *Tog*'s anti-Zionist editor): "Sh. Lakerman demonstrated with all sort of examples, that despite the long weeks of terror, casualties, and uncertainty in the Land, Jewish youth there has not fallen prey to doubt and stands ready to defend the positions Jews have secured (in the agricultural colonies, they haven't changed out of day-clothes or slept much for ten weeks; they work by day and carry a rifle by night). And this—the lecturer holds—comprises the difference between the situation in Palestine and that of other lands with Jewish communities."[79] In making this claim, Lakerman was not embracing Zionism even in Lestschinsky's purely political sense. But he was articulating a Jewish political outlook very different from what had become the norm both in Diasporism and in Territorialism. Those movements bypassed the question of Zionism by insisting that because the Yishuv clearly could not meet the political needs of most Jews, it had to be excluded from consideration in search for a more encompassing politics. Lakerman confronted his listeners with the counterview that in searching for such a politics, Jews had to take into account the unsettling possibility that the Yishuv had become (for whatever reason) the *only* Jewish community where Jews still seemed able to mobilize some power, however trammeled, to affect their own fate.

Lakerman's readiness to negotiate an active engagement with his new society suggests a far more complicated relationship to Zionism than Astour's postwar history-cum-score-settling allowed. But what it tells us about Lakerman's *intentions* in moving to Palestine is less clear. Here, the testimony of his son Ezra Lahad offers a different account of his motivations. Shortly after his father's death, Lahad wrote a private letter to Yitshok Steinberg, still the active leader of the Yiddishist-Territorialist Frayland-Lige, in which he acknowledged that Lakerman's move to Palestine had meant a bitter loss of cultural identity: "The new conditions [in Palestine] were not comfortable for him and unfortunately my father could not find any place to live a culturally fulfilling life [*oystsulebn gaystik*]." Why, then, did Lakerman come to Palestine, and why did he choose to stay, rather than seeking a path to other Jewish communities with still vibrant Yiddishist circles—something that many other Yiddishists who felt exiled in Israel did indeed do as they headed to Paris, New York, Buenos-Aires, or Mexico City? Lahad, who had come with his family to Palestine

Figure 7.2 Ezra Lakerman (Lahad) with father Shmuel, mother Basya, and presumably sister (unnamed) on visit to TOZ Jewish public health organization camp outside Wilno, 1933. Ghetto Fighters' House Museum Archive, catalog no. 45397.

not as a boy but as a young adult, offered his own unambiguous answer: "But [my father] accepted [this lot] with love [*mekabel beahoveh geven*], being certain that this was the only way out for his children." On this telling, Lakerman's choice of Palestine was one that cost him dearly, however ready he was to try to be a part of the new society. It cost him his culture and identity. But in Lahad's account, this was a trade-off consciously made; not only coming but staying was the price to be paid for his children's future.[80]

Within Polish Zionism proper, it seems, there were rising questions already by the early 1930s concerning how the *limits* of what Palestine could do for Polish Jews bore differently on the older and younger generations. When Druyanov reported finding many Polish Jews gripped by dread regarding future prospects in 1931–1932, this was no less true of the Zionist subculture than any other. Druyanov worried especially about what he was seeing among those called the *stam-tsionim*, the "plain old Zionists," by which he meant a particular Zionist subculture of "householders": middle-class or formerly middle-class merchants who mixed some modicum of old-fashioned norms with lifelong Zionism. Druyanov wrote about them in part to defend them from what he deemed counter-productive attacks by prominent Yishuv figures. But actually Druyanov was also concerned by what he found. He found the *stam-tsionim* he met in scores of cities and towns exhausted, ground down, and frightened—and sometimes angry. In particular, many were beset by a double feeling of suspicion and resentment toward the movement leadership, on the one hand, and toward Polish Zionist youth, on the other.[81]

This was partly framed as *Kulturkampf* between religiosity and so-cialism, but the other thing that set the youth and the leadership apart from the *stam-tisonim* was that the former were the ones most able to grab at the golden ring and get out of Poland for Palestine, or so it seemed. That Druyanov saw that many of these *stam-tsionim* would have liked to be able to leave for Palestine themselves was evident from his warning to his readers in the Yishuv not to offer them false hopes, lest this turn their "love" for Zionism into "hatred": "And even more necessary is a great measure of honesty and of refraining from cheap propaganda so as not to awaken in their hearts a tumult of exaggerated hopes for a quick salvation."[82]

But Druyanov also saw a countervailing nobility of spirit in these *stam-tsionim,* linked precisely to the same recognition that the Jewish home in Palestine for which they had worked and given for years would almost certainly not be for them but at best for the next generation, including the very youth whose sensibilities they execrated. In his defense of the *stam-tsionim* against those who charged that they were not truly ideal-istic Zionists but rather petty donors substituting donations for commit-ment, Druyanov challenged his Yishuv readers to recognize that this con-tinued financial support was evidence of a Zionist idealism greater than their own. "Far be it from me to diminish by even a grain the weight of the sacrifice of the pioneer boy or the pioneer girl who ascend to the Land," Druyanov wrote. But their sacrifice was one from which they themselves would benefit. The sacrifice of the rank-and-file adult Polish Zionist was by contrast a "burnt offering" that would be entirely con-sumed: "He himself does not enjoy any benefits from it."

Druyanov's text bears on adults—and parents—who were Zionists and whose Zionism (and its specific pathos in his view) consisted of building Palestine not for themselves but for their figurative or real children. Other sources, scattered but evidently only the tip of the iceberg, capture a final and far more direct triangular relationship among parents, children, and exit to Palestine. When the Prużana Yiddishist school principal and activist Gershn Urinsky wrote about the transformation of Jewish outlook in 1934 and the desperation of young Jews to emigrate, one of the things he underscored was that it was not only they who had come to see emigration as their only chance for a future. Prużana's *parents,* he reported, were now urging their children to join Zionist youth organizations and the town's Hehalutz "training kibbutz" in the hopes they might get one of the coveted Certificates.

In Urinsky's eyes, this clearly marked a notable shift. Other sources reported the same phenomenon and similarly registered it as a transformation in attitudes. In July 1932, one Hehalutz activist reported not only that "people are hungry for emigration to Palestine, hysterical to go." A new relationship between parents and children in relation to Palestine was also taking place: "Fathers [now] encourage their sons to join the training farms."[83]

The details of Urinsky's report coupled with his unique vantage as someone altogether distant from Zionism capture something essential: the protagonists he saw were not Zionists at all, or even close to Zionism, but elements hitherto distant from it or even antagonists. Urinsky's report indicated that there were in fact two kinds of non-Zionist parents suddenly looking to Palestine as a salvation for their children. First, attitudes had changed among more traditional parents: "A mother tells her oldest daughter: 'daughter, go join Hehalutz, go to the training kibbutz, with God's help you might get a Certificate, for your father has no dowry to give you.'"[84] The background to Urinsky's observation, a background that would have been familiar to all, was the well-attested worry among traditionally minded Polish Jewish parents that Hehalutz training kibbutzim were sites of moral and sexual license, or that, at any rate, their reputation for such meant that if their daughters were to involve themselves, it would mar their "respectability"—and marriageability. It was no accident that when a *shaliah* like Lova Levita came to Poland at the end of 1929, the young women he encountered in Hehalutz ranks struck him as more idealistic than the young men; in their case, as he noted, coming to Hehalutz had meant a genuine revolt against their home life and their parents. But by 1934, mothers in Prużana were not only overlooking the "immorality" of Hehalutz but betting on it. Hehalutz and marriage might give their daughters a ticket to Palestine; these mothers were choosing a future for their daughters over family virtue and reputation.

A still further political distance was being traveled by the other parents Urinsky clearly had in mind. The circles with whom Urinsky was most intimate were of course those in his own socialist-Yiddishist camp. It was the parents of these boys and girls with whom this school principal, leftist political activist, and tireless Yiddishist would have had intimate contact; it was their children who would have confided to him their desperation to leave. Urinsky's cri de coeur from Pružana, as good a candidate for a Polish Jewish Anytown as any, captures a familial micropolitics of parents urging their children to try for a new life in Palestine *despite* their own ideological indifference or hostility to Zionism, in the absence of any positive myth, and without any serious hope that Palestine would save them from whatever fate their children would be escaping.

Conclusion

"With a Cruel Logic"

In the 1930s, Polish Jewish political thought confronted unexpected forms and intensities of illiberal nationalism and political antisemitism and began to come to terms, belatedly, with just how little power Jews really had to determine their own fate. This book has tried to take seriously the shaping power of the Jewish Question in Jewish political life and thought, and in the history of what happened to Jews in the twentieth century. This was a power that was admittedly complex and intermittent. But it was also a power that was pervasive, profound, and above all *indifferent* to what Jews wanted or hoped for.

Most scholars of Jewish modernity want to investigate realms of thought and deed in which Jews set the terms of their engagement—realms of Jewish creativity, self-definition, freedom, and agency. Many histories of modern Jewish thought imagine modernity largely as an normative challenge to Judaism that compelled creative response. Even many histories of modern Jewish politics, though shot through with awareness of the larger factors limiting Jewish agency and choice, focus passionately on Jews' own ideologies and programs of self-construction and reconstruction, whether nationalist or antinationalist, Judaizing or integrationist, secular or religious, self-separating or self-hybridizing. Where my own previous work fit squarely in all those frames, *An Unchosen People* confronts a different history.

Engagement with the Polish Jewish 1920s and 1930s has forced me to think differently about Jewish modernity: less in terms of freedom than constraint, less in terms of dizzying possibility than new kinds and intensities of danger, less in terms of agency than painful satisficing under conditions of relative powerlessness. In the interstices of the era's great internal Jewish ideological debates, we find far less neat and tidy forms of Jewish thinking—jagged thinking driven by a terrified sense of the need to understand developments over which Jews had no control. In the interstices of the great Jewish political and cultural institutions that invested so much energy in shaping Jewish identities and worldviews in service of competing ideals, a growing multitude of skeptics at the grassroots searched instead for practical responses (including postcommunal ones) to danger and bad fate.

Living in historical time like everyone else, Jews necessarily interpreted the nature and implications of the Jewish Question through the refracting lenses of assumptions and ideologies. But some tried harder than others to understand phenomena indifferent to their will and likely decisive to their fate. This has been a history of such people and such efforts.

The Jewish Question before 1935 and After

To conduct such an inquiry through a focus on the Jews of Poland in the period of Piłsudski's rule between 1926 and 1935 particularly is, as I explained in the introduction, counterintuitive. Other interwar Jewish situations seem far more straightforward cases for thinking about Jewish engagements with danger, antisemitism, powerlessness, and limited choice—that of German Jews after 1933, obviously, or the neglected case of Romania's nearly one million Jews, so venomously maligned across so wide a swath of the political spectrum for so long even before the 1930s. By contrast, the Polish Jewish experience in the Piłsudski era was, as I have tried to register, not a simple story of antisemitism ascendant but a profoundly complex one in which enmity and tension were intermixed with dialogue and intimacy. Some historians go considerably further and treat this era as one defined by *possibilities:* of Jewish-Polish convergence under the banner of the republican ideal, or of a new dawning of socialist hopes.

But unlike those drawn to the Piłsudski years by a sense of complexity wedded to renewed *possibility,* I find the special significance of that period to inhere above all in the marriage of complexity and growing *uncertainty,* as the Depression set in and unrealistic hopes in the capacities of the new regime to defuse Poland's Jewish Question began to fade. I have tried to show that the period of Polish Jewish history spanning roughly 1928–1935 is of special interest for the history of modern Jewish political thought and choice because the particular dimensions of the political uncertainty under which the largest Jewish community in Europe lived in those years compelled new kinds of Jewish thinking about danger and vulnerability, social explanation and political prediction, minorityhood and majorityhood in a nationalist age, the nation-state, Diaspora, communal obligation, and individual choice.

It is for the same reason that I have chosen to close the present study in early 1936 rather than following the story through to what most historians would consider the normal terminus of the Polish Jewish interwar experience, the German and Soviet conquests of September 1939. To stop this study in 1936 may seem no less peculiar than to focus it on the Piłsudski years. For even in the deeply divided field of Polish history writing, most will agree that in the very last years of independent Poland, between 1936 and 1939, the Jewish fears on which this book has focused were substantially realized. First, 1936–1937 saw a massive "wave of anti-Jewish violence," albeit largely nonlethal, in Poland's universities, even in high schools, and in the centers of dozens of towns large and small, most of which had not previously seen anything of the sort, and not in the multiethnic eastern borderlands or *jacquerie*-prone Galicia but in the heart of Congress Poland, "in the areas where Poles were the majority."[1] One Jewish body sketched a few of these events from January 1937 thus:

> 5 January [1937]: pogrom at Czyżew—2 killed, 16 seriously injured; 60 slightly injured, pillage of Jewish shops and houses [. . .];14 January: pogrom at Piekuty [. . .] 21 seriously injured [. . .]; 30 January: "A Day Without Jews" at the University of Warsaw: all the entrances were guarded by Polish students, who forbade access to the Jewish lecturers and students; a group of 10 Jewish students who succeeded in entering the building were attacked by a great number of anti-Semitic students and beaten so long with iron bars that they were all left streaming with blood on the ground [. . .]. The students distributed the following appeal: "wherever you meet a Jew, knock his teeth out with iron. Don't worry even if it is a girl student [. . .]." At the Warsaw Polytechnic, where numerous Jewish auditors were beaten bloody, one of whom is in desperate condition, the Rector refused to receive a delegation of Jewish students [. . .]. At the Warsaw High School of Agriculture, Jewish women students were pricked with long needles by the Christian women students.[2]

Perhaps a more significant watershed was that the ruling Sanacja regime abandoned its commitment to the republican tradition within Polish nationalism and instead openly adopted a wide-ranging policy goal of "de-Judaization" involving open support for "nativization" of the economy and a commitment to the view that the emigration of most Polish Jews was the only solution to Poland's Jewish Question.[3] Even when the regime brought the anti-Jewish violence under control in 1938, it did not renounce its embrace of nationalist antisemitism's fundamental claim: that Poland's Jews were—sometimes by intention but always by their very presence—an obstacle and danger to Polish well-being. Behind the scenes, regime leaders sought Jewish allies who might help with mass emigration.[4] But publicly, by 1938, regime ideologist-publicists were ready to motivate policy in terms that could have been written by an Endek. It was not simply that "the Communist part of Jewry is the open enemy of our Nation and State." Jewish overrepresentation in "money exchange, the disposal of capital" was a clear and present danger too. Even the politically quiescent Orthodox population, "the conservative portion" whose leaders had so assiduously allied themselves with the Sanacja, was "through its cultural and ethical differences, a heavy burden upon our national life [. . .] a foreign body dispersed in our organism so that it produces a pathological deformation."[5] And the accession of the state to antisemitism's logic was not limited to the politicians. Although not everyone in the regime was convinced, neither was this new logic safely confined to a few leaders, planners, and publicists. On the ground, municipal authorities and police often manifested sympathy for the attackers over the victims. The antisemitic-nationalist diagnosis was embraced across wide swaths of Poland's judiciary, as literally thousands of court cases resulted in light sentences for pogromists, harsh sentences for Jewish self-defense activists, and even sentences against Jews who spoke up—their crime was "insulting the Polish nation."[6]

Then, too, the fact that the regime was operating partly out of the need to steal the Endecja's thunder was of little comfort, because it bespoke the terrifying fact that embracing antisemitism seemed the key to winning the hearts and minds of many, especially the youth. Historians of independent Poland's last years are locked in permanent dispute over the same questions that trouble historians of the 1920s and early 1930s: How wide and deep did the anti-Jewish sentiment now reach, how robust were countervailing currents of tolerance and liberal and radical alternatives to the nationalist-antisemitic dispensation, and—the question nobody can answer but historians cannot leave alone—where would everything have gone if not for the war? In this historiography, the "optimists" tend to look past the regime and the organized Right alike to "society," and find various reassuring signs. A pioneering historian of the regime's official antisemitism, Edward Wynot Jr., averred that "the vast majority of Poles [. . .] resisted this overt appeal to baser instincts and thereby thwarted the regime's designs of dividing and ruling along lines of hatred, passion, and alienation."[7] Other historians see little grounds for this happy vision of a tolerant "vast majority," for reasons we will soon see, but more guarded "optimists" can point to concrete data like the impressive showing of the Polish Socialist Party in December 1938 municipal elections: clearly, substantial numbers of Poles had not thrown in with either the Right or the regime.[8]

But other historians see a darker trajectory playing out. The eminent historian of interwar Poland Jerzy Tomaszewski ultimately concluded that "if one takes into account the situation that prevailed at the end of the 1930s, the prospects for lasting solutions" to the Jewish Question "must seem doubtful." Antony Polonsky agrees that "the conclusion has to be pessimistic."[9] Some such "pessimists" simply disagree with the happy view that Polish civil society remained largely resistant to antisemitism. Contra views like Wynot's, Emanuel Melzer cites evidence of widespread anti-Jewish pressure *on* the state *from* society. In March 1936, Foreign Minister Jan Szembek confided to his diary: "Even though the proposed law conflicts with the constitution, the government must confine itself to suggesting amendments, for no jurist will be found who would dare to find the law unconstitutional in the face of the antisemitic sentiments of most of the public."[10] Melzer argues that when indeed the government took its turn toward defining Poland's Jews as a problem that had to be solved on the policy front, "Polish public opinion was widely supportive of the government's efforts."[11] Historians who take this view may point to the continued spread of ideologically far-reaching antisemitism among educated youth, the fact that much of Poland's influential Catholic Church establishment continued to propound the view that Jews were a threat to Polish souls and bodies, the embrace of anti-Jewish politics by the Catholic Youth League with its 350,000 members, the decision of Polish professional associations in medicine, law, engineering, and business to adopt "Aryan clauses," and the ever-growing evidence that antisemitic violence was more widespread than is often thought.[12]

Historians' effort to gain clarity on the spread and intensity of anti-Jewish sentiment and countervailing tolerance in Polish society can only be asymptotic. Clearly the situation remained complex. One can easily find sources that emphasize the persistence of widespread decency: the

Wilno Jewish actor Yehiel Burgin's year of military service in Lida in 1936–1937 was marked by sporadic antisemitic encounters, but mostly he recalls fair treatment of the Jewish men by the officers and decent relations with fellow conscripts, mostly peasant youth. But Czesław Miłosz and Aleksander Hertz, who worked together in Warsaw between 1937 and 1939, experienced that time as a period in which "chauvinism, anti-Semitism [. . .] baseness and absurdity" ran wild in public life and "seemed to encounter no open resistance." We might read the gap between such sources—which can be endlessly replicated—as reassuring evidence that matters remained mixed. But we might also note that Burgin's experience took place among peasants in the provinces, whereas Miłosz and Hertz were speaking of the capital and the ruling classes, those wielding power or primed to inherit it.[13] And degree of *hatred* is not the sole measure of where civil society was headed; Zofia Trębacz's wide-ranging examination of public discourse about mass Jewish emigration/expulsion finds that "negative attitudes toward Jewish emigration could only be found on the Polish left, and even then not in all its circles."[14]

Moreover, as Benjamin Nathans observes, the "unspoken assumption" that frames so much of the historiographical debate I am characterizing here—namely, that the factor that would have proved most decisive for the future of Polish Jews was "the balance of sentiment in society at large" vis-à-vis Jews—is itself questionable. The outcomes of sociopolitical conflicts in the modern era, he notes, seem to be just as much, if not more, the product of the enthusiasms of mobilized ideological minorities or of "the position taken by the state [. . .] with all the awesome powers and resources at its disposal." Seen from this perspective, there is yet more reason for pessimism given what we know about the energized Right, its reach among young people, the populist-nationalist turn of policy visions among Poland's ruling stratum, and the general reach and power of the sense not only in Poland but across Europe that the time had come to solve difficult questions with decisive action.[15]

Sharing Nathans's intuitions, some of the "pessimists" in this field-consuming debate about futures that might have been derive their grim intuitions by looking past the balance of attitudes in Polish society to more structural problems. For historians like Tomaszewski, it seems sadly clear that interwar Poland simply faced too many objective problems of poverty and capacity, and that the sheer size and centrality of the Jewish presence in Poland's underdeveloped commercial economy was too big a scandal in a nationalist age and too tempting a target for too many others seeking a piece of the same small pie, to realistically expect that the baleful metastases of the 1930s could have resolved happily.

Sometime in early 1937, Yoysef Tshernikhov took part in a meeting of Jewish lawyers from across Poland. He summarized his colleagues' grim reflections thus:

> The next day, almost all of us congregate in Café Europejski [. . .]. Thoroughly assimilated Jewish "men of affairs" from the Congress Kingdom [. . .] talk naturally in Polish about Jewish woes [. . .]. They are not even angry. Almost all of them emphasize that regardless of everything that has happened in the past few months, relations with their non-Jewish colleagues are generally good—in some places, even quite good. But then again: every one of us gathered here has concluded after sober reckoning that personal relations are one thing while the general situation playing out with a cruel logic is something else altogether. The roof is not yet on fire, perhaps, but there is so much tinder piled up.[16]

Here was a double analytical insight. Polish society still featured much decency, goodwill, and humanism, but the malignity of some and the frustration and fear of many had "piled up" so much "tinder" that it was foolish to hope that conflagration could be avoided in the near term. Then, too, Tshernikhov's interlocutors could not escape the sense that something deeper was playing out: a "cruel logic" whereby the Jewish Problem conceived as a problem had grown so interwoven with the woes, hopes, interests, and needs of so many—problems that any Polish state *had to* address—that a politics of economic and social extrusion directed against Jews might be the easiest, most exigent option and effective resistance to it (whether in society or indeed government) a difficult path.

This book cannot stake a strong claim one way or another as to where Polish political culture might have gone. It does offer some perspective on a second question that historians of modern Poland revisit ceaselessly—namely, whether the mainstreaming of anti-Jewish visions in the political life of the late 1930s marked a *deviation* from a Polish national politics defined primarily by tolerance, or rather a *culmination* of processes at work in Polish political culture well before 1935. One thing this book helps demonstrate is that already in the Piłsudski years, plenty of Jewish participant-observers coming from a wide variety of perspectives discerned powerful currents carrying Polish political society toward extrusionary nationalism.

Polish Jewish Thought and Choice

But Polish political culture is not the primary concern of this book; Jewish political culture is. I have sought here to find new ways to think about the history of Jewish political thought and choice—and perhaps the larger history of minority political thought in the age of the nation-state and eth-nonationalist populism—in a period marked by a unique constellation of cultural complexity, economic disaster, political danger, and a peculiar possibility of Jewish exit. Culturally, the 1928–1935 period saw the Po-lonization of Polish Jewry reach new heights. But that period also dramatized as never before that cultural integration and political integration were two very different things, and that the former would not automatically bring the latter and might even be weaponized as an argument against it. Economically, Poland was gripped by the Depression, and this intensified the question of who really belonged to the commonweal and whom the state should serve. Politically, a thin membrane of semiauthoritarian quiet was stretched across vast economic suffering and hopelessness, renewed violent tensions between the Polish state and its minorities, the persistent draw of ethnic visions of nationhood within Polish political society despite the 1926 regime's commitment to the civic alternative, an intensification of the nationalist Right's commitment to radically extrusionary antisemitism, and disturbing signs that the Right's core contentions about the Jews as a problem demanding resolution through concerted national action were resonating across society: being echoed in the church and the press, mobilizing masses of youth, becoming common sense for masses of upstanding citizens. And it was also not lost on anyone that parallel phenomena could be seen elsewhere in Eastern and Central Europe, leading in some cases to startlingly fast transformations of the Jewish condition.

The particularities of this 1928–1935 constellation both destabilized and provoked Jewish political thought. As Chapters 1, 2, 4, and 5 demonstrated from various perspectives, unforeseen developments of the era provoked a building wave of skepticism toward all well-established forms of Jewish political faith and strategy, on the one hand, and toward the old certainties of Jewish social thought, on the other—particularly all the strategies built on liberal faith in Polish political culture's better angels, progressive faith in human improvement, or socialist faith in redemption through the dialectic. And as some Jews struggled to understand the linkages of economic crisis, majoritarian nationalism, democracy, and antisemitic enmity, they also struggled toward new and painful understandings of what might become of them and their children under these new circumstances and what they should seek to do about it.

Then, too, in 1932 another key factor peculiar to this period moved to the center of Polish Jewish debate and thought: for reasons that had nothing to do with Poland or its Jews, the British Empire opened up its Palestine Mandate to unprecedented levels of Jewish immigration, which in turn revitalized and consolidated the Zionist project and the radically distinctive Jewish (sub)society that had been gaining form and strength in Palestine under Zionism's auspices for several decades. After 1932 especially—though signs were visible as early as 1928–1929—the question of whether it made sense to hope for a better Jewish future in Poland was yoked to the question of what kind of alternative Palestine's Yishuv might offer. The impact on Jewish thought and choice of this concrete possibility of exit for a not-insignificant number of Polish Jews, disproportionately young, to what was perhaps a profoundly different kind of Jewish society, stood at the center of Chapters 2, 5, 6, and 7.

If this particular constellation of factors served as a forcing bed of new Jewish thought, what particular shoots of thought did it force to the surface? Chapters 1 and 2 sketched a revisionist social-historical account of grassroots Polish Jewish thinking about the future. Looking past the siloed histories of this or that movement, I brought to bear at least strongly suggestive evidence that, already in the Sanacja period, growing numbers of ordinary Jews began to move toward three intertwined conclusions: that there were few prospects for a decent future for themselves and their children in Poland; that none of the existing varieties of Poland-centered Jewish politics born in the 1920s—contestatory-nationalist, Orthodox-accommodationist, or socialist—could much affect that likelihood; and that Jews had as much to fear from unfolding political and cultural processes as from raw economic ruination.

Wide recognition that this spreading sense of futurelessness was itself a "social fact" converged with the larger political and economic worries that fed it to provoke some Jewish intellectuals—particularly those Diasporists unable to believe with perfect faith in the Revolution—toward new lines of thought about the prospects of Jewish identity and subjectivity under siege. Some heterodox Diasporist inquirers wrestled with a sense that the East European Jewish self was being undermined by emerging forms of *negative* identity born of stigmatization and felt powerlessness. Beneath the variety of their endeavors, from microloan management to cultural tourism to lyric poetry, these figures manifested a budding interest in whether means could be found to confront despair itself: to restore hope, change alternative aspirations, build endurance, or salve wounded subjectivity.

Other Jewish intellectuals, mostly Zionist or post-Diasporist, turned their gaze not inward but outward to the majority society. They sought to think past deep progressive and Marxian certainties about the determinative relationship between economic and political events and the arc of history toward Reason, and instead to wrestle with the problem that was beginning to confront all progressive social thought: why seemingly "irrational" forms of enmity were manifestly redefining the terms of social rationality and political interest. Where some thinkers began to grope toward a psychologistic account of how political enmities might be flowing from the inner needs of individuals, others groped in directions we might identify with mature political science to think about changing societal expectations of the state and resultant forms of state capture. Each of these forms of thought showed new appreciation for how nationalist ideology and imagination, and sometimes antisemitism's distinctive traditions, were channeling, shaping, and intensifying enmity.

Against this double backdrop, Chapters 5–7 sought to recapture lines of Jewish political thinking that began to emerge in the interstices of the long-established ideologies and movements, in ways that found little institutionalization but grew in the minds of individuals of various backgrounds drawn from across a fractured Polish Jewry. First, I highlighted the emergence of a new Polish Jewish orientation toward the Zionist project in Palestine defined neither by the canons of Zionism nor by those of anti-Zionism but by a posture of inquiry. For widening swaths of Polish Jewry, including many beyond organized Zionism of any sort, the "question of Zion" was no longer framed by old Zionist certainties of one sort or another or by the countervailing certainties of socialist-Diasporist, assimilationist, or Orthodox anti-Zionisms but by the complex fact of the Yishuv as a real place, possibly very different from Poland in what it could offer Jews and suddenly possibly significant for one's personal future and fate—or that of one's children.

Second, I began to excavate a dispersed and intimate history of how Polish Jewish individuals wrestled in new ways with competing claims of communal, individual, and familial need within the framework of two painful probabilistic conclusions: that for all the grand talk and quiet hopes of the 1920s, Poland's Jews were largely powerless to decide how the other 90 percent of Poland's population would choose to ask and answer the Jewish Question; and that there was too much evidence of rising danger to ignore. This dual recognition forced those afflicted by it toward one or all of three kinds of political thinking defined by a grim sense of the limits of the possible, the need to think in terms of emergency and rescue, and the need to approach the communal situation in terms of triage. First, it forced some to see that cherished visions of Jewish life, culture, and identity toward which they had long worked might have to be put aside or even given up for the sake of more elemental needs. Second, it forced some to accept that Jews had to frame their political calculations, tactics, and strategies in terms of the realities imposed by those who wielded power over them. Third, it bred a readiness to accept the hard truth that one could do little to help all or even most of the community, and that therefore questions of betterment—and rescue—contracted to the ugly question of whether and how one could help oneself, or at most some particular fellow Jews.

The 1936–1939 Denouement and Polish Jewish Thought

And what of 1936–1939? The processes that began to unfold in 1936 substantially disassembled the 1928–1935 constellation that had forced these lines of thought to crystallize. In Poland, as noted, fears that extrusionary antisemitism would conquer the political mainstream suddenly ceased to be fears. They became realities. Overseas, the idea that Palestine might offer an alternative for many was dealt a shattering blow. April 1936 saw the onset of what Palestinians would come to call the Great Revolt: an unprecedentedly large-scale military and civil insurrection by substantial parts of Palestinian society against the British Mandatory coupled with an intensifying campaign of attacks on Palestine's Jewish community.[17] In retrospect, the campaign, which Palestinian society sustained for three years, did not destroy the Yishuv. But many at the time imagined it would. In May 1936 the folklorist Menashe Unger received a letter from two Jewish friends in Palestine marked by certainty that the revolt would force the British to renounce the Balfour Declaration; the young Yiddish scholar Mordkhe Kosover decided to leave Palestine rather than waiting "for Ishmael" to drive him out.[18] The revolt also undermined many Diaspora Jews' hopes that Jewish society building in Palestine might truly be a meaningful alternative to the woes of the Diaspora. More concretely, already in 1936 the Palestinian campaign moved the British Mandatory to sharply reduce the number of Jewish immigrants it was willing to admit.[19] Thus the uncertainties and alternatives that had stimulated Jewish thought until 1936 melted into grim certainty that all possibilities were foreclosed.

Obviously, not everyone felt this way. The unmaking of the 1928–1935 constellation did not mean an end to Polish Jewish thinking. Some historians of Polish Jewry might reframe this point more forcefully and even argue that despite the ugliness of 1936–1939, growing numbers of Jews actually discovered new faith—or at least hope—that a better tomorrow was coming. To the degree this is true, some might argue further that this would constitute an event in Polish Jewish political culture so different from the sort of phenomena I have foregrounded for the 1928–1935 conjuncture as to demand some explanation on my part.

We might see such signs of renewed faith in the Polish Jewish future in various sites. Politically, this period saw a substantial drop in Polish Jewish engagement with organized Zionism: whereas 206,000 Polish Jews voted in the international Zionist Congress elections of 1935, only 116,000 did so in 1937 and 114,000 in 1939.[20] The same years brought a dramatic rise in Jewish electoral support for the socialist Bund: municipal elections in December 1938 and May 1939 brought commanding Bundist victories among Jewish voters in many major cities and even in some smaller locales.[21] Pointing to its status as the only Jewish party with an ally in the Polish political mainstream, the PPS, the Bund ran under a double banner of defiance against extrusionary antisemitism and Marxist confidence that a united front of socialist forces in Poland would overcome the reaction, that Jews had a great role to play in this struggle, and that Jews could look forward to equality and acceptance in Poland on the other end. Clearly, some of those who voted for the Bund in 1938–1939 were new supporters for whom much of its party program, culture, and ideology had previously been foreign. Were these latter simply supporting the Bund for its proud defiance of the Right and the regime alike, or were they moved by new hopes that the optimistic Bundist prognosis was right?[22]

Beyond the political sphere, some historians might point to the realm of continued Jewish economic self-help as a site where, perhaps, a rebirth of faith in Jewish agency was taking root. Jewish organs of economic self-help created in the Piłsudski years, like the large network of Jewish no-interest microloan kasses, continued to play a substantial ameliorating role through the late 1930s, and some deemed them highly effective (including unhappy antisemites).[23] Did this translate into an upwelling of Jewish confidence that such forms of communal self-defense offered a sustainable strategy of weathering prolonged siege? In June 1938, Majer Polner, an activist for the Jewish cooperative movement in the kresy, insisted to readers of *Moment* that Jews needed to organize on the model of Poland's Ukrainians. Having recognized that they had "no possibility of achieving something on the political front" in Poland, Ukrainian nationalists had "turned nearly their entire attention and all their powers to the economic front" and this had yielded "great, extraordinary achievements." Jews could achieve something too if only they shifted their efforts from fruitless political contestation to economic self-defense.[24]

No doubt some Polish Jews did retain or find faith in a better tomorrow even in the 1936–1939 period. Clearly, at least some of the support for the Bund reflected real investment in optimistic Bundist prognoses regarding both Jewish and Polish society—not least because the party had worked hard for years to build its own siloed counterculture through the Yiddish schools and trade unions it dominated, its youth movement, and a women's auxiliary.[25] Alternatively, historians of Poland's assimilated Jews and of its Hasidic Jews alike can no doubt find similar reservoirs of real confidence in Polish humanism or divine providence, respectively.

But it seems clear that when all is said and done, the mass sense of futurelessness that emerged in the Piłsudski years remained the most salient fact of Jewish political culture after 1936. It is undoubtedly true that masses of Polish Jews continued to wish to leave Poland. In mid-1936, Samuel Chmielewski, writing for a government-affiliated research initiative, averred that "the broad masses of Polish Jewry" were ready to grasp at *any* emigration possibility—including Palestine, but also Birobidzhan, Peru, Chile, and Manchuria—owing to "constantly intensifying economic crisis and the increase in antisemitic tendencies."[26] In the same year, the aforementioned activist Polner acknowledged unhappily that "the broad Jewish masses see their only salvation in emigration."[27] Crucially, he spoke from unusually wide direct experience, having worked for nearly a decade as a traveling inspector for the Jewish cooperative movement in northeastern Poland.[28] In the following year, Polish Jewish civil society grew uncomfortable with open discussion of mass emigration;

in late 1936, public pronouncements that only a mass exit by as many as a million Jews could defuse Poland's Jewish Question by the prominent Zionist leaders Grinboym and Jabotinsky drew angry rebuke from across the Jewish spectrum. But for many, this was clearly a matter of not wishing to play into the extrusionary program of the regime rather than a reflection of some sudden popular upwelling of *doik* hopes in Jewish civil society. After all, even activists for the YEAS Jewish emigration society rebuked Grinboym, noting that "the emigration-question [. . .] has recently become the expression of the antisemitic elimination idea," but this hardly reflected growing confidence in the Polish Jewish future in YEAS ranks.[29] Even some profoundly hostile to Zionism particularly and to the idea of Jewish mass exit generally acknowledged that masses of Polish Jews continued to dearly wish to leave. In May 1939, the veteran Bundist Dovid Mayer published a pamphlet inveighing against Zionism and proclaiming that the Polish working masses had embraced the Bundist view that Jews had every right to be in Poland and should therefore stay and fight. But he acknowledged that "a large part" of the Jewish population in Poland was "ready to leave because of economic, political, and national persecutions."[30] A quantitative source excavated by historian Joseph Marcus is also suggestive: over the course of 1937–1938, some 180,000 individuals registered their interest in leaving with YEAS. As Marcus observes, this is a strikingly large number given that registering with YEAS availed one of nothing more than advice and perhaps a bit of administrative aid; it offered no additional likelihood of actually getting out. It must be assumed that these 180,000 registrants were only part of a larger population keen to get out.[31]

And thus, too, there is much evidence to show that the new kinds of political thinking that I excavated for the 1928–1935 period did not disappear from Polish Jewish thought: thinking framed by a sense of danger and emergency, the painful limits of Jewish agency, a sharpening sense of the risks of Diaspora minorityhood, vernacular renegotiations of Zionism, and a creeping sense that the only practical politics available might be a politics of helping oneself. Between 1936 and 1939, hopes continued to fade that the Yishuv would offer rescue to large numbers of Polish Jews, or indeed that it would survive. This, though, did not mean that Polish Jews grew indifferent to the Zionist project. In mid-1939, Britain's formal renunciation of its commitment to the creation of a Jewish national home in Palestine called forth "massive street demonstrations" from Polish Jews.[32] Polonsky puts the number of Polish Jewish in Zionist youth movements "on the eve of the Second World War" between "70,000 and 100,000."[33]

Equally telling, a new line of thought about territory and sovereignty emerged across multiple circles of Polish Jews, provoked by an unexpected turn in the Palestine imbroglio. Over the course of 1937 it became clear that Britain was seriously considering pulling out of Palestine and partitioning it into separate Palestinian and Jewish states. Committed Zionists were sharply divided by the prospect, with some unwilling to compromise romantic- or religious-nationalist commitments to "the whole Land of Israel." But there is evidence that many Polish Jews in particular greeted the possibility of the immediate creation of a small Jewish state with desperate excitement—what Shmuel Dothan describes as a "largely spontaneous movement" of support. The Zionist activist Yaakov Helman recalled an event in Warsaw at which an impoverished Jewish man "attacked a Zionist journalist [. . .] whose newspaper opposed Partition," shouting, "We've swallowed enough *Tisha be-Av* [the holy day commemorating Jewish collective calamities], give us a bit of *Simhat Torah* [a holy day of celebration]."[34]

And clearly this enthusiasm for partition and a small state now over "the whole Land of Israel" later stemmed not from nationalist enthusiasm for "Hebrew letters on the stamps," as Weinreich had once dismissively put it, but from the popular recognition that Jewish sovereignty over a territory, even a small one, would mean the immediate expansion of mass immigration possibilities. Not only leading Polish Zionists like Moshe Kleinbaum and Aryeh Tartakover but also non-Zionists and even anti-Zionists were moved to think about the difference sovereignty might make for desperate Polish Jews. In October 1937, the Yiddishist Yisroel Yefroykin wrote to a friend in Palestine that leading Diasporist and Territorialist Yiddishists across Europe, including Wilno's Tshernikhov, had "altered their [dismissive] position on Palestine as soon as they heard the news about [the possibility of] the state."[35]

The prospect of partition led to fissures and new lines of thought among Orthodox leaders in Poland too. At the 1937 Marienbad meeting of the council of Hasidic and rabbinic leaders who determined the positions of the Agudas Yisroel party, some hewed to the established ultra-Orthodox view that "Torah-true" Jews had to actively oppose the creation of a state that would be dominated by "freethinkers, God forbid," as Rabbi Mordechai Rotenberg of Antwerp put it; he was not alone in demanding that "all the necessary steps be taken to prevent the creation of this state." But other participants were simply too concerned about the plight of Jews in Europe to accept this view, once hegemonic in *haredi* circles. When council chairman Rabbi Arn Lewin "propose[d] that [. . .] the political aspect of a Jewish state [*medinah yehudit*] should be kept out of our arguments and we should focus only on the religious question [of] whether a Jewish state is permitted by the Torah or not," Rabbi Zalman Sorotzkin of Lutsk protested that "the political aspect is also a matter of *pikuah nefesh*," the rule in Jewish religious law that saving a life overrides almost all other religio-legal injunctions. Another Polish participant, the Łódź Hasidic industrialist and communal leader Leib Mincberg, responded to Rotberg's unalloyed opposition with his famous sharpness. A Jewish state in Palestine, he suggested, would of course not be "the Beginning of the [Messianic] Redemption," but it would at least be "the beginning of redemption from troubles," and his fellow Orthodox leaders ought to relate to it with the same seriousness with which they would greet any other opportunity for large-scale Jewish evacuation. He laid out the *pikuah nefesh* argument for accepting a Jewish state under any circumstance: "Let us imagine that we could not bring in more than a few hundred or a few thousand. Even then it would be incumbent upon us to do and to help as much as our hands could."[36]

The 1937 upswell of hope for Jewish sovereignty was soon dashed. But the situation in Poland and Europe continued to drive individuals to look to Palestine as a possible solution if not for many then at least for some—or for oneself. One 1939 YIVO autobiography written by a young man in Węgrów records a suggestive double transition. His short-lived Zionist enthusiasms in the early 1930s had first given way to serious engagement with Bundist ideas. Participation in Bundist "lectures on political economy" led him to an active role as a "thinking activist" declaiming Bundist arguments on various questions "every Friday night" and to a strongly anti-Zionist outlook in accordance with "the [hard Left] stance of Khmurner." Yet by 1939 he was reconsidering once again: "In the framework of the Polish republic, we will not be able to win any national liberation. In Palestine, I think, there will eventually emerge an autonomous Jewish center."[37] The more radical self-rescue Zionism toward which Binyomen R. had been drawn also did not disappear. Ido Bassok pinpoints another 1939 autobiography in which the author declares himself an antinationalist but also acknowledges having come to see the Yishuv as a "place of refuge in the meantime, until I am able to fight for social equality and for cosmopolitanism."[38]

Beyond such continued engagement with Zionism, other forms of chastened political thought that had become visible in the Piłsudski years continued to evolve as well. This could be seen in emigration activism. Even as Jews across the political spectrum rejected regime visions of mass expulsion, some old opponents quietly concluded that mass self-removal from Poland was indeed essential. By 1939, the cooperative-movement activist Polner had grown convinced that there was little hope for a lessening of the anti-Jewish pressure given the mass of landless peasants eager for urban livelihoods still in Jewish hands, and joined the ranks of those trying to figure out how to persuade Western policy makers to open the doors wider.[39] Some writings on emigration displayed a growing sense of the need to reckon with anti-Jewish attitudes in potential receiving countries as facts that could not be argued or moralized away. A 1939 book-length policy study by Tartakover—still a Zionist, but apparently committed to a coordinated global Jewish effort to maximize emigration from Europe to anywhere else—called for a concerted public relations campaign to counter the view that Jews did not assimilate and become loyal citizens. He also argued that Jewish emigration activists had to pay more attention to "sprucing up" the potential emigrants themselves: to work on their attitudes and even "outward appearance" in order to combat prejudices against Jewish immigrants. This, Tartakover hoped, might help open the doors wider.[40] Polner went even further. He counseled that Polish Jews might increase their chances of getting out if they accommodated Euro-American white racism and the fact of its global power. Pointing to rising racist panic across the "White Pacific" about imagined East Asian demographic expansion (the "Yellow Peril"), Polner suggested that "even Jews" might qualify as "white" enough to be admitted to Australia in substantial numbers if—and only if—they undertook a large-scale program of retraining as agriculturalists and artisans, for "no country will accept a *Lumpenproletariat.*"[41]

Finally, perhaps we must indeed take seriously the notion—though it raises many historians' hackles—that 1936–1939 saw a fundamental contraction in Polish Jewish political culture jointly defined by recognition of Jewish powerlessness to shape the larger polity and by an accompanying turn inward. Of course, we find in the Polish Jewish internal discourse of the era a rich vein of defiance. In December 1937, the leadership of Grodno's Jewish community board wrote back to American friends about "your recommendation not to manifest signs of Jewishness on the envelopes lest this incite antisemitism." The Grodno Jews forcefully declined: "Concealing one's Jewishness has never been of any help to anyone, as evidenced by Germany. In our view, the only medicine that can provide the persecuted Jew with self-respect is endurance, and showing the whole world that despite everything we are not broken and that we 'wear the [figurative] yellow patch' with pride and we don't compromise even in small things."[42] But however moving, this defiance can hardly be conflated with sociopolitical confidence. The horizon toward which these anonymous respondents looked was, after all, the hell of Nazi Germany. Their talk of pride and bearing up points not toward a new belief in Jewish agency but toward the horizonless effort to shore up the embattled Jewish self with which figures such as Weinreich, Chaim Grade, and Mikhoel Burshtin had begun to reckon, gingerly, in the Piłsudski era.

And indeed, in the 1936–1939 period, such "pioneers" of the call to fortify inner life against despair were driven ever more fully toward the view that this was the only path left for most Polish Jews. Grade's 1934–1936 effort to achieve a world-affirming poetry that could repair the wounded self was short-lived; when his volume *Yo* finally appeared in 1936, the hard-won poems of affirmation that capped the "Yo" cycle were undercut by the unrelentingly grim "Yehezkel" (Ezekiel), which closed the volume. In many ways, his poetry thereafter was just as dark. And as Justin Cammy notes, Grade similarly continued to see nothing to hope for from organized Jewish politics; in 1937 he remarked in disgust that the Bundists and left-wing Zionist groups to whom he might otherwise have gravitated remained locked in internecine conflict, and lamented "[our national] anarchy." But Grade still hoped to find a poetry that would counter despair: in February 1939 he once again averred that "the poet must raise his voice in a song of faith."[43]

By the same token, Burshtin's last novel, *Bay di taykhn fun Mazovye*, appearing in 1937, was in some ways his most straightforward call to Polish Jews to bear up and endure. Like the 1931 *Ployne*, *Mazovye* was another highly textured and crushing portrait of small-town Jewish life—this time set in the present day of 1936 and culminating in a pogrom recognizably modeled on those that exploded across central Poland in that year. But unlike *Ployne*, *Mazovye* ended on a note of demonstrative defiance: as Sam Kassow reminds us, Burshtin gave the last word to the traditional Jewish everyman Hirsh Lustik, whose very name symbolizes vitality and who closes the novel with a vow to rebuild the town, his face flaming in the rising sun. This was certainly pathetic fallacy directed against despair, but was it a politics? In the meantime, Burshtin was now forced to earn his living from literature, having been removed from his teaching post "for a reason," as he put it in a letter to a Canadian friend, "you will surely intuit."[44]

Awareness that Jews would now be subject to a sustained siege, that it would not resolve soon, and that this necessitated a turn inward toward psychic endurance can be seen across the great divides that sundered Poland's Jewish community. In Poland's Orthodox community, many leading voices interpreted the late 1930s through a well-established theodicy that conceived Jewish travails and even antisemitic assault as God's tool—his "storm-wind"—to return straying Jews to the proper path.[45] Some others, including most famously the influential ultra-Orthodox leader Elkhonen Vaserman, averred that the irreversible apocalyptic travails of the Messianic advent had begun; the totality with which contemporary Jews had forsaken the "sovereignty of the Torah" to follow "dogs" preaching the "idols" of "liberalism [. . .], democratism, socialism, Communism," and above all Zionism was both cause and portent. Theurgically speaking, the former view held out the possibility of active response, whereas the latter demanded resignation. But in practice, both converged on the stance that the only path for Poland's Jews was religious devotion (and recognition that further political effort would be useless or worse—as Vaserman put it, "clutching at the skirts of a dying democracy" or participating in Zionism's "war" against "the Kingdom of Heaven"). Only hewing to faith might help, and at least it could offer, as Gershon Greenberg puts it, "psychological-spiritual strength to endure through the apocalyptic turmoil."[46]

If such a mythic and antipolitical relationship to worldly events was a deeply natural move to make within religious Judaism, it is perhaps more surprising—and telling—to see such trends among avowedly secular Polish Jews too. By the close of the 1930s, a number of prominent Yiddishist intellectuals who had moved through various modes of Diasporist and Territorialist political faith were speaking in unabashedly mythopoetic terms of Jews as fated—even called—to suffer toward national redemption; the most famous of these, Wilno's Kalmanovitsh, would eventually embrace Orthodox Judaism.[47] Less familiarly, a dawning sense of the need to turn inward and focus on helping Jews bear up under siege could be heard quietly even among socialists. In 1937, the left-leaning public health activist Hersh Matz, who only a few years earlier had authored a travel guide for Polish Jews marked by an optimistic vision of the country's multiethnicity, acknowledged that the situation was now defined by "efforts of a sort familiar to all to drive [Jews] out" of the economy and society, and that "the call of the hour across Jewish civil society" was "not to fall into despair and a mood of depression." Instead, he proposed, what was needed was a renewed focus on communal self-help and especially the long-term public health work of "making the Jewish people healthy physically and psychically."[48] Even some Communists and Bundists were willing to acknowledge an imperative to address the psychic situation, if only in class-bound terms. A 1937 children's book by Wilno poet and Communist activist M. Levin transformed a recent noble act (a Polish boy of twelve had tried to save a younger Jewish boy from drowning in a swollen river and had drowned as well) into a heavy-handed parable of interethnic friendship among "all Vilna inhabitants—Jews, Poles, Lithuanians, and Karaites."[49] A 1938 book of children's games by Bundist educators acknowledged that the book "appears in unquiet times" in which "terrible dangers loom over the working-class child, the child of the people." The book's task was "to give the children of the grey cellar and the narrow attic-apartment the greatest possible happiness, which they deserve and which is so often robbed from them by the dark contemporary life that surrounds us."[50]

Like their Polish history colleagues, many Polish Jewish historians too cannot resist the urge to ask "what if," and it colors much of the discussion of the late 1930s especially. So what would have happened to Jewish political culture if, let us say, something like the situation of the late 1930s had persisted for a while? If the "optimists" are right that progressive sensibilities were in fact resurgent, no doubt this would have strengthened broad Jewish engagement with the Bundist strategy and its hopes. But if the "pessimists" are right that there was just "too much tinder"—too many elements in state and society primed to see the Jews as a serious problem for the tensions to resolve easily—it is hard to see how the spread of such hopes beyond the circles of the already convinced could have lasted. What would we have seen instead? Under a prolonged stasis of exclusion without removal, it seems likely that Polish Jewish identity would have come to look more and more like what Weinreich feared it was becoming already in the early 1930s: an identity substantially defined by rejection and exclusion from the larger culture and community based on ascribed alienness and malignity, ascriptions largely unchallengeable no matter what one did and likely reinforced regularly with ample doses of psychic and perhaps real extruding violence. And what of Polish Jewish thought, politics, and culture in such a frame? If we add to this imagined continuation of the late 1930s an imagined renewal of Zionist society building and settlement possibilities in Palestine, there seems little doubt that the vernacular Zionism of the sort I have explored in this book would have roared back to the center of Jewish political imagination. If, somehow, Territorialist options had gotten some traction, that too would have drawn mass interest. But what would have happened in the absence or frustration of both? It seems likely that Polish Jewish political culture would have contracted more and more to a mix of stubborn efforts at economic self-defense and ever greater exploration à la Grade of how culture might be used in the service of psychic resilience, interrupted only intermittently by periodic upwellings of emigration fever and defiant political radicalism—unless, of course, the push for extrusion in substantial parts of the larger society achieved substantial success.[51]

Polish Jews as Guides to Twentieth-Century Experience

Does the foregoing history of Polish Jewish thinking in the 1930s have something to offer other histories of diasporas and minority life exposed to political exclusion and enmity? I hope so. Of course every historical experience is unique, and every form of comparability partial. But many of the Polish Jews I have profiled here would have been the first to say that it was *not* some ostensible unique rottenness in *Polish* political culture that accounted for their worsening situation but something(s) more general and more structural. Some emphasized wider traditions of thought about "the Jews" that circulated far beyond Poland—let us call these structural and structuring traditions of culture. Others emphasized that this "something" was (also) structural in a different sense, involving demands perhaps intrinsic to postimperial nationalisms that the state serve "the people" through development, redistribution, and the clearing away of alien elements deemed privileged or powerful in order to make room for members of the "real nation." Others recognized that it was something related to the kinds of fears about the future bred by economic woes amid prolonged underdevelopment, and also to new kinds of political desires and proclivities to seek unity, psychic relief, personal power, or, in a sick sort of way, renewal and hope through demonization and conspiracy theories.

Whether and how inchoate Polish Jewish discoveries about the nature of illiberal nationalism and forces of extrusion can speak to other cases in this global history that remains very much with us today, I must leave to others to decide. One peculiarity of the Polish Jewish case resonates with what Hannah Arendt suggested many years ago about the fate of European Jews generally (and that we might usefully extend to some former Middle Eastern Jewish communities as well): the weird fact that, considered collectively, Jews were economically *powerful* and central to the commercial economy, or at least seemed so to many of their neighbors, but they combined this obtrusive significance and modicum of "money power" with actual political powerlessness when substantial parts of society mobilized against them. All this raises the question of whether Polish Jewish thought about the nature and trajectories of illiberal nationalism might inform the truly global history of political thought among those deemed "middleman minorities" both by sociologists and by their neighbors. Of course, there are good reasons to bridle at a term that reduces human subjectivity to economic function and that elides the relations of power that work to canalize certain people into certain roles over time. But then part of what Polish Jewish thought rediscovered in the 1930s was that the categories through which others saw Jews might prove determinative of much in their lives regardless of how fair those categories were.

Beyond this, perhaps there is one more general thing that the drama of Polish Jewish reckoning with nationalism can offer to a larger history of twentieth-century lives shaped by imposed minorityhood and violent exclusion. *An Unchosen People* closed by investigating forms of politics marked by a felt tension between obligations to one's community and obligations to one's own needs. Arguably, this is a story especially relevant among populations for whom the goods of community, culture, and identity were especially hard-won, the capacities of individuals to secure well-being especially limited and perpetually threatened, and the choice between them in the context of contracting resources and rising dangers especially stark. Most people want a decent life for themselves *and* their communities, and also hope that there is some universal value in their experience. The foregoing has been a history of people who found it impossible to hold these hopes together. A final feature of Polish Jewish thought under the sign of a future in doubt seems relevant too. Between the value of the self and that of the community there is a third realm of value on which this history has compelled us to dwell, the question of the chances that your choices will afford to your children.

For reasons born of our present moment, many historians of the Jewish twentieth century seem to take special interest in those Jews who in dark times did not lose old faiths in the better angels of their neighbors, in culture, or in Revolution. The figures who have stood at the center of this book—intellectuals like Weinreich and Lestschinsky, ordinary people like Binyomen R. and the anonymous parents of Prużana—reacted to dark times with considerably less faith. We may judge them as we wish, but they are not one whit less relevant to the historian's task of understanding the modern condition than their true-believer brethren, and perhaps considerably more relevant when all is said and done. They shaped their thought in relation to the world not as they wished it to be but as it seemed to be becoming. They confronted a situation in which the problem of political choice was a problem of *prediction* regarding what *others* would do in spite of them and, perhaps most urgently, *to* them. These Jews of Poland struggled to make choices under the pressure of their sense of contracting possibilities coupled with the sense that *not* choosing was itself dangerous too, and in recognition of their incapacity to affect their situation except at the margins. Their experience resonates with that of many modern subjects whose gravest political concerns relate to futurity, uncertainty, dangers that cannot be fully articulated but are already felt, and limited resources for response. Tragically, they and their informed fear may be our truest guides to what makes the history of the Polish Jewish 1930s relevant to the history of the twentieth century as a whole, and to a global history that is with us today.

NOTES

ACKNOWLEDGMENTS

INDEX

NOTES

INTRODUCTION

1. Mikhl Astour, "A shtim fun der yugnt," *Literarishe bleter* 42 (20 October 1933): 3–4.

2. On connections between the Jewish Question and the search for minority rights protections, Carole Fink, *Defending the Rights of Others* (Cambridge, 2004); James Loeffler, *Rooted Cosmopolitans* (New Haven, CT, 2018).

3. Astour, "A shtim," 4.

4. Astour, "A shtim," 4; for sharp critique of Bundist assumptions, Astour, "Vegn pauperizatsye, ir apologye un teritoryalizm," *Frayland* 1–2 (Warsaw) (September–October 1934): 65, 72ff.

5. Astour, "A shtim," 4.

6. See among many: Jack Jacobs, *Bundist Counterculture in Interwar Poland* (Syracuse, NY, 2006); Roni Gechtman, "Socialist Mass Politics through Sport," *Journal of Sport History* 26, no. 2 (Summer 1999): 326–352; Glenn Dynner, "Replenishing the '*Fountain of Judaism*,'" *Jewish History* 31 (2018): 229–261; Marci Shore, *Caviar and Ashes* (New Haven, CT, 2006); Anna Landau-Czajka, *Syn będzie Lech* (Warszawa, 2006); Kenneth B. Moss, "Negotiating Jewish Nationalism in Interwar Warsaw," in *Warsaw: The Jewish Metropolis*, ed. Glenn Dynner and Francois Guesnet (Leiden, 2015), 390–434 on sociological and spatial factors that might help account for the robustness of each of these subcultures in Poland's capital; Karen Underhill, *Bruno Schulz and Galician Jewish Modernity* (Bloomington, IN, forthcoming), ch. 7–8; Samuel Kassow, *Who Will Write Our History?* (New York, 2009); Karolina Szymaniak, *Być agentem wiecznej idei* (Kraków, 2006); Szymaniak, "On the Ice Floe: Rachel Auerbach," in *Catastrophe and Utopia*, ed. Ferenc Laczo and Joachim von Puttkamer (Berlin, 2017), 304–352; Mayer Kirshenblatt and Barbara Kirshenblatt-Gimblett, *They Called Me Mayer July* (Berkeley, CA, 2007); Samuel Kassow, "Travel and Local History as a National Mission," in *Jewish Topographies,* ed. Julia Baruch, Anna Lipphardt, and Alexandra Nocke (London, 2008), 241–264. Benny Mer's moving history of one street in Jewish Warsaw, *Smots'eh: biografyah shel rehov yehudi be-Varsah* (Tel Aviv, 2018), speaks powerfully to everyday vitality; so will Ula Madej-Krupitski's forthcoming work on leisure culture and Cecile Kuznitz on Polish Jewish urban construction. I

don't seek to deny currents of idealism and creativity through the 1930s, but to understand other currents of thought and choice that proceeded from an intuition of rising political danger and relative Jewish powerlessness to meet it. On the meta-historical weight that freights discussion of Polish Jewish vitality versus impasse: Antony Polonsky, *The Jews in Poland and Russia,* vol. 3, *1914–2008* (Oxford, 2012), 56–58, 77.

7. William Hagen, *Anti-Jewish Violence in Poland, 1914–1920* (Cambridge, 2018).

8. For a concise statement of "the optimistic account," Jeffrey Kopstein and Jason Wittenberg, *Intimate Violence* (Ithaca, NY, 2018), ch. 1, esp. 5–6, 37.

9. Timothy Snyder, *Sketches from a Secret War* (New Haven, CT, 2005); cf. Kathryn Ciancia, "Borderland Modernity: Poles, Jews, and Urban Spaces in Interwar Eastern Poland," *Journal of Modern History* 89, no. 3 (September 2017): 531–561; Waldemar Paruch, *Od konsolidacji państwowej do konsolidacji narodowej* (Lublin, 1997), 231–246. Thanks to Dan Heller for directing me to Paruch.

10. Moshe Landau, "Hafikhat Mai 1926," *Gal-Ed* 2 (1975): 255–264, esp. 258. On rising rightist strength in the early 1920s, Piotr J. Wróbel, "The Rise and Fall of Parliamentary Democracy in Interwar Poland," in *The Origins of Modern Polish Democracy,* ed. M. Biskupski et al. (Athens, OH, 2010), 133–134.

11. Anna Landau-Czajka, *Polska to nie oni* (Warszawa, 2015).

12. Landau-Czajka, *Polska to nie oni,* ch. 4; Landau-Czajka, *Syn będzie Lech,* 155–156, 172–193; Katrin Steffens, *Juedische Polonitaet* (Gottingen, 2004); Joseph Lichten, "Jewish Assimilation in Poland," in *The Jews in Poland,* ed. Chimen Abramsky et al. (Oxford, 1986), 106–129; Miri Freilich, "Irgun ha-mitbolelim 'Zjednoczenie' be-Polin," *Gal-Ed* 14 (1995): 91–107. Two recent works expand yet complicate this new picture of Polonization by showing that even as circles of Jews drawn to some version of Polishness widened, this expanded contact intensi-fied animosity toward Jews in parts of Polish civil society, especially among edu-cated young people: Kamil Kijek, *Dzieci modernizmu* (Wrocław, 2017); and Daniel Heller, *Jabotinsky's Children* (Princeton, NJ, 2017).

13. Indebted to so many, I want to underscore several decisive influences. David Engel and the late Ezra Mendelsohn particularly have modeled a history of interwar Jewish high politics centered on the incapacity of all Jewish political persuasions to decisively shape the Jewish situation—bringing to the fore the ques-tion of Jewish power and powerlessness in properly historicized fashion. See Men-delsohn, "Zionist Success and Zionist Failure," in *Essential Papers on Zionism,* ed. Jehuda Reinharz and Anita Shapira (New York, 1996), 171–190; Engel, "Jewish Diplomacy at a Crossroads," in *1929,* ed. Hasia Diner and Gennady Es-traikh (New York, 2013), 27–35; Engel, "Perceptions of Power—Poland and World Jewry," *Simon Dubnow Institute Yearbook* 1 (2002): 17–28. Four recent works highlight mass ideological impasse and a search for new options at the Polish Jewish grassroots. Kijek, *Dzieci modernizmu,* and Heller, *Jabotinsky's Children,* demonstrate how Polish Jewish youth culture was recast in the 1930s both by Polo-nization and felt exclusion. My approach to Polish Jewish Zionism is indebted to Irith Cherniavsky's investigation of the changing relationship of Polish Jews and the Zionist movement in the 1930s, *Be-or shineihem* (Tel Aviv, 2015) and Rona

Yona's study of socialist-Zionist youth outlooks in "Nihyeh kulanu halutsim" (PhD diss., Tel Aviv University, 2013), esp. 239–300. I have learned much from Anita Shapira's insight in *Land and Power* (Stanford, CA, 1999) that interwar Zionist thought about territory, power, and ethnic conflict never simply expressed preexisting ideologies but was also shaped by changing perceptions of the *time* that remained to alter the Jewish situation, in relation to the acceleration of other agendas (Palestinian, British, German) and to the dearth of Jewish resources. Guy Miron's *The Waning of Emancipation* (Detroit, MI, 2011) highlights Central European Jewish discourse about the loss of a future before the Holocaust.

14. On the Jews as a *kwestia,* Holly Case, *The Age of Questions* (Princeton, NJ, 2018), 46–47, 51, and esp. 123–124; Anna Landau-Czajka, *W jednym stali domu* (Warszawa, 1998), esp. 24–31.

15. Available in English in Arthur Hertzberg, ed., *The Zionist Idea* (Philadelphia, 1997). For the classic analysis, see Jonathan Frankel, *Prophecy and Politics* (Cambridge, 1981), ch. 2. Cf. Dmitry Shumsky, *Beyond the Nation-State* (New Haven, CT, 2018), 42–44, which, despite important revisions, agrees that *Auto-emancipation* marked a significant development in Pinsker's thought around precisely the matter flagged here.

16. "Proclamation of the Jewish Labor Bund" and "Proclamation of the Hebrew Writers' Union" in David Roskies, ed., *The Literature of Destruction* (Philadelphia, 1988), 154–159; cf. Steven J. Zipperstein, *Pogrom* (New York, 2019), ch. 3.

17. Key starting points: Frankel, *Prophecy and Politics;* Ezra Mendelsohn, *On Modern Jewish Politics* (Oxford, 1993); Scott Ury, *Barricades and Banners* (Stanford, CA, 2012); Simon Rabinovitch, *Jewish Rights, National Rites* (Stanford, CA, 2014); Yisrael Bartal, *Kozak u-Vedui* (Tel Aviv, 2007).

18. Steven J. Zipperstein, *Elusive Prophet* (Berkeley, CA, 1993); Kenneth B. Moss, *Jewish Renaissance in the Russian Revolution* (Cambridge, MA, 2009) and references therein.

19. For a crystalline late example, see the case of Avraham Levinson, Chapter 4.

20. Abraham Nowersztern, "Between Dust and Dance: Peretz's Drama and the Rise of Yiddish Modernism," *Prooftexts* 12 (1992): 71–90.

21. "Tshernovitser shprakh-koferents," in *Briv un redes fun Y. L. Peretz,* ed. Nakhman Mayzl (New York, 1944), 372.

22. Jonathan Frankel, "The Paradoxical Politics of Marginality," in idem, *Crisis, Revolution, and Russian Jews* (Cambridge, 2009), 133.

23. I thank Tony Michels for sharing essential chapters of his forthcoming work on the American Jewish Left between Communism and anti-Communism.

24. Natalia Aleksiun, "Regards from My 'Shtetl,'" *Polish Review* 56, no. 1/2 (2011): 57–71; but Aleksiun finds much performativity, skittishness about asserting equal citizenship, and demonstrative patriotism in these appeals.

25. Max Weinreich, *Der veg tsu unzer yugnt* (Vilna, 1935), 203–210, 243–277; Barbara Kirshenblatt-Gimblett, Marcus Moseley, and Michael Stanislawski, introduction to *Awakening Lives,* ed. Jeffrey Shandler (New Haven, CT, 2002), xxv.

26. Exact numbers are hard to establish but the general picture is clear. Yoav Gelber puts the total number of *olim* from 1932 through 1935 at 185,000 in "Hitgavshut ha-yishuv ha-yehudi be-erets yisrael, 1936–1947," in *Toldot ha-yishuv*

ha-yehudi be-erets yisrael, ed. Moshe Lissak (Jerusalem, 1995), 2:303. Aviva Halamish reports 91,122 *Polish* Jewish immigrants to Palestine between 1932 and 1938; most clearly came before 1936. She puts the Polish percentage of aliyah for 1933–1936 between 41 and 49 percent. Halamish, *Be-meruts kaful neged ha-zeman* (Jerusalem, 2006), 332.

27. Rona Yona, "Connecting Poland and Palestine," in *From Europe's East to the Middle East,* ed. Kenneth B. Moss, Benjamin Nathans, and Taro Tsurumi (Philadelphia, 2021), 194–218; Yisrael Oppenheim, *Tenuat ha-haluts be-Polin 1929–1939* (Sdeh Boker, 1993), 47ff; Emmanuel Melzer, "Betar," Melzer, "Revisionism," and Scott Ury "Zionism," in *YIVO Encyclopedia of Jews in Eastern Europe,* ed. Gershon Hundert (New Haven, CT, 2008); Cherniavsky, *Be-'or,* 99–100, 124.

28. Yankev Lestschinsky, "'Vu tut men zikh ahin,'" *Forverts,* 4 January 1931.

29. Rakhel Faygenberg, "Prisat shalom me-Polin," *Davar,* 3 November 1929; Faygenberg, "Yordim," *Davar,* 17 December 1930. On Faygenberg, Naomi Brenner, *Lingering Bilingualism* (Syracuse, NY, 2016), 168ff.

30. Binyomen R., "Bamerkungen un ibertrakhtungen tsum bukh fun Dr. M. Vaynraykh *Der veg tsu unzer yugnt,*" Weinreich Collection, Record Group 584, f. 368, YIVO Archive, Center for Jewish History, New York, 18 (hereafter Collection x, RG x:x, YIVO). This distinctive text along with Binyomen R's no less fascinating autobiography has just appeared in Polish translation, with supplements and commentary by Kamil Kijek: Beniamin R., *Płonęli Gniewem. Autobiografia młodego Żyda,* trans. Anna Kałużna and Anna Szyba, ed. Kamil Kijek (Warszawa, 2021).

31. Jerzy Tomaszewski, "Between the Social and the National—the Economic Situation of Polish Jewry, 1918–1939," *Simon Dubnow Institute Yearbook* 1 (2002): 55–70.

32. Stephanie Zloch, *Polnischer Nationalismus* (Koln, 2010), part II; Eva Plach, *The Clash of Moral Nations* (Athens, OH, 2006), 14.

33. *Historical Dictionary of Poland,* ed. Jerzy Jan Lerski (Westport, CT, 1996), s.v. "Camp for a Greater Poland"; Bogumił Grott, *Nacjonalizm Chrześcijański* (Kraków, 1996), 57; Zloch, *Polnischer Nationalismus,* 388–389, 585.

34. Marek Chodakiewicz, Jolanta Mysiakowski-Muszynska, Wojciech Muszynski, *Polska dla Polakow* (Poznań, 2015), 138–143; Olaf Bergmann, *Narodowa Demokracja a Żydzi, 1918–1929* (Poznań, 2015), 441.

35. Brian Porter, *When Nationalism Learned to Hate* (Oxford, 2002); Theodore Weeks, *From Assimilation to Antisemitism* (DeKalb, IL, 2006); Grzegorz Krzywiec, *Polska bez Żydow* (Warszawa, 2017); Krzywiec, *Chauvinism, Polish Style* (London, 2005), 266–296.

36. Alina Cała, *Żyd—Wróg Odwieczny?* (Warszawa, 2012), 343ff; Małgorzata Domagalska, *Antysemityzm dla Inteligencji* (Warszawa, 2004); Joanna B. Michlic, *Poland's Threatening Other* (Lincoln, NE, 2006), 126–127; Polonsky, *Jews in Poland and Russia,* 3:78; Grzegorz Krzywiec, "The Balance of Polish Political Antisemitism," in *Right-Wing Politics and the Rise of Antisemitism in Europe, 1935–1941,* ed. Frank Bajohr and Dieter Pohl (Göttingen, 2019), 65–71; Kamil Kijek, "'The Road to Przytyk': Agitation and the Sociotechnique of Violence in the Kielce Region, 1931–1936," *Gal-Ed* 26–27 (2021): 59–102. My thanks to Kijek for sharing this essential article with me in proofs.

37. Timothy Snyder, *Sketches from a Secret War* (New Haven, CT, 2005), 63; Joseph Rothschild, *East Central Europe between the Two World Wars* (Seattle, 1974), 38.

38. Grott, *Nacjonalizm Chrześcijański*, 57; Powszechny Uniwersytet Korespondencyjny [Aleksander Hertz and Łucja Kipowa], *W Poszukiwaniu nowych metod pracy oświatowej* (Warszawa, 1932), 9–10, 13, 23, 26–28; Torsten Lorenz and Katarzyna Stoklosa, "Einleitung," in Hertz, *Skizzen uber den Totalitarismus* (Göttingen, 2014), 7–11. Thanks to Margarita Cygielska for clarifying the nature of the sources used by Hertz and Kipowa.

39. Hertz and Kipowa, *W Poszukiwaniu*, 26–28, 31–32, 59–60.

40. Hertz and Kipowa, *W Poszukiwaniu*, 66–68.

41. Hertz and Kipowa, *W Poszukiwaniu*, 69.

42. Hertz and Kipowa, *W Poszukiwaniu*, 69–71.

43. Omer Bartov, *Anatomy of a Genocide* (New York, 2018), 116–122.

44. Key accounts of the Jewish Question in interwar Polish political culture include Cała, *Żyd*, ch. 7, esp. 343–351; Landau-Czajka, *W jednym stali domu;* Michlic, *Poland's Threatening Other*, ch. 1–2; William W. Hagen, "Before the 'Final Solution,'" *Journal of Modern History* 68, no. 2 (June 1996): 351–381; Krzywiec, "Balance of Polish Political Antisemitism."

45. Ireneusz Jeziorski, *Od Obcości do Symulakrum* (Kraków, 2009), 210–214.

46. Cała, *Żyd*, 335–337, 349.

47. Aleksander Hertz, *The Jews in Polish Culture* (Evanston, IL, 1988), 188–190. Tellingly, Hertz misremembers the book's initial publication date as 1933; it was actually 1932.

48. Anna Lysiak (Majdanik), "The Rev. Kruszynski and Polish Catholic Teachings about Jews and Judaism in Interwar Poland," *Kirchliche Zeitgeschichte* 16, no. 1 (2003): 52–75, citing 56.

49. Ronald Modras, "The Interwar Polish Catholic Press on the Jewish Question," *Annals of the American Academy of Political and Social Science* 548, no. 1 (1996): 184–185; Modras, *The Catholic Church and Antisemitism* (London, 1994); Cała, *Żyd*, 384–398; Brian Porter-Szücs, *Faith and Fatherland* (Oxford, 2011), 272–314; Krzywiec, *Polska*, underscores the convergence of Catholic-political discourse about Jews with the activist-eliminationist ideal of Endeks even before World War I.

50. Bergmann, *Narodowa*, 281–282.

51. Joanna Olczak-Ronikier, *Korczak* (Warszawa, 2011), 285; Betty Jean Lifton, *The King of Children* (New York, 2006), 199.

52. Beth Holmgren, "Cabaret Nation," *Polin* 31 (2019): 273–288; Marcos Silber, "Reassessing the Acculturation Paradigm," *Jewish Social Studies* (forthcoming).

53. Plach, *Clash of Moral Nations*, ch. 2.

54. Kazimierz Czapiński, *Faszyzm Współczesny* (Warszawa, 1932), 13, 16, 25ff.

55. Agnieszka Wierzcholska, "Relations between the Bund and the Polish Socialist Party from a Micro-historical Perspective," *East European Jewish Affairs* 43, no. 3 (2013): 297–313; Zloch, *Polnischer Nationalismus*, 375–376.

56. Szymon Rudnicki, *Żydzi w parlamencie II Rzeczypospolitej* (Warszawa, 2004), 415.

57. Cała, *Żyd,* 347.

58. Kijek, "'Road to Przytyk'" 10.

59. Modras, *Catholic Church,* xiv.

60. Landau-Czajka, *W jednym,* 24.

61. Rudnicki, *Żydzi w parlamencie,* 415, 570.

62. Czeslaw Miłosz, *Native Realm* (New York, 2002), 94.

63. Hertz, *Jews in Polish Culture,* 242.

64. Aleksander Hertz, "Sprawa antysemityzmu" (1934), repr. in *Socjologia nieprzedawniona* (Warszawa, 1992), 390–410. Thanks to Zofia Trębacz for translating this essential text; I have modified her translation in some places.

65. Ludwik Krzywicki, preface to *Pamiętniki chłopów: nr. 1–51* (Warszawa, 1935), v, ix.

66. Kate Lebow, "Autobiography as Complaint," *Laboratorium* 6, no. 3 (September 2014), 14.

67. Polonsky, *Jews in Poland and Russia,* 3:69.

68. Timothy Snyder, *The Reconstruction of Nations* (New Haven, CT, 2004), 59.

69. Polonsky, *Jews in Poland and Russia,* 3:69–70; Piotr Wrobel, "World War One: A Turning Point in the History of Polish Jewry," in *The Golden Age and Beyond,* ed. Jacques Kornberg (Toronto, 1997); Paul Brykczinski, *Primed for Violence* (Madison, WI, 2018); Kopstein and Wittenberg, *Intimate Violence,* 35.

70. Landau-Czajka, *W jednym,* 9–11; John Connelly, "Catholic Racism and Its Opponents," *Journal of Modern History* 79 (December 2007): 845.

71. Engel, "Jewish Diplomacy"; Yitshok Grinboym, "Dos minoritetn-problem," *Dos Pinsker vort,* 13 February 1931.

72. On Polish Jewish responses, Yfaat Weiss, *Etniyut ve-ezrahut* (Haifa, 2000).

73. Landau-Czajka, *W jednym,* 11.

74. Bergmann, *Narodowa Demokracja,* 289–304; Cała, *Żyd,* 343–345; Yankev Lestschinsky, "In klem fun an ibergang-tsayt," *Frayland* 3–4 (November–December 1934): 8.

75. Hagen, "Before the 'Final Solution'"; Emanuel Melzer, *No Way Out* (Cincinnati, 1997), 8–9.

76. Polonsky, *Jews in Poland and Russia,* 3:77; Heller, *Jabotinsky's Children,* 139–140.

77. The question of whether rhetorics about Jewish power were believed as they circulated through Polish political society—and by whom—is put provocatively in Engel, "Perceptions of Power," 26–28. Engel suggests that Polish political elites knew quite well just how little actual political power Jews wielded (implying that the constant invocation thereof was more a cynical justification than a spur to extrusionary efforts). Other sources suggest that some in the political elite were more firmly in the grip of such claims; thus, in 1930, even in a personal letter to a fellow Endek leader, Dmowski could write that ridding Poland of the "Jewish plague" would be doing "Poland a service to rival perhaps [St.] Batory's." Cited in Krzywiec, *Chauvinism,* 266.

78. Quoted in Hagen, "Before the 'Final Solution,'" 356.

79. Józef Chałasinski, *Młode Pokolenie Chłopów* (Warszawa, 1938), 2:114–116, 180.

80. For this and other hopeful possibilities, Zloch, *Polnischer Nationalismus,* 327ff, 372–383.

81. Marci Shore, "The Jewish Hero History Forgot," *New York Times,* 18 April 2013.

82. Thus Shore: Bundism was "much more grounded, sensible and realistic" than Zionism because the former staked its hopes on "a Jewish workers' party allied with a larger labor movement, a secular Jewish culture in Yiddish, the language already spoken by most Jews, a future in the place where Jews already lived, alongside people they already knew." Shore, "The Jewish Hero History Forgot." For an early work that argues for the irrationality of both Zionist and Bundist visions of radical intervention in Jewish life as against the essential reasonableness of stolid loyalism and economic self-help advocated by Orthodox Jewish politicians, see Joseph Marcus, *Social and Political History of the Jews in Poland, 1919–1939* (Berlin, 1983). Tellingly, the book's metahistorical logic is that before Piłsudski's death in 1935, Jewish efforts to transform their situation were stupid, whereas after 1935, the same people are to be condemned for not doing more to get Jews out of Poland.

83. I am not engaging here in a cultural history of what Jewish historical actors meant when they invoked "realism" or its cognates. For a compelling example of that approach, see Daniel Levine, " 'These Days of *Shoah*' " *Political Power and Social Theory* 32 (2017): 99–125, which reads discourses of *Realpolitik* in Zionist culture as a belated effort to master an early modern European *paideia* of political calculation, moderation, and amorality.

84. Henryk Erlikh, *Der iker fun Bundizm* (New York, 1934), 11, 15–16.

85. Wierzcholska, "Relations between the Bund and the Polish Socialist Party," 375–376.

86. Weinreich to Sol Liptzin, 20 March 1934, RG 584:345, YIVO.

87. As the Bundist Erlikh put it, there could be no talk of "*Burgfrieden.*" Erlikh to Yankev Lestschinsky, 1 October 1929, Lestschinsky Collection, RG 339:49, YIVO. On the Communists, Joanna Nalewajko-Kulikov, *A Citizen of Yiddishland* (Berlin, 2020), 76. On several mavericks who broke with Stalinist orthodoxies, see Jack Jacobs, "Communist Questions, Jewish Answers," *Polin* 18 (2005): 369–380.

88. Cecile Kuznitz, *YIVO and the Making of Modern Jewish Culture* (Cambridge, 2014); Kassow, "Travel and Local History"; Efrat Gal-Ed, *Niemandssprache* (Berlin, 2016), 197–378; Karolina Szymaniak, "Speaking Back," *Polin* 28 (2016): 153–172.

89. William Connelly, *Aspirational Fascism* (Minneapolis, MN, 2017) has helped me think about the emergence and temporalities of new political forms.

90. For thought-provoking consideration of how group exclusion may be built into projects of communal democratic self-rule, see Michael Hanchard, *The Spectre of Race* (Princeton, NJ, 2018).

91. Erlikh to Lestschinsky, 1 October 1929, RG 339:49, YIVO.

92. Natan Gross, *Toldot ha-kolno'a ha-yehudi be-Folin* (Jerusalem, 1990), 12.

93. Heller, *Jabotinsky's Children;* Binyomen R., "Oytobiografye," 1934, Youth Autobiography Collection, RG 4, YIVO, 21; my deep thanks to Kamil Kijek for sharing this essential source with me.

94. Ela Bauer, "The Ideological Roots of the Polish Jewish Intelligentsia," *Polin* 24 (2012): 95–109; Marcos Silber, "Umah netulat medinah," *Tsion* 80 (2015): 473–502; Bartov, *Anatomy,* ch. 3.

95. Lova Levita to Comrades, 23 December 1929, Vaadat Hu"l shel ha-Kibuts ha-Meuhad Collection (hativah 2–12), m. 2, folder 7, Yad Tabenkin Archives, Ramat Efal (hereafter YT 2-12/x/x); repr. as "Ba-golat Polin," in *Sefer Klosowa,* ed. Haim Dan (Tel Aviv, 1978), 133–142, citing 134.

96. Eric Oberle, personal communication, June 2017. The argument that follows is deeply indebted to Oberle's work on twentieth-century critical thought struggling to make sense of what he calls "negative identity," both as a baleful structure of experience afflicting many moderns and as a special structure of enmity and violence attaching to minority communities. See Oberle, *The Century of Negative Identity* (Stanford, CA, 2018) for the titular concept.

97. I owe much of my thinking on this topic to a stimulating discussion with Tara Zahra, joined early in this project, about the place of Zionism in the gamut of East European nationalist population politics. See Zahra's "Zionism, Emigration, and East European Colonialism," in *Colonialism and the Jews,* ed. Ethan Katz, Lisa Moses Leff, and Maud S. Mandel (Bloomington, IN, 2017), 166–192.

1. FUTURELESSNESS AND THE JEWISH QUESTION

1. Ha-lishkah ha-rashit Keren Kayemet le-Yisrael (KKL) to Alter Druyanov, 20 December 1931, Druyanov Collection (A10), Central Zionist Archives, Jerusalem (hereafter RG x, CZA).

2. Alter Druyanov, *Tsionut be-Polanyah* (Tel Aviv, 1932–1933); Druyanov, "Rishme ha-derekh," unpublished travel notebook, RG A10, CZA. Thanks to CZA staff for making this then-uncataloged source available.

3. Druyanov, *Tsionut be-Polanyah,* 6, 22.

4. Druyanov, "Rishme ha-derekh," 3.

5. Kh. Sh. Kazdan, "Di Y. L. Peretz-shul in Pruzhene un ir forzitser Gershn Urinsky," Zalman Uryevitsh, "Di bundishe bavegung in Pruzhene," Uryevitsh, "Ver zenen geven di kandidatn tsu der pruzhener kehile-farvaltung in yor 1929," and Khayim Yanish, "Di Pruzhener Y. L. Peretz 'TsYShO'-shul (zikhroynes)," in *Pinkes fun finf fartilikte kehiles: Pruzhene, Bereze, Maltsh, Shershev, Selts,* ed. Mordechai Wolf Bernstein and David Forer (Buenos Aires, 1958), 214, 259–264, 218, 269; Samuel Kassow, *Who Will Write Our History?* (New York, 2009), 80, 86; *Lerer-Yizker-bukh,* ed. Kh. Kazdan (New York, 1954), s. v. "Uryevitsh, Yente"; "Meldung" 1928, Pruzhene file, Poland Collection (Vilna Archives), RG 28, YIVO.

6. N. Urinsky, "Fun Kasrilevke biz Kabtsansk," *Frayland* (Varshe) 3–4 (November–December 1934), 111.

7. Report beginning "Pruzhani tseylt 8600 aynvoyner," [1937–1938], Territorial Collection, Poland RG 116, box 6, f. 27, YIVO. On Prużana Jews trying to get to the United States, see Avraham Harshalom, *Alive from the Ashes* (Tel Aviv, 1990).

8. Eva Plach, *The Clash of Moral Nations* (Athens, OH, 2006), 7–8.

9. Szymon Rudnicki, *Żydzi w parlamencie II Rzeczypospolitej* (Warszawa, 2004), 414–416, 570.

10. Max Weinreich, *Der veg tsu unzer yugnt* (Vilna, 1935), 211: "I have already had occasion to hear an extreme opinion: the fundamental difference [between Jewish and non-Jewish youth] consists of the fact that Jewish youth have fewer *illusions* that the state apparatus and the economic system will be able to absorb them. Were that indeed the case, we would be dealing with not a social-economic but merely a social-*psychological* specificity. Put it in such extreme terms, this is certainly a false claim. [. . .] Whoever comforts himself with the view that actually there is no difference [between the situation of Jewish youth and other youth cohorts], and that as soon as conditions change, the Jewish sector [. . .] will *automatically* fully regulate itself—such a person is not seeing what is going on around him."

11. Yosef Gorny and Shlomo Netzer, "'Avodat ha-hoveh ha-murkhevet' be-hashkafat olamam shel Yitzhak Grinboym ve-shel Moshe Sneh be-Folin ba-shanim 1918-1939," in *Olam yashan adam hadash*, ed. Eli Tzur (Sde Boker, 2005), 104–111.

12. M. Polakiewicz to Yitzhak Grinboym, 4 May 1932, Grinboym Collection, A127, f. 1685, CZA, accessed Ben Gurion University Archives, http://bgarchives .bgu.ac.il/archives/grin/grin.html.

13. Urząd wojewódzki w Łodzi, wydział bezp., "Sprawozdanie nr. 9 za miesiąc wrzesień 1932 roku," p. 3, in Archiwum Państwowe w Łodzi, Urząd Wojewódzki Łódzki (1918–1939) Collection (zespół 166), syg. 2507i (1932), accessed at the United States Holocaust Museum and Memorial, Washington, D.C. Thanks to Zofia Trębacz for working through these reports.

14. Arieh Tartakower, *The Migrations of Polish Jews in Recent Times* (New York, 1964), 18–19; Kenneth B. Moss, "Thinking with Restriction," *East European Jewish Affairs* 44, nos. 2–3 (2014): 205–224.

15. "Vos tuht oyf YEAS far der yidisher emigratsye," *Haynt*, 10 January 1932; *Tsen yor "YEAS" 1924–1934* (Varshe, [1934]), 25; Irith Cherniavsky, "Aliyat yehudei Polin be-shnot ha-shloshim shel ha-meah ha-esrim" (PhD diss., Hebrew University of Jerusalem, 2010), 133; Urinsky, "Fun Kasrilevke biz Kabtsansk"; Norman Salsitz, *A Jewish Boyhood in Poland,* cited in Jerzy Tomaszewski, "Between the Social and the National—the Economic Situation of Polish Jewry, 1918-1939," *Simon Dubnow Institute Yearbook* 1 (2002), 65.

16. Patrick Weil, "Races at the Gate," in *Migration Control in the North Atlantic World,* ed. Andreas Fahrmeir, Olivier Faron, and Patrick Weil (New York, 2003), 279–280; Aristide Zolberg, *A Nation by Design* (New York, 2006), 264ff.

17. Gideon Shimoni, *Jews and Zionism* (Oxford, 1980), 97–108; Sally Peberdy, *Selecting Immigrants* (Johannesburg, 2009), 63–67.

18. William W. Hagen, "Before the 'Final Solution,'" *Journal of Modern History* 68, no. 2 (June 1996): 356.

19. Giterman to Senator, 12 June 1935, Collection of the Section for the Organization of Non-Zionists (Sokhnut), S29, f. 51, CZA.

20. H. N. Bialik to Manya Bialik, 2, 15, and 22 November 1931, in *Igerot el raayato Manya* (Jerusalem, 1955), 254–261.

21. Yankev Lestschinsky, "Masn idishe yungelayt loyfen fun Poyln v'u di oygen trogen zey," *Forverts,* 30 August 1934.

22. Quoted in Rona Yona, "Connecting Poland and Palestine," in *From Europe's East to the Middle East,* ed. Kenneth B. Moss, Benjamin Nathans, and Taro Tsurumi (Philadelphia, 2021), 210.

23. Anita Shapira, *Israel* (Waltham, 2012), 112; Shulamit Carmi and Henry Rosenfeld, "Immigration, Urbanization and Crisis," *International Journal of Comparative Sociology* 12 (1971): 53–55. How much of a crisis it was is debated: Jacob Metzer, *The Divided Economy of Mandatory Palestine* (Cambridge, 2002), 77. On the impact in Poland: Yisrael Oppenheim, *Tenuat he-haluts be-Polin (1917–1929)* (Jerusalem, 1982), 379–409; Jacek Walicki, *Ruch Syjonistyczny w Polsce w latach 1926–1930* (Łódź, 2005), 99–108.

24. Duvdavani to Shoshana, 27 April 1929, YT 2-12/2/4.

25. "Yeshivah be-inyanei Galitsyah," 5 January 1933, YT 2-12/3/5.

26. "5 yor poalei-tsien tetitkayt (1936)," repr. in Leyb Shpizman, ed., *Halutsim in Poyln* (New York, 1959), 1:324.

27. Henry Near, *The Kibbutz Movement: A History,* vol. 1 (London, 1992), 102ff, 120, 145–146.

28. Rona Yona, "Nihyeh kulanu halutsim" (PhD diss., Tel Aviv University, 2013), 244, 250.

29. Polakiewicz to Grinboym, 29 June 1932, Grinboym Collection, A127/1685, accessed Ben Gurion University Archives, http://bgarchives.bgu.ac.il/archives/grin/grin.html.

30. Moyshe Kligsberg, *Yugnt-psikhologye un sotsyalistishe dertsiung* (Warsaw: Kultur-Lige, 1938), esp. from 284. In the postwar United States, Kligsberg produced valuable scholarship on interwar Polish Jewish youth culture and psychology using the YIVO autobiographies: "Di yidishe yugnt-bavegung in Poyln tsvishn beyde velt milkhomes: a sotsiologishe shtudye," *Studies on Polish Jewry, 1919–1939,* ed. Joshua A. Fishman (New York, 1974), 137–228.

31. "Lerer-konferents fun Bialystoker raion, in Bialystok dem 23. Februar 1935," in *Shul-vegn* (Warsaw, April–May 1935), 251.

32. [Shmuel Murshteyn], "In hundert yor arum," *Khaver* (Vilna, March 1933): 71–74. An introduction by editor Sh. Bastomski notes that the text was written in 1929 when Murshteyn was a student in the seventh grade; it is telling that Bastomski deemed the piece relevant for young readers four years later.

33. Weinreich, *Veg,* 206, 210.

34. Weinreich, *Veg,* 244.

35. "Ershter proyekt far a gliderung fun der yugnt-forshung," 12 November 1933, Youth Autobiography Collection, RG 4:3881, YIVO, 2–3.

36. Lova Levita to Comrades, 19 March 1930, YT 2-12/2/7.

37. Tomaszewski, "Between the Social and the National," 62–63.

38. Kh. Sokolovsky (Kovel) to ORT Central Committee, 11 October 1930, ORT Collection: f. 172, Central Archive for the History of the Jewish People, Jerusalem. Thanks to Jaclyn Granick for recommending this collection.

39. Omer Bartov, *Anatomy of a Genocide* (New York, 2018), 95–96.

40. M. B-n, "Di Nalevkes," *Landkentenish / Krajoznawstwo,* 1 (April 1935): 9–10.

41. L. Vulman, *10-yor yidishe gezuntshuts-arbet in Poyln* (Warsaw, 1933), 34–35.

42. Ezra Mendelsohn, *Jews of East Central Europe between the World Wars* (Bloomington, IN, 1983), 25.

43. "Forget-Me-Not," in *Awakening Lives,* ed. Jeffrey Shandler (New Haven, CT, 2002), 123–140.

44. Ben-Adir, "Vi azoy iz dos geshen (tsu der katastrofe in der sotsialistisher velt)," *Fraye shriftn far yidishn sotsialistishn gedank* 17 (October 1935): 18.

45. Jakob Appenszlak, "Ghetto istnieje!," *Nasz Przegląd,* 1 January 1930.

46. Samuel Hirszhorn, "Kwestia żydowska w Polsce w r. 1929," *Nasz Przegląd,* 1 January 1930.

47. See Natalia Aleksiun, "Jewish Students and Christian Corpses in Interwar Poland," *Jewish History* 26 (2012): 327–342.

48. Rudnicki, *Żydzi w parlamencie,* 416n209.

49. Rudnicki, *Żydzi w parlamencie,* 416–417.

50. Mikhoel Burshtin, "Vi azoy hob ikh ongehoybn shraybn," in *Erev khurbn* (*Musterverk fun der yidisher literatur* 40), ed. Shmuel Rozhanski (Buenos-Aires, 1970), 248–250; Burshtin to Yoysef Opatoshu, 26 January 1932, image attached to "Burshtin, Mikhoel," *The YIVO Encyclopedia of Jews in Eastern Europe Online,* https://yivoencyclopedia.org/article.aspx/Burshtin_Mikhoel, last accessed 6 November 2020.

51. Chone Shmeruk, "Responses to Antisemitism in Poland, 1912–1936," in *Living with Antisemitism,* ed. Jehuda Reinharz (Waltham, 1988), 275–295.

52. M. Burshtin, *Iber di khurves fun ployne* (Vilna, 1931).

53. Burshtin, *Iber di khurves,* 185–191.

54. Burshtin, *Khurves,* 142–147.

55. Burshtin, *Khurves,* 205–206.

56. Burshtin, *Khurves,* 162–167.

57. Jeffrey Kopstein and Jason Wittenberg, *Intimate Violence* (Ithaca, NY, 2018), 37.

58. Rosa Lehmann, *Symbiosis and Ambivalence* (New York, 2001); Alina Cała, *Image of the Jew in Polish Folk Culture* (Jerusalem, 1995).

59. William Hagen, *Anti-Jewish Violence in Poland, 1914–1920* (Cambridge, 2018), esp. 46–47, 516–517.

60. Władysław Grabski, "Pamiętniki chłopów i środowisko społeczne wsi polskiej," *Przegląd Socjologiczny* 4, nos. 3–4 (1936): 326–327.

61. Diary 12 in Ludwik Krzywicki, ed., *Pamiętniki chłopów: nr. 1–51* (Warszawa, 1935), 160–162. Thanks to Margarita Cygielska for her assistance with this knotty text, and for clarifying the final Biblical flourish.

62. Burshtin, "Vi azoy," in *Erev khurbn* 248; Meylekh Ravitsh, "M. Burshtin," in *Mayn Leksikon* (Montreal, 1945), 40–41.

63. Ravitsh, "M. Burshtin," 42.

64. "Di yidishe emigratsye fun Poyln," in Farband fun di yidishe koopera-tive gezelshaftn in Poyln, *Di ekonomishe lage fun di yidn in Poyln un di yidishe*

kooperatsye (Vilna, 1926), 85–86, 90. On anti-Jewish efforts in the cooperative movement, Cornelius Groeschel, *Zwischen Antisemitismus und Modernisierungspolitik* (Marburg, 2010), ch. 4.

65. Weinreich, *Veg*, 203–204.

66. Fishl Shneurson, *Yidn un felker-psikhologye* (Warsaw, 1936), part II.

67. Binyomen R., "Oytobiografye," RG 4:29–31, 42, 48, YIVO; Binyomen R., "Bamerkungen un ibertrakhtungen tsum bukh fun Dr. M. Vaynraykh *Der veg tsu unzer yugnt*," Weinreich Collection, RG 584:368, 15, YIVO.

68. Rosalind H. Williams, *Dream Worlds* (Berkeley, CA, 1991).

69. Sheila Skaff, *Law of the Looking Glass* (Athens, OH, 2008), 37–42, 98–101, 141–143, 169–172; Natan Gross, *Toldot ha-kolno'a ha-yehudi be-Folin* (Jerusalem, 1990), 12.

70. Eddy Portnoy, "Freaks, Geeks, and Strongmen," *Drama Review* 50, no. 2 (Summer 2006): 117–135.

71. Weinreich, *Veg*, 9–13.

72. Weinreich, *Veg*, 245, 203.

73. Weinreich, *Veg*, 250–252.

74. "Rex," in Ido Bassok, *'Alilot neurim* (Tel Aviv, 2011), 149–154.

75. Gabriel Weinreich, *Confessions of a Jewish Priest* (Cleveland, OH, 2005), 29–30.

76. Binyomen R., "Bamerkungen," RG 584:368, 18, YIVO.

77. Binyomen R., "Bamerkungen," 21.

78. Binyomen R., "Oytobiografye," 32, 57–59.

79. Anna Landau-Czajka, *Polska to nie oni* (Warszawa, 2015), 238.

80. Binyomen R., "Oytobiografye," 17–18.

81. Kamil Kijek, "'The Road to Przytyk,'" *Gal-Ed* 26–27 (2021): 59–102.

82. Kijek, "'Road to Przytyk,'" 95–96 and 96fn101; Joseph Rothschild, *East Central Europe between the Two World Wars* (Seattle, 1974), 31; Antony Polonsky, *The Jews in Poland and Russia*, vol. 3, *1914–2008* (Oxford, 2012), 78.

83. Kassow, *Who Will Write Our History?*, 96–97.

84. Hagen, "Before the 'Final Solution,'" 356.

85. Emanuel Melzer, *No Way Out* (Cincinnati, OH, 1997), 4; for an example of such an indictment, I. Dizhur, *Di moderne felker-vanderung* (Berlin, 1929), 69–70. See Groeschel, *Zwischen Antisemitismus*, ch. 5; but also Stephan Stach's review in *Zeitschrift für Ostmitteleuropa-Forschung* 62 (2013): 525–527.

86. Hagen, "Before the 'Final Solution,'" 356.

87. Druyanov, *Tsionut be-Polanyah*, 4.

88. "Fun der redaktsye," *Landkentenish/Krajoznawstwo* 1 (Varshe, 1933), 4; Mikhoel Burshtin, "Landkentenish arbet af di koloniyes un vanderlagern," *Landkentenish: Yedies* 2, no. 20 (June 1935): 1–2. ZTK statistics between 1929 and 1934 recorded that 40–50 percent of the summer colony attendees were "office workers and commercial employees" and 20 percent were teachers or "free professions." Based on this and personal involvement, Burshtin noted that "socially speaking, this is the Jewish middle stratum," and remarked on its fairly high level of modern—that is, Polish—education.

89. Y. Toyb, "Lovitsh," *Landkentenish/Krajoznawstwo* 1, no. 19 (April 1935). In fact, the 1927 guidebook does mention a recently constructed synagogue at 53 Zduńska St., noting that Łowicz had no older synagogue building because an archbishop had forbade Jewish settlement in the town in 1505. Aleksander Bluhm-Kwiatkowski, *Przewodnik po Łowiczu i okolicy* (Łowicz, 1927), 31. I have not combed through the guidebook systematically, but it certainly seems that Jews are otherwise almost entirely absent.

90. Y. Ts. Toybenfeld, "Lovitsh—a shtot in Mazovye," in *Lovitsh*, ed. G. Shayak-Tsharnezon (Melbourne, 1966), 57–58.

91. Kazimierz Czapiński, "Z problemów turystycznych," *Landkentenish/Krajoznawstwo* 1 (19) (April 1935).

2. TOWARD A POLITICS OF DOUBT AND EXIT

1. Lova Levita to Comrades, 19 March 1930, YT 2-12/2/7 and 23 December 1929, YT 2-12/2/4.

2. On Jews in the kresy: Kathryn Ciancia, "Borderland Modernity," *Journal of Modern History* 89, no. 3 (September 2017): 531–561; Rebecca Kobrin, *Jewish Białystok and Its Diaspora* (Bloomington, IN, 2010); Felix Ackermann, *Palimpsest Grodno* (Wiesbaden, 2010), 32–91; Shimon Redlich, *Together and Apart in Brzezany* (Bloomington, IN, 2002).

3. Levita to Comrades, 22 January 1930, YT 2-12/2/7.

4. Levita to Comrades, 23 December 1929, YT 2-12/2/4; 19 March 1930, YT 2-12/2/7.

5. Levita to Comrades, 23 December 1929, YT 2-12/2/4.

6. Levita to Comrades, 22 January 1930, YT 2-12/2/7.

7. Avraham Zemba, "'Shtiblakh' be-Varshah," in *Mosadot Torah be-Eiropah,* ed. Shmuel Mirski (New York, 1956), 358.

8. Kenneth B. Moss, "Negotiating Jewish Nationalism in Interwar Warsaw," in *Warsaw: The Jewish Metropolis,* ed. Glenn Dynner and Francois Guesnet (Leiden, 2015), 410–425.

9. Daniel Heller, *Jabotinsky's Children* (Princeton, NJ, 2017); Eli Tzur, *Lifne bo' ha-afelah* (Sde Boker, 2006).

10. In Shmuel Nitzan, *Tenuat 'Dror' be-Galitsiyah* (Tel Aviv, 1984), 115–116.

11. Rona Yona, "Nihyeh kulanu halutsim" (PhD diss., Tel Aviv, 2013), 149–155.

12. Yona, "Nihyeh kulanu," 248; cf. 114.

13. Miriam [Shlimovits] to Comrades, 30 June 1933, YT 2-12/3/5.

14. "Mikhtavim shel Haim ben-Asher (1930–1931)," YT 2-12/3/1.

15. Circular #37, Białystok, 24 September 1933, Poland (Vilna Archives) Collection, RG 28, YIVO.

16. Hehalutz branch Koluszki, communique, 31 March 1933, YT 2-12/3/5.

17. "Me-tokh mikhtavim me-ha-bikurim be-ayarot Volin": report by Miriam [Shlimovits] [undated but between mid-1933 and early 1934], YT 2-12/25/10.

18. Yisrael Oppenheim, *Tenuat he-haluts be-Polin 1929–1939* (Sde-Boker, 1993), 50.

19. Jack Jacobs, *Bundist Counterculture in Interwar Poland* (Syracuse, NY, 2006); Magdalena Kozłowska, *Świetlana przyszłość?* (Kraków-Budapest, 2016); Gertrud Pickhan, *Gegen den Strom* (München, 2001); Samuel Kassow, "Left Poalei Tsiyon in Interwar Poland," in *The Emergence of Modern Jewish Politics,* ed. Zvi Giterman (Pittsburgh, PA, 2003), 71–84; Jaff Schatz, *The Generation* (Berkeley, CA, 1991); on anarchists and Jews, see Eliezer Hirshauge, *Troym un farvirklekhung* (Tel Aviv, 1953).

20. Glenn Dynner, "Replenishing the '*Fountain of Judaism,*'" *Jewish History* 31 (2018): 229–261; for the older declensionist account, Mendl Piekarz, *Hasidut Polin bein shtei ha-milhamot u-begezeirot Ta"Sh-Ta"ShaH (Ha-Shoah)* (Jerusalem, 1990). For accounts of Hasidic ideological creativity (which is not the opposite of defensive retrenchment), see Gershon Bacon, "Ha-yahadut ha-ortodoksit be-Polin ve-Rusiah, 1850–1939," in *Kiyyum ve-shever,* vol. 2, ed. Yisrael Bartal and Yisrael Gutman (Jerusalem, 2001), 470–480; Iris Brown, "Triumphs of Conservatism" in *From Europe's East to the Middle East,* ed. Kenneth B. Moss, Benjamin Nathans, and Taro Tsurumi (Philadelphia, 2021), 143–173.

21. Shaul Stampfer, "Hasidic Yeshivot in Inter-War Poland," *Polin* 11 (1998): 3–24; Asaf Kaniel, "Bein hilonim, masortiim ve-ortodoksim," *Gal-Ed* 22 (2010): 95, 105–106; Marcin Wodziński, *Hasidism* (Oxford, 2018), 265–277; Kalonymous Kalmish Shapiro, *Sefer hovat ha-talmidim* (n.p., 1997; Warsaw, 1931–1932), 12.

22. Agnieszka Wierzcholska, "Relations between the Bund and the Polish Socialist Party from a Micro-historical Perspective," *East European Jewish Affairs* 43, no. 3 (2013): 297–313.

23. Moss, "Negotiating Jewish Nationalism," 410–416, and sources therein.

24. Kh. Biber, report, 25 February 1934, YT 2-12/25/10; Avraham Tarshish, Yoske Rabinovits, and Haim Dan, eds., *Dror: Min ha-mahpekhah ha-rusit el ha-mahpekhah ha-ivrit* (Tel Aviv, 1980–1981), 157. Notably, even in this setting with no public framework to support Zionist activity, a Hehalutz ha-Tsair *snif* had formed, and its members, who impressed Biber intellectually, included students from the local "Yiddishist school."

25. Celia Stopnick Heller, "Poles of Jewish Background," in *Studies on Polish Jewry 1919–1939,* ed. Joshua A. Fishman (New York, 1974), 266–270; Anna Landau-Czajka, *Syn będzie Lech* (Warszawa, 2006), 176–193.

26. For a comparison of assimilationism in Warsaw, Kraków, Lwów, and Poland's smaller towns, see Landau-Czajka, *Syn,* 92, 104, 107–115.

27. Andrzej Pilch, *Studencki Ruch Polityczny w Polsce w Latach 1932–1939* (Warszawa, 1972), 145; Miri Freilich, "Irgun ha-mitbolelim 'Zjednoczenie' be-Polin," *Gal-Ed* 14 (1995): 100–103.

28. See the memoiristic comments by Aleksander Hertz, *The Jews in Polish Culture* (Evanston, IL, 1988), 140–141.

29. Joseph Lichten, "Jewish Assimilation in Poland," in *The Jews in Poland,* ed. Chimen Abramsky, Maciej Jachimczyk, and Antony Polonsky (Oxford, 1986), 119.

30. See especially Kamil Kijek, *Dzieci modernizmu* (Wrocław, 2017); also Landau-Czajka, *Syn,* 155ff.

31. "Esther" in *Awakening Lives,* ed. Jeffrey Shandler (New Haven, CT, 2002), 321–343.

32. Kijek, *Dzieci modernizmu*, ch. 5; Heller, *Jabotinsky's Children*, ch. 4.

33. Joanna Olczak-Ronikier, *Korczak* (Warszawa, 2011), ch. 32; Korczak also lectured for the Jewish *landkentenish* organization: "Program fun instruktorn-kurs far firer iber Varshe," in RG 28: f 438, YIVO.

34. See my introduction, note 6; on the *Sygnały* group, Andrij Bojarov, Paweł Polit, and Karolina Szymaniak, *Montages* (Łódź, 2017).

35. Karen Underhill, "Bruno Schulz's Galician Diasporism," *Jewish Social Studies* 24, no. 1 (Fall 2018): 1–33.

36. Moss, "Negotiating Jewish Nationalism." There I propose, for the case of Warsaw, that the sociospatially variegated character of Jewish political experience itself played an important role in shaping how Jews of various sorts did and did not see their political situation. Class-based settlement and employment patterns (Jewish workers working for Jewish masters in small workshops) may have helped ensure that lower-class Jews in Warsaw would experience the woes of the 1930s first and foremost as class conflict rather than interethnic conflict.

37. Max Weinreich, *Der veg tsu unzer yugnt* (Vilna, 1935), 13.

38. Binyomen R., "Bamerkungen un ibertrakhtungen tsum bukh fun Dr. M. Vaynraykh *Der veg tsu unzer yugnt*," Weinreich Collection, RG 584, f. 368, YIVO, 1–2.

39. Binyomen R., "Bamerkungen," 1–2.

40. Unsigned copy to va'ad ha-poel shel ha-histadrut, 14 April 1933, YT 2-12/25/7.

41. *Pinkes fun der shtot Pruzhene* (Prużana, 1930), 270–271. Given that most of the rest of the 2,629 votes cast were divided between lists identified with "Polish intelligentsia and officials" and "Christian Householders," the 1,762 votes cast for the Radical Group and the Zionists clearly constituted the large part of the Jewish vote.

42. See handbills in RG 28, "Pruzhene," YIVO; Dov Kirshner, "Dertsiungs-antshtaltn bay 'Tarbut' in Pruzhene," in *Pinkes fun finf fartilikte kehiles*, 240.

43. "Mikhtavim shel Haim ben-Asher," YT, 2-12/3/1. Poalei Tsion Left was a splinter party that combined a certain kind of theoretical Zionism with a hard-edged Marxist political outlook, meaning that in practice it was far from organized Zionism and largely affiliated with Yiddishist and indeed Diasporist-socialist institutions.

44. Dov Kirshner, "Tsionistishe bavegung in Pruzhene," in *Pinkes fun finf far-tilikte kehiles*, 228; Zelig Geyar, "Zikhronot al he-haluts ve-al he-haluts ha-tsair be-Pruzhany," in *Pinkes fun finf fartilikte kehiles*, 240; Yosef Fridlander, "Tenuat ha-noar ha-halutsi-amami 'Gordoniah,'" in *Pinkes fun finf fartilikte kehiles*, 238.

45. Zelig Kalmanovitsh to Shmuel Charney, 16 October 1934, Shmuel Niger Collection, RG 360:34, YIVO.

46. Sima Meyerovitsh, "6ster meydl-ring 'Bin'" [movement notebook], April 1928, Territorial Collection, RG 116, box 3, f. 1, YIVO.

47. Avrom Golomb, 27 June 1934, cited as "*rosh-kesher* of the Vilna Bin [writing] in the Bin circular," in Leyzer Ran, "'Bin' ('Ha-Dvorah')—irgun tsofim sotsialisti," *Gal-Ed* 3 (1976): 205n51. Ran, a central figure in Bin, saw all of this up close and endorses Golomb's testimony.

48. Max Weinreich, "Ver zenen mir—vos viln mir," in *Binishe lider* (Vilna, 1932), 15.

49. Mikhl Astour, "A shtim fun der yugnt," *Literarishe bleter* 42 (20 October 1933): 4.

50. Ben-Tikvah, autobiography, 9 July 1934, Youth Autobiographies Collection, RG 4, f. 3623, YIVO.

51. I first discovered the richly illustrative case of Czyżew-Osada/Tshizsheve through the collaborative online translation *Czyzewo Memorial Book* (https://www.jewishgen.org/yizkor/Czyzew/Czyzew.html). In what follows, I cite from the original *Yizkor-bukh nokh der khorev-gevorener yidisher kehile Tshizsheve*, ed. Shimon Kanc (Tel Aviv, 1961), but am guided by Gloria Berkenstat Freund's fine translations.

52. Yitzhak Gura, "Der ershter oyfshprots fun komunizm," in *Yizkor-bukh Tshizsheve*, 405, following Gloria Berkenstat Freund, "The First Buds of Communism."

53. Aryeh Tsvik, report, 27 February 1934, YT 2-12/25/10.

54. *Sprawozdanie Dyrekcji Państwowego Gimnazjum im. A. Mickiewicza w Prużanie za rok szkolny 1927/28*, 15, https://www.pbc.rzeszow.pl/dlibra/show-content/publication/edition/2577?id=2577, accessed March 2018; see also "Gimnazjum im. Adama Mickiewicza w Prużanie," https://pl.wikipedia.org/wiki/Gimnazjum_im._Adama_Mickiewicza_w Prużanie, last modified 29 April 2020.

55. The fact that in the class of 1927–1928 some 113 pupils declared themselves "of the Mosaic religion" but only 81 of those declared themselves "Jewish" by nationality means that a nonnegligible number of these students saw themselves as Poles.

56. Fridlander, "Tenuat ha-noar ha-halutsi-amami 'Gordoniah,'" 238.

57. Giterman to Senator, 12 June 1935, Collection of the Section for the Organization of Non-Zionists (Sokhnut), S29, f. 51, CZA.

58. Yisrolik Kopit, undated fragment [probably 1933 or early 1934], YT, 2-12/25/10; Aryeh Tsvik, "Reshamim me-bikuri," YT 2-12/2/25. On Radun in the early 1920s, Bernard Wasserstein, *On the Eve* (New York, 2012), 267.

59. Piekarz, *Hasidut Polin*, 233–234.

60. Berl Szajes, "Mayn Aleksander shtibl," in *Yizkor-bukh Tshizsheve*, 225.

61. Gershn Gura, "Agudas Yisroel," in *Yizkor-bukh Tshizsheve*, 388.

62. Malka Shayman, "Di bavegung farn arbetndikn E'Y," in *Yizkor-bukh Tshizsheve*, 372–373.

63. Shayman, "Di bavegung," 371; cf. Gura, "Agudas Yisroel."

64. Szajes, "Mayn Aleksander shtibl"; Shayman, "Di bavegung"; and Leah Dimentman, "Frayhayt," in *Yizkor-bukh Tshizsheve*, 235, 373, 384.

65. Cited in Yosef Fund, *Pirud o hishtatfut* (Jerusalem, 1999), 99–101.

66. Alter Druyanov "Rishme ha-derekh," unpublished travel notebook, Druyanov Collection, RG A10, CZA.

67. Cited in Fund, *Pirud*, 101–102.

68. David Frankel, "Kibbutz Hakhsharah: A Memoir (c. 1935)," in *The Jew in the Modern World*, 3rd ed., ed. Paul Mendes-Flohr and Jehuda Reinharz (Oxford, 2011), 681.

69. YIVO autobiography 3680, in Ido Bassok, ed., *Alilot neurim* (Tel Aviv, 2011), 130.

70. Dimentman, "Frayhayt," 384.

71. "Rex"' in Bassok, *Alilot neurim*, 154.

72. Ben-Adir, "Vi azoy iz dos geshen (tsu der katastrofe in der sotsialistisher velt)," *Fraye shriftn far yidishn sotsialistishn gedank* 17 (October 1935): 18.

73. Giterman to Senator, 12 June 1935, S29:51, CZA.

74. Vidrovits to Druyanov, 22 January 1933, A10/27/2, CZA.

75. Vidrovits to Druyanov, 22 July 1935, A10/27/2, CZA.

3. MINORITYHOOD AND THE LIMITS OF CULTURE

1. Moyshe Goler [Golomb], "Loynt tsu shraybn vegn dem?," *Literarishe bleter* 26 (30 June 1933): 413–415; Goler, "Vuhin geyen mir?," *Literarishe bleter* 18 (5 May 1933): 285–286.

2. Goler, "Loynt," 415.

3. Moyshe Goler, "Vu haltn mir?," *Literarishe bleter* 43 (27 October 1933): 677–679.

4. Abram Perelman, *Przyczynek do psychologii młodzieży żydowskiej* (Warszawa, 1932), 16–25.

5. Yitshok Bernshteyn, "Dreyst un ofn," *Literarishe bleter* 38, no. 489 (20 September 1933): 608.

6. Alter Druyanov, "Rishme ha-derekh," unpublished travel notebook, RG A10, CZA, 14.

7. Alter Druyanov, *Tsionut be-Polanyah* (Tel Aviv, 1932–1933), 3–5, 15–16.

8. Moyshe Knaphays, introduction to *Mokem: Poeme fun altshtot* (Warsaw, 1936), 3 (preface dated December 1935); on Knaphays' turn toward Communism, see Kh. Sh. Kazdan, *Moyshe Knaphays* (Buenos Aires, 1972), 31.

9. "Greyno," in *Awakening Lives*, ed. Jeffrey Shandler (New Haven, CT, 2002), 52–63, 76–96, 100–103, 107; Bundist autobiography cited in Max Weinreich, *Der veg tsu unzer yugnt* (Vilna, 1935), 252, 275.

10. Hirsh Gutgeshtalt, "Ven goyroles vign zikh," in *Erev khurbn*, ed. Shmuel Rozhanski (Buenos-Aires, 1970), 213–220.

11. Samuel Kassow, *Who Will Write Our History?* (New York, 2009), 96–97; Yehuda Bauer, *My Brother's Keeper* (Philadelphia, 1974), 36–45.

12. Yitshok Giterman, "Der moes fun di gmiles-khsodim-kases," *Haynt*, 25 December 1932; Giterman, "Tsi iz di arbet fun di gmiles-khsodim-kases a konstruktive?," *Moment*, 25 December 1932.

13. Giterman to Senator, 12 June 1935, Collection of the Section for the Organization of Non-Zionists (Sokhnut), S29:51, CZA.

14. Zilberfarb, "'ORT'-idee un 'ORT'-organizatsye," (1930), repr. in *Gedenkshrift tsum tsentn yortsayt nokh Dr. Aron Singalovski, 1956–1966* (Geneva, 1966), 16.

15. Yisrael Klausner, *Vilnah, Yerushalayim de-Lita : dorot aharonim 1881–1939* (Tel Aviv, 1982/83), 561.

16. Max Weinreich, "Ver zenen mir—vos viln mir," in *Binishe lider* (Vilna, 1932), 13–15.

17. Weinreich, "Ver zenen mir," 15.

18. Mikhl Astour, "A shtim fun der yugnt," *Literarishe bleter* (20 October 1933), 3.

19. Mikhoel Burshtin, "A nayer faktor in yidishn lebn," *Landkentenish/Krajoznawstwo* 1 (1933): 9–13.

20. Mikhoel Burshtin, *Iber di khurves fun ployne* (Vilna, 1931).

21. Chone Shmeruk, "Responses to Antisemitism in Poland, 1912–36," in *Living with Antisemitism,* ed. Jehuda Reinharz (Waltham, 1988), 276–288.

22. M. Burshtin, "A gast fun erets-yisroel," *Haynt,* 12 April 1936.

23. Samuel Kassow, "Travel and Local History as a National Mission," in *Jewish Topographies,* ed. Julia Baruch, Anna Lipphardt, and Alexandra Nocke (London, 2008), 241–264.

24. Burshtin, "A nayer faktor," 9.

25. M. B., "Der moes fun regionalizm," *Landkentenish/Krajoznawstwo* 2 (Varshe, 1934), 31.

26. Karolina Szymaniak, "Speaking Back," *Polin* 28 (2016): 163–164.

27. Burshtin, "A nayer faktor," 13.

28. Luks, "Di rasn-problem in Amerike," in Weinreich Collection, RG 584:305, YIVO. I learned of this piece from Leila Zenderland, "Social Science as a 'Weapon of the Weak,'" *Isis* 104 (2013): 742–772; warm thanks to Eddy Portnoy for making the clipping available.

29. Weinreich, *Veg,* 190.

30. A note on terminology: Weinreich consistently used *"neger,"* the Yiddish cognate of the term "Negro," both as a noun ("the Negro in America") and an adjective ("a Negro doctor"). The term itself has a complex history in American parlance, needless to say. But in Yiddish, and certainly in East European Yiddish, it was the term used by progressive elements of all stripes and was clearly intended to be a neutral and (hence) respectful ethnic designation. On the understanding that the term "Negro" had the same connotations of respect in the eyes of some (though not all) African Americans in the 1930s, but also in recognition that we need to understand what sort of race discourse framed and limited the thought of Weinreich and his contemporaries, whatever their intent, I have chosen to preserve the term "Negro" when quoting Yiddish text. My thanks to Nathan Connolly for guiding me through some of this vexed terminological-conceptual history.

31. Weinreich, *Veg,* 190–195; Max Weinreich, "Tuskegee, Ala." and other notes, RG 584:345, YIVO; Jennifer Young, "Race, Culture, and the Creation of Yiddish Social Science," in *Choosing Yiddish,* ed. Shiri Goren, Hannah Pressman, and Lara Rabinovitch (Detroit, MI, 2013), 217–232.

32. Weinreich, *Veg,* 22–23, 192.

33. This reading is suggested by Kamil Kijek, "Max Weinreich, Assimilation, and the Social Politics of Jewish Nation-Building," *East European Jewish Affairs* 41, nos. 1–2 (2011): 37ff.

34. "Murzyn Warszawski" debuted in 1928 and was published in the Polish literary journal *Skamander* in mid-1935 (starting with volume 9 [May 1935]: 116–136); Weinreich likely read it then. It must be remarked that in fact the thoughtful African American students whom Weinreich encountered in interviews and diaries at Fisk are nothing at all like Słonimski's characters, ridiculous two-

dimensional send-ups defined by an unthinking desire to belong to Polish high society and a complete incapacity for reflection.

35. Weinreich, *Veg,* 190–192.

36. Weinreich, *Veg,* 191–192.

37. Weinreich, *Veg,* 171–172.

38. Here Weinreich used not "atake" but "araynris," a tearing-into.

39. "Ershter proyekt far a gliderung," 12 November 1933, Youth Autobiography Collection, RG 4:3881, YIVO, 2–3.

40. Lux, "Di rasn-problem," RG 584:305, YIVO; cf. Zenderland, "Social Science," for a different reading.

41. Yfaat Weiss, *Etniut ve-ezrahut* (Jerusalem, 2001).

42. Weinreich, *Veg,* 192.

43. Weinreich, *Veg,* 193–196.

44. Weinreich, *Veg,* 196.

45. Weinreich, *Veg,* 190.

46. Weinreich, *Veg,* 250, 207–210.

47. Weinreich, *Veg,* 194–196.

48. Daryl Michael Scott, *Contempt and Pity* (Chapel Hill, NC, 1997).

49. Goler, "Vuhin geyen mir," 286.

50. Goler, "Vuhin geyen mir," 285.

51. Y. Gotlib, "Minderhayt-kompleks," *Haynt,* 29 September 1934.

52. Weinreich, *Veg,* 277.

53. Zaromb, "Tsu keynem nisht" (Warsaw, 1929), and Tsaytlin, "Ver iz unz shuldik?" (Warsaw, 1933), repr. in Rozhanski, *Erev khurbn,* 212, 245. Thanks to Miriam Trinh for introducing me to Tsaytlin's poem and to Sholem Berger for working on the translation with me. Yisroel Rabon, *Groyer friling* (Varshe, 1933).

54. Justin Daniel Cammy, "'Yung-Vilne': A Cultural History of a Yiddish Literary Movement in Interwar Poland" (PhD diss., Harvard University, 2003), ch. 4.

55. Cammy, "'Yung-Vilne,'" ch. 4; Avraham Nowersztern, "Yung Vilne," in *The Jews of Poland between Two World Wars,* ed. Yisrael Gutman (Hanover, NH, 1989), 383–398.

56. The key poems are grouped together in Grade, *Yo,* available in Khayim Grade, *Doyres* (New York, n.d.): "Koshmar," "Balade," "Sdom," "Kratn," "Vin," "Velt in nayntsn firundraysik."

57. In Grade, *Yo:* "Mayn mame"; "Mayn toyter tate"; "Balade"; "Mayn khaver—der poet"; "Likht un shney"; "A tog in vald."

58. Cammy, "'Yung-Vilne,'" 234–235.

59. Cammy, "'Yung-Vilne,'" 234–235.

60. Grade, *Yo:* "Ikh zing fun shney-badektn barg arunter"; "Baym shayn fun der lavone"; "Yo."

61. Grade, *Yo:* "A tog in vald"; "Mayn khaver—der poet," "Likht un shney."

62. *Groyser verterbukh fun der yidisher shprakh,* ed. Yuda A. Yofe and Yudl Mark (New York, 1961), s.v. "Oysbenkn": "To gain something by longing for it for a long time. 'Through supplicatory prayers, she gained-through-longing a child.'"

63. Grade, *Yo:* "Kidush levone"; "Kratn"; "Vin."

64. Byron Ellsworth Hamann, "How Maya Hieroglyphs Got Their Name," *Proceedings of the American Philosophical Society* 152, no. 1 (March 2008): 14.

65. Thanks to Anne Eakin Moss and Sholem Berger for translation advice. I have learned from Cammy's acute reading of this poem in "'Yung-Vilne,'" 255–257, but do not see it as "a series of paradoxes."

66. Dr. Debora Vogel-Barenbluth, "Legenda współczesności w literaturze dziecięcej," *Przegląd Społeczny* (Lwów) 8, no. 3 (March 1934): 41–46; translated as "The Legend of Modernity in Children's Literature" in Andrij Bojarov, Paweł Polit, and Karolina Szymaniak, *Montages* (Łódź, 2017), 407–410.

67. Shloyme Belis, "Bay di onheybn fun Yung-Vilne," *Di Goldene Keyt* 101 (1980): 44–45.

68. Avrom Sutzkever, "Marts," in *Blonder baginen,* repr. in Sutzkever, *Poetishe verk* (Tel Aviv, 1963), 41; translated with Sholem Berger.

69. Sutzkever, "Heymishe felder" (1935), in *Blonder baginen,* repr. in Sutzkever, *Poetishe verk,* 30; translated with Sholem Berger.

70. Cora Diamond, "Missing the Adventure," in *The Realistic Spirit* (Cambridge, 1995), 312.

71. Robert Magidoff, ed. *Negry poiut* (New York, 1934). For a new history of Jewish Communist engagement with the African American experience, see Amelia Glaser, *Songs in Dark Times* (Cambridge, MA, 2020), ch. 3.

72. Zeev Latski-Bertoldi, "*Der neger zingt,*" *Haynt,* 17 August 1934.

73. V. Latski-Bertoldi, *Di idishe lage in mizrekh-eyrope un der ufboy fun erets-yisroel* (Riga, 1931).

74. A Yiddish-language volume of Bialik's pogrom poetry was titled *Fun tsaar un tsorn* (Berlin: Klal-farlag, 1922).

75. Kenneth B. Moss, *Jewish Renaissance in the Russian Revolution* (Cambridge, MA, 2009), 197, 215.

76. Dan Haruv, "Latzky-Bertholdi, Ya'akov Ze'ev" in *YIVO Encyclopedia of Jews in Eastern Europe,* ed. Gershon Hundert (New Haven, CT, 2008).

4. ANTISEMITISM, NATIONALISM, ELIMINATIONISM

1. Latski to Lestschinsky, 28 June 1934, Lestschinsky Collection, RG 339, f. 36, YIVO.

2. Yankev Lestschinsky, "Vu tut men zikh ahin," *Forverts,* 4 January 1931.

3. Max Weinreich, *Der veg tsu unzer yugnt* (Vilna, 1935), 293.

4. H. Erlikh to Lestschinsky, 13 September 1927 and 30 April (?) 1928, RG 339:49, YIVO

5. Henryk Erlikh, *Der iker fun Bundizm* (New York, 1934), 11, 15–16.

6. Published in book form in 1931; now translated by Robert Brym, *The Economic Situation of the Jews in Interwar Poland* (Lexington, KY, 2021). Citing here page 12; see Brym's insightful introduction, 5–6.

7. Yankev Lestschinsky, "Ofener un erlekher," *Literarishe bleter* 33, no. 484 (18 August 1933): 526.

8. Yankev Lestschinsky, "Yidn faln in gas khaloshes fun hunger," written November 1932, reprinted in *Oyfn rand fun opgrunt* (Buenos Aires, 1947), 76–86.

9. Key texts: "Geto un vanderung in yidishn lebn," *YIVO-Bleter* 5, no. 1 (January 1933): 1–6 and "In klem fun an ibergang-tsayt," *Frayland* 3–4 (November–December 1934), 1–10.

10. Ben-Adir, "Af di vegn tsu teritoryalizm," *Frayland* 1–2 (September–October 1934): 50.

11. A. Menes, "Der matsev fun yidn in shayn fun der konyunktur-antviklung," *YIVO-Bleter* 3, no. 3 (March 1932): 193–207.

12. Levinson, *La-bisus ha-tsionut, kh. 2: antishemiut* [= *Antishemiut*] (Warsaw, 1932), 30.

13. Rachel Faygenberg, "Yordim," *Davar* (Tel Aviv), 17 December 1930.

14. Il'ya Dizhur, *Di moderne felker-vanderung* (Berlin, 1929), 69–70.

15. Levinson, *Antishemiut*, 30.

16. "Całuń, Tomasz," in *Słownik biograficzny działaczy polskiego ruchu robotniczego, A–D*, 2nd ed., ed. Janina Balcerzak and Feliks Tych (Warsaw, 1985), 203.

17. Zarząd gminy wyznaniowej żydowskiej w Ostrowcu, Wojew. Kielck. to Abr. Lewinzon, 9 August 1931, and reply by Levinson, undated, Levinson Collection, IV-104-656: f. 4, Lavon Institute, Tel Aviv.

18. Całuń to Levinson, 27 August (?) 1929, Lavon IV-104-656:4. Thanks to Zbigniew Janowski for deciphering this letter.

19. A. Kaplan, "Der rezultat fun di magistrate-vahle in Brisk," clipping from unidentified newspaper, and Yitzhak [illegible] to Levinson, 20 January 1929, Lavon IV-104-656:4.

20. Levinson, "Shalosh tekufot be-Brisk d'Lita," in *Kitve Avraham Levinson* (Tel Aviv, 1956), 1:260.

21. T. Gubkin, "Topolawa 12," and B. Kastrinsky, "Di tsionistishe organizatsye," in *Brisk d'Lita* (Jerusalem, 1958), 448, 462; ORT to Levinson, 27 February 1931, Lavon IV-104-656:4.

22. Levinson, *Antishemiut*, 58–62.

23. Levinson, *Antishemiut*, 58–62.

24. Levinson, *Antishemiut*, 38–40.

25. Levinson, *Antishemiut*, 65.

26. Cited in Maria Antosik-Piela, "Feminizm po żydowsku," *Midrasz*, December 2008, http://wiadomosci.onet.pl/feminizm-po-zydowsku/6ywxw.

27. Levinson, *Antishemiut*, 45; Oskar Schmitz, "Zur Psychologie des Judenhasses," *Abwehrblaetter* 3 (May 1931): 67–69; Paul Mendes-Flohr, "Messianic Radicals," in *Gustav Landauer*, ed. Mendes-Flohr and Anya Mali (Berlin, 2015), 28; Franziska Krah, *"Ein Ungeheuer, das wenigstens theoretisch besiegt sein muß"* (Berlin, 2017), 207ff.

28. Yitzhak Grinbaum, "Hitgavrut ha-antishemiut: 3," March 1933, repr. in *Milhamot yehudei Polanyah 1918-1940* (Jerusalem, 1941), 325.

29. Grinbaum, "Hitgavrut ha-antishemiut: 1," December 1932, in *Milhamot*, 318.

30. Grinbaum, "Hitgavrut ha-antishemiut: 2," February 1933, in *Milhamot*, 320–322.

31. Grinbaum, "Hitgavrut: 2," 320–322.

32. Sigmund Freud, *Di psikhologye fun di masn un der analiz fun mentshlekhn 'ikh,'* trans. Sarah Lehrman (Varshe, 1931).

33. Sigmund Freud, *Group Psychology and the Analysis of the Ego,* trans. James Strachey (1922; New York, 1959), 41.

34. *Stowarzyszenie Humanitarne "Braterstwo—B'nei-B'rith" w Warszawie 1922–1932* (Warsaw, 1932), 44.

35. Martin Wangh, "Gustav Bychowski, M.D.—1895–1972," *Psychoanalytic Quarterly* 41 (1972): 60–61; "Gustav Bychowski," https://pl.wikipedia.org/wiki /Gustaw_Bychowski, accessed 22 January 2018; Evan Osnos, "Meet Dr. Freud," *New Yorker,* 10 January 2011.

36. Gustaw Bychowski, "Rozmowa z Freudem," *Wiadomosci literackie* (Warsaw), 10 May 1936, 4.

37. Weinreich, *Veg,* 171.

38. F. Bernstejn, "Istota antisemityzmu i walki z nim," *Miesięcznik Żydowski* 3, no. 4 (April 1933): 285–288.

39. Peretz [Fritz] Bernstein, *The Social Roots of Discrimination,* trans. David Saraph (New Brunswick, NJ, 2011); F. Bernstein, *Der Antisemitismus als Gruppenerscheinung* (Berlin, 1926), 182, 183–184, 207.

40. Avrom Golomb, "Psikhologye fun kas," *YIVO-Bleter* 3, nos. 4–5 (April–May 1932): 300–312; Golomb, "Kas un dertsiung," *YIVO-Bleter* 5, no. 1 (January 1933): 47–52.

41. Moyshe Zilberfarb, "'ORT'-idee un 'ORT'-organizatsye," in (1930), repr. in *Gedenk-shrift tsum tsentn yortsayt nokh Dr. Aron Singalovski, 1956–1966* (Geneva, 1966),18.

42. Lestschinsky, "Yidn faln," 76–86.

43. Lestschinsky, "Yidn faln," 76–83.

44. Lestschinsky, "Yidn faln," 76–79, 82–83.

45. Lestschinsky, "Yidn faln," 82–83.

46. Druyanov, *Tsionut be-Polanyah,* 4.

47. Hagen, "Before the 'Final Solution,'" 356.

48. A. R. [Ben-Adir], "Vos azoyns iz 'ORT'?" *Virtshaft un lebn* 2 (5) (April 1929): 59–60.

49. A. R., "Fun der prese," *Virtshaft un lebn* 3 (August 1928): 53.

50. A. R., "Fun der prese," 53.

51. Cf. Etienne Balibar, "The Nation Form: History and Ideology," *Review* (Fernand Braudel Center) 13, no. 3 (Summer 1990), 347, which suggests that "the process of unification" that leads to the creation of a modern nation begins with "a more elementary process [. . .] of fixation of the affects of love and hate and representation of the 'self'" and thus is always primed to give way to a situation in which a "symbolic difference between 'ourselves and 'foreigners' [. . .] wins out and is lived as irreducible."

52. Ludwik Oberlaender, "Współczesne ruchy nacjonalistyczne a antysemityzm," *Miesięcznik Żydowski* 2, nos. 7–8 (July 1932): 1–25. Thanks to Zofia Trębacz for translating key parts of this essay; in what follows, I have modified the translation in some places and translated some parts directly.

53. Oberlaender, "Współczesne," 18.

54. Oberlaender, "Współczesne," 2.

55. Oberlaender, "Współczesne," 2, 24–25.

56. Oberlaender, "Współczesne," 25.

57. Lestschinsky, "Yidn faln," 85.

58. Lestschinsky, "In klem fun an ibergang-tsayt," 2–3.

59. Lestschinsky, "In klem, 6–8.

60. M. Klaynboym, "Der antisemitizm in Poylen shtaygt oyf," *Haynt* (Warsaw), 16 May 1934; transl. as "Goveret ha-antishemiut be-Polin" in Moshe Sneh, *Ketavim 1: 1928–1939,* ed. Emanuel Melzer (Tel Aviv, 1995), 164–166.

61. Klaynboym, "Der antisemitizm."

62. Klaynboym, "Der antisemitizm" and Melzer, note 11 to "Goveret," 367.

63. Klaynboym, "Der antisemitizm."

64. Oberlaender, "Współczesne," 25.

65. Latski to Lestschinsky, 28 June 1934, RG 339:36, YIVO.

5. FROM IDEOLOGY TO INQUIRY

1. Rakhel Faygenberg, "Prisat shalom me-Polin," *Davar* (Tel Aviv), 3 November 1929. On Hasidim and Otwock, see Ben-Zion Gold, *The Life of Jews in Poland before the Holocaust* (Lincoln, NE, 2007), 111–114.

2. Barbara Kirshenblatt-Gimblett, Marcus Moseley, and Michael Stanislawski, introduction to *Awakening Lives,* ed. Jeffrey Shandler (New Haven, CT, 2002), xxv.

3. Max Weinreich, ed., *Der alveltlekher tsuzamenfor fun yidishn visnshaftlekhn institut* (Vilna, 1936), 63–64; Jennifer Young, "Race, Culture, and the Creation of Yiddish Social Science," in *Choosing Yiddish,* ed. Shiri Goren, Lara Rabinovitch, and Hannah S. Pressman (Detroit, 2012), 217–232; "Maks Vaynraykh shildert di merkvirdige perzenlekhkayt fun dem idishn revolutsioner Virgili," *Forverts,* 12 March 1936.

4. Yankev Leshtshinsky, "Ofener un erlekher," *Literarishe bleter* 33, no. 484 (18 August 1933): 525.

5. Yankev Leshtshinsky, "In klem fun an ibergang-tsayt," *Frayland* 3–4 (November–December 1934): 8.

6. Ezra Mendelsohn, *On Modern Jewish Politics* (Oxford, 1993), ch. 5; Kamil Kijek, *Dzieci modernizmu* (Wrocław, 2017); Daniel Heller, *Jabotinsky's Children* (Princeton, NJ, 2017); Irith Cherniavsky, *Be-'or shineihem* (Tel Aviv, 2015); Rona Yona, "Nihyeh kulanu halutsim" (PhD diss., Tel Aviv, 2013).

7. Mikhl Astour, "A shtim fun der yugnt," *Literarishe bleter* 42 (20 October 1933): 4.

8. Binyomen R., "Bamerkungen un ibertrakhtungen tsum bukh fun Dr. M. Vaynraykh *Der veg tsu unzer yugnt,*" Weinreich Collection, RG 584:368, YIVO. Key loci in the text for the following argument: 1–2, 17–25, 29–41.

9. Binyomen R., "Bamerkungen," 25–28.

10. Binyomen R., "Oytobiografye," 1934, Youth Autobiography Collection, RG 4, YIVO. Key loci in the text for the following argument: 5, 7–13, 17–19, 28–30, 32, 36–37, 42, 46–58, 60–83.

11. Binyomen R., "Oytobiografye," 75–77.

12. Binyomen included in his own autobiography a citation of this other youth's letter to Hehalutz regarding why he wanted to leave the Bundist Tsukunft

movement, and Weinreich included and commented on it (as on Binyomen himself) in *Der veg tsu unzer yugnt* (Vilna, 1935), 259.

13. Binyomen R., "Oytobiografye," 17.

14. Typewritten summary of I. Gamlieli autobiography, Brańsk, 1934, RG 4:3548, YIVO.

15. Avrom Meirkevitsh, *Eseyen, dertseylungen un dokumentatsyes* (Tel Aviv, 2006), 29–35.

16. Autobiography of "Jezik Tomszow," Łódź, 1934, RG 4:3701, YIVO, 10–43.

17. "Mikhtavim shel Haim ben-Asher," YT 2-12/3/1.

18. Moshe Kliger to Gershon, reports, 12 August–14 August 1933, YT 2-12/3/5. Ela Bauer's forthcoming work on young women in Hehalutz ha-tsair in this period will be illuminating.

19. Yisrolik Kopit, undated report, 1934 or 1935, YT 2-12/25/7.

20. Miriam Shalev [Shlimovits], "Meshek ha-poalot be-Nahalat Yehudah," in *Sefer ha-Aliyah ha-Shlishit*, ed. Yehudah Erez (Tel Aviv, 1964), 2:752–753.

21. Shlimovits to Liliah, 6 May 1933, YT 2-12/3/5.

22. Miriam [Shlimovits] to Gershon, 7 May 1933, YT 2-12/3/5.

23. "Me-tokh mikhtavim me-ha-bikurim be-ayarot Volin," report by Miriam [Shlimovits], YT 2-12/25/10. This excerpt dates from late 1933 or early 1934; a photo from the archives of Kibbutz Lohamei ha-Getaot captures Shlimovits in nearby Nowostaw in March 1934; see fig. 11.

24. "Me-tokh mikhtavim me-ha-bikurim be-ayarot Volin"; Y. Kosoy to ha-vaad ha-poel shel ha-histadrut, 24 March [May?], [no year but filed with materials from 1933], YT 2-12/3/14.

25. Binyomen R., "Bamerkungen," RG 584:368, 29, YIVO.

26. Astour, "Shtim," 4.

6. PALESTINE AS POSSIBILITY

1. Yisrael Oppenheim, *Tenuat he-haluts be-Polin (1917–1929)* (Jerusalem, 1982), 379–409, 387n69; Jacek Walicki, *Ruch Syjonistyczny w Polsce w latach 1926–1930* (Łódź, 2005), 99–108; Liebman Hersh, *Di aliye un yeride* (Varshe, 1927); Avrom Golomb, "Tsionizm un palestinizm," *Fraye shriftn farn yidishn sotsyalistishn gedank* 7–8 (March 1930): 199–204.

2. Rona Yona, "Nihyeh kulanu halutsim" (PhD diss., Tel Aviv, 2013), 244ff.

3. Irith Cherniavsky, *Be-'or shineihem* (Tel Aviv, 2015), 99–100; Aviva Halamish, *Be-meruts kaful neged ha-zeman* (Jerusalem, 2006), ch. 8.

4. Rona Yona "Connecting Poland and Palestine," in *From Europe's East to the Middle East*, ed. Kenneth B. Moss, Benjamin Nathans, and Taro Tsurumi (Philadelphia, 2021), 194–218; Emmanuel Melzer, "Betar," Melzer, "Revisionism," and Scott Ury, "Zionism," in *YIVO Encyclopedia of Jews in Eastern Europe*, ed. Gershon Hundert (New Haven, CT, 2008); Yona, "Nihyeh kulanu," 300; Cherniavsky, *Be-'or*, 99–100, 124.

5. Alter Druyanov, "Rishme ha-derekh," unpublished travel notebook, Druyanov Collection, RG A10, CZA.

6. Cherniavsky, *Be-'or*, ch. 2.

7. Yona, "Nihyeh kulanu," 149–155.

8. Daniel Heller, *Jabotinsky's Children* (Princeton, NJ, 2017).

9. Yisrolik Kopit, report [undated but between mid-1933 and early 1934], YT 2-12/25/10; "Me-tokh mikhtavim me-ha-bikurim be-ayarot Volin": report by Miriam [Shlimovits] [undated but between mid-1933 and early 1934], YT 2-12/25/10.

10. "Maks Vaynraykhs ershter brif fun Palestine," *Forverts* (New York), 7 April 1936; Max Weinreich, *Der veg tsu unzer yugnt* (Vilna, 1935), 276n155: "I cite here a story I heard about Tel Aviv."

11. Max Weinreich, "Di mentshn vos shlisn zikh in di arbeyter-kolonies in Erets-Yisroel," *Forverts*, 10 April 1936.

12. Yoysef Tshernikhov, "Tsum tsveytn mol in Erets-yisroel: Ayndruken, begegenishen un shmuesn," pt. 7, "A tog in Sharon," *Haynt*, 8 September 1933.

13. Based on search of "Palestine" and "Erets-yisroel" in *Unzer ekspres* and *Haynt* in the Historical Jewish Press database (http://web.nli.org.il/sites/JPress/English/Pages /default.aspx). Currently, the HJP cannot offer any useful measure of the amount of coverage because it lacks *Nasz Przegląd* and *Moment* after December 1930; it also lacks other key Polish-language titles including the Lwów *Chwila* and Kraków's *Nowy Dziennik*. Characterization of *Unzer Ekspres*: Natan Cohen, "Unzer express," accessed 7 October 2016, http://web.nli.org.il/sites/JPress/English/Pages/Unzer.aspx. The Yishuv drew growing interest in Poland's *non*-Jewish public as well. Thus, in 1933, the journal *Słowo* carried detailed reportage on Jewish settlement in Palestine by Ksawery Pruszyński, which appeared that year as the book *Palestyna po raz trzeci;* see François Guesnet, "Sensitive Travelers: Jewish and Non-Jewish Visitors from Eastern Europe to Palestine between the Two World Wars," in "East European Jewry, Nationalism and the Zionist Project," ed. Kenneth B. Moss, special section, *Journal of Israeli History* 27 (September 2008): 178–181.

14. Cherniavsky, *Be-'or,* 49–79.

15. Cherniavsky, *Be-'or,* 68–70

16. Lova Levita, "Ba-golat Polin," in *Sefer Klosowa,* ed. Haim Dan (Tel Aviv, 1978), 133–142.

17. Marcin Kula, *Autoportet rodziny X* (Warszawa, 2007), 9, 16, 325, 327, 328, 331, 334. Thanks to Kamil Kijek for bringing this book to my attention and for his comments regarding its significance.

18. Kula, *Autoportet rodziny X,* 341–342.

19. Cited in Weinreich, *Veg,* 256.

20. Duvdavani, 15 January 1930, YT 2-12/2/7.

21. Hershl Pinski, 6 February 1930, YT 2-12/2/7.

22. Syjonistyczny Związek Państwowców (Judenstaatspartei): Wydział Turystyczny, "Tsirkular vegn turistn-rayzes tsum Mizrekh-Yarid," 3 April 1934, Poland Collection, RG 28:438, YIVO.

23. B. Yeushzohn, "A shpatsir keyn Erets-Yisroel," pt. 1, *Haynt,* 22 April 1934.

24. Kobi Cohen-Hattab, "Zionism, Tourism, and the Battle for Palestine," *Israel Studies* 9, no. 1 (2004): 61–85.

25. Syjonistyczny Związek Państwowców, "Tsirkular," 3 April 1934, RG 28:438, YIVO.

26. "Ufruf tsu di yidishe froyen un tekhter in Belkhatov," RG 28: 'B,' YIVO.

27. Cohen-Hattab, "Zionism, Tourism," 76. The records of various Jewish Agency bodies from the Section for the Organization of Non-Zionists to the Immigration Department reveal fitful efforts to measure, anticipate, or coordinate tourism. Lishkat ha-modi'in ha-tsionit le-tayarim to Werner Senator, 5 January 1937, S29, f. 88, CZA; misrad erets-yisraeli merkazi, Warsaw to mahlakah le-aliyah, Jewish Agency, Jerusalem, 27 January 1932, S6, f. 187/1, CZA.

28. Emanuel, "Turistn-sezon," *Moment,* 5 April 1935.

29. B. Yeushzohn, "A shpatsir keyn Erets-Yisroel," pt. 2, *Haynt,* 24 April 1934.

30. Guesnet, "Sensitive Travelers"; Yaad Biran, talk at the conference "Yiddishism: Mythologies and Iconographies," Jewish Historical Institute, Warsaw, 15–16 November 2015; Roni Gechtman, "The Rise of the Bund as Reflected in the *Naye Folkstsaytung,* 1935–1936," *Gal-Ed* 17 (2000): 29–55.

31. Ben-Shemen would later become famous as a starting point for such members of Israel's elite as Yigal Allon, Shulamit Aloni, Shimon Peres, and Dan Ben-Amotz; it is also a fraught site of Jewish-Palestinian memory struggles because some of its students took part in the violent expulsion of Lydda/Lod's Palestinian population in 1948. Ari Shavit, *My Promised Land* (New York, 2015), 101ff.

32. Helena Khatskels, *In erets-yisroel* (Vilna, 1931). On Khatskels's Communism, see her 1922 speech in "2ter Kehiles Tsuzamenfor," *Nays* (Kaunas/Kovne), 23 February 1922; on the Kovne Kinder-hoyz, Y. Lubinski, "Dos kinder-hoyz in Kovne," in *Shriftn far psikhologye un pedagogik,* ed. Leibush Lehrer (Vilna, 1933), 443–450 and Akiva Yishai, "Beit-ha-yeladim be-Kovnah," in *Yahadut Lita,* ed. Natan Goren (Tel Aviv, 1959–1984); on Khatskels's Palestine writing, Kerstin Hoge, "Don't Mention the Language War!," *Slavic Almanach* 13, no. 2 (January 2007): 146–169.

33. Weinreich to Cahan, 24 June 1932, Cahan Collection, RG 1139:70, YIVO.

34. Remarks in transcript of YIVO's *Alveltlekher kongres,* 96.

35. Yoysef Tshernikhov, "Tsum tsveytn mol in erets-yisroel," in ten Friday installments in *Haynt,* August–September 1933.

36. Tshernikhov, "Tsum tsveytn mol in erets-yisroel," 2, *Haynt,* 4 August 1933.

37. Tshernikhov, "Tsum tsveytn mol in erets-yisroel," 5, *Haynt,* 26 August 1933.

38. Cecile Kuznitz, personal communication, May 2017.

39. "Dr. Max Vaynraykhs ershter brif fun Palestine," *Forverts,* 7 April 1936.

40. Chapters 2–12 of the travelogue: "Tsugast in Deganiah, di eltste arbayter komune in Erets-Yisroel," "Di arbeyter kolonies in Erets-Yisroel," "Di mentshn vos shlisn zikh in di arbeyter-kolonies in Erets-Yisroel," "Tel Aviv un Yerushalayim," "Iden in Erets-Yisroel shpirn zikh zikherer vi andershvu—farvos iz dos azoy?" "Vos yidn in Erets-Yisroel hobn tsu zogn vegn der arabisher frage," "Daytshe iden in Erets-Yisroel," "Idish un hebreyish in Erets-Yisroel," "Idish in Erets-Yisroel mer treyf vi ale andere shprakhn," "Di Histadrut—di yidishe arbeyter organizatsye in Erets-Yisroel," "Erets-Yisroel vi an ideal un Erets-Yisroel in der praktik," *Forverts,* 8, 9, 10, 11, 13, 14, 16, 17, 20, 21, 24 April 1936, respectively.

41. Weinreich to Cahan, 24 June 1932, RG 1139:70; Weinreich, "Tsugast in Deganiah."

42. Weinreich, "Tsugast in Deganiah"; and Weinreich, "Di Histadrut." He explained the latter problem through the example of Tel Aviv's worker-owned Jewish bus cooperative, whose founding driver-members—Jewish workers and Histadrut members but also joint owners themselves—were faced with the problem of whether they should hire nondriver assistants (ticket takers, for example) at wages equal to their own despite the fact that this might be ruinous and cost them their own initial investment.

43. Weinreich, "Idish un hebreyish in Erets-Yisroel." Thanks to Israel Bartal for identifying Chizhik; the accuracy of Weinreich's characterization of Chizhik (who goes unnamed in the column) suggests that other "characters" similarly unnamed in Weinreich's reports were also real people with whom he engaged in real conversation.

44. Weinreich, "Tsugast in Deganiah."

45. Weinreich, "Tel Aviv un Yerushalayim."

46. "Rex," in *Alilot neurim*, ed. Ido Bassok (Tel Aviv, 2011), 153–154.

47. Weinreich, *Veg*, 276.

48. YIVO autobiography 3680, in Bassok, *'Alilot neurim*, 130. This is not to say that such leaps could only be made in the 1930s. A Skernevitser Hasidic memoirist describes his own motivations during the Fourth Aliyah thus: "I began to reveal to [the rebbe] the story of my long-developing longings for the Land of Israel, because life among the wicked Poles had become repugant to me." K. A. F[renkel], "Yahaso shel Admor me-Skernevits [Skierniewice] le-aliyah le-E'Y," in *Be-ohalei tsadikim*, ed. K. A. Frenkel (Tel Aviv, 1967), 382.

49. A. Gershom to vaad ha-poel shel ha-histadrut, 10 September 1936, YT 2-12/3/6; Levita to Dear Comrades, 23 December 1929, YT 2-12/2/4.

50. Avrom Golomb, *A halber yorhundert yidisher dertsiung* (Rio de Janeiro, 1957), 190.

51. Apollinary Hartglas, "Palestinizm: A nay bashefenish af der yidisher gas," *Haynt*, 9 February 1936.

52. Yeushzohn, "A shpatsir," pt. 2.

53. Giterman to Senator, 12 June 1935, Collection of the Section for the Organization of Non-Zionists (Sokhnut), S29:51, CZA.

7. REASON, EXIT, AND POSTCOMMUNAL TRIAGE

1. Ruth Wisse, introduction to *The Glatstein Chronicles*, trans. Maier Deshell and Norbert Guterman (New Haven, CT, 2010), vii–viii; Avraham Nowersztern, *Kan gar ha-am ha-yehudi* (Jerusalem, 2015), 474.

2. Citations are drawn both from *The Glatstein Chronicles*, 337–346 and from Yankev Glatshteyn, *Ven Yash iz gekumen* (New York, 1940), 240–254.

3. Glatshteyn, *Ven Yash iz gekumen*, 253.

4. This is embodied in his name, "Newfield," which stands in contradistinction to Yash's other main interlocutor, Shteynman/"Stoneman," who articulates Polish Jewish steadfastness in the face of antisemitic pressure.

5. *Glatstein Chronicles*, 343–344.

6. Wisse, introduction, ix.

7. Glatshteyn, *Ven Yash iz gekumen,* 258–259, 276; cf. Nowersztern, *Kan gar,* 597.

8. Max Weinreich, "Tsugast in Deganiah," *Forverts,* 8 April 1936.

9. Cf. Elizabeth Imber on Haim Arlosorov's analytical thought about the difference British state power could make in "Jewish Political Lives in the British Empire" (PhD diss., Johns Hopkins University, 2018), ch. 2.

10. There were of course many other lines of critique well developed by this point; see Walter Laqueur, *History of Zionism* (New York, 1972), ch. 8. These included critiques of Zionism as colonialism and of Zionist relations to the Palestinians as aggressive. Weinreich was certainly familiar with such critiques; they were mounted in Bundist circles to which he stood close, and he took an interest in Jewish-Arab relations, as we saw in Chapter 6. But he seems to have focused primarily on the plight of Jews in Europe.

11. Jacek Walicki, *Ruch Syjonistyczny w Polsce w latach 1926–1930* (Łódź, 2005), 102.

12. Yankev Lestschinsky, "Teritorializm un tsienizm," *Dos fraye vort* (Łódź), 16 November 1934.

13. For the young Lestschinsky's intellectual-ideological transition, see Jack Jacobs, *On Socialists and the Jewish Question after Marx* (New York, 1993). For recent histories of the Territorialist impulse, Adam Rovner, *In the Shadow of Zion* (New York, 2014); Gur Alroey, *Zionism without Zion* (Detroit, 2016).

14. A. R-n [Rozin], "Fun noentn un vaytn," *Frayland* 3–4 (November–December 1934): 82–90.

15. A. R-n [Rozin], "Fun noentn un vaytn"; see also Arn Singalovsky, "Gezelshaft oder bavegung," (1930), repr. in *Gedenk-shrift tsum tsentn yortsayt nokh Dr. Aron Singalovski, 1956–1966* (Geneva, 1966), 27; Yankev Lestschinsky, "Ofener un erlekher," *Literarishe bleter* 33, no. 484 (18 August 1933), 525.

16. Lestschinsky, "Teritorializm."

17. *Tsen yor "YEAS," 1924–1934* (Warsaw, [1934]), 3–14.

18. *Tsen yor "YEAS,"* 12–13.

19. Il'ya Dizhur, typescript for *Yidn loyfn,* 72–73, Dizhur Collection, RG 589, mf. 1, YIVO; Zofia Borzymińska, "Alter Leon," Delet Portal, https://delet .jhi.pl/pl/psj?articleId=17059, accessed 29 May 2021.

20. *Tsen yor "YEAS,"* 2–6; Tartakover to Natan Meltser, 10 December 1933, Tartakover Collection IV-104-565, Lavon Institute.

21. Tara Zahra, *The Great Departure* (New York, 2017), 106–119.

22. *Tsen yor "YEAS";* "Farn peryod 1/1/1929–31/3/1930," ICA-YEAS Collection (VII-227), Lavon Institute.

23. *Tsen yor "YEAS,"* 6–9.

24. *Leksikon fun der nayer Yidisher literatur,* ed. Shmuel Niger and Yankev Shatsky (New York, 1956–81), s.v. "Valk, Yitshok"; "Geulat-ha-arets-ring," *Haynt,* 27 March 1927; Valk, "Di shul in der provints," *Leben* (Vilna) 3–4 (June 1920): 21–24.

25. *Tsen yor "YEAS,"* 6.

26. Y. Valk, "Vilner opteylung fun der yidisher tsentraler emigratsye-gez. 'YEAS,'" in *Vilner Almanakh,* ed. A. Y. Grodzensky (1939; repr., Vilnius, 1992), 275.

27. *Tsen yor "YEAS,"* 13; "Tsuzamenfohr fun 'YEAS' in Poylen," *Haynt,* 6 May 1935.

28. *Tsen yor "YEAS,"* 30.

29. Shlimovitsh [date unclear, probably 1933 (though in 1934 folder)], YT 2-12/25/10 [mistakenly listed as Miriam Lutsk in finding aid].

30. "Rex," in *Alilot neurim,* ed. Ido Bassok (Tel Aviv, 2011), 153.

31. Compare Ido Bassok's insightful commentary: "One can see just how measured, rational," and disinclined to "ideological intoxication this writer is in his relationship to Zionism [particularly]," Bassok argues, precisely in the ways Rex located "the option of *aliyah* to the Land of Israel within a sociopolitical analysis of the Polish Jewish situation," in relation to not only "present considerations" but also future ones, and "in relative terms" rather than as a "complete solution." Bassok, *Alilot neurim,* 138.

32. Yoysef Tshernikhov, "Tsum tsveytn mol in Erets-yisroel" 7, "A tog in Sharon," *Haynt,* 8 September 1933.

33. Aviva Halamish, *Be-meruts kaful neged ha-zeman* (Jerusalem, 2006), 47.

34. Tshernikhov, "Tsum tsveytn mol," 2, *Haynt,* 4 August 1933.

35. Binyomen R., "Bamerkungen un ibertrakhtungen tsum bukh fun Dr. M. Vaynraykh *Der veg tsu unzer yugnt,*" Weinreich Collection, RG 584, f. 368, YIVO, 39.

36. Max Weinreich, "Erets-yisroel vi an ideal un erets-yisroel in der praktik," *Forverts,* 24 April 1936.

37. Max Weinreich, "Vos idn in erets-yisroel hoben tsu zogen in der arabisher frage," *Forverts,* 14 April 1936.

38. Weinreich, "Erets-yisroel vi an ideal."

39. Eliahu Dobkin, lecture in the Aliyah Bureau, 29 November 1934, Gruenbaum Collection, A127, f. 1817, CZA, accessed online through Ben-Gurion University 2011.

40. Dobkin, lecture, 29 November 1934, CZA A127:1817.

41. Halamish, *Be-meruts kaful,* 413–416; Aviva Halamish, "A New Look at Immigration of Jews from Yemen to Mandatory Palestine," *Israel Studies* 11, no. 1 (2006): 59–78.

42. A. R-n [Rozin], "Fun noentn"; and Mikhl Astour, "Vegn pauperizatsye, ir apologie un teritoryalizm," in *Frayland* 1–2 (Varshe) (September–October 1934).

43. Mikhl Astour, "A shtim fun der yugnt," *Literarishe bleter* 42 (20 October 1933): 3.

44. See his remarks about the late Tsemakh Shabad's ideological journey from Diasporism to Territorialism in *Der alveltlekher tsuzamenfor fun yidishn visnshaftlekhn institut,* ed. Max Weinreich (Vilna, 1936), 96.

45. Kalmanovitsh to Shmuel Charney, 16 October 1934, Shmuel Niger Collection, RG 360:34, YIVO.

46. M. Ravitsh, "A idee oder an ideal, a teritorye oder teritoryes," *Frayhayt* 3–4 (November–December 1934), 55–61.

47. Shoyl Gutman, in *Y. N. Shteynberg Bukh* (New York, 1961).

48. Zelig Geyar, "Zikhronot al he-haluts ve-al he-haluts ha-tsair be-Pruzhani," in *Pinkas Pruzhani,* ed. Yosef Fridlander (Tel Aviv, 1983), 239–240.

49. Miriam to Comrades, 7 August 1933, YT 2-12/25/7.

50. *Mitn ponem tsu zikh* (Warsaw, 1935), 7–46.

51. "Mikhtavim shel Haim ben-Asher," YT 2-12/3/1; Avraham Grebov [?], [unclear date but physically attached to a letter from Breslavski from 27 December 1933], YT 2-12/3/5.

52. Yisrael Guter's recollections in *Tenuat "Dror" be-Galitsyah,* ed. Shmuel Nitzan (Tel Aviv, 1984), 141–142.

53. Binyomen R., "Oytobiografye," 1934, Youth Autobiography Collection, RG 4, YIVO, 25, 29–30; Binyomen R., "Bamerkungen," 4–5; for direct evidence of his excellent Hebrew, see "Oytobiografye," 37, 44–46.

54. Binyomen R., "Bamerkungen," 15–17, 27, 29.

55. Binyomen R., "Oytobiografye," 29–30, 42; Binyomen R., "Bamerkungen," 10.

56. Binyomen R., "Bamerkungen," 30.

57. See the description of the Grodno talk in Avner Holtzman, *Hayim Nahman Bialik* (New Haven, CT, 2017), 200–201. A Polish translation of the talk Bialik gave in Warsaw during the same trip resonates closely with Binyomen R.'s description: Chaim Nachman Bialik, "O kulturze, książce, i polityce," *Miesięcznik żydowski* 1, nos. 11–12 (November–December 1931): 481–489; see the note there about Bialik's polemic with Grinboym.

58. Binyomen R., "Oytobiografye," 54–55.

59. Binyomen R., "Oytobiografye," 57–58.

60. Binyomen R., "Oytobiografye," 28.

61. Binyomen R., "Oytobiografye," 14.

62. Binyomen R., "Oytobiografye," 29.

63. Max Weinreich, *Der veg tsu unzer yugnt* (Vilna, 1935), 206.

64. Weinreich, *Veg,* 218.

65. Weinreich, *Veg,* 276.

66. Binyomen R., "Bamerkungen," 18–20.

67. Weinreich, *Veg,* 277.

68. Weinreich, *Veg,* 215.

69. Binyomen R., "Bamerkungen," 18–19.

70. Max Weinreich, "Daytshe yidn in erets-yisroel," *Forverts,* 16 April 1936.

71. "Forverts korespondent Dr. Maks Vaynraykh shraybt fun shif afn veg keyn Palestine," *Forverts,* 29 November 1935; also carried in *Vilner Tog.*

72. Max Weinreich, "'*Di idee fun Poyln*': Prof. Władysław Grabski's bukh vegn Piłsudski'n, Sanacja, dem bund mit Hitler-daytshland, un di yidn," *Vilner Tog,* 7 November 1935.

73. Avraham Barkai and Paul Mendes-Flohr, *German Jewish History in Modern Times* (New York, 1998), 4:320.

74. Max Weinreich, "Vos voltn mir gekent vayzn af der velt-oysshtelung: yidn, yidish, un yidishe kultur," *Tog* (Vilna), 2 July 1937; "A yidishe natsyonale program oyf nokh der milkhome" (New York), [undated but probably 1942], RG 584:602, YIVO, where Weinreich insists that although Palestine "has in the course of the past half-century absorbed a half million Jews," "as long as millions of Jews remain in Europe, it is against the interests of the Jewish people to present the Land of Israel as a cure for all Jewish problems," that even to speak about "an

exodus from Europe" was traitorous because it "strengthens the position of the enemy [and] paralyzes the will of Jews," and that reconstruction of Jewish life in Eastern Europe should be the centerpiece of international Jewish postwar policy because of the "rootedness of the East European Jew."

75. B. Yeushzohn, "A shpatsir keyn Erets-Yisroel," pt. 2, *Haynt,* 24 April 1934.

76. Basya Lakerman to Y. N. Shteynberg, 5 January 1951, Steinberg Collection, RG 366, f. 286, YIVO.

77. Mikhl Astour, *Geshikhte fun der frayland-lige* (New York, 1967), 76, 796.

78. "Men lebt mit bitokhn," *Der vilner tog,* 14 July 1936.

79. Editorial note to "Men lebt mit bitokhn," *Der vilner tog,* 14 July 1936. The unhappy editorial hand added a note that listed matters "Lakerman didn't mention," including the Histadrut's ostensible role in provoking Palestinian anger, and noted pointedly: "Something else is clear to everyone, with or without Sh. Lakerman's report from Palestine, namely, that with faith alone, one doesn't build countries."

80. Ezra Lahad to Y. N. Shteynberg, 8 January 1951, I. N. Steinberg Collection, RG 366:286, YIVO.

81. Alter Druyanov, *Tsionut be-Polaniah* (Tel Aviv, 1932–1933), 17ff.

82. Druyanov, *Tsionut be-Polaniah,* 7.

83. Cited in Henry Near, *The Kibbutz Movement: A History* (Oxford, 1992/2007), 1:220.

84. N. Urinsky, "Fun Kasrilevke biz Kabtsansk," *Frayland* (Varshe) 3–4 (November–December 1934), 110; cf. ch. 1.

CONCLUSION

1. Antony Polonsky, *The Jews in Poland and Russia,* vol. 3, *1914–2008* (Oxford, 2012), 85–86.

2. "The Situation of the Jews in Eastern Europe," [1937], Territorial Collection, RG 116:3:10, YIVO.

3. Polonsky, *Jews in Poland and Russia,* 3:80–90; Emanuel Melzer, *No Way Out* (Cincinnati, OH, 1997), ix–x, 20–31; Timothy Snyder, *Black Earth* (London, 2015), 58–59; Zofia Trębacz, *Nie tylko Palestyna* (Warszawa, 2018), ch. 1.

4. For a recent treatment emphasizing OZON engagement with the rightist Zionism of Zeev Jabotinsky's NZO, see Snyder, *Black Earth,* 62–69.

5. Edward Wynot Jr., "'A Necessary Cruelty,'" *American Historical Review* 76, no. 4 (October 1971): 1048–1052.

6. Polonsky, *Jews in Poland and Russia,* 3:89; Melzer, *No Way Out,* 63–65, 73, 91.

7. Wynot Jr., "'Necessary Cruelty,'" 1058.

8. Melzer, *No Way Out,* 108.

9. Polonsky, *Jews in Poland and Russia,* 3:97.

10. Cited in Melzer, *No Way Out,* 83

11. Melzer, *No Way Out,* 22–26, 92–93, 105, 133–134.

12. Melzer, *No Way Out,* 43–47, 77–78, 90–91; Polonsky, *Jews in Poland and Russia,* 3:80–90; Snyder, *Black Earth,* 69–70; Grzegorz Krzywiec, "The Balance of Polish Political Antisemitism," in *Right-Wing Politics and the Rise of*

Antisemitism in Europe, 1935–1941, ed. Frank Bajohr and Dieter Pohl (Göttingen, 2019), 61–79.

13. Yehiel Burgin, *Fun Vilne biz Yisroel* (Tel Aviv, 1988), 73–80; Czesław Miłosz, foreword to *The Jews in Polish Culture,* by Aleksander Hertz (Evanston, IL, 1988), ix–x.

14. Zofia Trębacz, *Nie tylko Palestyna* (Warsaw, 2018), 281.

15. Benjamin Nathans, personal communication, January 2021.

16. Yoysef Tshernikhov, "Tsvishn yidn inteligentn," [probably 1937], Tshernikhov Collection, IV-104-909:17, Lavon Institute, Tel Aviv.

17. Benny Morris, *Righteous Victims* (New York, 2001), 130–133, 137, 145, 150.

18. [Unclear] and Kosover to Unger, 13/14 May 1936, Menashe Unger Collection, RG 509:50, YIVO.

19. Morris, *Righteous Victims,* 130, 138.

20. Melzer, *No Way Out,* 110; Jehuda Reinharz and Yaacov Shavit, *The Road to September 1939* (Waltham, 2018).

21. Melzer, *No Way Out,* 109–111.

22. Anatomizing who voted for the Bund and why is difficult. Older work attributed much of the upswing in support to protest voters distant from the Bund before and after. More recent work argues that a good part of this upswing derived from expansion of the Bund's base rooted in long-standing Bundist institution building, recruitment, and indoctrination efforts. Compare Melzer, *No Way Out,* 111; Antony Polonsky, "The Bund in Polish Political Life, 1935–1939," in *Jewish History,* ed. Ada Rapoport-Albert and Steven J. Zipperstein (London, 1988), 562–564; Jack Jacobs, *Bundist Counterculture in Interwar Poland* (Syracuse, NY, 2006), 99–101. Clearly, though, the former camp was nonnegligible. To my mind, that very fact raises questions of ideological reorientation no less interesting than the fact of an expanding base.

23. Samuel Kassow, *Who Will Write Our History* (New York, 2009), 99–101; Polonsky, *Jews in Poland and Russia,* 3:96; Melzer, *No Way Out,* 45–46.

24. Meir Polner, "Brif tsu kooperatorn," *Moment,* 12 June 1938.

25. Jacobs, *Bundist Counterculture.*

26. S. Chmielewski, "Zagadnienie emigracji do nowych terenów w świetle opinji żydowskiej w Polsce: Biro-Bidzan, Peru, Chili, Equador, i in.," Archiwum Akt Nowych (Warsaw; accessed at United States Holocaust Museum and Memorial): Ministerstwo Spraw Zagranicznych w Warszawie nr. z. 322, nr. serii 6, syg. jed. arch. 2288, p. 2.

27. M. Polner, "Mit eygene koykhes," *Moment,* 31 May 1936.

28. Majer Pollner, *Emigracja i przewarstwowienie żydów polskich* (Warsaw, 1939), 5.

29. Melzer, *No Way Out,* 134–139; "A delegatn-konferents in der gezelshaft 'YEAS,'" *Moment,* 2 February 1937.

30. Dovid Mayer, *Tsienizm un yidishe emigratsye* (New York, 1939), 6.

31. Joseph Marcus, *Social and Political History of the Jews in Poland, 1919–1939* (Berlin, 1983), 518n43.

32. Kassow, *Who Will Write Our History?*, 48.

33. Polonsky, *Jews in Poland and Russia*, 3:94.

34. Shmuel Dothan, *Pulmus-ha-halukah be-tkufat ha-mandat* (Jerusalem, 1980), 83–84.

35. Yisroel Yefroykin to Zeev Latski-Bertoldi, 9 October 1937, Latski-Bertoldi Collection, IV-104-80: f. 22, Lavon Archive.

36. Protikhol me-yeshivat ha-va'ad ha-poel shel moetset gedolei ha-Torah, 8 Elul TaRTs'aZ/15 August 1937, Isaac Breuer Collection P173, f. 5, 10–11, Central Archive for the History of the Jewish People.

37. Autobiography of "Samuil Boroslavsky," Youth Autobiography Collection, RG 4:3648, YIVO, 137731–137737.

38. Quoted in *Alilot neurim*, ed. Ido Bassok (Tel Aviv, 2011), 703n9.

39. Aryeh Tartakover, *Yidishe emigratsye un Yidishe emigratsye-politik* (Vilna, 1939); Pollner, *Emigracja i przewarstwowienie*, 17–21.

40. Tartakover, *Yidishe emigratsye*, 189–190.

41. Pollner, *Emigracja i przewarstwowienie*, 42–45. For the accuracy of his perception about racist panic and population policy in the "White Pacific," see Marilyn Lake and Henry Reynolds, *Drawing the Global Colour Line* (Cambridge, 2008), 312–331.

42. Vaad ha-kahal Grodnah, 27 December 1937, RG 116:1:415, YIVO.

43. Justin Daniel Cammy, "'Yung-Vilne': A Cultural History of a Yiddish Literary movement in Interwar Poland" (PhD diss., Harvard University, 2003), 224, 258.

44. Samuel Kassow, "Travel and Local History as a National Mission," in *Jewish Topographies*, ed. Julia Baruch, Anna Lipphardt, and Alexandra Nocke (London, 2008), 256; Burshtin to Gershn Pomerants, 29 November 1938, *Tint un Feder* (Toronto) (January 1949): 52.

45. For example, Rebbe Avrom Mordkhe Alter of Gur, "Kriat hitorerut be-khnisiah ha-gedolah ha-shlishit (Marienbad, Elul 1936)," and R. Hayim Oyzer Grodzenski, introduction to *Sh"uT Ahiezer*, in *Le-Or ha-Emunah*, ed. Moshe Prager (New York, 1958), 17, 27.

46. Elkhonen Vaserman, "Ikveta de-meshiha," in Prager, *Le-Or ha-Emunah*, 28–30; Wasserman, *Epoch of the Messiah* (Los Angeles, 1985), 10–15; Gershon Greenberg, "Ontic Division and Religious Survival," *Modern Judaism* 14, no. 1 (February 1994), 46–49.

47. Joshua Karlip, *The Tragedy of a Generation* (Cambridge, 2013), ch. 4.

48. Hersh Matz, *Di oyfgabn fun 'TOZ'* (Vilna, 1937), 6; cf. Matz, *Kurerter un turistik in Poyln* (Warsaw, 1935), 203–223.

49. M. Levin, *A denkmol baym taykhl* (Varshe, 1937).

50. M. Gilinski, Yisroel-Borekh Grundman, and K. Vapner, *Shpil un farvaylung* (Warsaw, 1938), 1–2.

51. In her history of African American civic culture and thought from the 1890s through the 1930s, *Righteous Propagation* (Chapel Hill, NC, 2004), Michele Mitchell underscores a striking pattern. Initially, as African American hopes for integration after emancipation were drowned in violence, interest in plans for mass emigration, colonization, and self-determination flourished. But as it became

painfully clear that there was not only no clear way into American society but also no clear way out, Mitchell suggests, African American political-cultural energy turned inward toward a mix of practical communal uplift and a search for new cultural techniques to shore up the assaulted self, one's own and that of one's children, under attack by white society. Without wishing to blur the profound differences between the decades-long postemancipation African American case, with its enormities of mass violence and systematic oppression, and the much shorter and unquestionably different Polish Jewish case discussed here, I find Mitchell's model suggestive for thinking about how communal-cum-individual emigrationism and a turn toward an essentially psychosocial struggle of shoring up in the absence of other options may be said to exist in an ongoing state of tension and oscillation in twentieth-century history. Note that this reading of Mitchell's argument neglects her critical concern with the way these projects of self-defense were also efforts at communal discipline, control over women's bodies, and not least the internalization of the race idea—all issues that surely also bear comparative extension for the Jewish case. Thanks to Nathan Connolly for directing me to this work.

ACKNOWLEDGMENTS

Many colleagues and friends have shaped this book, and it could never have come to fruition without the extraordinary store of knowledge and insight that has been put at my disposal so generously for so long by so many.

Several people have aided me so extensively that they must be deemed cocreators of this work, though they are in no way responsible for its flaws. Anne Eakin Moss, Dan Moss, and Sholem Berger were essential interlocutors from the start, thinking with me day in and day out. In the field of Jewish history, Jim Loeffler and Tony Michels were true companions; their conviction that our shared field still had much to learn from the Polish Jewish 1930s kept mine from flagging, and insofar as I have articulated the stakes of this work, it is much thanks to them. Early in the research process I had the good fortune to meet a colleague in Polish Jewish history who seemed to already know everything I wanted to discover and was happy to share his extraordinary knowledge: Kamil Kijek put essential sources in my hands, read the entire manuscript at a critical stage, and guided me toward a new understanding of the relationship between the Jewish thought we both seek to understand and the larger political culture of interwar Poland. Patiently opening up new worlds of history and critical inquiry to me for a decade, Nathan Connolly has profoundly shaped my understanding of the interplay of cultural and political thought under pressures of exclusion and real or potential violence. This book owes a tremendous amount to his vision, and it is hard to imagine writing another book without regular meetings in his office. Eric Oberle's vision of how the Polish Jewish case fits within what he has named "the century of negative identity" helped me understand that the true concern of this study was not nationhood or identity but the thought and strivings of people trying to comprehend a world they could not determine and searching for a way through it. Eric's critical intelligence and bottomless learning have shaped every aspect of this book.

Eli Lederhendler, Norman Naimark, Joanna Nalewajko-Kulikov, Gabriella Safran, Marek Wierzbicki, and Tara Zahra read the entire manuscript and offered essential insights and correctives. Gabriella and Tara helped me rethink the book's first chapters. Olga Borovaya, Holly Case, Francois Furstenberg, Michael Hanchard, Daniel Levine, Pawel Maciejko, David Myers, and my student turned friend and colleague Elizabeth Imber offered essential comments on the introduction. Pawel helped me with translation tangles. The crystalline intelligence and sympathy of Ben

Nathans and Derek Penslar shaped early formations of this project and clarified its conclusions. Leora Auslander and Ben Sax read a more freewheeling version of the conclusion, and their enthusiasm points toward horizons I hope someday to reach.

Many scholars shared knowledge I cannot hope to attain and critical insight for which I can only be grateful. At a key early juncture, Tara Zahra shared her manuscript on the politics of East European emigration that became *The Great Departure,* and the stimulating correspondence that ensued reshaped my approach to Jewish discourses of danger in the age of nationalist population politics. Karolina Szymaniak and Karen Underhill have guided me through the Polish-Yiddish cultural borderlands they are rediscovering. Ela Bauer, Irith Cherniavsky, Dan Heller, and Rona Yona guided me toward the right sources and questions about Zionism in Poland. Avrom Novershtern, Miriam Trinh, Marc Caplan, Hannah Wirth-Nesher, and Efrat Gal-Ed helped me investigate what the Yiddish literature of the era sought to say. Discussions at Brown University in 2014 with Maud Mandel, Rachel Rojansky, and my first teacher, Omer Bartov, among others, proved a turning point. David Myers posed probing questions about nationalism and the 1920s, Malachi Hacohen and Scott Ury about Revisionist Zionism, Jonathan Boyarin about the Depression. David Engel and Antony Polonsky offered essential commentary on my earliest effort in 2014 to understand the impasses of 1930s Polish Jewish sociological thought; other conversations with David over the years have been equally vital. A 2016 conversation with Natalia Aleksiun about the politics of exit brought clarity. Grzegorz Krzywiec shared his essential work on the Jewish Question in Polish political culture. Beth Holmgren and Stephan Stach offered insights into the inner world of disparate sorts of Jewish Poles. Howard Brick was an inspiring interlocutor. Robert Brym pushed me take Polish Jewish sociology seriously. Zbygniew Janowski tried to teach me Polish. Zofia Trębacz provided translations of several crucial sources and helped me work through others even as she was completing her own important work. Margarita Cygielska copyedited and double-checked some translations while doing far more essential work as a front-line medical worker during Covid-19. Jaclyn Granick, Ula Madej-Krupitski, Marcos Silber, and Elhanan Reiner identified essential sources.

Samuel Kassow, Israel Bartal, David Fishman, and Cecile Kuznitz have long embodied for me how vast knowledge of East European Jewish life can flow from vast love for what was lost. I hope that some of the knowledge I have gleaned from them over many years is reflected here, and some of the love too.

This book was begun and finished at the Johns Hopkins University, which I now leave after eighteen years. I thank my wonderful colleagues in the History Department, the Stulman Jewish Studies Program, and beyond. It has been an incredible privilege to shape this project in dialogue with such extraordinary scholars.

My thinking about Jewish history, whatever the topic, remains indebted to the uniquely probing critical imaginations of Aron Rodrigue and Steven Zipperstein.

This work took shape through presentations at numerous conferences and workshops, and each time colleagues, friends, and strangers refined it. I thank participants in the 4th Lavy Colloquium on "Nationhood and the Jews" at Johns Hopkins in

2008; the 2010 conference for Antony Polonsky at UCL organized by Francois Guesnet and Glenn Dynner; the 2010–2012 migration workshop at the Hebrew University of Jerusalem organized by Jonathan Dekel-Chen; the 2012 Kandersteg Seminar with Larry Wolff and Katherine Fleming; conferences on Jewish nationalism's histories organized at the Hebrew University by Dima Shumsky and UCLA by David Myers and Sarah Stein; a 2014 conference in honor of Israel Bartal organized by Scott Ury at the Hebrew University and a 2015 conference at Saitama University convened by Taro Tsurumi; a 2015 conference at the Jewish Historical Institute in Warsaw; the "Doikeyt, Diaspora, Borderlands" conference at the University of Illinois at Chicago convened by Karen Underhill in 2016; and a 2018 conference at the Heinrich Heine Universitaet-Dusseldorf organized by Marion Aptroot, Efrat Gal-Ed, and Andrea von Huelsen-Esch. I thank participants in the Jewish Studies seminars of Duke-UNC and Yale and audiences at YIVO, Brown, SUNY New Paltz, Tel Aviv University, the University of Maryland, the University of Michigan, the University of Toronto, and the University of Virginia. The chance to present the Clara Sumpf lectures at Stanford before beloved teachers in 2019 was also the chance to finally understand my own argument. This argument was once again sharpened in presentations at the University of Chicago before old friends like David Nirenberg and Na'ama Rokem and new ones, whom I am now privileged to call colleagues.

I thank the American Council of Learned Societies for its support of this project through a Charles A. Ryskamp Fellowship. I thank the many archivists who aided me with such generosity at the YIVO Archive of the Center for Jewish History in New York, the Archiwum Akt Nowych in Warsaw, the Central Zionist Archives and the Central Archive for the History of the Jewish People in Jerusalem, Yad Tabenkin in Ramat Efal, and the Lavon Institute in Tel Aviv.

Kathleen McDermott at Harvard University Press shepherded this book from mere proposal to finished product with insight and patience; it has been a privilege to work with her once again and with the talented staff at HUP.

All errors and flaws in this work are, of course, my own.

For ongoing scholarly stimulation and friendship not wholly connected to this book, my gratitude goes not only to many of the aforementioned but also to Eran Shalev, David Bell, Scott Ury, Yuval Tal, Magdalene Klassen, Neta Stahl, Itzik Melamed, Brukhe Lang, Sam Spinner, Taro Tsurumi, Frank Wolff, Arie Dubnov, Avery Robinson, and Christine Holbo. Jane Marinelli helped me immeasurably. I have learned so much from so many scholars, but no less from beloved friends Peter and Becky, Danny and Amy, Ben and Jenny, Nathan and Shani, Ian and Laura, Aaron and Yael, Zack and Celeste, Doodie and Ruti, and many others.

In Poland and Israel, old friends and new made my visits an encounter that was as informative as time in the archives. They helped show me how good people wrestle with a conflict-ridden present and with illiberal pathologies spreading like cancers through their own societies—something that is not confined to Poland or Israel, of course, but looms before us all. Special thanks to Miriam and Eliezer, Yuval and Noga, Ariel and Leigh, and to Miriam, *z'l*, a remnant of Polish Jewry who made a life and a family in Israel, and whom we remember with love.

Two men whom I loved and respected, my father, Robert Moss, and my father-in-law, David Eakin, passed away while I was writing this book. I am grieved to have lost the gift of their support, insight, and counsel. But I could not be more fortunate in family. My brother Dan's learning and talent is outweighed only by his love and support; I could not have written this without his critical but enthusiastic readings, good humor, and steady supply of books about something else. Lindsay and Shoshana, Nora and Yale, my mother-in-law, Tess Eakin, and my mother and fellow historian, Sandra Moss, all have a share too. So do my children, Isaac, Aaron, and Celia. Aaron did me proud when he pronounced informed and stern judgment on a long and pointless discussion of Itsik Manger's *Megile-lider* in an earlier draft of Chapter 3. Isaac responded to my explanation of Chapter 5's portrait of ideology-skeptical young people by drawing an informed contrast with Perchik in *Tevye der milkhiger*. We must be doing something right. My daughter, Celia, joined our family while this book was being written and cannot claim to have shaped it intentionally. But every day, she and her brothers reground our faith in the future while embodying the need to fight for it. Finally, my wife, Anne, has, once again, made everything possible and worthwhile.

INDEX

Page numbers in italics indicate illustrations.

Adam Mickiewicz Gymnasium, Prużana, 106
African American experience (in Polish
  Jewish thought), 71, 128–134, 136, 141,
  148, 151–153, 175–176, 348n30, 363n51.
  See also culture; Golomb, Avrom; Jewish
  people, the; Latski-Bertoldi, Zeev-Volf;
  literature; minorityhood; race and racism;
  Weinreich, Max
agency, Jewish (posited collective Jewish
  capacity to substantially determine outcome
  of political processes affecting Jews): as
  central assumption of modern Jewish
  politics in Eastern Europe, 10–12; vs.
  growing recognition of relative powerlessness, 1–2, 36, 287–305. *See also* Astour
  (Tshernikhov), Mikhl; Binyomen R.; danger;
  ideologies, Jewish; inquiry; Lestschinsky,
  Yankev; politics, Jewish; realism; socialism;
  Zionism
Agudes Yisroel (Agudat Israel) party (the
  Agudah), 33, 94, 108, 110, 320. *See also*
  Hasidism; Orthodoxy
Aleksiun, Natalia, 13, 98, 99
Al ha-Mishmar faction, 251
aliyah. *See* Fifth Aliyah; Fourth Aliyah; Third
  Aliyah
Alter, Avrom Mordkhe (Gerer Rebbe),
  363n45
Alter, Leon, 264
anarchism, 96–97, 210, 244, 344n19.
  See also socialism

antisemitism (Judeophobia, Jew-hatred):
  abject Jewish political status as contri-
  buting factor to, in Tsarist Russia, 9–10;
  across interwar Europe, 6, 8, 296; Jewish
  analyses of character, sources, and trajectory
  of, 19–21, 24–25, 58–70, 74–79, 157–159,
  160–172, 174–192, 219; Jewish outlooks
  reshaped by rising, 69–78, 85–87, 110–113,
  134–137, 196, 217, 250, 253; and the
  Jewish Question in Polish politics and
  culture, 8, 13, 18–30, 39, 44–45, 65–67,
  79–86, 164–165, 171–190, 308–311;
  rejection of and resistance to, in Polish
  politics and culture, 5, 22–24, 58, 86–87,
  162–163, 311; and Ukrainian population
  in Poland, 27, 78, 178, 184–185; and
  violence, 9, 12, 18, *38*, 77–78, 80–81,
  85, 156, 169–171, 178, 187, 246, 308;
  in younger generation, 27–29, 186–189;
  and anti-Zionism, 22, *38*, 39. *See also*
  Appenszlak, Jakob; Arendt, Hannah;
  Burshtin, Mikhoel; Bychowski, Gustav;
  Czapiński, Kazimierz; danger; Dmowski,
  Roman; future, outlooks on the likely East
  European Jewish; Giterman, Isaac; Golomb,
  Avrom; Hertz, Aleksander; Hirszhorn,
  Samuel; Jewish Question; Kipowa, Łucja;
  Lestschinsky, Yankev; Levinson, Avraham;
  middleman minority, Jews as; minority-
  hood; nationalism; Oberlaender, Ludwik;
  Poland; progressivism; race and racism;

antisemitism (Judeophobia, Jew-hatred) (*continued*)
realism; Right, the European radical; Right, the Polish nationalist; social theory, East European Jewish; state capture; Weinreich, Max
Appenszlak, Jakob, 57–58, 69
Arab-Jewish conflict. *See* Jewish-Palestinian conflict
Arab population of Mandate Palestine. *See* Palestinians
Arendt, Hannah, 7, 9, 327
Argentina, 42–43, 166. *See also* emigration; exitism
Aronovitsh, Ezriel, 206
Ashkenazy, Szymon, 107
Assimilation. *See* Polonization
assimilationism (Jewish self-Polonization and integrationism as ideological program): commitment to ideology of, 4, 97–98, 264; disillusionment with political promise of, 6, 33, 102, 105–107; historiography of, 30; and Palestine, 232, 252; psychic vulnerability and suffering attributed to, 72, 129–130, 196–197; Yiddishism contrasted with, 130. *See also* Alter, Leon; Bychowski, Gustav; Hertz, Aleksander; Joselewicz, Berek; Korczak, Janusz; Polish Socialist Party (PPS); Polonization; Sanacja; Tuwim, Julian; Związek Akademickiej Młodzieży Zjednoczeniowej (ZAMZ)
Astour (Tshernikhov), Mikhl, 1–7, 13, 27, 30, 104, 122, 197, 219–220, 279, 299
Auerbach, Rokhl, 4
Australia, 322. *See also* emigration; exitism
Austria, gains of the radical Right in, 27, 32, 57, 112–113, 141–142, 155, 189. *See also* Nazism; Right, the European radical
Ayzenberg, G., 50

Baden-Powell, Robert, 94, 120
Baginen (journal), 205
Balfour Declaration, 278, 316
Balibar, Etienne, 181, 352n51
Bassok, Ido, 111, 268, 321
Bastomski, Shloyme, 52

BBWR. *See* Sanacja
Będzin, 48, 88
Bełchatów, 231
Belis, Shloyme, 149
Ben-Asher, Haim, 95, 103, 106, 211–212, 218, 219, 224–225, 229, 283
Ben-Gurion, David, 49, 152, 153, 207, 275, 278, 284
Ben-Shemen Youth Village, Palestine, 233, 356n31
Bernshteyn, Yitshok, 115
Bernstein, Fritz, 175–176
Betar, 14, 93, 98, 197, 200, 207, 217–218, 221. *See also* Binyomen R.; Jabotinsky, Ze'ev; Revisionist Zionism; Zionism
Bialik, Chaim Nahman, 48–49, 152, 286–287, 291
Białystok, 88, 95, 166, 187, 189, 207
Białystok area, 18, 45, 81
Biber, Haim, 97
Bielsko, 48
Bielsk Podlaski, 16, 43, 76–77, 79, 101, 201–208. *See also* Binyomen R.
Bin (The Bee: youth movement), 103–104, 120–122, *121*. *See also* Astour (Tshernikhov), Mikhl; Diasporism; Golomb, Avrom; Ran, Leyzer; Shabad, Tsemakh; Sutzkever, Avrom; Weinreich, Max; Yiddishism
Binyomen R. (Binyomen Rotberg) [pseudonym], 16, 30, 43, 72, 75–81, 100–101, 111–112, 198–208, 219, 270–271, 285–288, 290–294, 297, 321, 328. *See also* Communism; exitism; inquiry; Palestinism / Yishuvism; realism; Weinreich, Max; youth, Polish Jewish; Zionism
Birobidzhan, Soviet Union, 43, 255, 267, 280, 318. *See also* Communism; emigration; exitism; Zionism
Black experience in Polish Jewish thought. *See* African American experience
Błaszczyk, Adam, 18
Błonie, 60–61. *See also* Burshtin, Mikhoel
Bluhm-Kwiatkowski, Aleksander, 85
Bnai Brith, 174
Borochov, Ber, 10

Brandes, Georg, 130
Brown, Sterling, 151
Brześć, 163–164
Buczacz, 54, 118
Buehler, Charlotte, 32, 139
Bund (Algemeyner yidisher arbeter bund in
    Poyln): approach to Jewish Question, 2, 9,
    15, 32–33, 36, 51, 112, 116–117, 155, 193,
    279, 317, 321, 325; critiques of, 2, 193,
    279, 323; and Diasporism, 15, 31, 104;
    Diasporist intellectuals' relationships to,
    32, 35, 120, 155, 157, 194, 261; doubts
    within and defection from, 42, 51–52, 90,
    100–105, 201, 206, 321; historiography
    of, 31, 96; optimism bred by ideology
    of, 116–117; PPS and, 23, 32, 317–318;
    reach and support of, 35, 42, 93, 96–97,
    104, 116–117, 218, 236, 283, 317–319,
    362n22; recent celebration of, 31; and
    Zionism, 209, 218, 228, 236, 273, 275, 321.
    See also Astour (Tshernikhov), Mikhl;
    Bin; class; Diasporism; Erlikh, Henryk;
    Gutgeshtalt, Hirsh; Left, Polish; Lestschinsky,
    Yankev; Marxism; Menes, Avrom; Polish
    Socialist Party (PPS); socialism; Tsukunft;
    TsYShO; Urinsky, Gershn; Uryevitsh,
    Yente; Weinreich, Max; Zilberfarb, Moyshe
Burgin, Yehiel, 311
Burshtin, Mikhoel, 67–69, 123–127,
    323–324; Bay di taykhn fun Mazovye,
    323; Goyrl (Fate), 68; Iber di khurves fun
    Ployne, 60–65, 61, 67–68, 124, 184
Bychowski, Gustav, 174
Bychowski, Jan Ryszard, 174
Byelorussian population in kresy, 78

Cahan, Ab., 240
Cała, Alina, 18, 22, 23–24, 25
Całuń, Tomasz, 163. See also Sanacja
Cammy, Justin, 140–142, 144, 147–148, 323
Case, Holly, 8
Catholic Church in Poland (approaches to
    Jewish Question in), 22–24, 310. See also
    Christianity
Catholic University, Lublin, 22
Catholic Youth League, 310

Celine, Louis–Ferdinand, 23
Certificates (allowing immigration to
    Palestine), 14, 42–43, 50–51, 94, 101, 110,
    200, 213, 215, 278, 291
Chałasiński, Józef, 28–29. See also peasants
Cherniavsky, Irith, 14–15, 94, 196, 221–223,
    227–228
children (future of, as a stake in Polish
    Jewish thought and decision-making), 40,
    298–299, 301–305. See also Druyanov,
    Alter; exitism; Lahad, Ezra; Lakerman,
    Shmuel; Urinsky, Gershn
Chile, 318. See also emigration; exitism
Chizhik, Baruch, 243
Chmielewski, Samuel, 318
Christian Democrats, 165
Christianity (and Jewish Question), 22–25,
    75, 110, 167–168, 181–182. See also
    Catholic Church in Poland
class: and Jewish communal and political
    life, 11, 14–15, 42, 51–52, 53–55, 57, 94,
    103, 113, 118, 211, 221, 232, 236, 242,
    282, 292, 303, 342n88, 345n36; in Jewish
    political and social thought, 2, 9, 32–33,
    36, 51–52, 55–56, 101, 103, 112, 118,
    121, 123–125, 155, 158, 165–171, 175,
    200, 210, 228, 234–236, 240, 242, 260,
    325; and the Jewish Question in Eastern
    Europe, 8, 13, 19, 23, 25, 26, 35, 44, 60,
    78, 112–113, 160–161, 165–166, 170, 177,
    179–181, 185–186, 264, 327. See also
    declassing; ideologies, Jewish; middleman
    minority, Jews as; poverty; socialism
colonialism and imperialism (Polish Jewish
    thought about), 184–185, 237–238,
    245–248, 262–263, 273–274, 300, 322,
    358n10. See also Jewish-Palestinian conflict;
    kresy; territorialization
Communism (Polish Jewish engagement with):
    anti-Bundism of, 55, 104; anti-Zionism
    of, 55, 226; attraction of, 14, 55; approach
    to Jewish Question of, 2, 32–33, 325;
    critiques of, 2, 55–56, 78, 142, 287–288,
    291; disillusionment with and defection
    from, 56–57, 90, 102–105, 112–113, 201,
    210, 337n87; effects of investment in

Communism (Polish Jewish engagement with) (*continued*)
ideology of, 55, 116, 203, 280, 283; historiography of, 96; Jewish religious anti-, 324; supporters of and nature of support for, 97, 100–101, 104, 116, 200–203, 206–207, 209–210, 233, 235, 280, 292; in Yiddish literature, 123, 141, 151–152; discourse about Jews and, 80, 210, 309. *See also* Binyomen R.; class; Forget-Me-Not; Greyno; ideologies, Jewish; Khatskels, Helena; Knaphays, Moyshe; Marxism; Naymark, Yoelke; socialism

community (exitism and considerations of), 256–260, 292–294, 297–298. *See also* children; realism

compensation (psychological), 139, 175, 194, 199, 289, 291; Jewish culture and, 133–137

Connelly, John, 26

conservatism, Polish, 24, 45. *See also* liberalism

conspiracy theories: Jews as subject of, 8, 21–22, 24–25, 59, 79–80, 164–165, 171, 182, 296; Zionism as subject of, 22

correspondence to/from Yishuv, 229–231

critical inquiry. *See* inquiry

Cullen, Countee, 151

culture: capacities of, as a problem of interwar Polish Jewish thought and praxis, 117, 124, 139–153, 323–325; Jewish, (as Jewish nationalist project), 7, 10, 84, 139; Jewish, (in anthropological sense) in Eastern Europe and Poland, general characteristics and trends, 3–5, 41–42, 55–75, 88–91, 93–101, 114–139, 193–220; Polish cultural sphere, 4, 22–23, 36, *38*, 98–99, 126, 148, 162–163, 174. *See also* identity, Jewish; Binyomen R.; Burshtin, Mikhoel; Diasporism; film and cinema; Grade, Chaim; Hebraism; Hebrew; ideologies, Jewish; literature; Marxism; nature; Poland; Polonization; psychology; Shneurson, Fishl; subjectivity; Sutzkever, Avrom; Vogel, Debora; Weinreich, Max; Yiddish culture and literature; Yiddishism; Zionism

Czapiński, Kazimierz, 23, 86

Czas (journal), 24, 45

Częstochowa, 48, 79–80, 88, 90, 116

Czyżew-Osada, 104, *105*, 108–110, 308

danger (in Polish Jewish political thinking and experience): Jewish sense of growing, 1–2, 5–6, 54–71, 74–83, 184–192, 254–256, 262–264; political sources of, 13, 16–17, 21–30, 44, 54–75, 77, 83; and realism, 3, 6–7, 9, 13, 31, 37–38, 71, 75–82, 84, 87, 101, 111, 154, 186–192, 195–196, 256–258, 285–298; and rise of the Right, 5, 12–13, 17–18, 25–26, 58–59, 182–190; timing of Polish Jewish recognition of, 159–160, 190. *See also* antisemitism; children; diaspora; exitism; extrapolatory thinking; future, outlooks on the likely East European Jewish; Jewish Question; middleman minority, Jews as; nationalism; Poland; realism; Right, the European radical; Right, the Polish nationalist; Zionism

Davar (newspaper), 241

declassing (mass impoverishment of Jews previously in commercial sector), 53, 55, 118, 121, 124–125, 161, 177, 264, 268, 292

Depression. *See* Great Depression

Diamond, Cora, 150

diaspora (Jewish thought about), 114, 117, 125–127, 137–140, 240–249; dispersion and minorityhood vs. territorialization and ethnic concentration, 244–249. *See also* Diasporism; Jews, East European; Jews, Polish; middleman minority, Jews as; Zionism

Diasporism: and crisis of Polish Jewish subjectivity, 114–153; critiques of, 1–2, 138, 270, 279; disillusionment with parties advocating, 102–105, 234, 280; historiography of, 30; ideology and thought of, 1, 6, 11, 13, 15, 42, 114–127, 137–139, 157, 323, 325; Jewish–Polish special relationship in ideology of, 126–127; political outlooks among supporters of, 28, 42, 114; response of, to crisis in the 1930s, 34, 114–153; romanticism about Eastern

Europe in, 360n74; scholarly and popular engagement with, 30–31; Yiddishism as cultural ideology of, 1, 42, 68, 82, 139–140; Zionism compared to, 242–245, 247–249. *See also* Bin; Bund; Burshtin, Mikhoel; diaspora; economic self-help; Giterman, Isaac; Golomb, Avrom; Jewish Society for Knowing the Land; *kasses*; Lakerman, Shmuel; Lestschinsky, Yankev; minority-hood; public health, Jewish; Shabad, Tsemakh; socialism; state, the; Sutzkever, Avrom; territorialization; Weinreich, Max; Yiddishism; Zionism

Dimentman, Leah, 110, 111

Dizhur, Il'ya, 161

Dmowski, Roman, 17, 25–26; *Świat pow-ojenny i Polska*, 59, 164–165

Dobkin, Eliahu, 277–279

Doikeyt. See Diasporism

Dollfuss, Engelbert, 79, 112, 189

Dothan, Shmuel, 320

doubt about Jewish prospects in Eastern Europe. *See* future, outlooks on the likely East European Jewish

Druyanov, Alter, 41–43, 83, 110, 113, 115, 179, 222–223, 302–303

Dynner, Glenn, 96

Dzień Polski (journal), 24, 45

East European Jewry. *See* Jews, East European

economic self-help, 82, 118–119, *119*, 249, 317–318. *See also* Burshtin, Mikhoel; declassing; Giterman, Isaac; Joint Distri-bution Committee; *kasses*; ORT; poverty; public health, Jewish; Shalit, Moyshe; Zilberfarb, Moyshe

emigration: Certificates for, to Palestine, 14, 42–43, 50–51, 94, 101, 110, 200, 213, 215, 278, 291; desire for, regardless of destination, 15, 42–43, 47, 49, 89–92, 318–319; international restrictions on, 47–48, 267; mass, 221, 229, 255, 263–264, 266, 281, 309, 311, 318–319, 322; of 1905, 11; organizations seeking to facilitate, 263–267; to Palestine, 13–15, 37, 48–49, 221–222, 229–230, 298–305, 314; political

situation as source of the need for, 263–264. *See also* Argentina; Australia; Birobidzhan; children; exitism; Giterman, Isaac; Jewish Central Emigration Society; Palestine; South Africa; Yishuv; Zionism

emissaries, Zionist. *See shlihim*

Endecja, Endeks. *See* Right, the Polish nationalist

Engel, David, 7, 332n13, 336n77

Erlikh, Henryk, 32, 36, 155

escapism: among Polish Jewish youth, 73, 115, 123, 139; realism and rational judgment vs., 194–197; Zionism portrayed as, 242–243. *See also* fantasy; psychology; realism

Ewa (journal), 166

exitism (emigrationism, politics of exit): causes of, 110, 194, 196; increasing desire for, among Polish Jewry, 6, 15, 33, 42, 73, 88–92, 203, 319; individual vs. communal considerations and, 256–260, 292–294, 297–298; turn to Zionism and, 88–92, 102–103, 106–107, 203, 218, 250, 252, 276; Jewish Question and, 110–113, 276; as last-resort solution to 1930s crisis, 38, 42, 194, 252, 255–259, 263, 266, 282, 314, 319; transcending the diaspora-emigration-Zionism divide, 281–284; youth's embrace of, 103, 194, 293, 297–298. *See also* Binyomen R.; children; community; danger; emigration; Faygenberg, Rokhl; future, outlooks on the likely East European Jewish; Giterman, Isaac; Glatshteyn, Yankev; Hehalutz; ideologies, Jewish; inquiry; Jewish Central Emigration Society; Palestine; Polner, Majer; Tartakover, Aryeh; Urinsky, Gershn; Yishuv; Zionism

extrapolatory thinking, 184–192, 270, 273–276, 312. *See also* danger, future, outlooks on the likely East European Jewish; realism; social theory, East European Jewish

fantasy: as escapism vs. as a source of social energy, 242–243. *See also* subjectivity

fascism, 2, 56, 79, 185, 188, 219, 289. *See also* Austria; Germany; Right, the European radical

Faygenberg, Rokhl (Rachel), 15, *16*, 30, 43, 160, 172, 193–194, 219, 228
Faynshteyn, Mikhoel, 54
feminism, 166
Fifth Aliyah, 37, 94–96, 110, 214, 221, 223, 228, 229, 231, 253, 269, 333n26. *See also* Hehalutz; Palestine; Yishuv; Zionism
film and cinema, 36, 73, 77
Fisk University, 128
Folkstsaytung (journal), 209, 228
Forget-Me-Not (pseudonym), 55–56
Forverts (newspaper), 238, 240
Fourth Aliyah, 49, 221, 233, 248, 259, 269. *See also* Palestine; Yishuv; Zionism
Frankel, David, 110
Frankel, Jonathan, 12
Frayhayt, 39, *105*, 205, 206, 208–209, 283–284. *See also* Poalei Tsion Right; Zionism
Frayland (journal), 280
Frayland-Lige, 208, 260–261, 279–281, 299. *See also* Territorialism
Fraynd (newspaper), 209
Free-loan programs. *See* economic self-help; *kasses*
Freemasonry (in conspiracy theories), 22, 59, 164–165
Freud, Sigmund, 94, 173–174. *See also* psychology
Fridlander, Yosef, 106
Friedman, Filip, 124
Fuks, Tadeusz, 77, 112
future, outlooks on the likely East European Jewish: and decisions about family and children, 40, 298–299, 301–305; conviction of likely bad outcomes as common and spreading among Jews, 5–6, 12–17, 32–33, 41–55, 88–96, 100–110, 113–115, 123–124, 128, 154, 194–195, 199–202, 213, 235, 253–254; concrete factors and developments shaping conviction of likely bad outcomes in the early 1930s, 17–30, 44–45, 75–81; conviction of likely bad outcomes deriving from political experience and analysis of political and social developments in Poland and Europe, 1–2,

5–7, 17–19, 31–33, 34–35, 44–45, 57–87, 91–92, 110–113, 151–156, 161, 172, 177–181, 184–190, 194–195, 197, 219–220, 253, 255–256, 263–264; in the late imperial period, 9–12; and extrapolatory thinking, 1–2, 159, 184–192, 219–220, 262–263, 269–270, 287–305; and Yiddish literature, 139–140; and Zionism, 14, 42, 88–92, 100–103, 106–107, 203, 218, 250, 252, 276–279, 281–282, 287–292, 302–305. *See also* antisemitism; children; danger; diaspora; exitism; extrapolatory thinking; ideologies, Jewish; inquiry; Jewish Question; Marxism; middleman minority, Jews as; minorityhood; progressivism; realism; social theory, East European Jewish; Zionism
futurelessness. *See* danger; future, outlooks on the likely East European Jewish

Gafni, Sarah (née Strausberg), 94
Gal-Ed, Efrat, 34
Gazeta Polska (newspaper), 28
Gazeta Żywiecka (newspaper), 21
gender (as a factor in Polish Jewish political culture and thinking), 88, 199–200, 213, 225, 228, 304
General Jewish Labor Bund. *See* Bund
Ger, Gur, Góra-Kalwaria. *See* Hasidism
German Jews (in Polish Jewish thought), 175, 294–297
Germany: events in, 1–2; German anti-fascist thought, 167–168; German Jews, 294–297. *See also* German Jews; Nazism
Gershom, A., 250
Geyar, Zelig, 282–284
Giddens, Anthony, 238
Giterman, Isaac (Yitshok), 28, 48, 81–83, *81*, 106–107, 113, 117–120, *119*, 179, 253
Glatshteyn, Yankev, *Ven Yash iz gekumen*, 254–257, 285, 287
Goethe, Johann Wolfgang von, 149
Goldman, Emma, 240
Goldszmit, Henryk. *See* Korczak, Janusz
Golomb, Avrom, 103–104, 114, 138, 156, 176, 248, 251, 299

Gordon, A. D., 94
Gordonia youth movement, 103, 106. *See also* Zionism
Gotlib, Yehoshua, 138
Grabski, Władysław, 66
Grade, Chaim, 140–151, 153, 323, 326; "Baym shayn fun der levone," 143–146; "Ikh zing fun shney badektn barg arunter," 143–144, 146–147, 149; "Vin," 141–142; "Velt in nayntsn fir un draysik," 141; "Yehezkel," 323; "Yo," 143–150; *Yo*, 142–149, 323
Great Depression: effects of, 25, 44, 53–55, 118–119; in relation to political developments as source of 1930s crisis for Jews, 16–17, 25–29, 44–45, 55–57, 75–76, 83, 155–156, 177. *See also* antisemitism; Binyomen R.; class; declassing; Jewish Question; Krzywicki, Ludwik; Marxism; Poland; politics, Jewish; poverty
Greenberg, Gershon, 324
Greyno (pseudonym), 116, 210d
Grinboym, Yitzhak, 46–47, 60, 69, 156, 158, 168–172, 179, 182, 251, 277–279, 281–282, 287, 291, 319
Grodno, 204, 285–286, 322
Grodno Tarbut school, 205, 207, 285
Grodzenski, Rabbi Hayim Oyzer, 363n45
Grott, Bogumił, 19
Gura, Yitzhak, 104–105
Gutgeshtalt, Hirsh, 117, 140, 141
Gutman, Shoyl, 281

Habas, Brakha, 215. *See also* Hebraism; Shlimovits (Shalev), Miriam
Hagen, William, 28, 65, 82
Ha-Oved, 213
Harkavy, Alexander, 128
Hartglas, Apollinary, 251–253
Ha-Shomer ha-Tsair, 94, 199, 204, 207, 212, 282–283
Hasidism (and Polish Jewish political life), 15, 32–33, 94, 96–98, 102, 104–105, 108–111, 193, 230, 320–321, 357n48. *See also* Agudes Yisroel; Alter, Avrom Mordkhe (Gerer Rebbe); Czyżew-Osada; Druyanov,

Alter; Frankel, David; Mincberg, Leib; Orthodoxy; Shapiro, Rabbi Kalonymous Kalmish (Piaseczner Rebbe); Vaserman, Rabbi Elkhonen; Warsaw
Haynt (newspaper), 138, 151–152, 227, 228, 232, 234
Hebraism: as a centerpiece of ideologically serious Zionism, 49, 93, 215–216, 243; indifference to, among Zionists as mark of exitist and political-realism motivations over ideological motivations, 49, 91, 200, 216, 285–286; institutions of, 103, 106, 205, 207, 222–223. *See also* Binyomen R.; culture; Shlimovits (Shalev), Miriam; Zionism
Hebrew (language and culture in Polish Jewish society), 90, 93, 204, 211–212, 285, 360n53
Hehalutz, *216*; attractions and motivations for joining, 49–51, 90–91, 94–95, 101, 102, 103, 199–200, 203, 212–213, 218–219, 289–291; Hasidim and, 109; interest of Diasporists in model of, 120; and kibbutz movement in Palestine, 49–50; political involvement of, 39; popularity of, 14, 49–50, 88, 221; reports of *shlihim* about Polish, 88–97, 105, 107–108, 211–218, 224–225; Zionist ideology of, 49–50, 94. *See also* exitism; Hehalutz ha-Tsair; *shlihim*; Zionism
Hehalutz ha-Tsair, 95, 103, 106, 211, 213, 225, 283–284. *See also* Hehalutz; Frayhayt; *shlihim*; youth, Polish Jewish; Zionism
Heller, Daniel, 28, 98, 196–197, 223, 224
Helman, Yaakov, 320
Herder, Johann Gottfried, 151
Hertz, Aleksander, 19–20, 24–25, 29, 311
Hirszhorn, Samuel, 58–59, 69, 160–162, 172
Histadrut, 238, 239–242, 250. *See also* Weinreich, Max; Zionism
historiography, 2–5, 7–8, 13, 30–31, 92–93, 96–99, 196, 306–312, 317, 325–328
Hitahdut, 284
Hitler, Adolf, 1, 132, 154, 232, 255
Hughes, Langston, 151

identity, Jewish: commitments to, rendered irrelevant by political exigency, 39, 256–257, 276–277, 281, 285–287, 301–302, 316; chosen and unchosen, 7, 127–139. *See also* Binyomen R.; culture; danger; exitism; ideologies, Jewish; Lakerman, Shmuel; politics, Jewish

ideologies, Jewish (and camps, main Jewish political, in Poland and Eastern Europe): adherence to one of the, 4, 32, 93–94, 96–99; and presumption of Jewish agency, 10–12; skepticism and skeptical inquiry regarding claims of, search for alternatives to, and turn to forms of exitism or Zionism-as-Yishuvism, 1–2, 7, 13–15, 31–37, 88–92, 93–96, 99–113, 193–220, 223–253, 267–298, 303–305; transcending the diaspora-emigration-Zionism divide, 281–284. *See also* agency, Jewish; assimilationism; Diasporism; exitism; future, outlooks on the likely East European Jewish; identity, Jewish; inquiry; liberalism; Orthodoxy; Palestinism / Yishuvism; progressivism; realism; socialism; social theory, East European Jewish; Zionism

imperialism. *See* colonialism and imperialism

inquiry (in Polish Jewish political culture): into political situation, 30, 37, 195–220; as a praxis, 37, 203–218; about Yishuv, 224–233. *See also* Binyomen R.; youth, Polish Jewish

Instytut Gospodarstwa Społecznego, 25

integrationism. *See* assimilationism

Jabotinsky, Ze'ev, 319

Jackiewicz, Stepan, 77, 112

Jacobs, Jack, 96

Jewish Agency, 14, 106–107, 278

Jewish Central Emigration Society (YEAS), 47, 263–267, 277, 279, 284, 319

Jewish National Fund, 41, 222

Jewish-Palestinian conflict, 37, *38*, 39, 236–237, 250, 273–275, 299–301, 316, 320. *See also* colonialism and imperialism; Jewish Question; Kosover, Mordkhe; Lakerman, Shmuel; Levita, Lova;

nationalism; Palestine; Qassam, Izz ad-Din al-; self-defense; Tshernikhov, Yoysef; Weinreich, Max; Zionism

Jewish people, the (in Jewish thought): cultural compensatory resources available to, 133–137; and national oppression, 152; positive identity being replaced by sense of stigma, 131–133; as worldwide diasporic community, 114, 126–127, 138. *See also* African American experience; culture; East European Jewry; Golomb, Avrom; identity, Jewish; Latski-Bertoldi, Zeev-Volf; minorityhood; nationalism; Polish Jewry; subjectivity

Jewish Problem. *See* anti-Semitism; Jewish Question

Jewish Question, the: essential tensions in Jewish political thought concerning, 6, 306–307, 322; in Europe, 8, 13; and individual exit, 110–113, 255, 263–267, 322; Jewish confrontations with, 2, 6–13, 56–85, 154–192, 312, 318–322; in Polish political culture, 5, 8, 18–30, 44–45, 82–87, 160–161, 188, 307–312; Zionism as a partial answer to, 268–305. *See also* antisemitism; danger; future, outlooks on the likely East European Jewish; middleman minority, Jews as; minorityhood; nationalism; Zionism

Jewish Society for Knowing the Land (ZTK; Żydowskie Towarzystwo Krajoznawcze), 84–86, 124–125. *See also* Burshtin, Mikhoel; Diasporism

Jewish Workers' Party (YAP), 218, 226. *See also* socialism

Jews, East European: characteristics and historical trajectory general to, including Polish Jewry, 1–3, 8–12, 308; historiography of, 3, 7–8, 30–31, 306–308; Jewish sociological and political analysis concerning situation of, including Polish Jewry, 114, 154–157, 174–181, 184–187, 320–321. *See also* antisemitism; culture; Jewish people, the; Jewish Question; Jews, Polish; ideologies, Jewish; Poland; politics, Jewish; Yiddish culture and literature

Jews, Polish: characteristics and situation of, circa 1918, 1930, and 1935, 2, 4, 12, 14, 26, 46–55, 73, 113, 200–201; and children's future, 254, 298–305; constitutional rights of, 5; coup of 1926 and, 13, 17, 44; cultural habits of, 73; economic self-help of, 118, 317–318; emigration to Palestine of, 13–15, 37, 48–49, 221–222, 229–230, 298–305, 314; historiography of, 4–5, 13, 92–93, 96–99, 196, 307–312, 317, 325–328; ideologies and/vs. changing political views of, 1–2, 4–8, 13–17, 30–40, 41–46, 72, 82–83, 88–113, 145, 196, 200–201, 249–253; individual vs. communal considerations among, 39–40, 195–196, 256–260, 292–294, 297–298; in interwar period, 1–8, 307–308; minority rights for, 46–47, 138; political resources of, 1–3, 6, 7, 9–11, 13–14, 17, 29–38, 194–195, 220, 256–305, 313–316; Polonization of, 4–6, 72, 84, 97–98, 195–196; in post-1935 period, 316–328; poverty in, 48, 53–55; secularization of, 107–108; subjectivity of, 34, 114–142. *See also* antisemitism; assimilationism; culture; exitism; future, outlooks on the likely East European Jewish; ideologies, Jewish; inquiry; Jewish Question; Jews, East European; literature; minorityhood; Orthodoxy; Poland; politics, Jewish; Polonization; socialism; subjectivity; youth, Polish Jewish; Zionism
Jeziorski, Ireneusz, 21
Jezreel Valley, 95
Johnson, Helen, 151
Joint Distribution Committee, 48, 81, 117–118
Joselewicz, Berek, 66–67
Jude, Der (journal), 167

Kagan, Moyshe, 54
Kahan-Virgily, Arkady, 194
Kalisz, 48, 88, 90
Kalmanovitsh, Sholem. *See* Luria, Shalom
Kalmanovitsh, Zelig, 103, 280, 324
Kaplansky, Volf, 204–205

kasses (microloan institutions), psychological and political effects, 118–119. *See also* Diasporism; economic self-help; Giterman, Isaac
Kassow, Samuel, 4, 34, 98, 99, 323
Kazimierz-Dolny, 254, 257
Khatskels, Helena, 233, 240
Kibbutz Ein Harod, 215
kibbutzim, 49–50, 225, 230–231, 240, 245, 272, 304
Kielce, 18, 79, 91
Kielce region, 18, 45, 79, 80, 163
Kijek, Kamil, 18, 24, 37, 72, 79–81, 87, 98, 129, 196–197, 223
Kipowa, Łucja, 19–20, 24
Kishinev pogrom, 9
Kleck, 211, 283
Kleinbaum, Mojżesz, 187–190, 320
Kliger, Moshe, 213–214
Kligsberg, Moyshe, 51
Knaphays, Moyshe, 116
Kobryń, 283
Kolbe, Shabtai, 207
Kolki, 217
Koluszki, 95
Kondratieff cycles, 157
Koneczny, Feliks, 21
KOP. *See* Korpus Ochrony Pogranicza
Kopit, Yisrolik, 107–108, 214–215, 225–226
Korczak, Janusz (penname of Henryk Goldszmit), 22–23, 99
Korpus Ochrony Pogranicza (KOP; Border Protection Corps), 19–21
Kosover, Mordkhe, 317
Kosoy, Y., 219
Kowel, 54, 213
Krah, Franziska, 167
Kraków, 45, 48, 83, 84, 94, 97, 284
kresy (Poland's eastern borderlands), 21, 43, 91, 102, 104, 184–185, 224, 282, 318
Krzywicki, Ludwik, 25, 66
Krzywiec, Grzegorz, 18, 25
Kula, Marcin, 229
Kurier Poznański (newspaper), 22
Kuznitz, Cecile, 34

Labor Zionism, 49, 152, 264, 266, 278–279, 280, 283

Lahad, Ezra (né Lakerman), 299, 301, *302*

Lakerman, Basya, 299, *302*

Lakerman, Shmuel, 298–301, *300*, *302*

Landau-Czajka, Anna, 4, 8, 24, 26, 27

Landkentenish/Krajoznawstwo (journal), 85–86

Lapin, Chava, 207

Latski-Bertoldi, Zeev-Volf, 151–157, 191

League for a Laboring Land of Israel, 109, 200

Lebenzon, Micha Yosef, 285

Lebiedziew, 211

Left, Jewish. *See* anarchism; Binyomen R.; Bund; Communism; Forget-Me-Not; Gutgeshtalt, Hirsh; Marxism; socialism; Poalei Tsion Left; Poalei Tsion Right; progressivism; socialism

Left, Polish, 23, 97, 116, 165–166, 178, 186, 311. *See also* assimilationism; Communism; Hertz, Aleksander; Lestschinsky, Yankev; Marxism; Polish Socialist Party (PPS); socialism

Lehmann, Siegfried, 233

Lestschinsky, Yankev, 15, 27–28, 30, 35–36, 43, 49, 154–159, *155*, 177–179, 184–187, 191, 195–196, 260–263, 271, 285, 301, 328

Levin, Gershon, 171–172

Levin, Moyshe, 325

Levinson, Avraham, 156, 158, 162–168, 172, 182–183

Levita, Lova, 53–54, 88–93, *89*, 213, 228, 250, 304

Levita, Nimrod, *89*

Lewin, Rabbi Arn, 321

liberalism, 2, 4, 9–11, 24, 27, 128, 160, 173, 177, 182, 270, 324; and sites of Jewish liberal-Zionist dialogue, 174–175. *See also* Bernstein, Fritz; Bnai Brith; Bychowski, Gustav; conservatism, Polish; Oberlaender, Ludwik; progressivism; Zionism

Lichten, Joseph, 98

Lida, 88, 284, 311

Literarishe Bleter (journal), 195

literature (belles lettres): African American, 151–153; Polish, 23, 98–99, 126, 148, 162–163; Yiddish, 60–68, 139–152. *See also* culture; Yiddish culture and literature; Yiddishism

Łódź, 47–48, 66–67, 84, 115, 140, 166, 209, 260, 321

Łódź area, 18, 45, 95, 231

Łomża, 215

Łomża area, 214–215

Łowicz, 85–86

Lublin, 22, 230

Lublin region, 45, 293

Luck (Lutsk, town), 213, 321

Luria, Shalom, 280

Lux (pseudonym), 132–133, 137, 151–152

Lwów, 18, 58, 83, 97, 99, 169–171, 178–179

Malakh, Leyb, 233

Manchuria, 318. *See also* emigration; exitism

Mann, Michael, 238

Mapai (political party), 153, 235, 284

Marcus, Joseph, 319

Markowski, Florian, 80

Marxism: ideology of, as source of optimism and praxis, 6, 10, 12, 32, 35, 112, 116–117, 155, 157–158; and right-wing success in the 1930s, 35, 55–56, 113, 185; heterodox, 10, 34, 116, 155–156, 194; and social analysis, 157–158, 184–185; Zionism and, 10, 94. *See also* Bund; Communism; declassing; Erlikh, Henryk; Greyno; Gutgeshtalt, Hirsh; Lestschinsky, Yankev; middleman minority, Jews as; poverty; Rozin, Avrom; socialism; social theory, East European Jewish

Masaryk, Tomáš, 296

masculinity. *See* Zionism

Matz, Hersh, 324–325

Mayer, Dovid, 319

Mazyl, Nakhman, 195

McKay, Claude, 151

Meirkevitsh, Avrom, 208–209

Meltzer, Natan, 265

Melzer, Emanuel, 28, 310

men and boys, Jewish, as particular kinds of social actors. *See* gender; masculinity

Mendelsohn, Ezra, 54–55, 196

Mendelson, Shloyme, 51

Menes, Avrom, 157–158

Meyerovitsh, Sima, 104

Mickiewicz, Adam, 162

Middle Eastern and North African Jewries, historiography of, 3–4, 30, 322

middleman minority, Jews as, 8, 25, 35, 179–181, 263–264, 327

Miedziński, Bogusław, 28, 189

Miesięcznik Żydowski (journal), 175, 176, 181

Mikhalevitsh, Beynish, 104

Miłosz, Czesław, 24, 311

Mincberg, Leib, 321

Minorities Treaty, 27, 138

minorityhood: as political condition, 2–3, 7, 8, 25, 35, 179–181, 263–264, 327; as status, experience and consciousness, in Polish Jewish thought, 71, 127–139, 152–153. *See also* African American experience; culture; diaspora; psychology; subjectivity; Weinreich, Max

modernity: art, myth, and secular, 148; East European Jewry and, 6–12; scholarship on Jews and, 306. *See also* culture; ideologies, Jewish; minorityhood

Modras, Ronald, 22, 24

Moment (newspaper), 208, 228, 231, 318

Morgenshtern (sports club), 56

Moszczeńska, Iza, 166

Mucha (journal), 38, 39

Murshteyn, Shmuel, 52

Myśl Narodowa (newspaper), 22, 59

Nalevke, Sane, 206

NARA, 77, 79, 112, 187

Narutowicz, Gabriel, 26

Nasz Przegląd (newspaper), 57–58, 223–224, 227–228

Nathans, Benjamin, 311

National Democracy. *See* Right, the Polish nationalist

nationalism: analysis of, in Polish Jewish thought, 12–13, 35, 57, 154–159, 179–183, 185–186, 190–191; division within Polish, 5; inclusive tradition in Polish, 5, 12–13, 19–20, 22–23, 28, 36, 56, 162–163; right-wing and antisemitic traditions and trajectory of, in Poland and Europe, 5, 12–13, 17–19, 24–26, 29, 58–59, 66–67, 77, 79–81, 159, 161–172, 181, 183, 189, 191, 308–311. *See also* antisemitism; Jewish Question; Oberlaender, Ludwik; Poland; Right, the Polish nationalist; Zionism

national minorities in Poland, 5, 7, 21; hostility toward, 19–21, 29; regionalism and, 126; rights of, 46–47. *See also* antisemitism; minorityhood; Poland; politics, Jewish; Right, the Polish nationalist; Sanacja; Ukrainians

National Workers Party, 165

nation-state (Polish Jewish thought about), 7, 179–181, 320–321

nature (in Polish Jewish thought), 84–86, 144–151, 124–126, 255, 257. *See also* culture

Naymark, Yoelke, 201, 207

Nazism: exitism linked to rise and easy victory of, in Germany, 113, 253; and the Jewish Question in Polish political culture, 18, 27–28, 187–188; persecution of Jews by, 255; and Polish Jewish thought, 1–2, 26–27, 32, 56–57, 75, 113, 139–141, 155, 295–297. *See also* Błaszczyk, Adam; Right, the European radical

New Jew (of Zionism), 15, 101, 224

Niemojewski, Andzrej, 166

Nowersztern, Avraham, 140–141, 147

Nowogródek, 108

Nowogródek region, 45

Nowostaw, 216

Nowy Sącz, 95

Oberlaender, Ludwik, 156, 158, 181–183, 190–191

Oberle, Eric, 39

Obóz Wielkiej Polski (OWP; Camp for Greater Poland). *See* Right, the Polish nationalist

Opatoshu, Yoysef, 126, 233
Oppenheim, Yisrael, 94
Ordonówna, Hanka, 232
ORT (industrial training organization), 54, 120, 177, 180
Orthodoxy (traditionalist Jewry as an ideological camp in Polish Jewish life): approach to Polish Jewish situation advocated by spiritual and political leaders of, 32–33, 289, 320–321; changing political outlooks and rising political disillusionment among adherents of, 41, 102, 104–105, 107–111, 193; changing relationship to Zionism and the Yishuv within, 94, 104–105, 108–111, 193, 230, 320–321, 357n48; historiography of, as cultural and political force in Polish Jewish life, 4, 6, 30, 96–97; in post–1935 period, 324; and psychic resilience, 72; and theodicy, 289, 324. See also Agudes Yisroel; Alter, Avrom Mordkhe (Gerer Rebbe); Druyanov, Alter; Grodzenski, Rabbi Hayim Oyzer; Hasidism; Lewin, Rabbi Arn; Mincberg, Leib; Rotenberg, Rabbi Mordechai of Antwerp; Sorotzkin, Rabbi Zalman; Shapiro, Rabbi Kalonymous Kalmish (Piaseczner Rebbe); Vaserman, Rabbi Elkhonen
Osowa Wyszka, 217–218, 267
Ostrowiec-Świętokrzyski, 163
Otwock, 193
Oyerbakh, Rokhl. See Auerbach, Rokhl
OZON (Camp of National Unity), 160, 309–310

Palestine: analytical, empirical, non-Zionist, and post–anti-Zionist inquiry by Polish Jews into realities and possibilities of Jewish life in, 6–7, 222–253; Arab (Palestinian) population of, in Polish Jewish thought, 37, 224, 226, 235–237, 239, 250, 273–275, 299–301, 316; assimilationists and, 232, 252; economic investment in, 269–271, 275–276; interethnic violence in, 37, 38, 88, 236, 245, 248, 250, 273–275, 299–301, 316; growth and consolidation of Jewish national community and polity (Yishuv) in, 6–7, 229–238, 261–262, 269, 275–276, 333n26; and Jewish statehood, 236–238, 246, 249–250, 320–321; language question in, 243; 1905; Mandate, 14, 37, 48, 193, 221, 314, 316–317, 319–320; as partial solution to crisis facing Polish Jews, 232–233, 258–260, 267–277, 287–305; partition proposal for, 320–321; Polish Jews' emigration to, 13–15, 37, 48–49, 221–222, 229–230, 298–305, 314; self-defense in, 240, 243, 245–246, 250–251; tourism to, 231–233; travelogues about, 226–227, 234–249, 258–259, 268–269, 271–277, 294–297. See also Dobkin, Eliahu; Golomb, Avrom; Grinboym, Yitzhak; Jewish-Palestinian conflict; Lakerman, Shmuel; Mincberg, Leib; Palestinians; Palestinism/Yishuvism; Shabad, Tsemakh; territorialization; Tshernikhov, Yoysef; Weinreich, Max; Yishuv; Zionism
Palestinians (Arab community of Mandate Palestine): Polish Jewish thought about and encounters with, 224, 226, 235–237, 239, 250, 273–275, 299–301, 316. See also Jewish-Palestinian conflict; Lakerman, Shmuel; Palestine; Qassam, Izz ad-Din al-; Weinreich, Max; Zionism
Palestinism/Yishuvism, 14, 37, 251–253. See also children; exitism; Yishuv; Zionism
peasants (Poland): economic hardships of, in interwar Poland, 25, 54, 78; ideological and political sentiments of, 25, 28–29, 30, 65–67; and Jews, 18, 24–25, 28–29, 63–67, 78–79, 188; right–wing nationalism in Poland and, 18, 24, 79–80. See also Binyomen R.; Burshtin, Mikhoel; Chałasiński, Józef; Grabski, Władysław; Krzywicki, Ludwik; Piast Party
Perelman, Abram, 115
Peretz, Y. L., 11–12
Peretz School, Prużana, 102–103, 106
Peru, 318. See also emigration; exitism
pessimism. See danger; future, outlooks on the likely East European Jewish
Piast Party, 65

Piątnica, 214
Pickhan, Gertrud, 96
Piekuty, 308
Pieracki, Bronisław, 79
Piłsudski, Józef, 5, 13, 17, 23, 27, 98, 160, 307
Pinsker, Leon, *Autoemancipation*, 9–10
Pinski, Hershl, 230–231
Pinsk region, 230
Plach, Eva, 23, 44
Płock, 115
Poalei Tsion Left, 96, 103, 105, 109, 208, 210, 345n43. *See also* Marxism; Ringelblum, Emanuel; socialism; Tomszow, Jezik
Poalei Tsion Right, 207, 208, 283–284. *See also* Frayhayt; Zionism
poetry. *See* culture; literature
Polakiewicz, Moyshe, 46–47, 51
Poland: culture and literature of, and Polish Jews, 4, 22–23, 36, *38*, 98–99, 126, 148, 162–163, 174; as divided polity and society, 4–5, 8, 12–13, 17, 26, 44–45, 57–60; economic underdevelopment, underemployment, poverty, and Great Depression in, 8, 17, 25–27, 29–30, 48, 53–55, 118; ethnonationalist, intolerant, and anti-Jewish strains and trends in political culture of, 5, 18–22, 24–26, 44–45, 58–60, 65–67, 76–82, 85–86, 110–112, 165–166, 177–190, 308–312; Jewish population, general characteristics and situation in, circa 1918, 1930, and 1935, 2, 4, 12, 14, 26, 46–55, 73, 113, 200–201; Jewish Question and antisemitism in, 5, 8, 18–30, *38*, *39*, 60, 62, 75–86, 111–112, 172, 177–190, 309–312; the Left (Polish socialism) in, 23, 32, 57, 86, 97, 116, 186–187; map of, *xii*; moderate camp (Sanacja-supporting) in, 23, 24, 56, 57, 80, 163; multiethnic society of, 4–5; national minorities in, 20–21, 184–185; OZON, 308–312; religious actors (political views and influence of), 22–24, 26; the Right (National Democracy, organized ethnonationalist movement) in, 5, 8, 12–13, 17–19, 25–26, 44–45, 79–86, 164–165, 168–172; and Sanacja/Piłsudski regime, 5, 9, 17–18, 23–24, 28, 57–60, 80–83, 163–164, 188–19; tolerance and opposition to antisemitism in politics and culture of, 5, 22–23, 56, 86, 73, 98–99, 116, 162–163, 310–312; Ukrainian population in, 20–21, 27, 78, 178, 184–185; youth and right-wing politics in, 27–28, 79–80, 111, 186–189. *See also* antisemitism; Będzin; Bełchatów; Białystok; Bielsko; Bielsk Podlaski; Błonie; Brześć; Buczacz; Burshtin, Mikhoel; Catholic Church in Poland; Częstochowa; Czyżew-Osada; Giterman, Isaac; Grinboym, Yitzhak; Grodno; Hertz, Aleksander; Jewish Question; Jews, Polish; Kalisz; Kazimierz-Dolny; Kielce; Kipowa, Łucja; Kleck; Kobryń; Kolki; Koluszki; Kowel; Kraków; *kresy*; Krzywicki, Ludwik; Lebiedziew; Left, Polish; Lestschinsky, Yankev; Lida; Łódź; Łomża; Łowicz; Luck; middleman minority, Jews as; Levinson, Avraham; Nowogródek; Nowy Sącz; Osowa Wyszka; Ostrowiec-Świętokrzyski; Otwock; peasants; Piątnica; Piekuty; Płock; Prużana; Raduń; Right, the Polish nationalist; Równe; Sanacja; Siedlce, Sieradz; Smorgonie; Sosnowiec; state, the; Stołpce; Tarnów; Warsaw; Wilno; Włodzimierzec; Zawiercie; Żywiec
Polish Jewry. *See* Jews, Poland
Polish Socialist Party (PPS), 23, 26, 32, 165–166, 188, 310, 317. *See also* Czapiński, Kazimierz; Left, Polish
political ideologies. *See* ideologies, Jewish
politics, Jewish: critical inquiry and, 193–194, 196–220, 223–253; of existing camps, movements, and parties vs. skepticism about existing forms of, and search for alternative to, 33, 36–37, 88–113; as expression of ideals and ideology vs. as expression of assessment of Jewish situation and capacities to affect same, 1–2, 255, 267–298, 303–305; and future of Jewish children, 297–305; individual vs. communal considerations in, 39–40, 255–267, 292–294, 297–305; Jewish

politics, Jewish (*continued*)
  identity and cultural commitments overshadowed by exigencies of, 256–257,
  276–282, 285–287, 316; and the question
  of Jewish agency and resources, 1–2,
  35–36, 194–196, 258–263, 287–305.
  See also agency, Jewish; assimilationism;
  Binyomen R.; children; community; Diasporism; Druyanov, Alter; exitism; Faygenberg, Rokhl; future, outlooks on the
  likely East European Jewish; identity,
  Jewish; ideologies, Jewish; inquiry; Levita,
  Lova; liberalism; minorityhood; Orthodoxy; progressivism; realism; self-defense;
  Shlimovits (Shalev), Miriam; socialism;
  social theory, East European Jewish;
  Weinreich, Max; Zionism
politics of exit. *See* exitism
Polner, Majer, 318, 322
Polonization, 4–6, 68, 72–73, 84, 90–91,
  93, 97–99, 106, 126, 130, 164, 174, 196,
  313. *See also* assimilationism
Polonsky, Antony, 28, 310, 319
Porter, Brian, 18, 25
Pound, Ezra, 23
poverty, 48, 53–55, 118
PPS. *See* Polish Socialist Party (PPS)
progressivism: confidence in inevitability of
  historical progress and temporary character
  of political reaction as dominant strain in
  modern East European Jewish thought, 6,
  9–12, 162, 177, 182, 187, 190; critiques
  of political assumptions of, 2, 9–11,
  34–35, 165–166, 190; and social theory,
  35; and socialism, 10; and Zionism, 162.
  See also agency, Jewish; economic self-
  help; Hertz, Aleksander; ideologies, Jewish;
  Korczak, Janusz; Levinson, Avraham;
  liberalism; Marxism; Matz, Hersh; public
  health, Jewish; realism; Rozin, Avrom;
  Vulman, Leon; Zilberfarb, Moyshe
Prokop-Janiec, Eugenia, 99
Protocols of the Elders of Zion, 21, 25
Prużana, 41–43, 95, 102–103, 106, 282–283,
  304–305
Przegląd Katolicki (journal), 22

Przegląd Społeczny (journal), 148
psychology (as approach and concern in
  Polish Jewish thought): of antisemitism,
  159, 167–168, 173–176; and minority
  condition, 127–139; of Polish Jewish youth,
  127–139, 194, 199–200. *See also* Bernstein,
  Fritz; Bychowski, Gustav; compensation;
  escapism; fantasy; Freud, Sigmund; Golomb,
  Avrom; Perelman, Abram; realism;
  Shneurson, Fishl; subjectivity; Weinreich,
  Max
public health, Jewish (as form of activism),
  54, 82, 299, *302*, 324–325. *See also*
  Diasporism; Lakerman, Shmuel; poverty;
  progressivism; Shabad, Tsemakh;
  Vulman, Leon

Qassam, Izz ad-Din al-, 245

Rabon, Yisroel, 140
race and racism, 130–133, 137, 152, 173,
  322, 348n30
Raduń, 108
Ran, Leyzer, 345n47
rationality. *See* realism
Ravitsh, Meylekh, 68, 140, 280–282, 285
realism (in interwar Jewish political thought):
  as attempt to recalibrate Jewish politics
  around dual recognition of rising danger
  and of limited Jewish powers to meet
  same, as opposed to proceeding from
  doctrinal and ideological commitments,
  2–3, 6–11, 31–32, 256, 258–259, 262,
  287–305; about dangers to Jewish well-
  being, 3, 6–7, 9, 13, 31, 37–38, 40, 71,
  75–82, 84, 87, 101, 111, 154, 186–192,
  195–196, 256–258, 285–298; and limits
  of Jewish agency and resources, 31–32,
  36, 38, 141, 257–259, 262, 290–294;
  escapism and fantasy vs., 194, 196–197;
  in history, 31, 337nn82–83; intellectuals
  and, 156–157; and limits of Jewish agency
  and resources, 31–32, 36, 38, 141,
  257–259, 290–294; of Polish Jewish youth,
  197–220; transcending the diaspora-
  emigration–Zionism divide, 281–284.

See also Binyomen R.; danger; exitism; future, outlooks on the likely East European Jewish; Lakerman, Shmuel; Mincberg, Leib; Shabad, Tsemakh; Tshernikhov, Yoysef; Weinreich, Max; Zionism

regionalism, 126

Reinhold (Rinot), Hanoch, 296–297

Revisionist Zionism, 93, 101, 222. *See also* Betar; Jabotinsky; Zionism

Reyzen, Zalman, 97

Right, the European radical: Jewish analysis of the rise of, in interwar Europe, 1–2, 27, 32, 56, 112, 114, 141, 154–156, 174–175, 181–183, 219. *See also* Austria; fascism; Forget-me-Not; Germany; Lestschinsky, Yankev; Nazism; Oberlaender, Ludwik; Right, the Polish nationalist; Rozin, Avrom

Right, the Polish nationalist (National Democracy, the organized Polish ethnonationalist camp), 5, 8, 12–13, 17–19, 21–22, 25–26, 29, 44–46, 58–60, 79–82, 85–86, 111, 164–165, 308–311; eliminationist antisemitism and "the Jewish Question" in program of, 18, 23, 45, 58–59, 77, 79–82, 159, 161–172, 181, 183, 191; Jewish experience and analysis of, 74, 77, 116, 156, 160–165, 168–172, 181, 183, 191, 246, 254–255; resonance of ideology of, in wider society, 18–21, 23–24, 25–26, 27–29, 36, 45, 59–60, 67, 81, 181, 309–311; late nineteenth–century roots of, 18, 25–26; vs. Sanacja, 17–18, 28, 44, 58, 79–80, 161–162, 169–171, 189–190, 309; popularity, reach, influence, and vitality of, 17–19, 26, 45, 56, 59, 77, 79–80; younger generation's attraction to, 18, 24, 27–29, 36, 60, 77. *See also* antisemitism; Błaszczyk, Adam; Bluhm-Kwiatkowski, Aleksander; Chałasiński, Józef; Dmowski, Roman; Faygenberg, Rokhl; Grabski, Władysław; Grinboym, Yitzhak; Hertz, Aleksander; Jewish Question; Kipowa, Łucja; Lestschinsky, Yankev; Levinson, Avraham; Markowski, Florian; NARA; nationalism; Oberlaender, Ludwik; Poland

Ringelblum, Emanuel, 4, 99, 124

Rotenberg, Rabbi Mordechai of Antwerp, 320–321

Rotenstreich, Fiszel, 59

Rothschild, Joseph, 18, 81

Równe, 113, 213

Rozin, Avrom (Ben-Adir), 57, 157, 179–181, 261–263, 279. *See also* Territorialism

Rubinstein, Sarah, 215. *See also* Shlimovits (Shalev), Miriam

Rudnicki, Szymon, 23, 24, 45, 59

Sanacja (regime): ideology, goals, mixed composition of, extent and limits of support in Polish society for, and limits of efforts and capacity to reshape Polish political culture, 5, 8–9, 13, 17–19, 23–24, 27–28, 44, 80, 82–83, 86, 163–164, 308–311; Polish Jewish relationship to and views of intentions, capacities, and trajectories of, 5, 13, 58, 74–75, 82–83, 160–161, 168–172, 177–181, 184–190, 254–255. *See also* Całuń, Tomasz; Dizhur, Il'ya; Faygenberg, Rokhl; Grinboym, Yitzhak; Hertz, Aleksander; Jewish Question; Kipowa, Łucja; Kleinbaum, Mojżesz; Left, Polish; Lestschinsky, Yankev; Levinson, Avraham; Miedziński, Bogusław; nationalism; OZON; Poland; Piłsudski, Józef; Right, the Polish nationalist; Rozin, Avrom; Wysocki, Alfred

Schipper, Ignacy, 264

Schmitz, Oskar, 167–168

Schopenhauer, Arthur, 147

Schulz, Bruno, 99

Scott, Daryl Michael, 137

searchers and inquirers. *See* inquiry; youth, Polish Jewish

security, of life in the Yishuv, 244–245, 247–248, 250, 253, 298. *See* Palestinism / Yishuvism

self-defense: of East European Jews, 245–246, 309; in Palestine, 240, 243, 245–246, 250. *See* Weinreich, Max

Senator, Werner, 106–107, 253

Shabad, Tsemakh, *121*, 155, 233–234, 259

Shaf, Yisrael, *Akhsah bat Kalev*, 285

Shalit, Moyshe, 69–70, 264

Shapiro, Rabbi Kalonymous Kalmish (Piaseczner Rebbe), 96

shlihim (Zionist emissaries to Polish Jewish youth or communities), 37, 41–42, 88, 211–219, 222, 224–226, 228, 230, 284, 304. See also Ayzenberg, G.; Ben-Asher, Haim; Druyanov, Alter; Kliger, Moshe; Kopit, Yisrolik; Kosoy, Y.; Levita, Lova; Pinski, Hershl; Shlimovits (Shalev), Miriam; Tsvik, Aryeh

Shlimovits (Shalev), Miriam, 95, 215–219, 225–226, 228, 267–268, 283–284

Shmeruk, Chone, 62

Shneurson, Fishl, 72

Shore, Marci, 4, 31

Shteynberg, Yitshok (205), 279, 301

Siedlce, 91

Sienkiewicz, Henryk, 98

Sieradz, 88, 90

Skaff, Sheila, 73

skepticism. See future, outlooks on the likely East European Jewish; ideologies, Jewish; inquiry; politics, Jewish

Słonimski, Antoni, "Murzyn Warszawski" (The Warsaw Negro), 130

Słowacki, Juliusz, 174

Smorgonie, 211

Snyder, Timothy, 18–19, 25–26

socialism (as political ideology and movement): approach to Jewish Question of socialist parties and their supporters, 2, 9, 23, 31, 32, 36, 111–113, 116–117, 123, 162, 165–166, 178, 188, 201, 219, 287–289, 311, 325; Diasporist intellectuals and, 116–117, 140–142; disillusionment with political approach and capacities of, in Poland, 2, 6, 33, 55–56, 102–105, 112–113, 140–142, 186, 194, 219; historiography of, 96; myths of, 116–117; in post-1935 Poland, 311, 324–325; optimism provided by promises of revolutionary, 4, 32, 51, 116–117, 177, 317–318; reach of ideas and assumptions of, among Polish Jews, 4, 6, 93, 96–97, 104, 116, 140–142, 208; and Territorialism, 279–280; and

Zionism, 10, 162, 241–242, 283–284, 287–297. See also anarchism; Binyomen R.; Bund; Communism; Diasporism; Forget-Me-Not; Grade, Chaim; Gutgeshtalt, Hirsh; Jewish Workers' Party (YAP); Knaphays, Moyshe; Left, Polish; Marxism; Polish Socialist Party (PPS); Zionism

social theory, East European Jewish: challenges to progressive presumptions of secular, 2, 9–11, 34–35, 165–166, 190; dominance of progressive and Marxian assumptions in secular, 9–12, 32, 157–158; about middleman minorityhood in age of nationalism, 179–181, 189; presumptions about Jewish collective agency in secular, 10–12; Orthodox, 32–33, 320–321, 324; regarding territorial concentration (vs. dispersion), the state, and sovereignty, 238, 246–248, 320–321. See also antisemitism; Bychowski, Gustav; class; Golomb, Avrom; Hertz, Aleksander; inquiry; Kipowa, Łucja; Lestschinsky, Yankev; Levinson, Avraham; Marxism; Menes, Avrom; nationalism; Oberlaender, Ludwik; progressivism; Rozin, Avrom; Schmitz, Oskar; state, the; Weinreich, Max

Sorotzkin, Rabbi Zalman, 321

Sosnowiec, 48, 119

South Africa, 48, 166. See also emigration; exitism

stam-Zionists, 302–303

state, the (Polish Jewish thought about and experience of): capacities of, and of sovereignty/power over territory and infrastructure to reshape Jewish condition, 238, 246–248, 320–321; capture of, by popular ethnonationalist sentiment, 179–181, 189; federalism vs., 11–12; Palestine as potential Jewish, 236–238, 249–250, 320–321; relation of Polish, toward the Jews, 1, 5, 9, 11–13, 20, 24, 26–28, 35, 57–60, 69–70, 74–75, 82–83, 159–161, 163–164, 177–181, 186, 188–190, 310. See also Palestine; Poland; Rozin, Avrom; Sanacja; social theory, East European Jewish; Weinreich, Max; Zionism

state capture, 179–181, 189. *See also* antisemitism; nationalism
Steinberg, Isaac. *See* Shteynberg, Yitshok
Steinlauf, Michael, 99
Stołpce, 211
Strausberg sisters. *See* Gafni, Sarah; Vainshtein, Miriam
subjectivity (Polish Jewish): crisis of, 34, 114–116; defenses of, 115; Diasporism and, 116, 120–127, 135, 137; Grade's poetry and, 140–151; ideological support of, 116–117; as minority consciousness, 127–139; nourishment of the will in, 120–121; pathologies ascribed to, 120–123, 127–139; search for new meanings to nourish, 117–127; social thought in response to, 115–116. *See also* culture; identity, Jewish; minorityhood
Sutzkever, Avrom, 149–150, 153; "Heymishe Felder," 149; "Marts," 149
Świętochowski, Aleksander, 166
Szabad, Zemach. *See* Shabad, Tsemakh
Szajes, Berl, 108
Szajman, Malka, 109–110
Szembek, Jan, 310
Szymaniak, Karolina, 4, 34, 98, 99

Tarbut. *See* Hebraism
Tarnów, 48
Tartakover, Aryeh, 265–266, 320, 322
Tel Aviv, 231, 235–237, 239–241, 244, 246–247, 250
Territorialism, 39, 205, 233–234, 248, 259–261, 279–281, 301, 320. *See also* Astour (Tshernikhov), Mikhl; Communism; Diasporism; Frayland-Lige; Ravitsh, Meylekh; Rozin, Avrom; Shabad, Tsemakh; Shteynberg, Yitshok; socialism; Tshernikhov, Yoysef; Yiddishism; Zionism
territorialization (ethnic concentration and local majorityhood) in Jewish thought, 237–238, 244–249
Tetmajer, Kazimierz, 126
Third Aliyah, 215; *See also* Palestine; Yishuv; Zionism

Tog (newspaper), 97, 238, 295, 301
Tolstoy, Leo, 94
Tomaszewski, Jerzy, 310, 311
Tomszow, Jezik, 209–210
tourism, 84–86, 124–126, 231–233
Toybenfeld, Y., 85–86
TOZ. *See* public health, Jewish
traditionalism. *See* Orthodoxy
travelogues (about Palestine/Yishuv), 226–227, 234–249, 258–259, 268–269, 271–277, 294–297. *See also* Khatskels, Helena; Opatoshu, Yoysef; tourism; Tshernikhov, Yoysef; Weinreich, Max; Yishuv
Trębacz, Zofia, 311
Trotsky, Leon, 1, 56
Tsaytlin, Arn, 139–140
Tshernikhov, Yoysef, 224, 227, 233–238, 241, 268–270, 280, 312, 320
Tsukunft (youth movement), 97, 101, 102–103, 117, 200
Tsvik, Aryeh, 105, 108
TsYShO, 206, 208
Tuskegee Institute, 128, 132
Tuwim, Julian, 23

Ukrainians: economic politics of, 318; and Jewish Question, 27, 78, 178, 184–185; hostility toward, 19–20; nationalism of, 21, 98, 184; political unrest involving, 44, 79, 184
Underhill, Karen, 4, 98, 99
Unger, Menashe, 316
United Kibbutz movement, 231
United Peasant Party, 188
United States: immigration policy of, 47–48
Unzer ekspres (newspaper), 227
Urinsky, Gershn, 41–43, 102–103, 304–305
Uryevitsh, Yente, 42

Vainshtein, Miriam (née Strausberg), 94
Valk, Yitshok, 266, 279, 285
Vaserman, Rabbi Elkhonen, 324
Vaynig, Naftole, 4, 99, 124

Vidrovits, Leah, 113
Vilna. *See* Wilno
Vilner Tog (newspaper), 132
Viltshinski, Yehezkl, 126
violence: and Jews in Eastern Europe, 9,
  12, 18, *38*, 77–78, 80–81, 85, 156,
  169–171, 178, 187, 246, 308; in Palestine,
  38, 88, 236, 245, 248, 250, 273–275,
  299–301, 316; self-defense, 245–246,
  309
Virtshaft un lebn (journal), 180
Vogel, Debora, 4, 99, 148
Vohlman, Miriam, 228
Vohlman, Yehudah Leyb, 228
Volf, Leyzer, 140, 148
Vulman, Leon, 54, 124
Vygotsky, Lev, 139

Warsaw, 13, 18, 28, 31, 45, 46, 48,
  51, 54, 57–58, 62, 68, 84, 93, 97,
  105–107, 169–172, 298, 308, 311, 320,
  345n36
Washington, Booker T., 194
Weber, Max, 170, 256–260
Weeks, Theodore, 18, 25
Weinreich, Max, 13–16, 30, 32, 34, 43, 51–53,
  70–77, 100, 120–123, *121*, 150–152,
  154, 169, 194, 197, 226–227, 238–250,
  258–259, 270–277, 285, 286, 289–297,
  323, 325, 328; *Veg tsu unzer yugnt*, 16,
  71–73, 75–76, 100–101, 127–139, 175,
  194, 198–203, 242–244, 250, 270, 287,
  289–293, 297
Wilno (Vilna), 1, 18, 52, 76, 77, 103–104,
  120, 122, 140–142, 148, 169
Witos, Wincenty, 65
Włodzimierzec, 95–96
women and girls, Jewish, as particular kinds
  of social actors or subjects of ideology,
  88, 215, 228. *See also* gender
Wynot, Edward, Jr., 310
Wysocki, Alfred, 28

YEAS. *See* Jewish Central Emigration
  Society
Yefroykin, Yisroel, 320

Yeushzohn, B., 232, 298
Yiddish culture and literature (secular-modern),
  1, 116–117, 120–153, 286; in relation
  to Jewish condition and exigencies of
  Jewish question, 42, 285–287, 298–302,
  305. *See also* Auerbach, Rokhl; Burshtin,
  Mikhoel; culture; Diasporism; Glatshteyn,
  Yankev; Grade, Chaim; Jews, East European;
  literature; Rabon, Yisroel; Sutzkever, Avrom;
  Tsaytlin, Arn; Vaynig, Naftole; Vogel,
  Debora; Yiddishism; Zaromb, Shmuel
Yiddishism: assimilationism contrasted with,
  130; and culture, 139–152, 195; and
  Diasporism, 1, 42, 68, 82, 139–140;
  irrelevance of, to Polish Jewish fate,
  286–287, 301–302; in post–1935 period,
  324; resilience vs. despair relating to, 72,
  280; Territorialism and, 280; weakness of,
  135, 195–196; and the Yishuv/Zionism,
  233–234, 239, 301–302, 320. *See also*
  Astour (Tshernikhov), Mikhl; Bin; Binyomen
  R.; Burshtin, Mikhoel; Diasporism;
  Jewish Society for Knowing the Land;
  Ravitsh, Meylekh; Ringelblum, Emanuel;
  Territorialism; TsYShO; Urinsky, Gershn;
  Weinreich, Max; YIVO
Yishuv: information gathering about,
  224–233; interest in, 14, 37, 212, 222–225;
  language question in, 239; myths of, 218,
  224, 229; New Jews of, 15; Poland
  compared to, 49, 240, 245–250; positive
  accounts of, 236–249, 251, 269, 272;
  press coverage of, 227–229; security offered
  by, 92, 244–245, 247–248, 250–251, 253,
  298; travelogues about, 226–227, 234–249,
  258–259, 268–269, 271–277, 294–297.
  See also inquiry; Jewish-Palestinian conflict; Khatskels, Helena; kibbutzim;
  Lakerman, Shmuel; Palestine; Palestinians;
  Palestinism/Yishuvism; Tel Aviv; tourism;
  travelogues; Tshernikhov, Yoysef;
  Weinreich, Max; Zionism
Yishuvism. *See* Palestinism/Yishuvism
YIVO, 13, 15, 52–53, 55, 74, 75, 98, 114,
  197–198, 208–210, 230, 238–239, 268,
  286, 321

YIVO-Bleter (journal), 176

Yona, Rona, 94–95, 196, 223, 224

youth, Polish Jewish: autobiographical reflections of, 13–14, 52–53, 55–56, 70–72, 74–77, 98, 110–111, 114–116, 197–198, 208–210, 230, 249, 250, 268, 293, 321; Binyomen R. as case example of, 75–81, 198–208; doubt and pessimism among, 13–16, 48–49, 52–53, 70–75, 77, 88–91, 127–139, 196–198, 201–202, 254; emigration as response to crisis facing, 14–15, 42–43, 49–51; gendered motivations for political decisions of, 199–200; pathologies ascribed to, 114–115, 127–139, 196–197, 199, 289–290; political experience and engagement of, 73–81, 91, 198–208, 212–218; realism and rationality of, 197–220; searchers and inquirers among, 198–220. *See also* Bin; Binyomen R.; Communism; exitism; Faygenberg, Rokhl; Frayhayt; Hehalutz; Hehalutz ha-Tsair; inquiry; politics, Jewish; *shlihim*; subjectivity; Tsukunft; Weinreich, Max; Zionism

Youth Aliyah program, 296–297

Yudishe velt, Di (journal), 286

Zahra, Tara, 265

Zaromb, Shmuel, 139

Zawiercie, 90, 118

Zdziechowski, Marian, 23

Zenderland, Leila, 132

Żeromski, Stefan, 126, 162

Zilberfarb, Moyshe, 120, 177, 180

Zionism: antisemitism and, 22, *38*, *39*, 74–75, 249–251; anti- and non-Zionists turning to, 90, 92, 102–110; attracting mass support among Polish Jews, 6, 14, 37, 48–51, 88–91, 93–95, 211–218, 221–224, 320–321; attractions of, 14, 197, 199, 290; Bund's relationship with, 35–36; critiques of, 158, 221, 226, 235–236, 242, 259, 290, 292, 295; Diasporism compared to, 242–245, 247–249; efficacy of, as solution for Polish Jews, 233, 258–260, 267–284, 301–303; and emigration, 14, 48–51, 89, 95–96, 193, 213–215, 263–267, 277–284, 291; exitism and, 14, 42, 88–92, 100–103, 106–107, 203, 218, 250, 252, 276; ideological vs. emergency considerations in, 277–279, 281–282, 287–292; in interwar period, 6; labor policies of, 225–226, 235–236, 241–242; Labor Zionism, 49, 152, 264, 266, 278–279, 280, 283; masculinist/militarist aspect of, 224; motivations for interest in, 88–92, 100–101, 211–218, 222–224, 304–305; myths of, 93, 95, 101, 108, 212, 214, 218, 223–224, 224, 227, 229, 230, 238, 244–245; new adherents disinterested in cultural ideology of, 33, 48–50, 88–91, 94–95, 100–101, 211–218; New Jews of, 101, 224; and Palestinism/Yishuvism, 14, 37, 251–253; Polish interest in, 107, 309, 355n13; resilience and optimism provided by, 72, 242, 272, 289–291; Revisionist, 93, 101, 222; Territorialism in relation to, 259, 261–262, 279–284; and tourism, 231; transcending the diaspora-emigration-Zionism divide, 281–284. *See also* African American experience; Appenszlak, Jakob; Ben-Gurion, David; Bernshteyn, Yitshok; Betar; Bialik, Chaim Nahman; Bnai Brith; children; Czyżew-Osada; danger; Dobkin, Eliahu; exitism; emigration; fantasy; Faygenberg, Rokhl; Fifth Aliyah; Fourth Aliyah; Frayhayt; future, outlooks on the likely East European Jewish; gender; Gordonia youth movement; Gotlib, Yehoshua; Grinboym, Yitzhak; Ha-Oved; Ha-Shomer ha-Tsair; *Haynt*; Hebraism; Hehalutz; Hehalutz ha-Tsair; Histadrut; Hitahdut; Jabotinsky, Ze'ev; Jewish Central Emigration Society; Jewish-Palestinian conflict; Kishinev Pogrom; Kleinbaum, Mojżesz; Lakerman, Shmuel; Latski-Bertoldi, Zeev-Volf; Lestschinsky, Yankev; Levinson, Avraham; Levita, Lova; Mapai; *Miesięcznik Żydowski*; *Nasz Przegląd*; Oberlaender, Ludwik; Palestine; Palestinism/Yishuvism; Perelman, Abram; Pinsker, Leon; Poalei Tsion Left; Poalei Tsion Right; Polakiewicz, Moyshe; politics;

Zionism (*continued*)
realism; *shlihim*; Shalit, Moyshe; Shlimovits
(Shalev), Miriam; *stam*-Zionists; Tartak-
over, Aryeh; Tshernikhov, Yoysef; Valk,
Yitshok; Weinreich, Max; Yishuv; Zionist
Congresses; Zlotnicka, Beyle
Zionist Congresses, 22, 205, 222, 317
Zloch, Stephanie, 17

Zlotnicka, Beyle, 208
Zmierzch Izraela, 21–22
ZTK. *See* Jewish Society for Knowing the
Land
Związek Akademickiej Młodzieży
Zjednoczeniowej (ZAMZ), 97–98. *See also*
assimiliationism
Żywiec, 21